ADVANCE PRAISE FOR *MIND TO MIND*

"What a treasure trove this book is! It offers readers a detailed, and yet concise, summary of some of the most important cutting-edge thinking in psycho-analysis and developmental research. Its star-studded list of authors includes diverse perspectives and traditions, yet their contributions provide a themat-ically coherent account of where our field is today and where it is heading."

—**PAUL L. WACHTEL, Ph.D.**, CUNY Distinguished Professor,
Doctoral Program in Clinical Psychology

"Man is a mentalizing animal; to be fully human is to recognize that others, and oneself, have minds. Fonagy, Target, and colleagues have started from that simple but profound truth and developed concepts and theories that provide a new perspective on psychoanalysis. The foremost thinkers and workers in the field are assembled here to reflect on that perspective and provide us with a guide to this new domain. Early psychosocial development, attachment theory, neurobiology, and operational tools for measuring mentalization are all discussed. The theory is applied to psychotherapy, to parenting and parent–infant attachment, to international conflict resolution, and to clinical psycho-analysis. This volume takes us from the basic concepts to their formulation as central in contemporary psychoanalytic thought."

—**ROBERT MICHELS, M.D.**, Walsh McDermott University Professor of Medicine
and Psychiatry, Cornell University; Training and Supervising Analyst,
Columbia University Center for Psychoanalytic Training and Research;
Joint-Editor-in-Chief, *The International Journal of Psychoanalysis*

"This highly readable book takes us through a lively exploration of how a brain becomes a mind and how the mind becomes structured by the experience of relationships. The contributors weave together strands from evolutionary theory, neuroscience, psychoanalysis, and attachment theory to elucidate what makes humans (and perhaps other primates as well) capable of giving meaning to their own feelings and behaviors as well as those of others. Reading at times like a 'whodunit' of the mind, this exciting, thought-provoking collection leaves us grateful for what it teaches and eager for the knowledge that is still to come."

—**ALICIA F. LIE**~~~~~~, ~~~~ ~~~~~~~~ ~~~~~~ lowed Chair in
Infant Ment: an Francisco

"Splendidly conceived and beautifully edited, *Mind to Mind* brings together a regal cast of researchers and clinicians to explore the rich significance of mentalization. The papers in this volume offer a comprehensive course on topics that are vital to the future of psychoanalysis. Especially valuable is the in-depth exploration of the impact of trauma on mentalization and how this insight can be used effectively in treatment. Equally illuminating are the discussions of the relationship of mentalization to attachment, the wide-ranging examination of neurobiology and cognitive-affective processing in relation to trauma and borderline personality disorder, and the use of mentalization in both the assessment of clinical cases and in systematic research into the effectiveness of psychoanalytically based therapies. The volume as a whole is an outstanding testament to the generative power of the concept of mentalization to foster new insights into enduring theoretical and clinical concerns."

—SUSAN COATES, Ph.D., Clinical Professor of Psychology in Psychiatry, College of Physicians and Surgeons, Columbia University

"This is a fascinating and groundbreaking volume! It is truly interdisciplinary in scope, weaving together research on normality and pathology with clinical intervention from a multiple-levels-of-analysis perspective. Psychoanalysis, neuroscience, developmental psychology and psychopathology, cognitive psychology, and philosophy are brought to bear in order to examine and extend the boundaries of the concept of mentalization. Well-written, compelling, and thought-provoking, *Mind to Mind: Infant Research, Neuroscience, and Psychoanalysis* is a major contribution to science and practice."

—DANTE CICCHETTI, Ph.D., Professor and McKnight Presidential Chair, Institute of Child Development and Department of Psychiatry, University of Minnesota

"This is an outstanding compendium that elaborates in original ways on the work of Fonagy, Target, Gergely, and Jurist. The chapters are clearly written, detailed, sophisticated, and equally useful to clinicians and researchers."

—BEATRICE BEEBE, Ph.D., Clinical Professor of Psychology in Psychiatry, College of Physicians and Surgeons, Columbia University

MIND TO MIND

INFANT RESEARCH, NEUROSCIENCE, AND PSYCHOANALYSIS

EDITED BY

Elliot L. Jurist, Arietta Slade, and
Sharone Bergner

OTHER PRESS • NEW YORK

"A Neurobiological Perspective on Mentalizing and Internal Object Relations in Traumatized Borderline Patients" by Glen Gabbard, Lisa Miller, and Melissa Martinez reprinted by permission of John Wiley & Sons Limited from *The Handbook of Mentalization-Based Treatment*, John G. Allen and Peter Fonagy, eds., Hoboken, NJ: Wiley. Copyright © 2006 John Wiley & Sons Limited.

"Mentalization as a Frame for Working with Parents in Child Psychotherapy" by Arietta Slade reprinted by permission of the Taylor & Francis Group from *Mentalization: Theoretical Considerations, Research Findings, and Clinical Implications*, Fredric N. Busch, ed., NY: Analytic Press. Copyright © 2008 by Taylor & Francis Group, LLC.

Production Editor: Yvonne E. Cárdenas

Book design: Natalya Balnova

This book was set in 11.2 pt. Bembo by Alpha Graphics of Pittsfield, NH.

10 9 8 7 6 5 4 3 2

Library of Congress Cataloging-in-Publication Data

Mind to mind : infant research, neuroscience, and psychoanalysis / edited by Elliot L. Jurist, Arietta Slade, Sharone Bergner.
    p. cm.
    Includes bibliographical references.
    ISBN 978-1-59051-251-7
    1. Psychoanalysis.   2. Mental healing.   I. Jurist, Elliot L., 1953-   II. Slade, Arietta.
III. Bergner, Sharone.
    [DNLM: 1. Psychoanalytic Theory.   2. Mental Processes.   3. Object Attachment.
4. Psychoanalytic Therapy—methods.   5. Self Concept. WM 460 M6635 2008]
    RC506.M534 2008
    616.89'17—dc22

                                                                                2007052433

To Julia
—E.J.

In memory of my dear grandparents, John and Isis Steinberg
—A. S.

To Yaniv, Omri, and Odelya
—S. B.

CONTENTS

INTRODUCTION

Early in 2004, we began to plan a conference aimed at examining the impact of Peter Fonagy and Mary Target's notions of mentalization and reflective functioning upon current and future psychoanalytic theory and practice. The main purpose of the conference was to consider how (and whether) these constructs inform or have changed the ways psychoanalysts think about internalization, representation, and other central contemporary psychoanalytic ideas. We asked: How are the concepts of mentalization and reflective functioning related to psychoanalytic constructs? How are they distinct? What do these constructs add to questions of theory and technique? How do they change the ways we work with patients? Have these constructs changed the landscape of psychoanalysis in meaningful ways?

The conference opened lively discussion and even debate about the meaning, utility, and limits of the concepts of mentalization and reflective functioning, issues that are both far from settled and full of promise.

Although this volume is based on the papers presented at that conference, it is not simply a volume of conference proceedings, because we invited the contributors to expand upon and elaborate their presentations. In addition, new papers were added to those in the original conference by two of the editors, Arietta Slade and Elliot Jurist, rounding out the volume. The result is a broad and diverse array of reflections on the constructs of mentalization and reflective functioning as these relate to the current status of key psychoanalytic ideas and to the future of psychoanalysis.

The concept of mentalization has its roots in a range of disciplines. It was originally introduced to psychoanalysis by French psychoanalysts writing about so-called psychosomatic patients, who displayed a lack of symbolization of mental states. It is also derived from the theory of mind literature, which itself spans philosophy, cognitive psychology, and developmental psychology. Over the past twenty years, Peter Fonagy and his colleagues (notably Mary Target) have expanded upon these ideas in ways that have brought the construct of mentalization to the forefront of psychoanalytic theory and practice. They have defined mentalization as the process of interpreting (the behavior of) oneself and others in terms of mental states. In their view, to adopt a mentalizing stance is to conceive of one's self and of others as having a mind and acting in relation to feelings, beliefs, desires, and intentions. Thus, mentalization is a skill, capacity, or process that requires cognition; however, as several chapters in this volume emphasize, it is deeply shaped by the affective dimensions of experience, specifically the earliest affective and affect regulating attachment relationship between infant and caregiver. The construct of reflective functioning—which is essentially an operationalization of mentalization—was introduced by Fonagy, Target, and attachment researchers Miriam and Howard Steele.

The terms mentalization and reflective functioning refer to a crucial human capacity that develops out of the child's earliest attachment relationships, specifically the mother's capacity to represent the child's mind, and the child's internalization of this representation of himself as a mentalizing being. The mother's willingness and readiness to understand people (and specifically her baby) in terms of mental states (i.e., her own capacities for reflectiveness) set the stage for the development of reflective functioning in her baby.

Tracing the development and current status of the concept of mentalization is an exercise in interdisciplinary thinking and cross-methodological dialogue. Fonagy and his colleagues' current conceptualizations of mentalization combine insights and ideas derived from (a) neuroscientific research about the brain and the link between brain and mind, as well as about the way early relationships affect development, (b) attachment theory and research about the properties of early (and potentially also later therapeutic) relationships that promote, or hinder, the capacity for mentalization, and (c) theory of mind studies in developmental psychology and in philosophy. It thus provides a unique arena for fertile, mutually enriching collaboration between psychoanalysis and its neighboring disciplines.

The constructs of mentalization and reflective functioning promote a focus on the mind. In reflecting on the future direction of psychoanalysis, it is interesting to consider whether such a focus on the mind augurs a paradigm shift within psychoanalysis, echoing prior conceptual shifts in the field. Ego psychology's focus on the ego and superego, for instance, deepened our understanding of character and of the importance of defenses. At the same time, however, it produced a more normalizing version of psychoanalysis that threatened to soft-pedal the power of the unconscious. Likewise, the turn to a focus on the self, brought by object relations theory and self psychology, provided a richer account of subjective experience and directed attention to the affective bond between the self and both its internal and external objects; at the same time, it ushered in less specificity about defenses and a downgrading of the role of the superego. The current turn to the mind directs psychoanalysis to find a common language with other disciplines and to seek a comprehensive approach to mental functioning that does not minimize cognition or the interaction between cognition and affect.

Of course, the mind is not a new concept in psychoanalysis; terms like "mind" and "mental" have always been around. It is no betrayal of any psychoanalytic orientation to seek to understand the mind as a whole, without dwelling exclusively on various elemental features at the expense of others. Still, there remains something problematic and unresolved about the psychoanalytic conception of the mind. The classical view of the structural model of id, ego, and superego no longer guides even Freudians in the way it once did. The relational movement, despite its contributions to technique, has conspicuously lacked a model of the mind. The growing interest in the mind within psychoanalytic circles augurs, in our view, the possibility of a fruitful engagement with the world beyond psychoanalysis, paving the way toward a lively and less isolated future.

The chapters in this volume attest to the value of dialogue and collaboration between psychoanalysis and related fields. Although we have divided the book into parts, many of these contributions synthesize ideas and findings from overlapping domains in describing the development, psychopathology, and treatment of the mentalizing self. Considerations of the limits of mentalization theory for psychoanalytic thinking as well as variations of its clinical applications are also here, reflecting a collective effort to push and prod ideas and collaboration along. We think this is most fitting for a volume on mentalization and psychoanalysis, as it captures the spirit of the work of fathoming the minds of others and embracing the process of reflection in the context of otherness.

The chapters in Part I of the book, Mentalization and Attachment, address the concept of mentalization in relation to attachment in two ways. First, these chapters consider the construct of mentalization itself, placing it in the context of attachment theory and research and articulating ways in which it links psychoanalysis, as well as other domains, with attachment theory. In this sense, these chapters help us to map the construct of mentalization against the backdrop of a number of fields—primarily, though not only attachment theory—and to understand how it contributes to the evolution of ideas germane to psychoanalysis. Second, these chapters address the development and vicissitudes of the skill or function of mentalization within a relational, or attachment-based context. In this sense, they help us understand how and why the development of the mentalizing self is facilitated, as well as how the mentalizing function and the object relational world interrelate.

Peter Fonagy and Mary Target's opening chapter sets the stage by deftly weaving together psychoanalytic theory, attachment theory, and neuroscience research. These multiple perspectives provide a backdrop for discussing the concept of mentalization and its relation to the pathologies of trauma. The authors begin and end with clinical material, opening with two disturbing examples of the devastation caused by trauma, and culminating with a touching illustration of how to work productively and successfully with a traumatized patient. Their main claim is that trauma impairs mentalization: victims have difficulty in understanding others and themselves, and especially have difficulty in discerning the boundary between external and internal reality (the psychic equivalence mode) and in making sense of others beyond motivation that has to do with physical constraints and observable goals (the teleological mode). The authors underscore the enormous psychic cost of trauma to the normal functioning of the mind and self. They pay special attention to the relation between attachment and mentalization: on the one hand, mentalization is seen as growing out of secure attachment; on the other, the systems are recognized as distinct.

Attachment is about security and relies on trust, whereas mentalization has its evolutionary source in competition and social survival. Trauma patients lack both the benefit of being able to rely on attachment (thereby allowing mentalization to be off-line) and to access mentalization when it is needed.

Gergely and Unoka's chapter opens up crucial questions about mentalization. The main focus is a discussion of the relation between attachment and mentalization in humans. On the basis of recent research suggesting that mentalization begins as early as 1 year of age (rather than 4 or 5, as had previously been outlined in the developmental literature), Gergely and Unoka argue that the notion that mentalization flourishes as a result of secure attachment must be revised. Along these lines, they urge us to be cautious and indeed skeptical in our interpretations of studies that link attachment and mentalization. Their perspective suggests that mentalization contributes to affective development by facilitating secondary (cognitive) appraisals that in turn foster affect regulation. Along the way, Gergely and Unoka review their previous work on affect mirroring, contingency detection, and affect regulation, and introduce a fascinating new idea: natural pedagogy, the parental stance that initiates infants into the realm of culture.

Jurist's chapter explores the concept of mentalization in terms of its various meanings, seeking to clarify but also address problematic areas and thus to push the concept along toward greater articulation and specificity. He focuses on the complex relation between attachment and mentalization, and turns to the theory of mind literature in philosophy to introduce a key distinction between low and high levels of mentalization. Jurist suggests that the psychoanalytic concept of mentalization is unique in its particular emphasis on development. Mentalization is about self-understanding as well as the understanding of others; it involves emotions and emotional styles in a fundamental way; and it is not, by definition, accurate. Jurist's chapter culminates with a discussion of his concept of "mentalized affectivity," the process of reevaluating the *meaning* of emotions that occurs in psychoanalytic psychotherapy. This chapter directly addresses and seeks to begin to resolve an issue raised by a number of our contributors, namely, the place of affect in mentalization theory.

Steele, Kaniuk, Hodges, Henderson, Hillman, and Steele's chapter addresses mentalization across a variety of contexts—childhood and parenting, attachment research and clinical insights, narrative, and observation.

The authors describe their longitudinal study of intergenerational patterns of attachment in adoptive parents and their late-placed, previously maltreated adopted children. They explore the links between the adoptive mothers' reflective functioning in the pre-adoption Adult Attachment Interview, which taps representations of childhood, and these mothers' representations of the evolving relationship with the child, as assessed by the Parent Development Interview administered after the adoption. The authors identify specific dimensions of the mothers' representations of the adopted child and the experience of parenting—including the capacity for acknowledging difficulty—that correlate most strongly with mothers' capacity to reflect on their own childhoods. Their findings shed light on the aspects of parental reflective functioning that allow for robust adaptation even in the exceedingly challenging context of late adoption of a maltreated child, and offer insights that are useful for identifying appropriate adoptive parents and developing supports for such parents and the children they adopt.

Part II of this book, Mentalization in Clinical and Neuroscience Research, brings together a variety of research methodologies and domains in order to consider the development of mentalization, the processes and factors that hinder such development, and the pathology that results and is entrenched by defects in mentalization, as well as treatment approaches that aim to target such deficits.

In the chapter that opens this part, Fonagy and Bateman discuss their treatment program for borderline personality disorder, Mentalization-Based Treatment (MBT). In their view, deficits in mentalization are at the heart of the affective, interpersonal, and regulatory disturbances that characterize borderline personality disorder. In line with this thinking, Fonagy and Bateman have developed an approach to working with borderline patients that is aimed specifically at developing or enhancing disrupted and disabled mentalizing capacities. Many of the accepted psychodynamically oriented approaches to working with borderline patients may actually induce instability and severe regression, they argue, as these require patients to think about mental states and about the mental states of the therapist in ways that they are not able to do. Such approaches also activate the attachment system without providing the patient with the requisite mentalizing skills to make use of and internalize that attachment. Only the development of mentalizing capacities within the framework of the treatment itself, and within the framework of the transference, will allow the patient to be able ultimately to tolerate and make sense of his mental experience, and decrease his reliance on pathological modes of relatedness and defense. Fonagy and Bateman describe the findings of a randomized clinical trial that compared MBT with Dialectical Behavior Therapy (DBT) and treatment as usual; it showed significant and enduring changes in mood states and interpersonal functioning after an 18-month treatment.

Kernberg, Diamond, Yeomans, Clarkin, and Levy examine Transference Focused Psychotherapy (TFP), their own manualized psychodynamic treatment for borderline personality disorder, and compare it to the other central psychodynamic manualized approach for such patients, Fonagy and Bateman's Mentalization-Based Treatment (MBT). The authors discuss TFP's interpretive approach in detail, and use research data on the efficacy of their treatment model along with detailed case material from one of their studies to explain their finding that TFP is associated with improvements in the capacity for mentalization in borderline patients, as well as with attachment status and symptomatology changes, including a reduction in aggression. The interpretive process that is unique to TFP is based upon Kernberg's object relations model, and the particular theoretical formulations regarding the etiology and structure of borderline pathology that are derived from it. Through their explication of features that are central to their understanding of such pathology, as well as of those features of their treatment approach that are unique and mutative, the authors highlight both their common ground and disagreement with Fonagy's approach, including points related to the centrality of affect and to the structure of the borderline patient's object-relational world. The chapter also offers a critique of the concept of mentalization as it is used in MBT, and puts forth a view of the process of mentalization as a multistaged one involving transformations in both cognitive and affective ego and superego structures.

Gabbard, Miller, and Martinez identify various neurobiological correlates of borderline object relations and internalized object representations. In particular, they suggest that the relationship between amygdalar abnormalities on the one hand, and decreased activity in the prefrontal cortex on the other, create a challenge to mentalization as well as to the articulation of coherent and integrated self-states. Also implicated in the phenomenology of borderline syndromes, particularly in patients who have suffered early abuse and neglect, are hippocampal abnormalities that have an impact on working and other crucial forms of memory that are involved in forming new relationships. The authors use such neurobiological underpinnings to explain the tenacity with which borderline individuals cling to destructive patterns of relatedness, and suggest that it is only through sustained effort in long-term psychotherapy that problematic links in activated networks can be deactivated, and newer circuits be created to override old ones. They emphasize the complex point that while brain dysfunction from neglect and abuse should not be underestimated, internalized object relations continue to influence brain function; thus, altering internalized object relations *within the context of treatment* is the central challenge in treating borderline patients.

In their chapter, Blatt, Auerbach, and Behrends address the relationship between representation, internalization, and mentalization. For the past 30 years, representation and internalization have been viewed by psychoanalysts as key to crucial developments in the self, in relationships, and in affect regulation, and have been at the heart of much of contemporary developmental psychoanalysis. Blatt and his colleagues, who have long been at the forefront of study in this area, consider the relationship of mentalization to these key processes. They suggest that mentalization is intrinsically linked to representation and internalization, and depends—as those functions do—upon crucial relationship experiences for its development. They suggest that two core aspects of a mutative relationship are gratifying involvement, which promotes intimacy, and experienced incompatibility, which promotes separation and autonomy. Both are crucial to the development of these three processes, and occur within the context of early development as well as the psychotherapeutic relationship. Using narrative data from the longitudinal study of patients in long-term, psychoanalytically oriented inpatient treatment, the authors examine the development of mentalization, representation, and internalization over the course of a lengthy hospitalization. Shifts in these processes, which are presumed to result from the gratifying involvement and experienced incompatibility with the therapist, are reflected across descriptions of a number of key relationships.

In their chapter, Swain, Thomas, Leckman, and Mayes consider a number of the complex psychological, neurological, and biological aspects of parenting. The importance of adequate parenting is obviously implicated in the development of mentalization, and thus seems a particularly crucial area of investigation. Swain and his colleagues discuss recent advances in understanding the genetic, epigenetic, and neurobiological substrates of maternal behavioral in model mammalian species, and explore the relevance of these findings for understanding risk and resiliency. They suggest, for instance, that maternal preoccupation may be correlated with the release of the hormone oxytocin, itself linked to parturition and nurture, and which triggers a range of caregiving behaviors. Other studies reviewed suggest that aspects of maternal behavior are nongenomically transmitted from one generation to the next and that the nature of the maternal care received in infancy may "program" aspects of infants' responses to stress later in life and have enduring consequences affecting their approach to the world. They argue that the increasing evidence for the intergenerational transmission of parenting, both at the behavioral and the neural level, underscores the importance of early intervention programs, and provides a model for understanding vulnerability and resilience.

In the third and final part of this volume, Mentalization in Practice, we consider the applicability of mentalization theory to work in the consulting room and the world at large. While many of the chapters in the other parts synthesize findings from clinical work with research-based insights, the chapters in this last part focus in greater detail on some of the ways mentalization theory enriches applied psychoanalysis as well as individual clinical work.

In her chapter, Slade considers the development of a mentalizing stance in work with parents. She describes the parent work that is central to many child therapies in light of mentalization theory, and suggests that often parents whose children come for psychotherapy are themselves struggling to make sense of and reflect upon their children's emotional lives. The therapist's work with a child's parents invariably involves helping them to mentalize aspects of their child's experience that they have been unable to recognize or regulate. She emphasizes the notion that the capacity to imagine another— in this case the child—from a different point of view is essential to resolving conflict and promoting development. Using a series of clinical vignettes, Slade suggests that there are many ways that a therapist can help the parent develop a reflective stance, as by (a) creating a "playspace" in which the therapist and parent can contemplate the child's mind together, (b) allowing the parent her own space in the treatment, such that her experience can be held in mind by the therapist, (c) modeling the reflective stance for the parent, (d) working only at the level the parent can manage, and (e) maintaining flexibility and openness to both the child's and parent's needs throughout the course of treatment.

The chapter by Leary, which ventures to explore the uses of mentalization theory outside the realm of the consulting room, offers a creative and original view of the ways these core constructs can be helpful in understanding and even changing political and social conflict. She offers a case study of applied psychoanalysis, describing how the development of mentalizing capacities among long-standing enemies was key to the successful negotiation between the Indonesian government and the Free Aceh movement, a rebel group seeking independence. Leary uses her own highly refined clinical skills to focus on key moments in which the successful negotiation turned on the capacity to imagine oneself from another's point of view and to entertain new perspectives. In her chapter, Leary makes abundantly clear that taking a mentalizing stance is essential to solving problems that extend far beyond the realm of clinical psychoanalysis and psychotherapy.

The final four chapters in this part explore the clinical applications of mentalization theory. Seligman's chapter uses mentalization theory to illuminate elements of the analytic treatment of a traumatized woman with significant character pathology. The patient began treatment in a "nonmentalized state," experiencing the world and her inner life in a way that dramatically evokes Fonagy's notion of psychic equivalence. Her difficulties in mentalization not only affected her relationships outside the treatment but profoundly compromised the development of a stable therapeutic alliance. This came to a head when Seligman inadvertently disappointed her, leading to a prolonged crisis that nearly ended the treatment. This experienced incompatibility, to use the term introduced by Blatt and his colleagues, was almost unbearable for the patient, and the therapist's gratifying involvement was central to riding out the transference and countertransference storms that accompanied this breach. Over time, the patient slowly began to see the therapist as having a mind of his own, and became more able to imagine others' as well as her own states of mind. As a consequence of these shifts in the treatment relationship, she became more flexible, empathic, and reflective in her relationships outside of the treatment.

Gilmore's chapter similarly uses material from a single analytic case to illustrate the clinical utility of mentalization theory. Here too a breach in the treatment led to growth and change. In the wrenching case Gilmore describes, the analysis of a man adopted in infancy reveals the myriad ways that adoption and its multiple complexities challenge mentalization and in particular thinking the unthinkable about parenting figures. The patient's striking inability to mentalize is further complicated by the death of his adoptive mother when he was 14, and his adoptive father's relentless need to co-opt his son's mind so that he could fulfill his dreams for his "own" biological son. Indeed, the impact of his adoptive father's inability to value and appreciate this child as an individual (i.e., to see him as separate and as having a mind of his own) harks back to Steele and her colleagues' report on the impact of insecure parental attachment and distorted parental representations on adoption outcomes. Interestingly, it is only through threatening to terminate the treatment, thus fully evoking the patient's fear of abandonment, that the analyst is able to move the treatment forward and qualitatively shift the patient's relentless need to enact primitive internalized representations in the transference. Echoing Blatt and Seligman, Gilmore provides compelling clinical evidence that rupture facilitates change and growth in mentalizing and other capacities.

Stern, by contrast, asks us to consider the limitations and failures of mentalization theory. While he appreciates the importance of this perspective, he recommends that we learn to love those "dark places," the sphere of nonmentalization, or the domain of what Stern himself has termed "unformulated experience." In particular, Stern argues that mutual enactments, which appear to be departures from mentalization, actually facilitate change. Stern punctures the superficial notion of the analyst as chief mentalizer, and offers a probing clinical account of breaking new ground with a patient through mutual enactment. At the same time, referring to his experience as a conference participant, Stern readily acknowledges the evolution of his own understanding of mentalization, and seeks to find a balance between the strengths of this perspective and the areas in which complexity and texture are as yet lacking.

A volume on mentalization would be incomplete without at least some attention to the themes of playfulness and humor, and Bromberg's chapter amply supplies this. Bromberg teases us with his title, "MENTALIZE

THIS!" a play on the film *Analyze This* (1999), starring Billy Crystal as the analyst and Robert De Niro as a gangster who makes an unlikely but engaging patient. Bromberg is not, of course, just joking around: he makes serious points about this humorous film, having to do with the recognition of painful dissociated feelings and the negotiation of otherness. Bromberg asserts that mentalization depends upon "affective safety"; this safety precludes a retreat into dissociation in confronting others. He also presents a harrowing, honest case vignette in which he, as the analyst, contributed to the patient's experience of not feeling safe, although he was able to restore her sense of safety and move her toward mentalization. As does Stern's, Bromberg's essay illustrates both the value and the limits inherent in the construct of mentalization in the clinical arena.

Part I

MENTALIZATION AND ATTACHMENT

Chapter 1

Attachment, Trauma, and Psychoanalysis

Where Psychoanalysis Meets Neuroscience

Peter Fonagy and Mary Target

WHY DO WE DO THIS TO EACH OTHER?

Trauma is puzzling, as the following vignettes exemplify. James, who is currently in prison for armed robbery, frequently used to suffer violent attacks from his father in the name of punishment. For example, at the age of 9, James was punished for stealing. This is how he describes the incident: "He [James's father] put the gas cooker on, right, and um—I will always remember this—he put a hand on top of the gas cooker, and roasted our hands [your hand?] yeah, my hand, and uhm—the next day I went to school with gloves on, because they [were] really, really bad. . . ." James's reaction to this and dozens of other traumatic experiences is telling: "I used to have a drink and sleep and when I woke up I was a different person." When asked to describe if he ever felt upset, James is completely unable to understand the question: "When I was young I never really got upset because I had everything I wanted really, and when you get everything that you want you don't really get upset." When asked how his childhood experiences might have affected his adult personality, his response is totally without insight: "I cannot explain, I can't, it's not even up there for me to explain."

James is not a special case. Stuart, also a robber, and also violent and dangerous, was brought up by his mother and a succession of stepfathers, the second of which, who lived with the family for almost 10 years, in particular traumatized him. In Stuart's and in his mother's mind, the stepfather just wanted to "straighten him out." If Stuart behaved badly, his stepfather would beat him when he came home—and every night afterward for a week. Stuart describes what happened after he had been caught shoplifting and was brought home by the police: "He tied me to the bed . . . and he got a screwdriver, and he was stabbing me in the hands with it, because they [my hands] were what stole . . . and I was just laughing at him, 'cause I was . . . I don't know. . . . And then he went downstairs, and he got a hammer and nails, and he nailed one of my hands to the board of the bed, like. Just stuck a nail straight through my hand, like. Like, so I was howling, I couldn't move, and the blood was . . . and I was screaming then. I had to cry then, I couldn't handle it. And after they [sic] had done it, my hands went numb, so I couldn't feel it. And I looked at my hands, and I started laughing at myself. And I felt I was going mad, like, cause I was going 'Ha ha,' you know, and I was thinking, '*I had done that.*'"

As with many severe trauma victims, Stuart attacks himself when he is upset, hitting the walls with all his considerable force: "The amount of times I've broken my hands, my arms, you know. Five times, in six months. Different arms." Like other abused children, Stuart expresses gratitude to his stepfather for hardening him, enabling him to take violence from others.

Stuart's story also illustrates the total disorganization of the attachment system that inevitably accompanies such cases of prolonged trauma. When he was 11 he witnessed his stepfather beating his mother, apparently trying to choke her to death. Seizing the first thing that came to hand, Stuart attempted to stab his stepfather in the chest with a screwdriver. When Stuart was 12 his stepfather threatened to shoot him and had to be disarmed by the police. His mother then arranged for Stuart to be taken into care, explaining that this was for his own protection. A few weeks before the interview with Stuart, this stepfather, long estranged from Stuart's mother, committed suicide. His reaction to hearing the news was paradoxical: "I just started being sick. And, and I just . . . I was standing there for about an hour, like, shocked. And then I just, you know, I just cracked up, man, I went mad, like. I did, I went berserk. And the police just, like, there was about five of them got ahold of me, like, you know, to try to calm me down. And I was trying to hit them, you know what I mean." At the inquest into his stepfather's death, Stuart's mother screamed across the courtroom that it was all Stuart's fault: "she starts screaming in the court. And then I went, I flipped my lid there, I jumped out of the dock, I grabbed a hold of her by the hair, like and I was banging her head off, the police had to get me off her." Stuart, like many others we have interviewed, shows a bizarre lack of understanding of what makes him, his mother, his stepfather, or indeed anyone else, tick. When asked about the effects of his attachment trauma on his adult personality, Stuart admits to "going over the top," but also says: "I mean, I am not a danger to anyone, I am a danger to myself, not other people." He seems genuinely unaware of how other people experience his violent outbursts. In prison, not only the guards but also his fellow inmates are scared of him, and his behavior often results in extremely severe punishments from the system.

A PSYCHOANALYTIC DEVELOPMENTAL PHENOMENOLOGY OF THE RESPONSE TO ATTACHMENT TRAUMA

In adults with a history of childhood attachment trauma there often seems to be an acquired failure of the capacity to conceive of how people think or feel. We call this a failure of mentalization. Mentalization is a concept originally introduced by French psychoanalysts working with psychosomatic patients (Luquet, 1981, 1987, and others; Marty, 1968, 1990; Marty & De M'Uzan, 1963).[1] They noted a lack of symbolization of mental states in such individuals, a lack of freedom in free association, and a characteristic way of thinking that was too close to sensations and primary unconscious fantasies. Following on from the French, but also incorporating a tradition in philosophy of mind established by Brentano (1973/1874), Dennett (1978), and others, we define mentalization as a form of mostly preconscious *imaginative* mental activity, namely, interpreting people's actions in terms of "intentional" mental states. This activity is "imaginative" because we have to imagine what other people might be thinking or feeling; an important indicator of high-quality mentalization is the awareness that we do not know for sure what is in someone else's mind. The same kind of imaginative leap can be required to understand one's own mental experience, particularly in relation to emotionally charged issues or irrational (perhaps unconsciously driven) reactions. To adopt this stance, to conceive of self and others as having a mind, the individual needs a symbolic representational system for mental states. With regard to the neuroscientific manifestations of mentalization, it seems that, although mentalization probably involves numerous interconnected cortical systems, it is commonly associated with activation of four (Frith, 2007): in the middle prefrontal areas of the brain, in particular the paracingulate area (recruited when thinking about beliefs, and representing the implicit ability to infer mental states); the posterior superior temporal sulcus (pSTS) and temporo-parietal junction (TPJ) (responsible for perspective taking and for recognizing motion in a social context, as for example when a person is making gestures within a social scene (Morris, Pelphrey, & McCarthy, 2005); the amygdala (used in attaching reward values to stimuli and decoding the emotional content of facial expressions); and the temporal poles (recruited when social scripts are invoked to understand interpersonal interaction).

What is the clinical picture like when trauma brings about a partial and temporary collapse of mentalization? The difficulty traumatized patients have in understanding themselves and others (i.e., their failure to mentalize) struck me (PF) forcibly over 15 years ago while I was treating borderline women and violent men (Fonagy, 1989). A later study of the psychoanalytic treatment of 30 young adults with violent and suicidal behavior, led by Anne-Marie Sandler at the Anna Freud Centre, reinforced my conclusions (Gerber, 2004; Perelberg, 1999);[2] 83% were in analysis (with 29% in psychotherapy). In these studies we observed something that seemed like a lack of imagination about the mental world of others, a naiveté or cluelessness about what others think or feel that can verge on confusion. Corresponding to this was an absence of insight into the way that the traumatized person's own mind worked. James describes thinking thus: "I keep doing these crazy things. Why am I doing these things? I was confused. I used to just sit down for hours sometimes and drive myself mad, thinking. And I just didn't get anywhere. It used to wind me up."

Research has shown that the capacity for mentalization is undermined in most people who have experienced trauma. Young, maltreated children manifest certain characteristics that might suggest problems with mentalization: (a) like blind children, they engage in less symbolic and dyadic play (Alessandri, 1991); (b) at times they fail to show empathy when witnessing distress in other children (Howes & Espinosa, 1985; Klimes-Dougan & Kistner, 1990; Main & George, 1985); (c), they have poor affect regulation (e.g., Maughan & Cicchetti, 2002); (d) they make fewer references to their internal states, and specifically, discuss emotions less frequently with their mothers (Beeghly & Cicchetti, 1994; Shipman & Zeman, 1999); (e) maltreated toddlers have difficulty in learning to use internal state words (Beeghly & Cicchetti, 1994) and (f) have difficulty in understanding (particularly facial) emotional expressions (Camras, Grow, & Ribordy, 1983), masked negative emotional facial expressions (Camras et al., 1988), and adult facial expressions (During & McMahon, 1991), even when controlled for verbal IQ (Camras et al., 1990). Maltreated children tend to misattribute anger (Camras, Sachs-Alter, & Ribordy, 1996) and maltreated 6- to 12-year-olds show elevated event-related potential (ERP) to angry faces (Cicchetti & Curtis, 2005; Pollak, Klorman, Thatcher, & Cicchetti, 2001; Pollak & Sinha, 2003). In a recent, as yet unpublished study we used Baron-Cohen's Reading the Mind in the Eyes stimuli to test mentalization in 147 adults, half of whom were individuals with a history of childhood maltreatment histories. The adults with histories of maltreatment achieved lower scores on the Eyes Test, but this effect varied with the severity and type of maltreatment. A history of moderate sexual or physical abuse was most strongly associated with low scores on difficult items in the test.

A second aspect of the phenomenology of the response to attachment trauma is that the collapse of mentalization entails a loss of awareness of the relationship between internal and external reality (Fonagy & Target, 2000). Modes of representing the internal world reemerge that developmentally precede the awareness that thoughts, feelings, and wishes are part of the mind. The 2- to 3-year-old, not yet experiencing his mind as truly representational, assumes that his thoughts have a reality equivalent to that of objects in the physical world. This generates a lack of flexibility, which we have termed *psychic equivalence*: mental states are equated with physical reality (Fonagy & Target, 1996; Target & Fonagy, 1996). Not only is there an omnipotence of subjectivity ("I know what is right") but also everything that is "out there" is felt to be known ("You can't tell me anything"). This of course leaves no room for alternative perspectives.

19

The 3-year-old's fantasy that there is a tiger under his bed generates acute, compelling fear. Post-traumatic subjective experiences (flashbacks) are similarly compelling to the trauma victim; such experiences are resistant to argument, and feel dangerous until they can be mentalized. Often, survivors of trauma simply refuse to think about their experience because to think about it means to relive it. Furthermore, in addition to this failure to mentalize when facing their trauma, patients often show marked psychic equivalence in other contexts. James, for example, talks about writing letters in the following manner: "When you write to someone, it's like, you're going in that letter, you put your hand in the letter, or your whole body's in the letter. And when they open the letter, the words, you are the words—so, you know, it's like you're outside, but you're still in, still in prison." It is interesting to note that aspects of psychic equivalence overlap with descriptions of paranoid-schizoid forms of thinking, particularly those formulated by Wilfred Bion in *Elements of Psychoanalysis* (Bion, 1963; Hobson, Patrick, & Valentine, 1998), and the concept of symbolic equation as formulated by Hanna Segal (1957).

Separation from reality is the third aspect of the phenomenology of attachment trauma. The *pretend mode* is a developmental complement to psychic equivalence, and it, too, recalls the child's experience. Because he is not yet able to conceive of internal experience as mental, when a child plays his fantasies have to be dramatically divided off from the external world so that they are not experienced in the mode of psychic equivalence as terrifyingly real. Small children cannot simultaneously pretend (even though they know it is not real) and engage with normal reality; asking them if their pretend gun is a gun or a stick spoils the game. Following trauma and the constriction of mentalization, we see the reemergence of the pretend mode, particularly in dissociative experiences. In dissociated thinking, nothing can be linked to anything—the principle of the pretend mode, in which fantasy is cut off from the real world, is extended so that nothing has implications (Fonagy & Target, 2000). The compulsive search for meaning (hyperactive mentalization), what James describes as "driving himself mad," is a common reaction against the sense of emptiness and disconnection that the pretend mode generates. Patients report "blanking out," "clamming up," or remembering their traumatic experiences only in dreams. The most characteristic feature of traumatization is the oscillation between psychic equivalence and pretend modes of experiencing the internal world.

A further pre-mentalistic aspect of psychic reality is the reemergence of what we describe as a teleological mode of thought, which is characterized by the attitude "I believe it only when I see it." In this mode others' actions are understood in terms of physical constraints and observable goals rather than mental states. This mode of understanding the world antedates even language. Infants as young as 9 months are able to attribute goals to people and to objects that seem to behave purposefully, but these goals are not yet truly mental; they are tied to what is observable.

The return of this teleological mode of thought is perhaps the most painful aspect of a subjectivity stripped of mentalization following trauma. In this mode, verbal reassurance means little. Interacting with others at a mental level has been replaced by attempts at altering thoughts and feelings through action. Changes in mental states are assumed to be real only when confirmed by physically observable actions that are contingent with the patient's wish, belief, feeling, or desire. In therapy, someone who is functioning in the teleological mode may put pressure on his therapist to show concrete (physical) evidence of concern by deviating from the therapeutic protocol, for example by offering extra sessions or allowing phone calls between sessions as physical proofs of commitment. These patients are forced to try and provoke visible evidence of concern from others because of their limited capacity to experience concern in circumstances in which others whose mentalizing capacity was intact would not find any reason to doubt it. Most trauma, certainly physical and sexual abuse, is almost by definition teleological in that it involves a physical experience with physical consequences. However, everyone recognizes that it is the psychological context of these physical consequences that generates problems, precisely because they undermine standard social scripts, generate inappropriate and intense affect, fail to take the perspective of the victim into consideration, and confound the victim's efforts to infer the mental states of the perpetrator. It is hardly surprising that the victim feels that the mind of another can only be altered in this same mode, through a physical act, threat, or seduction. Stuart describes his feelings about being sent to live in a hostel at the age of 11 as follows: "I tried to make them understand that I was upset so I was throwing things quite a lot, I threw my bed out of the window, I broke all the windows in the room, the only way I could make them understand that I did not like it." It is not just those who are severely traumatized who find physical modes of expression more persuasive than words—words that are all too easily experienced as meaningless within a pretend mode. Following trauma, we all need physical assurances of security. In fact, some of the more effective therapies offered for acute trauma reactions involve an element of bodily manipulation as well as psychological interventions (van der Kolk, 2003).

A NEUROSCIENTIFIC ATTACHMENT THEORY UNDERSTANDING OF THE LOSS OF MENTALIZATION ASSOCIATED WITH TRAUMA

Attachment Theory and Trauma

Attachment theory and research offer a useful starting point for understanding the impact of trauma. *Trauma triggers the attachment system.* As John Bowlby pointed out (Bowlby, 1969), trauma inhibits exploration and activates affectional bonds. We feel distressed and we want to be hugged. The events of 7/7 triggered the need to belong to a community of Londoners, as did 9/11 in New York and 3/11 in Madrid. Such crises are most challenging for those whose capacity for relationships is weakest, while a history of secure attachments increases the chances of responding to trauma in relatively adaptive ways. Why? Classical attachment and some object relations theories contend that templates of relationships are established in infancy and are enacted in later development (Bretherton & Munholland, 1999; Crittenden, 1994; Sroufe, 1996). Early traumatic experiences establish such early relationship expectations, and later traumas activate and interact with those early expectations. A child from a background of parental conflict, whose attachments have been disrupted and sense of security undermined, perhaps often expects to be rejected. Such a child might dismiss a helper in much the same way as the infant in the strange situation feels she cannot afford to turn for comfort to the caregiver.

From a psychoanalytic perspective the above is an overly simplistic model of attachment-trauma. To understand adult violence as a mere repetition of attachment trauma fails to reflect the extent of the devastation that attachment trauma causes to a child's psychological integrity. To understand this devastation more fully, we have to go back in time, not just through the child's life, but right back through 2 million years of human evolution, a development that has now been illuminated by a combination of fossil and neuroscientific investigations.

The Evolution of the Social Brain

The most generally accepted model of how humans evolved was proposed by Richard Alexander (1989). Alexander suggests that our exceptional intelligence evolved not to deal with the hostile forces of nature, but rather to deal with competition from other people. This occurred only after our species had achieved relative dominance over its environment. At that point it seems we became our "own principal hostile forces of nature" (Alexander, 1989, p. 469). All species face competition from within, but humans are special with respect to the role that social groups play in achieving success in this type of competition.[3] A kind of "evolutionary arms race" took place among ever more effective social groups (Flinn, Geary, & Ward, 2005). This effectiveness depended on skill in social cognition, which has much in common with the psychoanalytic concept that we have called mentalization, and which is the symbolic representation of mental states: to understand other people also allows one to outsmart them.[4] As the intelligence of the opposition increased, so did the requirement for ever greater ability for communication, imaginative social and emotional understanding, and the anticipation of others' reactions—capacities finely honed in most psychoanalysts.

Brain studies and fossil records suggest that self-awareness most likely evolved to aid other-awareness. Closely associated with evolutionary changes in social intelligence were changes in human brain structure. There was a modest proportional expansion in parts of the prefrontal cortex (about 10%; Semendeferi & Damasio, 2000), accompanied by increased richness of interconnections between neurons in these areas. There are unique features of human neuroanatomy, such as increased lateralization, which underpin social interpretation. There was also a disproportionate expansion of the right prefrontal cortex and the frontal pole (Holloway, 1996; Zilles et al., 1996). These areas of the brain have been shown by imaging studies to be involved in self-awareness, the ability to remember personal experiences, and to project oneself into the future (Tulving, 2002). Self-awareness enables

23

us to modify the way we wish to present ourselves, and also to mislead. The right prefrontal cortex may be there "to allow us to see ourselves as others see us so that we may cause competitive others to see us as we wish them to" (Alexander, 1990, p. 7). Thus the original evolutionary function of subjective experiences such as daydreams and fantasies might have been to allow individuals to form goals and carry out plans, and to integrate these within a seamless knowledge of their life histories (Levine, 1999).

It seems that self-awareness and awareness of the mental states of others are closely linked, certainly in terms of the brain areas involved. Mentalization does not simply facilitate collaboration and positive relationships, but, more importantly, it facilitates social survival. Mentalization serves competition: it is more like the antlers of a reindeer (used to fight other reindeer) than the eyes of the hawk (used to find prey). What are the implications of this for our understanding of attachment trauma?

As the mind needs to adapt to variable conditions, the capacity for mentalization is influenced, but not fixed, by genetics. Increased sophistication in social cognition evolved hand in hand with greater helplessness in infancy, the prolongation of childhood, and the emergence of intensive parenting (Geary & Huffman, 2002; Hrdy, 2000; Siegal & Varley, 2002). Evolution, it seems, has charged attachment relationships with ensuring the full development of the social brain and has made the infant-parent relationship into a training ground for teaching the infant about minds. The selective advantage conferred by the intensive multi-adult parenting that human infants receive (Hrdy, 2000) is the opportunity it affords for the full development of neurocognitive social capacities. The child discovers minds in his objects as he tries to find representations of himself as thinking and feeling in their actions. The child's capacity to represent mental states symbolically has long been assumed by psychoanalysts to be acquired within the primary object relationship. The idea is clearest in Bion's work, but it is also implicit in Fairbairn, explicated in Winnicott, restated in Kohut, and rediscovered with new emphases by relational writers such as Stephen Mitchell.[5] The infant learns about the nature of mental states and learns to represent specific mind states symbolically.

Modern attachment theory identifies important developmental functions of attachment beyond the physical protection of the child (Belsky, 1999; Polan & Hofer, 1999). Stress and affect regulation (Champagne et al.,

2004; Cicchetti & Walker, 2001; Plotsky et al., 2005; Zhang, Chretien, Meaney, & Gratton, 2005), the establishment of attention control mechanisms (particularly effortful control) (Fearon & Belsky, 2004; Posner & Rothbart, 2000) and the development of mentalizing capacities (Bateman & Fonagy, 2004; Fonagy, Gergely, Jurist, & Target, 2002) are perhaps the most important. The social brain is "experience expectant" (Siegel, 1999), in that it relies on normative kinship experiences for its normal development. The disruption of early affectional bonds not only sets up maladaptive attachment patterns but also undermines a range of capabilities vital to normal social development, including mentalization.

The Neurobiology of Attachment

Recent neuroimaging studies cast an intriguing light on the association of attachment with the development of mentalization. The neurobiology of attachment is now fairly well understood.[6] In brief, it seems that changes in attachment behavior, such as falling in love, which are stimulated by social/sexual activity, entail the activation of an oxytocin- and vasopressin-sensitive circuit within the anterior hypothalamus (MPOA) linked to the ventral tegmental area (VTA) and the nucleus accumbens shell (Insel, 2003). Functional imaging studies indicate that the same pathways in the brain are activated both when a person sees their own baby and when they see their partner; these pathways are not activated when they see another familiar baby or other people's partners (Nitschke et al., 2004).

In two separate imaging studies, Bartels and Zeki (Bartels & Zeki, 2000; 2004) reported that the activation of areas mediating maternal and/or romantic attachments appeared simultaneously to suppress brain activity in regions associated with making social judgments and mentalizing. This suggests that being in an intense, emotionally attached state inhibits mentalizing and the capacity accurately to see the attachment figure as a person.

These findings are extremely important and their implications deserve detailed consideration. In particular, the system defined by the temporal poles, parietotemporal junction, amygdala, and mesial prefrontal cortex, including the paracingulate, has been consistently implied to be active when judgments of social trustworthiness, moral judgments, considering other people's beliefs, and attention to one's own emotions are called for (Brunet,

Sarfati, Hardy-Bayle, & Decety, 2000; Castelli, Happe, Frith, & Frith, 2000; Gallagher & Frith, 2003; Gusnard, Akbudak, Shulman, & Raichle, 2001; Lane, Fink, Chau, & Dolan, 1997). Taking the evolutionary perspective elaborated above, it would appear that the presence of an attachment bond implies a less pressing need to create a mental model of what the other might be thinking since the emotional bond identifies them as potentially facilitative rather than in competition. This is why trust and attachment are so closely linked. To be attached to someone is to trust them implicitly, not to feel the need to identify the thoughts and beliefs behind their actions, and to assume that these are obvious and invariably benign in relation to oneself. Because of the complementarity of the activation of attachment and mentalization the mental states of attachment figures will always be hard to comprehend fully and perhaps will always remain somewhat enigmatic. Perhaps psychoanalytic therapy provides a much-needed opportunity for clarification and elaboration of the thoughts and feelings of attachment figures in the past and present precisely because the "heat" of attachment has moved from them to the analyst in the transference.

The configuration described by Bartels and Zeki has critical developmental implications precisely because the mentalizing capacity is *not* normally vital in the context of the attachment relationship. With an attachment relationship, errors carry little in the way of penalty. Explicitly revealing one's own state of mind to an attachment figure does not increase the individual's vulnerability. The attachment context is a practice ground for the acquisition of mentalization, a kind of sanctuary. From an evolutionary perspective, mentalization is a weapon to be used in the struggle for survival, and it is dangerous to play war games with loaded weapons. Taking a sociobiological perspective helps us understand why secure attachment in infancy might facilitate the development of mentalization (Fonagy, Redfern, & Charman, 1997; Fonagy, Steele, Steele, & Holder, 1997; Fonagy & Target, 1997; Meins, Fernyhough, Russell, & Clark-Carter, 1998; Meins & Russell, 1997) at the same time as feeling attached inhibits the capacity of mentalization. Missing out on early attachment experience (as happened for the Romanian orphans, e.g., O'Connor, Marvin, Rutter, Olrick, & Britner, 2003; Rutter & O'Connor, 2004) creates a long-term vulnerability from which the child may never recover. The capacity for mentalization is never fully established, leaving the child vulnerable to later trauma and unable to cope fully with attachment relationships. More importantly, trauma, by activating attachment, will cause the suppression of the capacity for mentalization. This of course is greatly exacerbated when the trauma is attachment trauma. We now turn to three related clinical aspects of this issue.

The first of these is the hyperactivation of the attachment system. Attachment is normally the ideal training ground for the development of mentalization because it is safe and noncompetitive. This biological configuration, which is so adaptive in the context of normal development, becomes immensely destructive in the presence of attachment trauma. Attachment trauma hyperactivates the attachment system because the person to whom the child looks for reassurance and protection is the one causing fear. The devastating psychic impact of attachment trauma is therefore the combined result of the inhibition of mentalization by attachment and the hyperactivation of the attachment system by trauma. This context demands extraordinary mentalizing capacities from the child, yet the hyperactivation of the attachment system will have suppressed the (limited) capacity that he has.

The coincidence of trauma and attachment creates a biological vicious cycle. Trauma normally causes a child to seek safety by gaining proximity to the attachment figure. This generates a characteristic dependency on the maltreating figure, with the real risk of an escalating sequence of further maltreatment, increased distress, and an ever greater inner need for the attachment figure. The inhibition of mentalization in a traumatizing, hyperactivated attachment relationship is always likely to lead to a pre-mentalistic psychic reality, largely split into psychic equivalence and pretend modes. The memory of the trauma feels real, so there is a constant danger of retraumatization from inside. The traumatized child often begins to fear his own mind, needing the attachment figure even more. The inhibition of mentalization is often an intrapsychic adaptation to traumatic violent attachment. The frankly malevolent mental state of the abuser terrifies the helpless child. The parents' abuse undermines the child's capacity to mentalize, because it is no longer safe for the child, for example, to think about wishing, if this implies recognizing his parent's wish to harm him. In reality of course it is never a single figure who is involved but an entire family dynamic that is nonmentalizing (Hill, Fonagy, Safier, & Sargent, 2003). We know from cross-sectional research that family atmosphere is a powerful predictor of precociousness in mentalizing (Cassidy, Parke, Butkovsky, & Braungart, 1992; Denham, Zoller,

& Couchoud, 1994). In the situations we have described for James and Stuart, it was trauma in an attachment context, rather than the abuse perpetrated by a primary attachment figure, that is likely to have led to the mentalizing difficulties that ensued for both these men. In that kind of family scenario of the problem is inevitably multilayered as well as multiply determined. The fear of the mind of the abuser is increased by the apparent inability of the primary attachment figure, often the mother, to protect the child. The child invariably experiences this as a failure on the mother's part to perceive his suffering. The experience of being confronted by blankness while experiencing extreme terror may in itself generate an intense wish to avoid minds, or to see the attachment figure as incapable of mirroring one's own mental state. Thus an important component of interpersonal violence is the violent person's explicit rejection of knowledge of mental states. More generally, the tragedy of transgenerational transmission of attachment trauma is based on the undermining of mentalization in the abused child, who will then become the abuser of children in the context of his or her own parenting.

A further complication follows because the child with attachment trauma who phobically avoids the mind of the parent cannot use the other as a mirror to understand the self, and diffusion of identity and dissociation can be the consequence. Even more pernicious is the state in which, owing to the individual's desperate need for some kind of self-awareness, psychic reality comes to be experienced through incorporating the other as part of the self. Recall Stuart's description of how, after feeling numb, he looked at his hands, and started laughing at himself: "I was going 'Ha ha,' you know, and I was thinking, *'I had done that.'*" Of course this process, taking the perspective of the other intent on destroying him, is very similar to what Anna Freud described as the process of identification with the aggressor.

The second aspect of attachment trauma concerns arousal, or the "biology of being frazzled." In all our investigations of trauma we have been impressed that loss of mentalization is partial, even in those whose trauma is pervasive. The impact of trauma on mentalization is intermittent: sometimes the disappearance of mentalization has to do with the intensification of an attachment relationship, for example in the course of an analysis; at other times, being stressed (for example touching on a sensitive issue) can trigger what feel like wild, unjustified reactions. Ten years ago, in a hallmark paper in *Science* entitled "The biology of being frazzled," Arnsten (1998) gave an explanation that, at the risk of simplifying highly complex pioneering neuroscientific work, works as follows: Arnsten's Dual Arousal Systems Model delineates two complementary, independent arousal systems, the prefrontal and posterior cortical and subcortical systems (Arnsten, 1998; Arnsten, Mathew, Ubriani, Taylor, & Li, 1999; Mayes, 2000). The system that activates frontal and prefrontal regions inhibits the second arousal system that normally kicks in only at quite high levels of arousal, when prefrontal activity goes offline and posterior cortical and subcortical functions (e.g., more automatic or motor functions, not thinking so much as running) take over. The switch-point between the two arousal systems may be shifted by childhood trauma. Undoubtedly, as mentalization involves the prefrontal cortex, this accounts for some of the inhibition of mentalization in individuals with attachment trauma, in response to increases in arousal that would not be high enough to inhibit mentalization in the majority of people. As James says: "I just snap, you know what I mean. It's like a switch. But I don't like it, I hate it. But I just can't help myself for doing it."

In light of this phenomenon, it is important for analysts to monitor the traumatized patient's readiness to hear comments about thoughts and feelings. As arousal increases, in part in response to interpretative work, traumatized patients cannot process talk about their minds. Interpretations of the transference at these times, however accurate they might be, are likely to be way beyond the capacity of the patient to hear. The clinical priority has to be to reduce arousal so that the patient can again think of other perspectives (i.e., mentalize).

The third and final aspect of attachment trauma, which is clinically the most significant, is *projective identification,* which can become a matter of life and death. The first of Bion's elements of psychoanalysis is "the essential feature of Melanie Klein's conception of projective identification . . . the dynamic relationship between container and contained" (Bion, 1963, p. 3). Jacobson (1954) and Winnicott (1956) independently noted that the internalization of the representation of another before the boundaries of the self have been fully formed undermines the creation of a coherent sense of self. The infant is forced to internalize the other not as an internal object but as a core part of his self. If the caregiver fails to contain the infant's anxieties, to metabolize them, and to mirror the self-state, the infant, rather than gradually constructing a representation of his internal states through mirroring and normal projective identification, is forced to accommodate the object, an alien being, within his self representation. Such incoherencies in self-structure are not features found only in profoundly neglected children. Even the most sensitive caregiver is insensitive to the child's state of mind more than 50% of the time. Thus we all have alien parts to our self-structure. The coherence of the self, as many have noted, is somewhat illusory. This illusion is normally maintained by the continuous narrative commentary on behavior that mentalization provides, which fills in the gaps and weaves our experiences together so that they make sense. In the absence of a robust mentalizing capacity, in the wake of trauma, the underlying fragmentation of the self-structure is likely to be clearly revealed in all of us.

Of course in traumatized individuals these introjections are colored by the traumatic context in which they occur.[7] What is internalized as part of the self is a caregiver with terrifying intentions. We have seen how Stuart, in desperation, opted to adopt his father's stance of vindictiveness and denigration toward himself. The tragic consequence of this manner of self-protection is the modification of self-organization so that the self now incorporates the abusive intention. This can generate momentary experiences of unbearable psychic pain when the self feels attacked literally from within and almost overwhelmed by an experience of badness that is impossible to mitigate by reassurance. Experienced in the mode of psychic equivalence, the feeling of badness translates directly into actual badness, from which, in a teleological mode of functioning, self-destruction might appear the only escape. In our view, this state is commonly the trigger for acts of self-harm and suicide, which are often associated with attachment trauma.

The only way the person can deal with such introjections is by constantly externalizing these alien parts of the self-structure into a container. Through projective identification, the persecutory parts are experienced as "outside." At this point, it is essential to the traumatized person that the alien experiences are owned by another mind, so that another mind is in control of the intolerable parts of the self—intolerable because they are set upon the self's own destruction. Thus, children who before the trauma were well-behaved and controlled suddenly become coercive and controlling.

They appear so because their attempts at control are crude. They may appear to have lost a previous level of subtlety of relating, based in an awareness of their own and others' feelings. Such a child may be contemptuous, provoking rage in the object, a rage which itself had originally been internalized in infancy in response to the insensitivity of the caregiver, and which becomes experienced as alien and intolerable following the trauma.

Many have noted that this mechanism can engender repetition of the traumatic experience in adult survivors. A woman who had been severely sexually abused in childhood by her father was sent to boarding school for her own protection and found herself in a very similar violent relationship with a teacher she trusted. Analysis revealed how she experienced respite from the unbearable state of self-hate by creating situations where she was debased, violated, and exploited. Paradoxically, while the need for projective identification is a matter of life and death for those with a traumatizing component within their self-structure, the particular constellation—of self with an aspect of self-experience that must be gotten rid of and attributed to another—creates a dramatic need for the object, a dependence that has many features of addiction. Neuroscience is helpful here in explaining that the triggering of the attachment system by the need to find a container for traumatized, alien parts of the self will once again inhibit mentalization, since, as discussed above, the hyperactivation of the attachment system—in the frantic dependence upon the object—inhibits those brain regions and processes that are the constituent parts of the capacity to mentalize. This will in turn reduce the chances that alternative solutions may be accepted, or that a nonteleological (nonphysical) solution can be found.

The following extract from a patient interview offers a striking illustration of the experience of externalizing the alien self. Sexually abused by his stepfather and brothers, the patient is now making a living as a male prostitute:

> The more you experience, the more immune you become to anything. If you get lured into a gang of queers and then you're abused, you don't fear queers no more. You just probably revenge against them. Cause you can turn your mind into their

activity and use it against them. I'm not getting into fights or anything like that, but I do happen to get into people's heads and hurt them, do you know what I mean?

Clinical Implications

What should be the object of psychoanalysis with traumatized patients? Traumatized individuals come to seek psychoanalytic help not simply to deal with the adversity they have experienced. The devastation of psychic function that attachment trauma leaves in its wake impairs the capacity to cope with *all* of the ordinary vicissitudes of mental life: unconscious conflicts over aggression, oedipal desires and defenses mounted against them, narcissistic vulnerabilities, conflicts in relation to ambivalently cathected objects, and more. All of the inescapable pains of the human condition are experienced with the rawness of an open wound unprotected by the "skin" that mentalization provides. While some of these derivatives will interact with the trauma suffered, the intensity of the associated feelings should not mislead the analyst into thinking that these later conflicts are the underlying cause of the patient's mental anguish; they have been amplified and prolonged by the patient's difficulty in mentally processing all painful experiences.

The overall aim of treating trauma patients is therefore to help them to establish a more robust, mentalizing self so that they can (try to) mentalize trauma and conflict and develop more secure relationships. Mentalizing provides a buffer between feeling and action, which is necessary if impulses are to be caught before they become overwhelming, and if motivations of self and other are to be monitored and understood. Enhancing mentalization bridges the gap between affects and their representation, especially with current mental states. However, this is not necessarily accomplished via work on the trauma itself. Most trauma-linked mental disorder involves specific dysfunctions of mentalization. As we have seen, attachment trauma creates psychological disturbance by interfering with mentalization, leading the mind to misperceive and misrepresent the status of its own contents and its own functions. Thus borderline personality disorder may be seen as a fear of minds, while depression might entail an overinvolvement with negative cognitions experienced in psychic equivalence mode as real and true. More generally, psychopathology seen as a trauma-generated collapse of mentalization entails that the traumatized individual in some sense loses contact with his mind. Psychoanalysis fosters mentalization in relation to the patient's self, not just in relation to his trauma. It entails finding or recovering mentalization through a developmentally appropriate process; that is, finding one's psychological self through the mind of a benign attachment figure. But how can we help a patient with memories of attachment trauma to become more able to mentalize about these experiences? The mental shift required of the analyst, which involved moving from a long tradition of aiming to provide insight to an alternative approach that focuses on the more modest aim of enhancing mentalization, should not be underestimated. The challenge for the analyst is to maintain a mentalizing therapeutic stance in the context of countertransference responses that may provoke the therapist to react rather than to think. In fact countertransference enactments are inevitable, and it is necessary to be permissive (non-self-persecutory) about them while trying to guard against them. The therapist has to accept that in order to stay in mental proximity with a patient he will occasionally find himself acting in a manner that would normally be uncharacteristic of him (e.g., being critical of the patient, losing his or her temper, becoming excessively familiar, etc.). We cannot consider technique at length here and shall discuss only one controversial topic, the role of memory and the recovery of traumatic experience in the context of therapy.

Recovering Memories of Trauma

Research on memory shows that childhood memories are very fallible, but the gist of recalled experience is mostly accurate (Christianson, 1992; Heuer & Reisberg, 1992; Riccio, Rabinowitz, & Axelrod, 1994), particularly for traumatic events (Usher & Neisser, 1993). While episodic memory does not develop until age 5, children can probably encode and store many experiences that they are unable to describe, although this does not mean that systematic reconstruction of such experiences would necessarily be helpful in the treatment of trauma. The reason for this is that trauma, in particular early trauma, interferes with autobiographical memory. We have known this for some decades, particularly from studies of combat veterans suffering from post-traumatic stress disorder (Bremner et al., 1992; Christianson

& Nilsson, 1989; Fisher, 1945; Kazniak, Nussbaum, Berren, & Santiago, 1988; Sargant, 1967). In particular, early trauma may disrupt the normal functioning of the memory system (Teicher, Ito, Glod, Schiffer, & Gelbard, 1994). Repeated experience of maltreatment have been shown to generate hippocampal damage (Bremner et al., 1993), and the hippocampus is critically important in the integration of experiences in memory. In the absence of its integrative function, patients are likely to be left with fragmented images and emotions that they are unable to combine with their life narrative or self-schema.

In terms of the neurology of memory, the frontal lobes appear to play a key role in monitoring the source of a memory image, including distinguishing true and false memories; prior expectations can create an unusually vivid set of ideas or images. The hyperactivation of the attachment system in individuals with trauma and the likely associated inhibition of mentalizing may compromise the ability to know or discover where an image comes from. Any pressure by the therapist to recreate and revive memories would be likely to introduce a further bias and inaccuracy. The therapist must be aware that the cognitive functions that are normally available to prevent confusion between fantasy and memory will be specifically compromised in traumatized individuals due to the hyperactivation of the attachment system, and that these functions may be specifically compromised by the therapeutic process itself.

Some, and we are not among these, might argue that using reconstruction to identify a child within the patient, one traumatized by (say) rejection at the time of her sibling being born, serves to collude with the patient's need to avoid the massive depressive anxiety associated with her hatred of her own child and the multifarious roots of her self hatred. In that sense, these clinicians might argue that reconstruction is invariably somewhat collusive with the patient's defenses, to the extent that it serves to displace primitive and intense guilt from the present into the past while also making others (rather than the patient) culpable. We believe that reconstruction does indeed carry such a risk. But so does any effective psychoanalytic intervention. Analysts using any psychoanalytic technique must be cognizant of the patient's defenses (and thus address the conflict from the point of view of the ego), and in addition ensure that the technique is (broadly) acceptable to the patient in the way it presents material that we know to be inherently impossible to contemplate. We believe that reconstruction is essential to the therapeutic process because: (a) it provides a means of bringing the patient's mind into contact with what it has previously found intolerable; (b) it provides a place where threats to the ego and to the therapeutic goal are reasonably balanced; (c) it generates a coherent self narrative assuming a historical continuity of self, which may itself be of therapeutic value (Holmes, 1998; Schafer, 1980; Spence, 1994); and (d) most importantly, it can help in the primary task of the recovery of mentalization. It is this last point that we would like to illustrate with a clinical example.

CLINICAL ILLUSTRATION

Miss C. had originally presented with a mixture of quite severe anxiety and depression, and a history that included a psychotic episode and abuse from a psychotic stepfather. The abuse was severe enough for extensive social services involvement, and there was a realistic risk of the 11-year-old Miss C. being taken into care. The trauma was cumulative. Her stepfather systematically humiliated her in addition to being physically, but not explicitly sexually, abusive. For example, she recalled having to stand by her bed at night reciting her homework, knowing that any mistake would be followed by physical punishment.

Not surprisingly, in Miss C.'s analysis memories acquired great significance. At one level, she experienced her work with me (PF) as a masochistic submission to a mad and cruel man who was demanding that she remember her past in great detail no matter how painful and humiliating it felt. Also unsurprising was her reaction to this submission, which consisted of an enraged regression and an at times infantile state of withdrawal. For days, sometimes weeks, she would not speak to me. She came on time and seemed to value her time on the couch, but made no response to invitations to free associate or even to answer direct questions. She seemed to have cut off awareness of being in the room with me. While remembering was fraught, the present was unbearable. The longest periods of silence invariably followed any attempt I made to link the painful experiences she recalled to her current relationship with me. For example, she had brought a memory of a time when she had gone to bed hoping that her stepfather had forgotten about the testing that evening. She had been careful to keep especially quiet to make sure that she did not inadvertently draw attention

35

to herself. She recalled her terror when he burst into her room some time after she had gone to sleep. He demanded an explanation for her daring to go to bed without having been tested. I gently suggested that she might equally be fearful of how I might act or that I might say things that she did not anticipate, and that being silent might be the only way that she could feel safe during analysis. She acknowledged what I said with a vague shrug and said nothing for the rest of the session. She was more or less totally silent during the next session too.

With hindsight it is clear to me that Miss C. experienced my interpretations in a psychic equivalence mode. Even though gently put, the analogy in the transference to her stepfather's behavior seemed to become an actual threat of my behaving in unpredictable ways, and placed an implicit demand on her not to move or draw attention to herself. The current relationship with Miss C. was not an appropriate entry point into her inner world.

However, what did turn out to be most useful for Miss C. was what seemed like direct work with her experiences of trauma. She found it helpful when we talked about her terror of her stepfather, his moodiness, the way his gestures or facial expressions could indicate to her what to expect, the way the beatings felt, where her mother was and what she might have been thinking when the abuse occurred, Miss C.'s ways of trying to comply with his wishes, and the tricks that she was proud of developing and which she used to distract him from his wish to maltreat her. The remembering, as it occurred in this analysis, took quite some time (most of the first year of Miss C.'s treatment). This remembering took the place of an analysis as classically described. During this time there was a growing understanding of her traumatic experience but little apparent understanding of her self. Yet the impact on her was clearly positive and, as the year passed, she engaged with her treatment and the difficulties with her work also began to ease.

We have made reference to this case in order to show that our emphasis on mentalization is not inconsistent with reconstruction. To this day I remain unconvinced about the accuracy of Miss C.'s memories of abuse. I would remember that she had presented the same incidents in quite different ways at different times. The whole idea of remembering was so fraught, so loaded with unmetabolized affect, that I felt continually drawn into the abuse. Even mild questioning of her silence fixed me in that role. Yet my tolerance of her silence was vital, ultimately enabling her to speak without feeling that she was being compelled to "do her homework." But perhaps even more concretely, remembering allowed her to learn to mentalize her experience.

Miss C. worked through the same memories again and again, both screen memories and real memories. But with each recollection she would be able to depict with slightly greater clarity her thoughts and feelings, and, perhaps even more important, the putative thoughts and feelings of her tormentor. As she remembered what sounded like different accounts of the same events, I would realize that she was trying out different perspectives on the experience. When Miss C. remembered waiting in her bed, listening in terror, trying to identify her stepfather's footsteps, she was not only remembering trauma, but also making the imaginative leap of mentalization, putting herself into the mind of the 8-year-old girl listening to the sounds and remembering her constructions. When she recalled her stepfather's face contorted into a Kabuki grimace of rage, the therapeutic benefit came from stepping behind his mask and seeing the cruelty of a man struggling with his own internal demons, demons that probably persecuted him as mercilessly as he persecuted Miss C.

The quality of Miss C.'s memories underwent a change; from static pictures of the past, they became moving and even talking pictures, where Miss C.'s experience of herself and others was no longer either equated to the past or dissociated. In retrospect it seems clear that for Miss C. the memories of the trauma paradoxically created the safest context for the recovery of mentalization. The benefit was not from the recovery of memories or even the discovery of specific states of mind that were contained within them. It was in rediscovering the mere fact of thought and feeling, the layeredness of subjective experience. Miss C. came to describe this stage of her treatment as "remembering." On one occasion she added: "It's not enough to remember; you've got to make remembering count."

Of course this was not something that occurred from one day to the next. Miss C. was in analysis for three years, followed by psychotherapy twice and then once a week for a further two. Many issues besides her traumatic experiences needed to be addressed before she was ready to leave and move on with her life, which turned out to be a successful one by any standard. It is important to point out that dealing with her trauma-induced difficulty in thinking was by no means resolved when the trauma itself became mentalized. Even when she was able to think about the complexity of her object relations, colored as they were by experiences of maltreatment, she remained vulnerable to moments of regression, affect dysregulation, and psychic equivalent and pretend modes of experiencing her subjective reality. Interestingly, much of the significant improvement in her capacity to mentalize occurred once she had stopped intensive treatment. It seemed to both of us as if the analytic setting, with its features encouraging regression, at times made it apparently inevitable that she experienced her mental states as somewhat unreal. In once-weekly psychotherapy and then after the termination of her treatment she became far better able to function independently, and to think for herself and for others in creative and constructive ways.

THE ROLE OF "MEMORY WORK" IN PSYCHOANALYSIS

While reconstruction of how things actually were in childhood may significantly contribute to therapeutic action, this does not mean that the outcome of reconstruction, the remembering of (hypothetical) autobiographical events, is the key. It is the process of reworking current experiences in the context of other perspectives, that is, enhancing mentalization, that I believe to be curative in what we do. The other perspectives may be from the patient's childhood, but they could be the analyst's current experience, or the way the patient is experienced by others close to him in the present. Given the historical, theoretical, and even geographical specificity of psychoanalytic focus on particular historical reconstructions (taking up primal scene memories, sibling rivalry, birth trauma, toilet training, sexual abuse, separation trauma, etc.), it is most unlikely that reconstruction per se is essential, whereas the creation of a narrative and the deep exploration of subjectivity from alternative perspectives almost certainly are. The questioning of current ways of being and thinking, inevitably implied by any act of reconstruction, is no doubt therapeutic.

While the interpersonal situation created by those patients who desperately need external validation is certainly difficult, even for experienced therapists, it must be wrong to collude with the patient's attempt to use the therapist to reduce the unknowable to a fact. From our point of view the task of the therapist is to contain the patient and to show genuine understanding both of his state of uncertainty and of the hopes and conflicts that result from such uncertainty. It is far more difficult to empathize with the patient's not knowing than to reduce uncertainty by pretending to know. Ultimately, confirming a reality basis for the patient's vague sense that something inappropriate might have happened is the same sort of technical error as direct reassurance.

By giving reassurance, the analyst not only colludes with one side of a patient's ongoing conflict, but also communicates an inability to withstand the patient's demands for false certainty. In this way, his own incapacity to tolerate uncertainty is communicated. The patient is then obliged not only to live what may be a false reality, but, perhaps even more damaging, to support what he unconsciously perceives as the therapist's psychic fragility. Paradoxically, many therapists intend such interventions to show the patient something quite different—that is, an inner strength in facing up to unbearable images and in thinking the unthinkable.

CONCLUSION

We have suggested that the psychological consequences of trauma, in an attachment context and perhaps beyond, entail a decoupling of mentalization and a reemergence of nonmentalizing modes of representing internal reality. This situation is pernicious because the immediacy of a memory experienced in the nonmentalizing mode of psychic equivalence has the capacity to retraumatize again and again, further decoupling mentalization and making the experience ever more real. Trauma in the attachment context is most pernicious because the biological basis of attachment assumes trust, and part of this rests on the safety of not having to mentalize, of knowing that others are thinking for us and that we need not monitor our own or others' thinking. Trauma inevitably activates the attachment system. This activation (probably for evolutionary reasons) temporarily inhibits areas of the brain concerned both with remembering and mentalization. This is why mentalization comes to be so readily abandoned in the face of trauma, particularly attachment trauma. Unmentalized trauma endures and compromises mental function. Of course it also interferes with new relationships. When the self is experienced as being destroyed from within through identification with the aggressor, projective identification is felt to be imperative. The constellation of self and object that results from this imperative ends up retraumatizing the person who, addicted to the object, needs to draw the other ever closer and to select relationships that will permit such an unhealthy structure to be lived out. In this way, the individual loses a possible route by which to be freed from the shackles of a traumatic past that is constantly relived. In order to escape from the grip of trauma, the individual needs help to recover mentalization. Fortunately there are many means to achieve this; remembering in the context of an enduring psychoanalytic relationship is one such means, but not the only one.

NOTES

1. French psychoanalysts developed a notion of mentalization largely formulated from the economic point of view. Pierre Marty discussed mentalization as a protective buffer in the preconscious system that prevents progressive disorganization (Marty, 1968). He considers mentalization as connecting drive excitations and mental representations, thereby creating both "fluidity" and "constancy" (Marty, 1990, 1991). Mentalization ensures freedom in the use of associations, as well as permanence and stability. At the same time, Pierre Luquet (1981, 1988) discussed the development of different forms of thinking and the reorganization of inner experience alongside this development. In his chapter on a theory of language (Luquet, 1987), he distinguished primary mentalization (which we would consider the absence of reflective functioning) with secondary symbolic mentalization. While this form of mentalization was still seen as closely connected to sensory data and primary unconscious fantasies, it was nevertheless also seen as representative of these processes and observable in dreams, art, and play. His third level was verbal thought, which he considered most distant from bodily processes. Similar ideas have been proposed by Green (1975), Segal (1957), and McDougall (1978), and more recently by Frosch (1995), Busch (1995), and Auerbach (1993; Auerbach & Blatt, 1996).

2. Incidentally, the statistical analysis of the results of these treatments was recently completed and underscored the effectiveness of the psychoanalytic approach. In this sample of young adult personality-disordered subjects who were sequentially assigned to psychoanalysis and psychodynamic psychotherapy, 63% improved significantly on a very conservative composite measure of

psychiatric diagnosis, depression, and anxiety. Of those who were treated with psychoanalysis 83% showed improvements, compared to only 29% of those treated in psychotherapy. Only 9% of subjects in psychoanalysis for whom post-termination follow-up data were available did not maintain the gains of treatment.

3. These are normally negotiated, dynamic, multilevel kinship groups.

4. The more cognitively, socially, and behaviorally sophisticated individuals are able to outmaneuver and manipulate other individuals in order to gain control of resources and to gain control of the behavior of other people. But why such (in evolutionary terms) rapid development? Most evolutionary adaptations have a downside that makes them self-limiting (e.g., an increase in the size of a reindeer's antlers will help in combating other males, but only up to a point, after which the laws of physics make them an obstruction and a handicap). There is no such constraint on social intelligence other than the possibility of totally destroying our ecology (Flinn et al., 2005). The increasing coherence and organization of hominid groups and the ever more sophisticated cognitive capacities that underpin these groups bring increasing ecological advantages rather than costs. A virtuous cycle was created of ever-increasing ecological dominance and ever higher social intelligence and social complexity. Linguistic and social cognitive capacities were favored because they enabled our ancestors to anticipate and influence social interactions with other increasingly intelligent humans.

5. Children develop a malleable system that enables them to adapt to the particular mental structures that have evolved within a cultural group as specific adaptations to that environment (Bloom, 2000).

6. It is linked to the mesocorticolimbic dopaminergic reward circuit, which also plays a key role in mediating the process of physical (as well as emotional) addiction (Insel, 1997; MacLean, 1990; Panksepp, 1998). It is highly unlikely that nature created a brain system specifically to subserve cocaine and alcohol abuse. It is more likely that addictions are the accidental by-product of the activation of a biological system that underpins the crucial evolutionary function of attachment (Insel, 1997; MacLean, 1990; Panksepp, 1998). Attachment, then, is an 'addictive disorder' (Insel, 2003).

7. Trauma thus contributes to the foregrounding of self-fragmentation (identity diffusion) because traumatized individuals can make use of discontinuities within the self to adapt to incomprehensible assaults from someone connected to them by attachment bonds by "identifying with the aggressor" (Freud, 1936). One individual, who had been sexually abused as a child and was in prison for rape, vividly describes how this happens in answering a question about how his childhood experiences affected his adult personality: "I don't think none of it's been a setback I think it's all been, everything has been more positive because it's just like let's take, let's take slavery for example errm not from a racist point of view but from a realistic point of view[,] you take a man and you make him work for you, you feed him what you don't want to eat you put him in places you wouldn't want your dog to live but yet still he makes that home his castle he

makes gourmet meals out of your trash[,] one man's trash is another man's treasure one man's nightmare is another man's pleasure see and when you have a situation and you know that you are not going to get out of it well you start feeling good in it quicker than you can imagine."

REFERENCES

Alessandri, S. M. (1991). Play and social behaviours in maltreated preschoolers. *Development and Psychopathology, 3,* 191–206.

Alexander, R. D. (1989). Evolution of the human psyche. In P. Mellars & C. Stringer (Eds.), *The Human Revolution: Behavioural and Biological Perspectives on the Origins of Modern Humans* (pp. 455–513). Princeton, NJ: Princeton University Press.

Alexander, R. D. (1990). *How did humans evolve? Reflections on the uniquely unique species. Museum of Zoology (Special publication no. 1).* Ann Arbor, MI: University of Michigan.

Arnsten, A. F. T. (1998). The biology of being frazzled. *Science, 280,* 1711–1712.

Arnsten, A. F. T., Mathew, R., Ubriani, R., Taylor, J. R., & Li, B.-M. (1999). Alpha-1 noradrenergic receptor stimulation impairs prefrontal cortical cognitive function. *Biological Psychiatry, 45,* 26–31.

Auerbach, J. S. (1993). The origins of narcissism and narcissistic personality disorder: A theoretical and empirical reformulation. In J. M. Masling & R. F. Bornstein (Eds.), *Psychoanalytic Perspectives on Psychopathology* (pp. 43–110). Washington, DC: American Psychological Association.

Auerbach, J. S., & Blatt, S. J. (1996). Self-representation in severe psychopathology: The role of reflexive self-awareness. *Psychoanalytic Psychology, 13,* 297–341.

Bartels, A., & Zeki, S. (2000). The neural basis of romantic love. *Neuroreport, 11*(17), 3829–3834.

Bartels, A., & Zeki, S. (2004). The neural correlates of maternal and romantic love. *Neuroimage, 21*(3), 1155–1166.

Bateman, A. W., & Fonagy, P. (2004). *Psychotherapy for borderline personality disorder: Mentalization based treatment.* Oxford, UK: Oxford University Press.

Beeghly, M., & Cicchetti, D. (1994). Child maltreatment, attachment, and the self system: Emergence of an internal state lexicon in toddlers at high social risk. *Development and Psychopathology, 6,* 5–30.

Belsky, J. (1999). Modern evolutionary theory and patterns of attachment. In J. Cassidy & P. R. Shaver (Eds.), *Handbook of Attachment: Theory, Research and Clinical Applications* (pp. 141–161). New York: Guilford.

Bion, W. R. (1963). *Elements of psycho-analysis.* London: Heinemann.

Bloom, P. (2000). *How Children Learn the Meaning of Words*. Cambridge, MA: MIT Press.

Bowlby, J. (1969). *Attachment and Loss, Vol. 1: Attachment*. London: Hogarth Press and the Institute of Psycho-Analysis.

Bremner, J., Southwick, S., Brett, E., Fontana, A., Rosenheck, R., & Charney, D. (1992). Dissociation and posttraumatic stress disorder in Vietnam combat veterans. *American Journal of Psychiatry, 149*, 328–332.

Bremner, J. D., Scott, T. M., Delaney, R. C., Southwick, S. M., Mason, J. W., Johnson, D. R., et al. (1993). Deficits in short-term memory in posttraumatic stress disorder. *American Journal of Psychiatry, 150*, 1015–1019.

Brentano, F. (1973/1874). *Psychology from an empirical standpoint*. London: Routledge.

Bretherton, K., & Munholland, K. A. (1999). Internal working models in attachment relationships: A construct revisited. In J. Cassidy & P. R. Shaver (Eds.), *Handbook of attachment: Theory, research and clinical applications* (pp. 89–114). New York: Guilford.

Brunet, E., Sarfati, Y., Hardy-Bayle, M. C., & Decety, J. (2000). A PET investigation of the attribution of intentions with a nonverbal task. *Neuroimage, 11*(2), 157–166.

Busch, F. (1995). Do actions speak louder than words? A query into an enigma in analytic theory and technique. *Journal of the American Psychoanalytic Association, 43*, 61–82.

Camras, L. A., Grow, G., & Ribordy, S. (1983). Recognition of emotional expressions by abused children. *Journal of Clinical and Consulting Psychology, 12*(3), 325–328.

Camras, L. A., Ribordy, S., Hill, J., Martino, S., Sachs, V., Spaccarelli, S., et al. (1990). Maternal facial behavior and the recognition and production of emotional expression by maltreated and nonmaltreated children. *Developmental Psychology, 26*(2), 304–312.

Camras, L. A., Ribordy, S., Hill, J., Martino, S., Spaccarelli, S., & Stefani, R. (1988). Recognition and posing of emotional expressions by abused children and their mothers. *Developmental Psychology, 24*(6), 776–781.

Camras, L. A., Sachs-Alter, E., & Ribordy, S. C. (1996). Emotion understanding in maltreated children: Recognition of facial expressions and integration with other emotion cues. In M. D. Lewis & M. Sullivan (Eds.), *Emotional Development in Atypical Children* (pp. 203–225). Mahwah, NJ: Erlbaum.

Cassidy, J., Parke, R. D., Butkovsky, L., & Braungart, J. M. (1992). Family-peer connections: The roles of emotional expressiveness within the family and children's understanding of emotion. *Child Development, 63*(3), 603–618.

Castelli, F., Happe, F., Frith, U., & Frith, C. (2000). Movement and mind: A functional imaging study of perception and interpretation of complex intentional movement patterns. *Neuroimage, 12*(3), 314–325.

Champagne, F. A., Chretien, P., Stevenson, C. W., Zhang, T. Y., Gratton, A., & Meaney,

M. J. (2004). Variations in nucleus accumbens dopamine associated with individual differences in maternal behavior in the rat. *Journal of Neuroscience, 24*(17), 4113–4123.

Christianson, S. (1992). Remembering emotional events: Potential mechanisms. In S. Christianson (Ed.), *The Handbook of Emotion and Memory: Research and Theory* (pp. 307–340). Hillsdale, NJ: Erlbaum.

Christianson, S., & Nilsson, L. (1989). Hysterical amnesia: A case of aversively motivated isolation of memory. In T. Archer & L. Nilsson (Eds.), *Aversion, Avoidance, and Anxiety: Perspectives on Aversively Motivated Behavior* (pp. 289–310). Hillsdale, NJ: Erlbaum.

Cicchetti, D., & Curtis, W. J. (2005). An event-related potential study of the processing of affective facial expressions in young children who experienced maltreatment during the first year of life. *Development and Psychopathology, 17*(3), 641–677.

Cicchetti, D., & Walker, E. F. (2001). Editorial: Stress and development: Biological and psychological consequences. *Development and Psychopathology, 13*, 413–418.

Crittenden, P. M. (1994). Peering into the black box: An exploratory treatise on the development of self in young children. In D. Cicchetti & S. L. Toth (Eds.), *Disorders and Dysfunctions of the Self. Rochester Symposium on Developmental Psychopathology, Vol. 5* (pp. 79–148). Rochester, NY: University of Rochester Press.

Denham, S. A., Zoller, D., & Couchoud, E. A. (1994). Socialization of preschoolers emotion understanding. *Developmental Psychology, 30*, 928–936.

Dennett, D. C. (1978). Beliefs about beliefs. *Behaviour and Brain Sciences, 4*, 568–570.

During, S., & McMahon, R. (1991). Recognition of emotional facial expressions by abusive mothers and their children. *Journal of Clinical and Consulting Psychology, 20*(2), 132–139.

Fearon, R. M., & Belsky, J. (2004). Attachment and attention: Protection in relation to gender and cumulative social-contextual adversity. *Child Development, 75*(6), 1677–1693.

Fisher, C. (1945). Amnesic states in war neurosis: The psychogenesis of fugues. *Psychoanalytic Quarterly, 14*, 437–458.

Flinn, M., Geary, D., & Ward, C. (2005). Ecological dominance, social competition, and the coalitionary arms races: Why humans evolved extraordinary intelligence. *Evolution and Human Behavior, 26*, 10–46.

Fonagy, P. (1989). On tolerating mental states: Theory of mind in borderline patients. *Bulletin of the Anna Freud Centre, 12*, 91–115.

Fonagy, P., Gergely, G., Jurist, E., & Target, M. (2002). *Affect Regulation, Mentalization and the Development of the Self.* New York: Other Press.

Fonagy, P., Redfern, S., & Charman, T. (1997). The relationship between belief-desire reasoning and a projective measure of attachment security (SAT). *British Journal of Developmental Psychology, 15,* 51–61.

Fonagy, P., Steele, M., Steele, H., & Holder, J. (1997). Attachment and theory of mind: Overlapping constructs? *Association for Child Psychology and Psychiatry Occasional Papers, 14,* 31–40.

Fonagy, P., & Target, M. (1996). Playing with reality: I. Theory of mind and the normal development of psychic reality. *International Journal of Psycho-Analysis, 77,* 217–233.

Fonagy, P., & Target, M. (1997). Attachment and reflective function: Their role in self-organization. *Development and Psychopathology, 9,* 679–700.

Fonagy, P., & Target, M. (2000). Playing with reality III: The persistence of dual psychic reality in borderline patients. *International Journal of Psycho-Analysis, 81*(5), 853–874.

Freud, A. (1936). *The Ego and the Mechanisms of Defence.* New York: International Universities Press, 1946.

Frith, C. D. (2007). The social brain? *Philosophical Transactions of the Royal Society of London, Series B, Biological Sciences, 362*(1480), 671–678.

Frosch, A. (1995). The preconceptual organization of emotion. *Journal of the American Psychoanalytic Association, 43,* 423–447.

Gallagher, H. L., & Frith, C. D. (2003). Functional imaging of "theory of mind." *Trends in Cognitive Sciences, 7*(2), 77–83.

Geary, D. C., & Huffman, K. J. (2002). Brain and cognitive evolution: Forms of modularity and functions of mind. *Psychological Bulletin, 128*(5), 667–698.

Gerber, A. J. (2004). Psychodynamic psychotherapy for severe personality disorders: A quantitative study of treatment process and outcome. Unpublished doctoral thesis, University of London, England.

Green, A. (1975). The analyst, symbolisation and absence in the analytic setting: On changes in analytic practice and analytic experience. *International Journal of Psycho-Analysis, 56,* 1–22.

Gusnard, D. A., Akbudak, E., Shulman, G. L., & Raichle, M. E. (2001). Medial prefrontal cortex and self-referential mental activity: Relation to a default mode of brain function. *Proceedings of the National Academy of Sciences of the USA, 98*(7), 4259–4264.

Heuer, F., & Reisberg, D. (1992). Emotion, arousal, and memory for detail. In S. Christianson (Ed.), *The Handbook of Emotion and Memory: Research and Theory* (pp. 151–180). Hillsdale, NJ: Erlbaum.

Hill, J., Fonagy, P., Safier, E., & Sargent, J. (2003). The ecology of attachment in the family. *Family Process, 42*(2), 205–221.

Hobson, R. P., Patrick, M. P., & Valentine, J. D. (1998). Objectivity in psychoanalytic judgements. *British Journal of Psychiatry, 173*, 172–177.

Holloway, R. L. (1996). Evolution of the human brain. In A. Lock & C. R. Peters (Eds.), *Handbook of Human Symbolic Evolution* (pp. 74–116). New York: Oxford University Press.

Holmes, J. (1998). Defensive and creative uses of narrative in psychotherapy: An attachment perspective. In G. Roberts & J. Holmes (Eds.), *Narrative and psychotherapy and psychiatry* (pp. 49–68). Oxford, UK: Oxford University Press.

Howes, C., & Espinosa, M. P. (1985). The consequences of child abuse for the formation of relationships with peers. *International Journal of Child Abuse and Neglect, 9*, 397–404.

Hrdy, S. B. (2000). *Mother Nature.* New York: Ballantine Books.

Insel, T. (1997). A neurobiological basis of social attachment. *American Journal of Psychiatry, 154*, 726–735.

Insel, T. R. (2003). Is social attachment an addictive disorder? *Physiology and Behavior, 79*(3), 351–357.

Jacobson, E. (1954). The self and the object world: Vicissitudes of their infantile cathexes and their influence on ideational affective development. *The Psychoanalytic Study of the Child, 9*, 75–127.

Kazniak, A. W., Nussbaum, P. D., Berren, M. R., & Santiago, J. (1988). Amnesia as a consequence of male rape: A case report. *Journal of Abnormal Psychology, 97*, 100–104.

Klimes-Dougan, B., & Kistner, J. (1990). Physically abused preschoolers' responses to peers' distress. *Developmental Psychology, 25*, 516–524.

Lane, R. D., Fink, G. R., Chau, P. M., & Dolan, R. J. (1997). Neural activation during selective attention to subjective emotional responses. *Neuroreport, 8*(18), 3969–3972.

Levine, B. (1999). Self-regulation and autonoetic consciousness. In E. Tulving (Ed.), *Memory, Consciousness and the Brain: The Talinn Conference* (pp. 200–214). Philadelphia: Psychology Press.

Luquet, P. (1981). Le changement dans la mentalization. *Revue Français de Psychoanalyse, 45*, 1023–1028.

Luquet, P. (1987). Penser-Parler: Un apport psychanalytique à la theorie du langage. In R. Christie, M. M. Christie-Luterbacher, & P. Luquet (Eds.), *La parole troublée* (pp. 161–300). Paris: Presses Universitaires de France.

Luquet, P. (1988). Langage, pensée et structure psychique. *Revue Français de Psychoanalyse, 52*, 267–302.

MacLean, P. (1990). *The Triune Brain in Evolution: Role in Paleocerebral Functions.* New York: Plenum.

Main, M., & George, C. (1985). Responses of abused and disadvantaged toddlers to distress in agemates: A study in the daycare setting. *Developmental Psychology*, *21*, 407–412.

Marty, P. (1968). A major process of somatization: The progressive disorganization. *International Journal of Psycho-Analysis*, *49*, 246–249.

Marty, P. (1990). *La psychosomatique de l'adulte*. Paris: Presses Universitaires de France.

Marty, P., & De M'Uzan, M. (1963). La pensée opératoire. *Revue Française de Psychanalyse*, *27 (Suppl.)*, 1345–1356.

Maughan, A., & Cicchetti, D. (2002). Impact of child maltreatment and interadult violence on children's emotion regulation abilities and socioemotional adjustment. *Child Development*, *73*(5), 1525–1542.

Mayes, L. C. (2000). A developmental perspective on the regulation of arousal states. *Seminars in Perinatology*, *24*, 267–279.

McDougall, J. (1978). *Plea for a Measure of Abnormality*. New York: International Universities Press.

Meins, E., Fernyhough, C., Russell, J., & Clark-Carter, D. (1998). Security of attachment as a predictor of symbolic and mentalising abilities: A longitudinal study. *Social Development*, *7*, 1–24.

Meins, E., & Russell, J. (1997). Security and symbolic play: The relation between security of attachment and executive capacity. *British Journal of Developmental Psychology*, *15*, 63–76.

Morris, J. P., Pelphrey, K. A., & McCarthy, G. (2005). Regional brain activation evoked when approaching a virtual human on a virtual walk. *Journal of Cognitive Neuroscience*, *17*(11), 1744–1752.

Nitschke, J. B., Nelson, E. E., Rusch, B. D., Fox, A. S., Oakes, T. R., & Davidson, R. J. (2004). Orbitofrontal cortex tracks positive mood in mothers viewing pictures of their newborn infants. *Neuroimage*, *21*(2), 583–592.

O'Connor, T. G., Marvin, R. S., Rutter, M., Olrick, J. T., & Britner, P. A. (2003). Child-parent attachment following early institutional deprivation. *Development and Psychopathology*, *15*(1), 19–38.

Panksepp, J. (1998). *Affective neuroscience: The foundations of human and animal emotions*. Oxford, UK: Oxford University Press.

Perelberg, R. J. (Ed.). (1999). *Psychoanalytic understanding of violence and suicide*. London: Routledge.

Plotsky, P. M., Thrivikraman, K. V., Nemeroff, C. B., Caldji, C., Sharma, S., & Meaney, M. J. (2005). Long-term consequences of neonatal rearing on central corticotropin-releasing factor systems in adult male rat offspring. *Neuropsychopharmacology*, *30*, 2192–2204.

Polan, H. J., & Hofer, M. (1999). Psychobiological origins of infant attachment and separation responses. In J. Cassidy & P. R. Shaver (Eds.), *Handbook of Attachment: Theory, Research, and Clinical Applications* (pp. 162–180). New York: Guilford.

Pollak, S. D., Klorman, R., Thatcher, J. E., & Cicchetti, D. (2001). P3b reflects maltreated children's reactions to facial displays of emotion. *Psychophysiology, 38*(2), 267–274.

Pollak, S. D., & Sinha, P. (2003). Effects of early experience on children's recognition of facial displays of emotion. *Developmental Psychology, 38*(5), 784–791.

Posner, M. I., & Rothbart, M. K. (2000). Developing mechanisms of self-regulation. *Development and Psychopathology, 12*, 427–441.

Riccio, D. C., Rabinowitz, V. C., & Axelrod, S. (1994). Memory: When less is more. *American Psychologist, 49*, 917–926.

Rutter, M., & O'Connor, T. G. (2004). Are there biological programming effects for psychological development? Findings from a study of Romanian adoptees. *Developmental Psychology, 40*(1), 81–94.

Sargant, W. (1967). *The unquiet mind*. London: Heinemann.

Schafer, R. (1980). Action and narration in psychoanalysis. *New Literary History, 12*, 61–85.

Segal, H. (1957). Notes on symbol formation. *International Journal of Psycho-Analysis, 38*, 391–397.

Semendeferi, K., & Damasio, H. (2000). The brain and its main anatomical subdivisions in living hominoids using magnetic resonance imaging. *Journal of Human Evolution, 38*, 317–332.

Shipman, K. L., & Zeman, J. (1999). Emotional understanding: A comparison of physically maltreating and nonmaltreating mother-child dyads. *Journal of Clinical Child Psychology, 28*, 407–417.

Siegal, M., & Varley, R. (2002). Neural systems involved in "theory of mind." *National Review of Neuroscience, 3*(6), 463–471.

Siegel, D. J. (1999). *The Developing Mind: Toward a Neurobiology of Interpersonal Experience*. New York: Guilford.

Spence, D. P. (1994). The special nature of psychoanalytic facts. *International Journal of Psycho-Analysis, 75*, 915–925.

Sroufe, L. A. (1996). *Emotional Development: The Organization of Emotional Life in the Early Years*. New York: Cambridge University Press.

Target, M., & Fonagy, P. (1996). Playing with reality II: The development of psychic reality from a theoretical perspective. *International Journal of Psycho-Analysis, 77*, 459–479.

Teicher, M. H., Ito, Y., Glod, C. A., Schiffer, F., & Gelbard, H. A. (1994). Early abuse, limbic system dysfunction, and borderline personality disorder. In K. R. Silk (Ed.), *Biological and Neurobehavioral Studies of Borderline Personality Disorder* (pp. 177–207). Washington, DC: American Psychiatric Press.

Tulving, E. (2002). Episodic memory: From mind to brain. *Annual Review of Psychology, 53*, 1–25.

Usher, J. A., & Neisser, U. (1993). Childhood amnesia and the beginnings of memory for four early life events. *Journal of Experimental Psychology: General, 122,* 155–165.

van der Kolk, B. A. (2003). The neurobiology of childhood trauma and abuse. *Child and Adolescent Psychiatric Clinics of North America, 12*(2), 293–317, ix.

Winnicott, D. W. (1956). Mirror-role of mother and family in child development. In D. W. Winnicott (Ed.), *Playing and reality* (pp. 111–118). London: Tavistock.

Zhang, T. Y., Chretien, P., Meaney, M. J., & Gratton, A. (2005). Influence of naturally occurring variations in maternal care on prepulse inhibition of acoustic startle and the medial prefrontal cortical dopamine response to stress in adult rats. *Journal of Neuroscience, 25*(6), 1493–1502.

Zilles, K., Dabringhaus, A., Geyer, S., Amunts, K., Qu, M., Schleicher, A., et al. (1996). Structural asymmetries in the human forebrain and the forebrain of non-human primates and rats. *Neuroscience and Biobehavioral Reviews, 20*(4), 593–605.

Chapter 2

Attachment and Mentalization in Humans
The Development of the Affective Self

György Gergely and Zsolt Unoka

INTRODUCTION: ATTACHMENT AND THE DEVELOPMENT OF MENTALIZATION IN HUMANS

It has been often proposed that humans may be unique in having evolved a specialized inferential and representational *system for mindreading* (or "theory of mind"); (see Baron-Cohen, 1995; Baron-Cohen, Leslie, & Frith, 1985; Dennett, 1978, 1987; Fodor, 1992; Perner, 1991). This cognitive adaptation functions to efficiently predict, interpret, and manipulate other conspecifics' actions in a variety of competitive as well as cooperative situations through inferring and attributing causal intentional mind states (such as desires, intentions, and beliefs) to them that are considered to drive their behavior.

At the same time, humans are just one of the many social animal species with an *attachment instinct system* where the quality of early caregiving (Bowlby, 1969; Harlow, 1961; Hofer, 1995; Polan & Hofer, 1999; Suomi, 1995, 1999) has a formative effect on the organism's later capacity to adaptively function in affiliative relationships. In fact, it can be argued that attachment and mindreading are two independent adaptations that have been selected to serve qualitatively different evolutionary functions. This is suggested, for example, by the fact that many social species (e.g., rodents or

50

rhesus monkeys, see Hofer, 1995; Polan & Hofer, 1999; Suomi, 1999) that apparently lack the capacity for mindreading, nevertheless possess an innate infant–caregiver attachment system. According to Bowlby's (1969) original proposal, the basic evolutionary function of the biosocial attachment instinct is to provide an efficient interactive mechanism to ensure predator evasion for the immature offspring through a specialized pre-wired, goal-directed signal system serving proximity seeking and maintenance between caregiver and infant. This basic function certainly seems independent of and qualitatively different from the primary function served by the specialized social cognitive adaptation for mentalizing, which is to predict and interpret the actions of other conspecifics during adult competitive and cooperative situations through attributing causal intentional mind states to them.

In spite of this, in recent years several attachment theorists and developmental psychologists have put forward different versions of the general hypothesis that—in the case of humans—there is an inherent causal and functional link between the quality of early infant attachment on the one hand, and the development of the ability for mindreading on the other. In particular, the acquisition of explicit mentalization skills by about 4 years of age (as indicated by passing the standard verbal false belief attribution tasks; see Perner, 1991; Wellman, Cross, & Watson, 2001; Wimmer & Perner, 1983) has been suggested to be causally linked to and developmentally facilitated by the security of early attachment relationships in general and the quality of species-unique types of mother–infant attachment interactions in particular. These factors are often interpreted as providing mentalistic "precursors" or component structures for the later-emerging explicit capacity for mindreading in humans (e.g., Fonagy & Target, 1997; Fonagy, Redfern, & Charman, 1997; Hobson, 1993, 2002; Meins, Fernyhough, Russell, & Clark-Carter, 1998; Meins, Fernyhough, Wainwright, Clark-Carter, Das Gupta, Fradley et al. 2003). One way to interpret such developmental proposals is to suggest that they are attempts to provide an adequate response to two basic empirical and theoretical challenges that are raised by the unique characteristics of early socio-emotional and cognitive development of humans.

On the one hand, according to the view shared by many theory of mind researchers (e.g., Gopnik & Meltzoff, 1997; Gopnik & Wellman, 1994; Perner, 1991; Wellman, 1990; Wellman et al. 2001), it is not before 4 years of age that an explicit capacity for mindreading is acquired, as indicated by younger children's general failure to pass the standard battery of verbal false belief tasks (Wellman et al., 2001; Wimmer & Perner, 1983). This has presented a challenge in identifying the early social environmental determining factors, initial precursor competences, and causal developmental mechanisms that may mediate or facilitate the relatively late ontogenetic acquisition of preschoolers' explicit mindreading abilities.

On the other hand, proposals for a hypothesized link between attachment and mentalization may have been motivated by the need to explain the evolutionary function of a number of species-unique structural features (listed below) that have come to characterize early mother–infant attachment interactions during hominin evolution. These features qualitatively enrich the structural organization of early attachment relations in the case of humans and as such may have been related to significant evolutionary changes in the functional nature of the human attachment system. Below is a short list of these species-unique characteristics of early human caregiver–infant interactions that are likely to have been selected for during hominin evolution as they seem conspicuously absent from the attachment relationships and interaction patterns that characterize the attachment system of other, nonhuman social species (including our closest primate relatives):

1. Early mother–infant interactions in humans exhibit a particular species-unique pattern of "proto-conversational" *turn-taking contingency structure* (Brazelton & Tronick, 1980; Brazelton, Koslowski, & Main, 1974; Sander, 1988; Stern, 1985; Trevarthen, 1979; Trevarthen & Aitken, 2001; Tronick, 1989; Tronick & Cohn, 1989) that seems absent in primates. Human infants show an early sensitivity to, preference for, and spontaneous motivation to engage in *highly response-contingent stimulus events* characteristic of the patterns of contingent interactive reactivity produced by infant-attuned social partners (Bahrick & Watson, 1985; Bigelow, 1999; Bigelow & De Coste, 2003; Bigelow & Rochat, 2006; Lewis, Allessandri, & Sullivan, 1990; Rochat & Morgan, 1995; Watson, 1972, 1985, 1994, 1995).

2. Human infants show a species-specific innate sensitivity to and preference for *ostensive-communicative cues* (Csibra & Gergely, 2006;

Gergely & Csibra, 2006) such as *eye contact* (Farroni, Csibra, Simion, & Johnson, 2002), *contingent reactivity* (Floccia, Christophe, & Bertoncini, 1997; Johnson, Slaughter, & Carey, 1998; Movellan & Watson, 2002; Watson, 1972, 1994, 1995), or the specific prosodic vocal intonation pattern of infant-directed speech or "*motherese*" (Cooper & Aslin, 1990; Fernald, 1985, 1992).

3. Young human infants also exhibit a sensitivity and spontaneous tendency to attend to and gaze-follow specific behavioral *referential cues* (such as gaze shift, or head movement), but only if these are presented in an ostensive-communicative cuing context (e.g., when being preceded by infant-oriented direct eye contact or infant-contingent turn-taking reactivity, Farroni et al., 2002; Johnson et al., 1998; Movellan & Watson, 2002; but not when they follow a slightly diverted eye-gaze, see Csibra & Gergely, 2006, for a review). Similarly, unlike apes, by one year of age human infants show a *communicative and referential understanding* and use of the *pointing* gesture (Behne, Carpenter, & Tomasello, 2005; Liszkowski, Carpenter, Henning, Striano, & Tomasello, 2004; Tomasello, Carpenter, & Liszkowski, in press; Southgate, Van Maanen, & Csibra, in press).

4. Early mother–infant interactions in humans are characterized by frequent *exchanges of a relatively rich and differentiated* (and ontogenetically quickly increasing) *repertoire of facial-vocal emotion displays expressing specific basic emotions* (including anger, joy, fear, sadness, disgust, and interest; see Cohn & Tronick, 1988; Ekman, 1992; Ekman, Friesen, & Ellsworth, 1972; Gergely, 2002, 2007a; Gergely & Watson, 1996; Izard & Malatesta, 1987; Malatesta, Culver, Tesman, & Shepard, 1989; Sroufe, 1996; Tronick, 1989). Infants automatically display such basic emotion expressions toward their caregiver with increasing regularity and specificity during the first year and onward (Bennett, Bendersky, & Lewis, 2004, 2005; Malatesta et al., 1989; Sroufe, 1996; Tronick, 1989). This contrasts with the small range and low frequency of exchange of specific affective displays in nonhuman infant–caregiver attachment interactions. Even in primates such caregiver-directed emotion-expressive displays are quite rare and tend to be restricted to basic

expressions of distress and protest triggered by loss of proximity, and to a few stereotyped affiliative displays (such as lipsmacking) signaling an intention to increase proximity to the mother (e.g., De Marco & Visalberghi, 2007).[1]

5. Human mother–infant attachment interactions are uniquely characterized by the production of *empathic affect-mirroring emotion displays* by the caregiver during affect-regulative face-to-face interactions (importantly, these sometimes include contingent mirroring of the infant's negative emotion expressions as well) (Bigelow, 1999; Cohn & Tronick, 1988; Fonagy, Gergely, & Target, 2007; Fonagy, Gergely, Jurist, & Target, 2002; Gergely, 2004, 2007a; Gergely & Watson, 1996, 1999; Malatesta et al., 1989; Tronick, 1989; Uzgiris, Benson, Kruper, & Vasek, 1989). The facial-vocal pattern of emotion-mirroring parental displays consists of specifically *"marked," transformed versions* of the stereotypic motor display patterns that are the normative default expressions of the mother's actual and "real" internal basic emotions (Gergely, 2007a; Gergely & Watson, 1996, 1999). Apart from their characteristic *"manifestative" features of markedness* (such as the exaggerated, slowed-down, schematic, or only partial motor execution of the canonical display pattern, see Gergely, 2007a), "marked" emotion-mirroring expressions are also typically contextually framed by a specific constellation of *ostensive-communicative and referential cues* (including eye contact, raised eyebrows, widening and shrinking of the eyes, "knowing" looks, infant-directed contingent reactivity, etc., see Csibra & Gergely, 2006; Gergely, 2007a, 2007b; Gergely & Csibra, 2005, 2006, for details) that are themselves species-specific features of human caregiver–infant interactions (see Points 2 and 3 above).

6. Human infants seem endowed with an innate *capacity and motivation to contingently and spontaneously reenact features of emotion-expressive and ostensive parental facial-vocal displays* during caregiver–infant interactions (such as tongue protrusion, frowning, raised eyebrows, lip protrusion, mouth opening, and some component features of basic emotion displays (see Field, Woodson, Cohen, Garcia, & Greenberg, 1983; Malatesta et al., 1989;

Meltzoff, 2002; Meltzoff & Moore, 1977, 1989; Tronick, 1989; Trevarthen & Aitken, 2001).

So what are the basic functions that these human-specific features of early mother–infant attachment interactions may have evolved to serve? In recent years several attachment theorists have proposed that secure attachment in early infancy and early forms of parental interactive styles that correlate with infant attachment security at 1 year of age (such as measures of maternal mind-mindedness at 6 months, see Meins, Fernyhough, Fradley, & Tuckey, 2001) play an important causal role in the early development of mentalization. This is indicated by the fact that they seem to significantly facilitate the precocious acquisition of explicit mindreading skills by early childhood (e.g., Fonagy, 2001; Fonagy & Target, 1997; Fonagy et al., 1997; Meins et al., 1998, 2003; Meins, Fernyhough, Wainwright, Das Gupta, Fradley, & Tuckey, 2002). The empirical evidence for this position consists mainly of correlational findings showing that secure infant attachment at 1 year (as well as its earlier correlates such as maternal mind-mindedness at 6 months) predicts earlier appearance of the ability to pass the standard verbal false belief tasks by preschoolers (e.g., de Rosnay & Harris, 2002; Fonagy & Target, 1997; Fonagy et al., 1997; Fonagy, Steele, Steele, & Holder, 1997; Meins et al., 1998, 2003; Ontai & Thompson, 2002).

Without questioning the validity of these data, we shall argue below that there are a number of good empirical and theoretical reasons to question the strong form of the hypothesis that postulates a specific evolutionary role and/or a direct ontogenetic causal and functional link between security of infant attachment and its early interactive predictors on the one hand, and the development of explicit mindreading abilities in later childhood on the other. Briefly, one problem lies in the fact that the correlational findings linking infant attachment security during the first year to earlier success by preschoolers in passing the explicit theory of mind tasks have not been supplemented with specific causal developmental models that would spell out the particular ways in which the secure quality of preverbal attachment and/or factors, such as parental talk involving mental state attributions to the baby at 6 months, would exert their facilitating effects on the acquisition of the cognitive skills involved in inferring, attributing, representing, and reasoning about epistemic mind states of others (such as beliefs). Given the lack of such specific models, one may always point to a number of possible and often plausible causal linking variables that appear only during later phases of development, but which—while they themselves may be positively correlated with preverbal attachment security—may turn out to be directly and specifically responsible for much of the actual facilitating influence that shows up in the correlations linking preverbal measures of attachment security to later mindreading skills. Such linking factors may include, for example, the frequency of perspective taking in caregiver–child linguistic exchanges (e.g., de Rosnay & Hughes, 2006; Harris, 2005; Lohmann, Tomasello, & Meyer, 2005), the amount of complementary role play in the family, the degree of family talk about conflicting emotions and the availability of differential conflict- and emotion-regulation strategies in the family (Cutting & Dunn, 1999; Dunn, Brown, & Beardsall, 1991; Ruffman, Perner, & Parkin, 1999; Sabbagh & Callanan, 1998; Vinden, 2001), the number of references to thoughts and beliefs, and the relationship specificity of children's real-life accounts of negative emotions (Hughes & Dunn, 2002), and so on. The independent effects of these (and other) factors on the earlier appearance of explicit theory of mind performance around 4 years are well documented in the developmental literature (for a review, see Fonagy et al., 2007). Furthermore, as it turns out, a variety of other factors also show a facilitating influence on passing standard false belief tasks even though they seem to have no obvious or demonstrated relation to early measures of infant attachment security. These include, for example, having older siblings (Perner, Ruffman, & Leekam, 1994; Ruffman, Perner, Naito, Parkin, & Clements, 1998), the relative frequency and precocity of using complex syntactic complement structures (Astington & Jenkins, 1999; de Villiers & de Villiers, 2000; de Villiers & Pyers, 2002), or the maturational development of executive function, selective attention, and response inhibition capacities (Leslie, 2000; Leslie, Friedman, & German, 2004; Perner & Lang, 2000).

It should also be noted that the demonstrated facilitating effects of early secure attachment on theory of mind development are not that strong. In fact, in several studies they only show up in theory of mind tasks that involve reasoning about emotions as well (such as belief–desire tasks) and not only purely epistemic states such as false beliefs (e.g., Fonagy et al., 1997; see Fonagy et al., 2007, for a review). Furthermore, there are strong recent arguments and supporting empirical demonstrations showing that the explicit verbal false belief tasks (Wimmer & Perner, 1983) that are standardly used to diagnose the developmental achievement of attaining "full" mindreading skills around 4 years (Wellman et al., 2001) involve several complex linguistic, pragmatic interpretational, and executive function requirements that are not specific to the ability to infer and represent intentional mind states. These factors make the standard theory of mind tasks rather hard to pass for young children, not because they still lack the capacity to mentalize (or at least some components of theory of mind), but rather because of their difficulties with one or more of the non-theory-of-mind related cognitive component skills that these tasks require (see Bloom & German, 2000; Leslie et al., 2004). Note that this in itself can account for the apparently late developmental emergence of the capacity to pass the explicit and verbal standard theory of mind tasks. This may have seriously distorted the validity of the standardly accepted estimates concerning the normal developmental timetable for the ontogenetic establishment of mentalizing abilities that are generally used and relied on in the developmental literature (Wellman et al., 2001). For these reasons some researchers have recently explicitly argued for the abandonment of the standard false belief tasks as a general diagnostic tool for establishing the attainment of theory of mind skills (see e.g., Bloom & German, 2000).

Complementary to these methodologically based doubts in the representativeness of the explicit standard false belief tasks for diagnosing the onset of theory of mind abilities, there is converging recent evidence (based on paradigms that are not plagued with the methodological problems outlined above) demonstrating mentalization abilities much earlier in human ontogeny. For example, in a series of intriguing studies Tomasello and his colleagues have demonstrated that 12-month-olds already spontaneously monitor another person's perceptual access to transformations of relevant aspects of reality, infer and attribute the corresponding epistemic mental states of informedness or ignorance to the other, and can rely on such mental attributions to differentially modulate their own goal-directed behaviors in the presence of or in relation to that person later (e.g., Tomasello & Haberl, 2003; Tomasello, Carpenter, Call, Behne, & Moll, 2005). Similarly, there is convergent new evidence coming from implicit nonverbal versions of the standard false belief attribution tasks using violation-of-expectation looking time paradigms showing that already infants as young as 13 months of age exhibit a spontaneous ability to monitor another agent's perceptual access to reality and infer, attribute, and represent the other's true *or false* beliefs about the situation accordingly, relying then on the representational content of such attributed mental states to predict the other's subsequent behavior (Csibra & Southgate, 2006; Onishi & Baillargeon, 2005; Onishi, Baillargeon, & Leslie, 2007; Southgate, Senju, & Csibra, in press; Surian, Caldi, & Sperber, in press). Finally, recent evidence from the comparative animal literature strongly calls into doubt the assertion that the basic ability for implicit mindreading is an exclusively human-specific capacity. These intriguing new studies suggest that some rudimentary and possibly highly domain-restricted forms of mentalization seem to have evolved independently and convergently in a number of different nonhuman social species that live in highly competitive social environmental niches (such as apes and goats, as well as several avian species including crows, ravens, and scrub jays, see Bugnyar & Heinrich, 2005; Emery & Clayton, 2004; Hare, Call, & Tomasello, 2001; Kaminski, Call, & Tomasello, 2006; Tomasello, Call, & Hare, 2003). These nonhuman species have been shown to spontaneously monitor specific conspecifics' perceptual access to where food is located or hidden, attribute to them and represent their mental states of informedness or ignorance about such facts, and can hang on to such person-specific epistemic information about the other's mental states for relatively long periods using it to efficiently direct or modify their own food-directed behavior when the other is present (such as choice of location for food caching, food displacement, or food approach).

To sum up: Based on this brief review, we argue that the currently popular view endorsed by a number of attachment theorists and infant researchers that assumes a possibly evolutionarily based and human-specific direct causal and functional link between the ontogeny of early security of infant attachment on the one hand, and the acquisition of explicit mentalizing skills on the other, must be significantly revised. The relevant developmental and comparative evidence of recent years seems more compatible with the alternative view that an implicit and automatic capacity for mentalizing about others is not a developmental achievement, but an innate social-cognitive evolutionary adaptation implemented by a specialized and pre-wired mindreading mechanism that seems active and functional at least as early as 12 months of age in humans. Furthermore, this capacity for implicit mindreading is unlikely to be a uniquely human competence either, since in its basic form it seems to have evolved independently and convergently in a number of nonhuman social species that also live in highly competitive niches.

It should be made clear, however, that the present argument does not imply that certain types of early interactive patterns characteristic of specific attachment relationships of human infants would have no developmental effect whatsoever on one's later ability to functionally and efficiently use the evolved capacity for mindreading in coping with interpersonal interactions and relationships during childhood or adulthood. There are, in fact, good empirical reasons to believe that certain dysfunctional types of early attachment relations involving severe neglect, abuse, dissociative, highly intrusive, or grossly unpredictable patterns of parental reactivity have significant and long-term detrimental and disruptive effects on one's later capacity to functionally use the innate competence for online mentalization as an adaptive interpersonal coping strategy to deal with the vicissitudes of affectively charged intimate and affiliative relationships of later life (see e.g., Fonagy et al., 2002, 2007; Fonagy, Target, Gergely, Allen, & Bateman, 2003, for relevant reviews).[2]

Thus, according to the present view, the specialized capacity for mentalization is likely to be an independent social-cognitive adaptation whose primary evolutionary function is separate and unrelated to the basic evolutionary function for which the attachment instinct system has been selected. To that degree it should not be surprising if security of early infant attachment in humans did not turn out to play a direct causal functional role in the ontogenetic development or acquisition of our explicit mindreading capacity. Nevertheless, as we have proposed elsewhere (Gergely & Unoka, in press, a, b), when maladaptive patterns of affective parental reactivity become the dominant features of the reoccurring interactive structure of the infant's primary attachment relationships, they can play a significant causal role in pathologically *undermining* the developing self's potential to rely on its innate mindreading capacity as its dominant social-cognitive strategy to cope with interpersonal situations and intimate and affiliative relationships during later life.

THE DEVELOPMENTAL ORIGINS OF (INTER)SUBJECTIVITY AND THE SOCIAL CONSTRUCTION OF THE REPRESENTATIONAL AFFECTIVE SELF

In this paper we shall argue that the species-unique aspects of early human infant–caregiver attachment interactions play a significant functional role in socio-emotional self development insofar as they constitute basic preconditions for the *social construction of the representational affective self* (Gergely, 2007a; Gergely & Unoka, in press, a, b) that forms the basis for the human-specific capacity for *emotional self-awareness and affective self-control* (Fonagy et al., 2002, 2007; Gergely, 2007a; Gergely & Watson, 1996, 1999). In particular, we hypothesize that the reoccurring patterns of species-unique infant–caregiver attachment interactions provide the necessary input conditions for specialized *representation-building and attention socialization mechanisms* (such as the causal contingency detection device, the social biofeedback mechanism, and natural pedagogy; see Csibra & Gergely, 2006; Fonagy et al., 2002, 2007; Gergely, 2007a, 2007b; Gergely & Csibra, 2005, 2006; Gergely & Unoka, in press, a, b; Gergely & Watson, 1996, 1999; Watson, 1985, 1994, 2001) that construct *cognitively accessible second-order representations* for the innate constitutional self's primary, nonconscious, and procedural basic emotional automatisms. We shall contrast this social constructivist view of affective self development with currently popular theories of primary "intersubjectivity."

Many recent developmental and attachment theories consider the species-unique features that enrich the structural organization of early human caregiver–infant affective attachment interactions (see Points 1 to 6 in the preceding pages of this chapter) as empirical evidence for their "rich" mentalistic interpretation in terms of primary intersubjectivity according to which the human infant already during the first months of life is able to identify, attribute, and be subjectively aware of mutually "sharing" a variety of internal mental states with others (such as emotions, goals, intentions, and motives) (see Bråten, 1988, 1992, 1998; Gianino & Tronick, 1988; Meltzoff, 2002; Meltzoff & Gopnik, 1993; Meltzoff & Moore, 1977, 1989, 1998; Hobson, 1993, 2002; Stern, 1985; Trevarthen, 1979, 1993; Trevarthen &

Aitken, 2001). Elsewhere we have provided detailed criticisms on a number of grounds of the overly rich mentalistic interpretation proposed for these early interactive phenomena by adherents of primary intersubjectivity theory who assume that the human infant basically from the beginning has differentiated subjective states of conscious awareness of its basic internal emotional arousal states (not to mention those of others) (see Fonagy et al., 2002, 2007; Gergely, 2002, 2007a; Gergely & Watson, 1996, 1999). In contrast to these theories, we have proposed an alternative model of early emotional self development (Fonagy et al., 2002, 2007; Gergely & Watson, 1996, 1999) within the framework of contingency detection theory and attachment theory (Watson, 1985, 2001) according to which infants' differentiated subjective sense of their internal affective self-states has important social interactional origins and has an individually variable developmental course of ontogenetic unfolding. It should be emphasized that according to our alternative approach subjective self-awareness and sense of differential internal self-states is viewed as a (relatively hard-won) developmental achievement. Similarly, the capacity for intersubjective recognition and awareness of (mutual) sharing of internal affective states with others is considered to be an emergent property of the subjective self rather than an initial and universal starting state of the human infant's mental life.

In particular, we have proposed that the subjective sense of differential self-states (e.g., awareness of being "angry," rather than just experiencing some undifferentiated negative state of tension) is established as a result of infants' repeated experience with the pattern of contingent parental reactivity and social "mirroring" feedback reactions that their automatic expressions of— initially nonconscious—basic emotional arousal states evoke from their attachment environment. Our model is based on two central assumptions:

1. *The introspectively "invisible" constitutional affective self.* We assume (together with many other emotion theorists, e.g., Ekman, 1992; Izard & Malatesta, 1987; Tomkins, 1995; and see also Darwin, 1872) that the infant's innate biological or constitutional self has a richly structured internal organization from the beginning. Though the constitutional self is characterized by significant genetically based individual temperamental differences (Kagan, 1994; Rothbart, 1989), it contains a basic set of pre-wired universal categorical emotions that are primary biological adaptations (Ekman, 1992; Ekman et al., 1972). These basic emotions are best understood as

consisting of pre-wired, stimulus-driven, procedural physiological and motor automatisms that are initially not accessible to conscious awareness and over which the baby has no voluntary control at first. Affect regulation at the earliest stages is carried out mainly by the attachment environment, as the caregiver, reading the infant's automatic emotion expressions, reacts to them with appropriate affect-modulating interactions and emotion displays (Gergely, 2002, 2004, 2007a; Gergely & Watson, 1996). Thus, while infants may be sensitive to the general (positive vs. negative) hedonic quality of their affective experience, we assume that babies at the beginning of their lives have no subjective awareness of their discrete basic emotion states as differentiated subjective categories of internal self-experience (for supporting arguments, see Gergely & Watson, 1996). It is in this sense that we consider the initial constitutional self to be introspectively invisible; while it contains discrete and categorically differentiable emotional states, these pre-wired automatisms are at first not accessible to introspective awareness and so they do not present themselves as subjectively experienced differential internal states of the self.

We also hypothesize (contrary to classical views such as Bruner, Olver, & Greenfield, 1966; Mahler, Pine, & Bergman, 1975; cf. Gergely, 2000) that at the beginning of life the human infant exhibits a primary, built-in bias toward actively attending to and learning about external events (that is, a primary sensitivity-bias toward exteroceptive stimulation), while showing little active introspective attentional orientation toward internal self-states to start with (Fonagy et al., 2002; Gergely & Watson, 1996, 1999).

2. *The social interactive origins of affective subjectivity: the development of introspectively accessible emotional self-representations.* We assume that for the categorical basic emotion states of the primary constitutional self to become introspectively accessible and subjectively differentially experienced, two basic conditions need to be established developmentally. On the one hand, the primary and procedural basic emotion programs of the constitutional self (which are pre-wired, initially nonconscious automatisms) need to become associated with *second-order representations* that, when activated, are cognitively accessible to introspectively oriented attentional self-monitoring processes. In other words, we suggest that the initially nonconscious primary emotion states become introspectively visible, differentiated affective self-states of subjective awareness through the activation of their associated

second-order representations only. For this to happen, it is also necessary that the primarily externally oriented attention system of the infant should become modified during early development. *Attentional monitoring processes need to become introspectively sensitized* and turned toward the self's internal states to a sufficient degree to allow for the active introspective monitoring and detection of the activation of second-order emotion representations. This would be possible when these second-order, cognitively accessible representations become triggered through the stimulus-induced automatic arousal of the basic emotion states of the constitutional self to which the second-order emotion representations are associatively linked. This can then lead to the introspective self-perception of being in a particular differentiated emotion state, giving rise to the discrete subjective awareness of that state.

The cognitively accessible and introspectively monitored second-order representations of the primary emotion states can then provide the basis for the establishment of a continuously updated representation of the dynamically changing affective states of the self. This allows for the possibility of internally generating self-predictions about one's likely emotion-induced actions by anticipating the automatic activation of the stereotypic motor-action tendencies that the self's basic emotion arousal state is likely to trigger. The ability to become subjectively aware of the current dispositional states of the self before the automatic activation of the emotion-based action-tendencies would take effect is a major precondition for the possibility of exercising affective self-control (Fonagy et al., 2002; Gergely & Unoka, in press, a, b; Gergely & Watson, 1996). This is so because by foreseeing and cognitively evaluating the likely external consequences of the self's anticipated actions even before those would become automatically executed, one can inhibit or modify them in an adaptive manner rather than being automatically induced to act them out.

CONTINGENCY DETECTION AND SOCIAL BIOFEEDBACK

Our central developmental proposal is that both of the above preconditions for the construction of the introspectively accessible subjective self become established as a result of, and to the degree to which, the social attachment environment of the infant provides *systematic contingent feedback reactions* to the automatic expressions of the initially nonconscious dynamic affect states of the constitutional self. In other words, it is the experience of one's current internal states being externally "mirrored" or "reflected" back through the infant-attuned contingent social reactions of the attachment environment that makes it possible to develop a subjective sense and awareness of one's primary affective self-states.

Of course, no amount of contingent social mirroring could result in the establishment of these two (representational and attentional) preconditions unless infants were equipped with an appropriate information-processing mechanism that could efficiently detect the contingent relatedness between their automatic state-expressive behavioral displays on the one hand, and the corresponding external mirroring reactions of the social environment on the other. Furthermore, some further mechanism is needed to internalize the representation of the external mirroring feedback signal, and to establish an association between this second-order representation and the primary self-states that have contingently evoked the external mirroring reaction in question.

In previous work on the contingency-based *social biofeedback theory* of parental affect-mirroring (Fonagy et al., 2002; Gergely, 2007a; Gergely & Watson, 1996, 1999), we have proposed that the human infant's causal *contingency detection device* (Watson, 1994, 2001) provides the right sort of analytic and representation-building mechanism that has the necessary structural properties to establish second-order emotion representations when applied to contingent affect-mirroring interactions. This pre-wired contingency perception device (Watson, 1985, 1994) automatically monitors and assesses over time the degree of contingent relatedness between the infant's responses and events in the external (social) stimulus environment. By monitoring three different aspects of contingent relatedness in parallel (the degree of temporal contingency, spatial similarity, and correspondence of relative intensity; see Gergely & Watson, 1999, for a review of supporting evidence), the contingency detection mechanism can identify those stimulus aspects of the social environment that are under (some specific degree of) *causal control* of the infant's state expressions and behavioral displays. One important developmental consequence of this causal contingency analysis is that, to the degree that the social environment exhibits systematic and differential contingent reactivity to the baby's particular types of responses, the consequent discovery of being in contingent control over particular aspects of the social environment generates a subjective sense of experience of causal efficacy and self-agency in the young infant.

"MARKED" AFFECT-MIRRORING AND ITS ROLE IN THE REPRESENTATIONAL DEVELOPMENT OF THE AFFECTIVE SELF

Earlier we have identified as one of the species-unique differentiating characteristics of human infant–caregiver interactions (see Points 5 and 6 above) the inclination of sensitive, infant-attuned caregivers to present their infants during affect-regulative interactions with empathic emotion-expressive displays that imitatively mirror their baby's automatic facial-vocal affect-expressions (including the empathic parental mirroring of negative affect displays as well).[3] Elsewhere (Fonagy et al., 2002; Gergely & Watson, 1996, 1999), we have emphasized the functional importance of the fact that such empathic emotion-mirroring displays tend to be executed in a saliently *marked* manner that perceptually clearly distinguishes them from the caregiver's corresponding realistic emotion expressions. Such "marked" affect-reflecting displays are *saliently transformed versions* of the normative motor display patterns of the corresponding realistic emotion expressions of the caregiver (see Point 5 above).[4] Some of the typical features of "markedness" involve (a) *exaggerated, slowed-down execution* of the spatial-temporal display pattern of the corresponding realistic, normative emotion expression; (b) *schematic, sometimes abbreviated or only partial execution* of the normative motor display pattern of the same emotion; (c) the mirroring display being *sometimes mixed with* simultaneous or quickly alternating *components of other emotion* displays; and (d) it being typically introduced or accompanied by *ostensive communicative "framing" cues as well as referential gestures*, including such direct eye contact as gaze-direction, eyebrow flashing, slightly tilted head, widely opened eyes, and so on (which, as we have argued in the Introduction, constitute further species-unique structural interactive features that are among the distinguishing characteristics of human caregiver–infant attachment interactions; see Points 2 and 3 above).

Our original interpretation of the function of this marking of parental affect expressions (Gergely & Watson, 1996) emphasized its importance as a cue signaling to the infant that the emotion display is "not for real," and that its expressed emotional content should be decoupled from the caregiver; or, in other words, that its attribution to her as her real emotion state should be inhibited. This was considered especially important in cases when the caregiver was mirroring a *negative* emotion display of the infant. When salient marking of the mirroring display is absent in such cases, the infant could easily confuse it with the corresponding normative emotion expression of the parent. This would lead to the attribution of the expressed emotion to the caregiver as her actual, realistic negative affect state. The consequent perception of the parent's being in, and expressing toward the infant, a realistic negative emotion state could then induce traumatic escalation, rather than soothing, of the baby's negative emotion state.

Lately (see Gergely, 2007a; Gergely & Unoka, in press, a, b), we have extended this functional characterization of markedness by generalizing it in two ways. First, we propose that ostensively framed marked emotional mirroring parental displays constitute a special kind of instance of the general class of communicative referential "teaching" manifestations generated by the human-specific cultural learning system called *natural "pedagogy"* (Csibra & Gergely, 2006; Gergely, 2007b; Gergely & Csibra, 2005, 2006; Gergely, Király, & Egyed, 2007). In particular, in this interpretation ostensively communicated infant-directed marked emotion-mirroring interactions can be conceived as pedagogical, cultural teaching manifestations where the relevant cultural information being conveyed for the infant to learn is that his or her currently expressed basic emotion (that is being contingently mirrored in a marked manner by the "teacher") belongs to those categorical emotions that are culturally shared by (and can be communicated to as well as shared with) other members of the cultural community that the infant belongs to.

This interpretation can provide a more principled and generalized explanatory account of why marked mirroring displays are interpreted self-referentially by the infant, leading to their referential *anchoring* (in the form of internalized second-order representations) to those primary procedural emotion states that the mirroring displays contingently reflect. Furthermore, this new interpretation of marked mirroring displays as a form of ostensive "pedagogical" communication that referentially identifies the infant's particular emotion state, as well as conveying relevant information about the categorical kind that the basic emotion in question belongs to, will also provide us with an improved account of why the perception of ostensive communicative cues that include the features of markedness of affect-mirroring expressions (together with cues of referent identification) help to establish an introspective orientation of the infant's (initially externally biased) attentional processes. Considering marked mirroring as a case of pedagogical communication referencing the infant's self-states also sheds further explanatory light on the consequent increase in sensitivity to subjective self-states and their contingent effects on the external social environment.

NATURAL PEDAGOGY: THE ROLE OF OSTENSIVE COMMUNICATION AND MARKED FORMS OF KNOWLEDGE MANIFESTATIONS IN EARLY CULTURAL LEARNING

Natural pedagogy is hypothesized to be a human-specific cognitive adaptation of mutual design whose evolutionary function is the facilitation of fast and efficient intergenerational transfer of relevant cultural information about referents from knowledgeable conspecifics to ignorant juveniles (Csibra & Gergely, 2006; Gergely, 2007b; Gergely & Csibra, 2005, 2006; Gergely et al., 2007). The initial domain in which such pedagogical communications first occur is that of the early infant–caregiver interactions that take place within the human attachment system. The types of new and relevant cultural knowledge that are typically transmitted through pegadogical communication include new words, gestural symbols, artifact functions, the stereotypic use of artifacts (Gergely, Bekkering, & Király, 2002; Gergely & Csibra, 2005, 2006), valence information about object kinds (Gergely, 2007b; Gergely et al., 2007), culturally habitual manners of actions, culture-specific emotion display rules, and so on. Here we argue that this list should be extended to include relevant knowledge about the universally and culturally shared categorical emotion states of the infant's constitutional self as well. This knowledge is initially made accessible to and becomes represented by the infant through the caregiver's pedagogical communicative interactions involving ostensively marked, contingent emotion-mirroring displays.

The hypothesis that the primary cognitive adaptation of human pedagogy has a built-in *mutual design* (Csibra & Gergely, 2006) implies specific biological preparedness on both the adult's and the infant's side for providing and receiving cultural information that is new and relevant for the infant. On the teacher's side, when knowledgeable caregivers take a pedagogical attitude toward their infant, they show a natural inclination to exhibit *ostensive communicative cues* and *marked forms of referential knowledge manifestations.* These pedagogical cues are hypothesized to trigger in the infant a specific type of attentional orientation and receptive fast-learning attitude. First, they convey to infants that the other has an overt "communicative intent" that is directly "addressed" to them (cf. Sperber & Wilson, 1986). Second, they evoke an expectation that the other is going to manifest new and relevant information about a referent and that the other's specific manner of knowledge manifestation will guide the infant to identify the referent and the relevant new information content to be learned about the referent. Third, the ostensive communicative cues put the infant into a receptive learning mode supporting fast mapping of the manifested information to its referent.

Two types of pedagogical communicative cues are produced by adults for which infants show specific receptivity: *cues of "ostensive communication"* and *cues of "referential knowledge manifestation."* Ostensive communicative cues have two major functions: (a) they inform the infant that the adult has an overt "communicative intent" (cf. Sperber & Wilson, 1986); and (b) they function as "addressing cues" signaling to the infant that the upcoming communicative manifestation of new and relevant knowledge is specifically addressed to him or her. Ostensive cues involve the establishment of direct eye-contact typically marked by further ostensive gestures such as knowingly raising one's eyebrows (the "eyebrow flash"), momentarily widening and shrinking one's eyes, and tilting one's head slightly forward toward the addressee. These are often accompanied by verbally addressing the infant by his or her own name using the salient and specific type of marked speech-intonation pattern of infant-directed speech or "motherese."

An important semantic feature of such ostensive cues, which differentiates them from the marked forms of the "referential knowledge manifestations" that they introduce or accompany, is that they do not encode or convey specific informational content about the relevant knowledge to be transmitted to the infant. Instead, the referential meaning that these ostensive cues express is simply (and only) the fact that the person producing them has an overt communicative intent that is specifically directed to the addressee.

As we have argued, the perception of ostensive communicative gestures triggers in the infant an active expectation that new and relevant knowledge will be manifested about some referent. Therefore, the infant will need to identify the intended referent of the communication in order to map the manifested new information onto it. This will induce a search for the intended referent entity by the infant. This referent-identification process is based on (and is directed by) the adult's presentation of *referential orienting cues* such as eye-direction, gaze-shift, or a pointing gesture, indicating the intended referent about which new knowledge is going to be manifested. For example, such referential orienting cues will lead the infant to identify the new object whose name is going to be demonstrated by the adult, as in fast-mapping word-learning situations (Tomasello, 1999), and to single out the referent object about which valence information is going to be provided by the object-directed emotional attitude manifestations by the adult, as in social referencing situations (Baldwin & Moses, 1996; Moses, Baldwin, Rosicky, & Tidball, 2001; Gergely et al., 2007; Mumme & Fernald, 2003), or to specify the referent object about whose new functional affordance properties the adult's goal-directed action manifestation is going to provide relevant information, as in situations of ostensively induced imitative learning about artifact functions (Gergely, 2007b; Gergely, Bekkering, & Király, 2002; Gergely & Csibra, 2005).

The second type of pedagogical communicative cues is provided by the specially *marked manner* in which the action demonstrations, serving as *referential knowledge manifestations*, are executed by the adult. The function of referential knowledge manifestations is to convey to the infant the content of the adult's "referential intention" (cf. Sperber & Wilson, 1986), that is, to communicate the content of the new and relevant knowledge about the intended referent that the infant should infer and map onto the representation of the referent. Marked manifestations involve a *modified and saliently transformed version* of motor execution of a primary motor scheme when it serves as a "referential knowledge manifestation." The cues of markedness of parental emotion-mirroring displays correspond to this special form of saliently exaggerated, slowed-down, schematic, and sometimes only partially executed versions of the habitual procedural motor pattern. Marked forms of knowledge manifestations serve several functions in pedagogical knowledge transfer. First, they cue the infant about the fact that the marked behavioral display is produced to achieve the communicative and referential goal of manifesting the relevant knowledge content to (and for) the infant to learn, rather than simply using the procedural motor routine in its everyday habitual manner to achieve its normative, primary function. Take the example of demonstrating to an infant how to eat with a spoon with the pedagogical intention to teach him about this curious—culturally habitual and shared—human manner of food intake. Clearly, you don't simply start to eat your soup, as you normally do, in front of the infant, passively letting it watch your smooth and efficient functional use of the spoon. Rather, after having established ostensive communicative contact with the infant through the production of the kind of ostensive addressing cues discussed earlier, you produce a saliently marked, modified, schematized, exaggerated, and transformed version of the primary motor scheme of eating with a spoon. Apart from cueing the infant about your referential communicative teaching intent, a further function that is served by performing the motor display in its marked and transformed version is to cue the infant to take the "pedagogical stance" toward your behavioral manifestation and to infer from it what the new and relevant information is that is being demonstrated for the child to acquire.

Furthermore, the production of ostensively cued, marked forms of referential knowledge manifestation is characterized by a *recipient design* that also serves several functions in human pedagogy. First, by taking into consideration the current state of knowledge and mobilizable inferential capacities of the infant, the adult can produce a "marked" transform of the primary motor scheme that foregrounds and saliently exaggerates those particular aspects of knowledge that are new and relevant for the infant. In this way, the demonstrator facilitates, constrains, and directs the infant's inferential processing of the referential knowledge manifestation by directing the child's attention to those aspects of the demonstrated action that convey new and relevant information. Second, by producing a "recipient-tailored" version of the motor manifestation emphasizing certain aspects of the procedural scheme over others, the adult can help the infant who is imitating or practicing the new skill by directing its attention to those relevant functional aspects of the procedure that the infant hasn't yet fully understood. This socially modulated relevance-guidance of the cultural learning process may be well served by the human-specific feature of infant–caregiver attachment interactions described under Point 6 above—

namely, that human infants show a spontaneous inclination to contingently reenact features of parental motor displays that are ostensively addressed to them.

Finally, the mutual design structure of pedagogical communication involves built-in, implicit assumptions that ostensive cues trigger in the infant. As a result the baby takes the pedagogical stance toward the ostensively communicating other treating him or her as a repository of relevant cultural knowledge. The infant "learner" expects the ostensive other to exhibit cooperative benevolence in communicating only trustworthy and indeed relevant information for the infant to learn (elsewhere we have termed this ostensively triggered receptive attitude the "basic epistemic trust"; see Gergely, 2007b; Gergely et al., 2007). Therefore, the infant can faithfully and quickly learn the content of the ostensively communicated knowledge or skill without any further need for testing its relevance or even for understanding why and how the demonstrated knowledge skill actually works to fulfill its relevant function. Note that these tacit assumptions built into the infant's pedagogical stance—about the communicator as a repository of relevant cultural knowledge, and as having a communicative attitude of cooperative benevolence (see Gergely, 2007b; Gergely et al., 2007)—are crucial for making possible the efficient and fast intergenerational transfer of *arbitrary* and *conventional* (and sometimes not transparently functional) forms of cultural knowledge, these being a species-characteristic feature of human culture (see Gergely & Csibra, 2006). Through pedagogy, such ostensively communicated, arbitrary aspects of cultural knowledge can become acquired and used (thereby also contributing to the stabilization of such forms of knowledge in human culture, Sperber, 1996), even when the nature of their causal or functional efficacy remains cognitively opaque to the learner.

THE ESTABLISHMENT OF SECOND-ORDER EMOTION REPRESENTATIONS: THE ROLE OF OSTENSION AND MARKEDNESS

If one looks at the characteristic formal features of empathic, "marked" affect-mirroring displays and the ostensive affective interactions in which they appear, it becomes apparent that both types of pedagogical cues described above are centrally involved in the affect-mirroring communicative acts performed by sensitive, infant-attuned caregivers. The manner of execution of marked emotion expressions shares the characteristic features of other types of ostensively communicated referential knowledge manifestations in that "marked" affect displays are themselves salient and schematically executed transformations of the corresponding normative, realistic emotion expressions (see Points 4 and 5 above). Also, marked emotion displays are typically accompanied by such ostensive cues of communicative intent as "raised eyebrows," "slightly tilted head," and "knowing looks" involving gestural "widening (or shrinking) the eyes." One of the consequences of the presence of these cues of "markedness" (Fonagy et al., 2002; Gergely & Watson, 1996, 1999) is that the infant inhibits the attribution of the emotion expressed as being the caregiver's real feeling by referentially decoupling the emotion display from her. In other words, the infant is cued by the markedness of the mirroring emotion expression and by the ostensive communicative cues accompanying it that the emotion display is not performed in its primary function as expressing the caregiver's actual and real emotion state. At the same time, the joint presence of cues of ostension and markedness will, by hypothesis, induce the referential interpretive attitude of the pedagogical stance in the infant. In other words, the infant will be induced to activate a search for the intended referent of the caregiver's marked behavioral manifestation and to construct a referential interpretation for the marked affect display (anchoring it to a referent state *other* than the caregiver's actual emotion state). In trying to identify the actual referent that the (decoupled) marked emotion display is about, the infant will rely on the cues of referent identification (such as eye-gaze direction) of the caregiver that accompany her communicative emotion display. Since the caregiver is looking at and being oriented toward the infant while producing such marked emotion mirroring displays (accompanied with the characteristic infant-directed vocal intonation of motherese), the infant's attention will be directed toward its own face and body, that is, its own physical self as the locus of the referent to which the marked (and decoupled) parental affect display should be referentially anchored. This ostensively indicated spatial locus of the intended referent also coincides with those proprioceptive cues of the infant's automatic motor emotion display that exercise a high degree of contingent control over the caregiver's emotion-mirroring response (as this is indicated by the output of the infant's contingency detection device, Gergely & Watson, 1996). These two sources of converging information then identify the referent of the marked parental mirroring display as being that of the infant's currently activated emotional self-state whose expressive behavioral components exert high contingent control over the caregiver's marked empathic mirroring response. As a result, the infant will referentially anchor (and associate) the marked mirroring display as referring to its own primary emotion state and internalize it as its second-order representation.

It is in this way, then, that by activating the infant's pedagogical stance, repeated experience with ostensively cued, marked affect-mirroring feedback reactions from infant-attuned caregivers can (a) "teach" the infant about its primary categorical emotions; (b) lead to the internalization of the caregiver's marked mirroring displays as second-order emotion representations associated with such automatic, basic emotional self-states; and (c) turn the infant's attentional system in an introspective direction and sensitize it to those internal-state cues that indicate the presence of categorical emotional self-states. This process (together with the sensitization effects of the contingency-based social biofeedback mechanism described by Gergely & Watson, 1996, pp. 1190–1196) also leads to a heightened awareness of the internal proprioceptive cues of emotional self-expressions and the potential instrumental effects of contingent control that the self's affective displays can exert over the reactivity of the social environment.

This is then, in short, the manner in which an infant-attuned social mirroring-environment contributes to the construction of the introspectively detectable subjective self, populating it with cognitively accessible second-order emotion representations that form the basis of a subjective sense of self-awareness and affective self-control.

MENTALIZATION IN THE SERVICE OF AFFECTIVE SELF-REGULATION AND EMOTIONAL SELF-CONTROL

Let us now examine the role that the ability to "mentalize" can play in the self's developing capacity to exercise top-down cognitive control over its emotional self-states in the service of affective self-regulation. Above we have briefly mentioned the primary evolutionary function and advantage that the selection of the specialized cognitive capacity for mindreading or "mentalizing" about others' causal intentional mind states conferred on humans by providing them with an efficient mechanism to anticipate and interpret others' actions in a broad variety of social interactive contexts. Clearly, insofar as the theory of mind mechanism allows one to make fast and efficient online predictions about the other's likely actions during competitive as well as cooperative situations, it can provide significant benefits and advantages for the mindreader in furthering his or her own interests. If the person can anticipate through mentalizing what the other is likely to do in a particular situation, he or she will be in a position to plan and carry out informed actions that will significantly increase the chances of realizing his or her *own* goals (whether those happen to be contradictory or complementary to those of the other). A further type of evolutionary advantage to be gained from a strategic use of one's mentalization capacity is provided by the possibility to control and modify others' expectable actions by directly manipulating the representational contents of their causal mental states that drive their behavior. This can be achieved by communicating to them new information (or, alternatively, by deceptively misinforming them) to change their beliefs about relevant aspects of the situation as a result of which they will be likely to change their goal-directed actions as well.

We speculate that the proper evolutionary domain (see Sperber & Hirschfeld, 2004) of the cognitive adaptation for mindreading may have originally been restricted to infer and represent the causal intentional mental states of *other minds* only. This was sufficient to cope with the evolutionary task of anticipating the likely goal-directed actions of other agents in primarily competitive interpersonal situations. However, we hypothesize that with the developmental construction of cognitively accessible second-order representations of internal self-states, the proper domain of the human mindreading capacity becomes ontogenetically extended to include in its actual domain the mind of one's own self as well. This can be expected to result in significantly better coping strategies in the realm of affective, competitive, and cooperative interactions and relationships by enabling the self to anticipate its *own* actions and reactions as well as those of others through introspectively detecting, self-attributing, representing, and reflecting about one's dynamically changing affective and intentional dispositional self-states and anticipate their likely action consequences.

So how can the inferential system of mentalizing be applied introspectively to the domain of emotional self-control during affectively charged interactive situations? Clearly, there are important cases when one's mind-reading abilities can provide highly useful and relevant information to instruct one's secondary cognitive reappraisal processes of emotion control (Ellsworth & Scherer, 2003; Lazarus, 1991; Lazarus & Lazarus, 1994; LeDoux, 1995, 1996, 2000; Ochsner & Gross, 2005; Posner & Rothbart, 2000; Thompson, 1994). Such could be the case when these top-down cognitive appraisal processes are applied to reevaluate the realistic significance for the self of the *causal triggering conditions* of one's basic emotional arousal reactions in situations where these conditions involve another person's actions, reactions, or emotion expressions directed toward one's self. In such cases, mentalizing processes can support the secondary cognitive reappraisals of emotional self-control by accessing and reasoning about relevant stored knowledge concerning the other person's enduring mental dispositions, self-related attitudes, long-term aspirations, temperamental or personality traits, or recent life events, or by picking up and interpreting relevant situational or behavioral cues to infer what particular current dispositions, desires, intentions, and (possibly false) beliefs may have induced the other's reactions that led to the triggering of one's automatic basic emotional arousal response.

Similarly, it should be equally clear how the generation of secondary cognitive evaluations of the likely *causal consequences* of automatically acting on or expressing one's basic emotional arousal reaction can be greatly facilitated by the self's mentalizing capacity. The validity and scope of the predictions generated by such cognitive appraisals can be qualitatively enriched by mentalistic reasoning about the other's likely mental states and reactions that one's own emotional responses might induce. Such mentalizing inferences can take into consideration a range of relevant situation- and person-specific motivational factors such as the other's temperament, personality traits, childhood history, current dispositional states, his or her quality of relationship with and available relevant knowledge about one's own self, and so on. Importantly, in generating predictions about the other's likely reactions to one's potential emotional outburst, a good mentalizer may also be able to take into account available knowledge about the quality of *the other's mentalizing skills* that the latter can be counted on to apply when evaluating the reasons behind one's own emotional reactions toward him or her in the given situation.

CONCLUSION

We have argued that it is the successful social developmental construction of cognitively accessible second-order emotion representations that provides the representational preconditions for the possibility of extending one's mentalizing ability to the domain of the self's own affective states in the service of emotional self-regulation and control. The ensuing ability to intro-spectively detect one's internal affective states makes it possible to anticipate, evaluate, and adaptively modify one's own emotion-induced instrumental and expressive action tendencies. In other words, it is the early social con-struction of the representational affective self and the introspective social-ization of attentional self-monitoring processes that provide the conditions for the self to take advantage of its mentalizing capacity in the service of emotional self-control and to enable it to cope more efficiently in affective interpersonal situations and long-term affiliative and intimate relationships in later life.

NOTES

1. In fact, recent research indicates that the relative frequency with which both infant and juvenile capuchin monkeys direct to and exchange facial emotion displays with other conspecif-ics is highest in relation to peers, and lowest in relation to their mothers or to the dominant male of the group (Visalberghi, personal comunication, June 1, 2006; De Marco & Visalberghi, 2007).

2. This is in fact a central topic pursued by much current-day clinical research on develop-mental psychopathology investigating the early social developmental and attachment origins of a variety of later mentalization deficits that are now recognized as characteristic core symptoms of several types of affective and self-pathologies as well as certain personality disorders such as BPD (see e.g., Fonagy et al., 2002, 2003, 2007; Fonagy, Target, & Gergely, 2000; Gergely, Fonagy, & Target, 2002). This new direction of clinical research is well exemplified by current investigations on the impact of attachment traumas, attachment disorganization, and severe neglect, as well as other highly atypical patterns of early attachment interactions, on later dysfunctions of mentalization

capacities in BPD, and also by the development of new mentalization-based treatment (MBT) techniques for BPD (see Allen & Fonagy, 2006; Fonagy & Bateman, 2006).

3. In Gergely & Watson (1996) and Fonagy et al. (2002) we provide a review of the developmental and psychoanalytic literature that both demonstrate and emphasize the centrality of parental empathic affect-mirroring during early affect-regulative mother–infant interactions.

4. It is noteworthy that the ways in which such displays of "marked" emotion transform the normative display patterns of realistic emotion expressions share a great deal of formal similarity with the marked "as if" manner of executing real expressive and goal-directed action schemes in pretend play, on the one hand (Gergely & Watson, 1996; Fonagy et al., 2002), as well as with the ways in which infant-directed speech or "motherese" transforms adult communicative speech patterns, on the other (Fernald, 1992; see Gergely & Watson, 1996, note 8, p. 1198).

REFERENCES

Allen, J. G., & Fonagy, P. (2006). *Handbook of Mentalization-based Treatment.* New York: Wiley.

Astington, J. W., & Jenkins, J. M. (1999). A longitudinal study of the relation between language and theory-of-mind development. *Developmental Psychology, 35,* 1311–1320.

Bahrick, L. R., & Watson, J. S. (1985). Detection of intermodal proprioceptive-visual contingency as a potential basis of self-perception in infancy. *Developmental Psychology, 21,* 963–973.

Baldwin, D. A., & Moses, L. J. (1996). The ontogeny of social information gathering. *Child Development, 67,* 1915–1939.

Baron-Cohen, S. (1995). *Mindblindness: An Essay on Autism and Theory of Mind.* Cambridge, MA: Bradford, MIT Press.

Baron-Cohen, S., Leslie, A. M., & Frith, U. (1985). Does the autistic child have a "theory of mind"? *Cognition, 21,* 37–46.

Behne, T., Carpenter, M., & Tomasello, M. (2005). One-year-olds comprehend the communicative intentions behind gestures in a hiding game. *Developmental Science, 8,* 492–499.

Bennett, D. S., Bendersky, M., & Lewis, M. (2004). On specifying specificity: Facial expressions at 4 months. *Infancy, 6*(3), 425–429.

Bennett, D. S., Bendersky, M., & Lewis, M. (2005). Does the organization of facial expression change over time? Facial expressivity from 4 to 12 months. *Infancy, 8*(2), 167–187.

Bigelow, A. E. (1999). Infants' sensitivity to imperfect contingency in social interaction. In P. Rochat (Ed.), *Early Social Cognition* (137–154). Hillsdale, NJ: Erlbaum.

Bigelow, A. E., & De Coste, C. (2003). Infants' sensitivity to contingency in social interactions with familiar and unfamiliar partners. *Infancy, 4*, 111–140.

Bigelow, A. E., & Rochat, P. (2006). Two-month-old infants' sensitivity to social contingency in mother-infant and stranger-infant interaction. *Infancy, 9*(3), 313–325.

Bloom, P., & German, T. P. (2000). Two reasons to abandon the false belief task as a test of theory of mind. *Cognition, 77*, B25–B31.

Bowlby, J. (1969). *Attachment and loss, Vol. 1: Attachment.* London, Hogarth Press and the Institute of PsychoAnalysis.

Bråten, S. (1988). Dialogic mind: The infant and the adult in protoconversation. In M. Carvallo (Ed.), *Nature, cognition, and system, vol. I* (pp. 187–205). Dordrecht: Kluwer Academic Publishers.

Bråten, S. (1992). The virtual other in infants' minds and social feelings. In H. Wold (Ed.), *The Dialogical Alternative* (pp. 77–97). Oslo: Scandinavian University Press.

Bråten, S. (Ed.). (1998). *Intersubjective Communication and Emotion in Early Ontogeny.* New York: Cambridge University Press.

Brazelton, T. B., & Tronick, E. (1980). Preverbal communication between mothers and infants. In D. R. Olson (Ed.), *The Social Foundations of Language and Thought* (pp. 299–315). New York: Norton.

Brazelton, T. B., Koslowski, B., & Main, M. (1974). The origins of reciprocity: The early mother–infant interaction. In M. Lewis & L. Rosenblum (Eds.), *The Effect of the Infant On Its Caregiver* (pp. 49–76). New York: Wiley.

Bruner, J. S., Olver, P. R., & Greenfield, P. M. (1966). *Studies on Cognitive Growth.* New York: Wiley.

Bugnyar. T., & Heinrich, B. (2005). Ravens, *Corvus corax*, differentiate between knowledgeable and ignorant competitors. *Proceedings of the Royal Society, 272*, 1641–1646.

Cohn, J. F., & Tronick, E. Z. (1988). Mother–infant face-to-face interaction: Influence is bidirectional and unrelated to periodic cycles in either partner's behavior. *Developmental Psychology, 24*, 386–392.

Cooper, R. P., & Aslin, R. N. (1990). Preference for infant-directed speech in the first month after birth. *Child Development, 61*, 1584–1595.

Csibra, G., & Gergely, G. (2006). Social learning and social cognition: The case of pedagogy. In M. H. Johnson & Y. M. Munakata (Eds.), *Processes of Change in Brain and Cognitive Development. Attention and Performance, XXI*, 249–274.

Csibra, G., & Southgate, V. (2006). Evidence for infants understanding false beliefs should not be dismissed. *Trends in Cognitive Sciences, 10*, 4–5.

Cutting, A. L., & Dunn, J. (1999). Theory of mind, emotion understanding, language, and family background: Individual differences and interrelations. *Child Development,* *70*(4), 853–865.

Darwin, C. (1872). *The Expression of Emotions in Man and Animals.* New York: Philosophical Library.

De Marco, A., & Visalberghi, E. (2007). Facial displays in young tufted capuchin monkeys (*Cebus apella*): Appearance, meaning, context, and target. *Folia Primatologica, 78*(2), 118–137.

Dennett, D. C. (1978). Beliefs about beliefs. *Behaviour and Brain Sciences, 4,* 568–570.

Dennett, D. C. (1987). *The Intentional Stance.* Cambridge, MA: MIT Press.

de Villiers, J. G., & de Villiers, P. (2000). Linguistic determinism and the understanding of false belief. In P. Mitchell & K. Riggs, (Eds.), *Children's reasoning and the mind* (pp. 191–228). Hove, UK: Psychology Press.

de Villiers, J. G., & Pyers, J. E. (2002). Complements to cognition: A longitudinal study of the relationship between complex syntax and false-belief-understanding. *Cognitive Development, 17,* 1037–1060.

de Rosnay, M., & Harris, P. L. (2002). Individual differences in children's understanding of emotion: The roles of attachment and language. *Attachment and Human Development, 4*(1), 39–54.

de Rosnay, M., & Hughes, C. (2006). Conversation and theory of mind: Do children talk their way to socio-cognitive understanding? *British Journal of Developmental Psychology, 24*(1), 7–37.

Dunn, J., Brown, J., & Beardsall, L. (1991). Family talk about feeling states and children's later understanding of others' emotions. *Developmental Psychology, 27,* 448–455.

Ekman, P. (1992). Facial expressions of emotion: New findings, new questions. *Psychological Science, 3*(1), 34–38.

Ekman, P., Friesen, W. V., & Ellsworth, P. (1972). *Emotion in the Human Face.* New York: Pergamon Press.

Ellsworth, P. C., & Scherer, K. R. (2003). Appraisal process in emotion., In R. J. Davidson, K. R. Scherer, & H. H. Goldsmith (Eds.), *Handbook of affective sciences* (pp. 572–595). Oxford, UK: Oxford University Press.

Emery, N. J., & Clayton, N. S. (2004). The mentality of crows: Convergent evolution of intelligence in corvids and apes. *Science, 306,* 1903–1907.

Farroni, T., Csibra, G., Simion, F., & Johnson, M. H. (2002). Eye contact detection in humans from birth. *Proceedings of the National Academy of Sciences of the United States of America, 99,* 9602–9605.

Fernald, A. (1985). Four-month-old infants prefer to listen to motherese. *Infant Behavior and Development, 8,* 181–195.

Fernald, A. (1992). Human maternal vocalizations to infants as biological signals: An evolutionary perspective. In J. H. Barkow, J. Tooby, & L. C. Cosmides (Eds.), *The adapted* mind: *Evolutionary psychology and the generation of culture* (pp. 391–428). Oxford, UK: Oxford University Press.

Field, T., Woodson, R., Cohen, D., Garcia, R., & Greenberg, R. (1983). Discrimination and imitation of facial expressions by term and preterm neonates. *Infant Behavior and Development*, *6*, 485–490.

Floccia, C., Christophe, A., & Bertoncini, J. (1997). High-amplitude sucking and newborns: The quest for underlying mechanisms. *Journal of Experimental Child Psychology*, *64*, 175–189.

Fodor, J. (1992). A theory of the child's theory of mind. *Cognition*, *44*, 283–296.

Fonagy, P. (2001). *Attachment Theory and Psychoanalysis*. New York: Other Press.

Fonagy, P., & Bateman, A. W. (2006). Mechanisms of change in mentalization-based treatment of BPD. *Journal of Clinical Psychology*, *62*, 411–430.

Fonagy, P. & Target, M. (1997). Attachment and reflective function: Their role in self-organization. *Development and Psychopathology*, *9*, 679–700.

Fonagy, P., Gergely, G., & Target, M. (2007). The parent–infant dyad and the construction of the subjective self. *Journal of Child Psychology and Psychiatry*, *48*(3/4), 288–328.

Fonagy, P., Redfern, S., & Charman, T. (1997). The relationship between belief–desire reasoning and a projective measure of attachment security (SAT). *British Journal of Developmental Psychology*, *15*, 51–61.

Fonagy, P., Target, M., & Gergely, G. (2000). Attachment and borderline personality disorder: A theory and some evidence. *Psychiatric Clinics of North America*, *23*(1), 103–123.

Fonagy, P., Gergely, G., Jurist, E., & Target, M. (2002). *Affect-Regulation, Mentalization, and the Development of the Self*. New York: Other Press.

Fonagy, P., Steele, H., Steele, M., & Holder, J. (1997). Attachment and theory of mind: Overlapping constructs? *Association for Child Psychology and Psychiatry Occasional Papers*, *14*, 31–40.

Fonagy, P., Target, M., Gergely, G., Allen, J. G., & Bateman, A. (2003). The developmental roots of borderline personality disorder in early attachment relationships: A theory and some evidence. *Psychoanalytic Inquiry*, *23*, 412–459.

Gergely, G. (2000). Reapproaching Mahler: New perspectives on normal autism, normal symbiosis, splitting, and libidinal object constancy from cognitive developmental theory. *Journal of the American Psychoanalytic Association*, *48*(4), 1197–1228.

Gergely, G. (2002). The development of understanding self and agency. In U. Goshwami (Ed.), *Blackwell handbook of childhood cognitive development* (pp. 26–46). Oxford, UK: Blackwell.

Gergely, G. (2004). The role of contingency detection in early affect-regulative interactions and in the development of different types of infant attachment. *Social Development*, *13*(3), 468–488.

Gergely, G. (2007a). The social construction of the subjective self: The role of affect-mirroring, markedness, and ostensive communication in self development. In L. Mayes, P. Fonagy, & M. Target (Eds.), *Developmental science and psychoanalysis*. London: Karnac.

Gergely, G. (2007b). Learning 'about' versus learning 'from' other minds: Human pedagogy and its implications. In P. Carruthers (Ed.), *Innateness, vol. III. Foundations and mechanisms*. Oxford, UK: Oxford University Press.

Gergely, G., & Csibra, G. (2005). The social construction of the cultural mind: Imitative learning as a mechanism of human pedagogy. *Interaction Studies, 6*(3), 463–481.

Gergely, G., & Csibra, G. (2006). Sylvia's recipe: The role of imitation and pedagogy in the transmission of cultural knowledge. In S. Levenson & N. Enfield (Eds.), *Roots of human sociality: Culture, cognition, and human interaction* (pp. 229–255). Oxford, UK: Berg Publishers.

Gergely, G., & Unoka, Z. (in press a). Attachment, affect-regulation and mentalization: The developmental origins of the representational affective self. In C. Sharpe, P. Fonagy, & I. Goodyer (Eds.), *Social cognition and developmental psychology*. Oxford, UK: Oxford University Press.

Gergely, G., & Unoka Z. (in press b). The development of the unreflective self. In F. Busch (Ed.), *The Reflective Self: Special Issue of* Psychoanalytic Inquiry.

Gergely, G., & Watson, J. S. (1996). The social biofeedback theory of parental affect-mirroring: The development of emotional self-awareness and self-control in infancy. *The International Journal of Psycho-Analysis, 77*, 1–31.

Gergely, G., & Watson, J. S. (1999). Early social-emotional development: Contingency perception and the social biofeedback model. In P. Rochat (Ed.), *Early Social Cognition* (pp. 101–137). Hillsdale, NJ: Erlbaum.

Gergely, G., Bekkering, H., & Király, I. (2002). Rational imitation in preverbal infants. *Nature, 415*, 755.

Gergely, G., Fonagy, P., & Target, M. (2002). Attachment, mentalization, and the etiology of borderline personality disorder. *Self Psychology, 3*(1), 73–82.

Gergely, G., Király, I., & Egyed, K. (2007). On pedagogy. *Developmental Science, 10*(1), 139–146.

Gianino, A., & Tronick, E. Z. (1988). The mutual regulation model: The infant's self and interactive regulation and coping and defensive capacities. In T. M. Field, P. M. McCabe, & N. Schneiderman (Eds.), *Stress and Coping Across Development* (pp. 47–68). Hillsdale NJ: Erlbaum.

Gopnik, A., & Wellman, H. M. (1994). The theory theory. In L. A. Hirschfeld & S. A. Gelman (Eds.), *Mapping the Mind: Domain Specificity in Cognition and Culture* (pp. 257–293). New York: Cambridge University Press.

Gopnik, A., & Meltzoff, A. N. (1997). *Words, Thoughts, and Theories*. Cambridge, MA: MIT Press.

Hare, B., Call, J., & Tomasello, M. (2001). Do chimpanzees know what conspecifics know? *Animal Behavior, 61,* 139–151.

Harlow, H. F. (1961). The development of affectional patterns in infant monkeys. In B. M. Foss (Ed.), *Determinants of infant behaviour, Vol. 1* (pp. 75–88). London: Methuen.

Harris, P. (2005). Conversation, pretence, and theory of mind. In J. Astington & J. Baird (Eds.), *Why Language Matters for Theory of Mind* (pp. 70–83). New York: Oxford University Press.

Hobson, R. P. (1993). *Autism and the Development of Mind.* Hillsdale, NJ: Erlbaum.

Hobson, P. (2002). *The cradle of thought: Exploring the origins of thinking.* Oxford, UK: Oxford University Press.

Hofer, M. A. (1995). Hidden regulators: Implications for a new understanding of attachment, separation, and loss. In S. Goldberg, R. Muir, & J. Kerr (Eds.), *Attachment Theory: Social, Developmental, and Cinical Perspectives* (pp. 203–230). Hillsdale NJ: Analytic Press.

Hughes, C., & Dunn, J. (2002). 'When I say a naughty word.' Children's accounts of anger and sadness in self, mother and friend: Longitudinal findings from ages four to seven. *British Journal of Developmental Psychology, 20,* 515–535.

Izard, C. E., & Malatesta, C. Z. (1987). Perspectives on emotional development. I. Differential emotions theory of early emotional development. In J. D. Osofsky (Ed.), *Handbook of Infant Development* (2nd ed., pp. 494–554). New York: Wiley.

Johnson, S. C., Slaughter, V., & Carey, S. (1998). Whose gaze will infants follow? The elicitation of gaze-following in 12-month-olds. *Developmental Science, 1,* 233–238.

Kagan, J. (1994). *Galen's Prophecy: Temperament in Human Nature.* New York: Basic Books.

Kaminski, J., Call, J., & Tomasello, M. (2006). Goats' behaviour in a competitive food paradigm: Evidence for perspective taking? *Behaviour, 143*(11), 1341–1356.

Lazarus, R. S. (1991). *Emotion and Adaptation.* New York: Oxford University Press.

Lazarus, R. S., & Lazarus, B. N. (1994). *Passion and reason: Making sense of our emotions.* New York: Oxford University Press.

LeDoux, J. E. (1995). Emotion: Clues from the brain. *Annual Review of Psychology, 46,* 209–235.

LeDoux, J. E. (1996). *The Emotional Brain: The Mysterious Underpinnings of Emotional Life.* New York: Simon and Schuster.

LeDoux, J. E. (2000). Emotion circuits in the brain. *Annual Review of Neuroscience, 23,* 155–184.

Leslie, A. M. (2000). "Theory of mind" as a mechanism of selective attention. In M. S. Gazzaniga (Ed.), *The New Cognitive Neurosciences* (2nd ed., pp. 1235–1247). Cambridge, MA: MIT Press.

Leslie, A. M., Friedman, O., & German, T. P. (2004). Core mechanisms in "theory of mind." *Trends in Cognitive Sciences, 8,* 528–533.

Lewis, M., Allessandri, S. M., & Sullivan, M. W. (1990). Violation of expectancy, loss of control, and anger expressions in young infants. *Developmental Psychology, 26*(5), 745–751.

Liszkowski, U., Carpenter, M., Henning, A., Striano, T., & Tomasello, M. (2004). Twelve-month-olds point to share attention and interest. *Developmental Science, 7,* 297–307.

Lohmann. H., Tomasello, M., & Meyer, S. (2005). Linguistic communication and social understanding. In J. Astington & J. Baird (Eds.), *Why language matters for theory of mind* (pp. 245–265). Oxford, UK: Oxford University Press.

Mahler, M., Pine, F., & Bergman, A. (1975). *The Psychological Birth of the Human Infant: Symbiosis and Individuation.* New York: Basic Books.

Malatesta, C. Z., Culver, C., Tesman, R. J., & Shepard, B. (1989). The development of emotion expression during the first two years of life. *Monographs of the Society for Research in Child Development, 54,* Serial No. 219.

Meins. E., Fernyhough, C., Russell, J., & Clark-Carter. D. (1998). Security of attachment as a predictor of symbolic and mentalising abilities: A longitudinal study. *Social Development, 7,* 1–24.

Meins, E., Fernyhough, C., Fradley, E., & Tuckey, M. (2001). Rethinking maternal sensitivity: Mothers' comments on infants' mental processes predict security of attachment at 12 months. *Journal of Child Psychology and Psychiatry, 42,* 637–648.

Meins, E., Fernyhough, C., Wainwright, R., Das Gupta, M., Fradley, E., & Tuckey, M. (2002). Maternal mind-mindedness and attachment security as predictors of theory of mind understanding. *Child Development, 73,* 1715–1726.

Meins, E., Fernyhough, C., Wainwright, R., Clark-Carter, D., Das Gupta, M., Fradley, E., et al. (2003). Pathways to understanding mind: Construct validity and predictive validity of maternal mind-mindedness. *Child Development, 74*(4), 1194–1211.

Meltzoff, A. N. (2002). Imitation as a mechanism of social cognition: Origins of empathy, theory of mind, and the representation of action. In U. Goshwami (Ed.), *Blackwell handbook of childhood cognitive development* (pp. 6–25). Oxford, UK: Blackwell.

Meltzoff, A. N., & Gopnik, A. (1993). The role of imitation in understanding persons and developing a theory of mind. In S. Baron-Cohen, H. Tager-Flusberg, & D. J. Cohen (Eds.), *Understanding other minds: Perspectives from autism* (pp. 335–365). Oxford, UK: Oxford University Press.

Meltzoff, A. N., & Moore, M. K. (1977). Imitation of facial and manual gestures by human neonates. *Science, 198,* 75–78.

Meltzoff, A. N., & Moore, M. K. (1989). Imitation in newborn infants: Exploring the range of gestures imitated and the underlying mechanisms. *Developmental Psychology*, 25, 954–962.

Meltzoff, A. N., & Moore, M. K. (1998). Infant intersubjectivity: Broadening the dialogue to include imitation, identity and intention. In S Bråten (Ed.), *Intersubjective Communication and Emotion in Early Ontogeny* (pp. 47–62). New York: Cambridge University Press.

Moses, L. J., Baldwin, D .A., Rosicky, J. G., & Tidball, G. (2001). Evidence for referential understanding in the emotions domain at twelve and eighteen months. *Child Development*, 72(3), 718–735.

Movellan, J. R., & Watson, J. S. (2002). The development of gaze following as a Bayesian systems identification problem. *UCSD Machine Perception Laboratory Technical Reports*, 2002(1).

Mumme, D. L., & Fernald, A. (2003). The infant as onlooker: Learning from emotional reactions observed in a television scenario. *Child Development*, 74(1), 221–237.

Ochsner. K. N., & Gross, J. J. (2005). The cognitive control of emotion. *Trends in Cognitive Sciences*, 9(5), 242–249.

Onishi, K. H,. & Baillargeon, R. (2005). 15-month-old infants understand false beliefs. *Science*, 308(5719), 255–258.

Onishi, K. H., Baillargeon, R., & Leslie, A. M. (2007). 15-month-old infants detect violations in pretend scenarios. In B. Hommel & S. Biro (Eds.), Becoming an intentional agent: The development of action control. *A Special Issue of Acta Psychologica, 124.*

Ontai, L. L., & Thompson, R. A. (2002). Patterns of attachment and maternal discourse effects on children's emotion understanding from 3 to 5 years of age. *Social Development, 11*(4), 433–450.

Perner, J. (1991). *Understanding the Representational Mind*. Cambridge, MA: MIT Press.

Perner, J., & Lang, B. (2000). Theory of mind and executive function: Is there a developmental relationship? In S. Baron-Cohen, H. Tager-Flusberg, & D. J. Cohen (Eds.), *Understanding Other Minds: Perspectives from Developmental Cognitive Neuroscience* (pp. 150–181). New York: Oxford University Press.

Perner, J., Ruffman, T., & Leekman, S. R. (1994). Theory of mind is contagious: You catch it from your sibs. *Child Development, 65*, 1228–1238.

Polan H. J., & Hofer, M. A. (1999). Psychobiological origins of attachment and separation responses. In J. Cassidy & P. R. Shaver, (Eds.), *Handbook of Attachment: Theory, Research, and Clinical Implications* (pp. 162–180). New York: Guilford.

Posner, M. I., & Rothbart, M. K. (2000). Developing mechanisms of self-regulation. *Development and Psychopathology, 12*, 427–441.

Rochat, P., & Morgan, R. (1995). Spatial determinants in the perception of self-produced leg movements in 3- and 5-month-old infants. *Developmental Psychology, 31*, 626–636.

Rothbart, M. K. (1989). Temperament and development. In G. A. Kohnstamm, J. E. Bates, & M. K. Rothbart (Eds.), *Temperament in Childhood* (pp. 187–247). New York: Wiley.

Ruffman, T., Perner, J., & Parkin, L. (1999). How parenting style affects false belief understanding. *Social Development, 8*, 395–411.

Ruffman, T., Perner, J., Naito, M., Parkin, L., & Clements, W. (1998). Older (but not younger) siblings facilitate false belief understanding. *Developmental Psychology, 34*(1), 161–174.

Sabbagh, M. A., & Callanan, M. A. (1998). Metarepresentation in action: 3-, 4-, and 5-year-olds' developing theories of mind in parent–child conversations. *Developmental Psychology, 34*, 491–502.

Sander, L. (1988). The event-structure of regulation in the neonate–caregiver system as a biological background for early organisation of psychic structure. In A. Goldberg (Ed.), *Frontiers in Self Psychology* (pp. 64–77). Hillsdale, NJ: Analytic Press.

Southgate, V., Senju, A., & Csibra, G. (in press). Action anticipation through attribution of false beliefs by two-year-olds. *Psychological Science.*

Southgate, V., van Maanen, C., & Csibra, G. (in press). Infant pointing: Communication to cooperate or communication to learn? *Child Development.*

Sperber, D. (1996). *Explaining culture: A naturalistic approach.* London: Blackwell.

Sperber, D., & Hirschfeld, L. (2004). The cognitive foundations of cultural stability and diversity. *Trends in Cognitive Sciences, 8*(1), 40–46.

Sperber, D., & Wislon, D. (1986). *Relevance: Communication and cognition.* Oxford, UK: Blackwell.

Sroufe, L. A. (1996). *Emotional development: The organization of emotional life in the early years.* Cambridge, UK Cambridge University Press.

Stern, D. N. (1985). *The Interpersonal World of the Infant.* New York: Basic Books.

Suomi, S. J. (1995). Influence of Bowlby's attachment theory on research on non-human primate biobehavioral development. In S. Goldberg, R. Muir, & J. Kerr, (Eds.), *Attachment Theory: Social, Developmental, and Clinical Perspectives* (pp. 185–201). Hillsdale, NJ: Analytic Press.

Suomi, S. J. (1999). Attachment in rhesus monkeys. In J. Cassidy & P. R. Shaver (Eds.), *Handbook of Attachment: Theory, Research, and Clinical Implications* (pp. 181–197). New York: Guilford.

Surian, L., Caldi, S., & Sperber, D. (in press). Attribution of beliefs by 13-month-old infants. *Psychological Science.*

Thompson, R. S. (1994). Emotion regulation. A theme in search of definition. *Monographs of the Society for Research on Child Development, 59*(2/3), 25–52.

Tomasello, M. (1999). *The Cultural Origins of Human Cognition.* Boston: Harvard University Press.

Tomasello, M., & Haberl, K. (2003). Understanding attention: 12- and 18-month-olds know what's new for other persons. *Developmental Psychology, 39,* 906–912.

Tomasello, M., Call, J., & Hare, B. (2003). Chimpanzees understand psychological states—the question is which ones and to what extent. *Trends in Cognitive Sciences, 7*(4), 153–156.

Tomasello, M., Carpenter, M., & Liszkowski, U. (in press). A new look at infant pointing. *Child Development.*

Tomasello, M., Carpenter, M., Call, J., Behne, T., & Moll, H. (2005). Understanding and sharing intentions: The origins of cultural cognition. *Behavioral and Brain Sciences, 28,* 675–691.

Tomkins, S. (1995). *Exploring Affect: The Selective Writings of Silvan Tomkins.* Cambridge, UK: Cambridge University Press.

Trevarthen, C. (1979). Communication and cooperation in early infancy: A description of primary intersubjectivity. In M. Bullowa (Ed.), *Before Speech: The Beginning of Interpersonal Communication* (pp. 321–347). New York: Cambridge University Press.

Trevarthen, C. (1993). The self born in intersubjectivity: An infant communicating. In U. Neisser (Ed.), *The Perceived Self* (pp. 121–173). New York: Cambridge University Press.

Trevarthen, C., & Aitken, K. J. (2001). Infant intersubjectivity: Research, theory, and clinical applications. *Journal of Child Psychology and Psychiatry, 42*(1), 3–48.

Tronick, E. Z. (1989). Emotions and emotional communication in infants. *American Psychologist, 44,* 112–119.

Tronick, E. Z., & Cohn, J. F. (1989). Infant–mother face-to-face interaction: Age and gender differences in coordination and the occurrence of miscoordination. *Child Development, 60,* 85–92.

Vinden, P. G. (2001). Parenting attitudes and children's understanding of mind: A comparison of Korean American and Anglo-American families. *Cognitive Development, 16,* 793–809.

Watson, J. S. (1972). Smiling, cooing, and "the game." *Merrill-Palmer Quarterly, 18,* 323–339.

Watson, J. S. (1985). Contingency perception in early social development. In T. M. Field & N. A. Fox (Eds.), *Social Perception in Infants* (pp. 157–176). Norwood, NJ: Ablex.

Watson, J. S. (1994). Detection of self: The perfect algorithm. In S. T. Parker, R. W. Mitchell, & M. L. Boccia (Eds.), *Self-awareness in Animals and Humans: Developmental Perspectives* (pp. 131–148). New York: Cambridge University Press.

Watson, J. S. (1995). Mother–infant interaction: Dispositional properties and mutual designs. In N. S. Thompson (Ed.), *Perspectives in Ethology, Vol. 11. Behavioral Design.* New York: Plenum Press.

Watson J. S. (2001). Contingency perception and misperception in infancy: Some potential implications for attachment. *Bulletin of the Menninger Clinic, 65*(3), 296–321.

Wellman, H. (1990). *The Child's Theory of Mind.* Cambridge, MA: Bradford Books, MIT Press.

Wellman, H. M., Cross, D., & Watson, J. (2001). Meta-analysis of theory-of-mind development: The truth about false belief. *Child Development, 72*(3), 655–684.

Wimmer, H., & Perner, J. (1983). Beliefs about beliefs: Representation and constraining function of wrong beliefs in young children's understanding of deception. *Cognition, 13*, 103–128.

Uzgiris, I. C., Benson, J. B., Kruper, J. C., & Vasek, M. E. (1989). Contextual influences on imitative interactions between mothers and infants. In J. J. Lockman & N. L. Hazen (Eds.), *Action in Social Context: Perspectives on Early Development* (pp. 103–127). New York: Plenum Press.

Chapter 3

Minds and Yours

New Directions for Mentalization Theory

Elliot L. Jurist

The mind is emerging as a main focus in psychoanalysis. This is not surprising, given how much has been learned about the brain in recent years and how much more we can expect to know in the near future. In one sense, Freud's dream of a scientific psychology in the *Project* (1895) is no longer merely speculative; in another sense, however, there is good reason to be wary of reductionist conclusions. The relation of the mind to the brain continues to be hotly debated in philosophy and the cognitive sciences. For proponents of AI (artificial intelligence), the relation of the mind to the brain can be analogized to the relation of software to hardware. Other philosophers, like Searle (1998) and Nagel (1979), as well as neuroscientists like Edelman (1992), though, have warned against such formulations, emphasizing that the mind is defined by subjective experience, which does not map onto brain function automatically or easily. At present, we are at a very early stage of being able to understand subjective experience scientifically.

Progress can be made by studying the evolution of the brain developmentally. The brain only becomes a mind as a result of appropriate input from caregivers. Thus, contemporary psychoanalytic theories of development increasingly have focused on the theme of intersubjectivity, although the emphasis has been primarily on the self rather than the mind. The theory of mentalization, introduced to psychoanalysis by Peter Fonagy, is an exception: it emphasizes precisely that the mind grows and fathoms itself by virtue of the capacity to read and interpret the mental states of others and oneself.

In the first section of this chapter, I describe the concept of mentalization with an emphasis on how it brings attachment theory and psychoanalysis together in an appealing way. In the second section, I focus on the relation between attachment and mentalization, an aspect of mentalization theory that remains unresolved. In the third section, I examine how mentalization has been conceived in the theory of mind literature, and argue that the distinction philosophers make between low and high levels of mentalization is crucial to understanding the full range of the concept as well as to addressing the relation between attachment and mentalization. In the fourth part, I take a closer look at differences in the conceptualization of mentalization across disciplines and specify the issues that are in need of further elaboration. In the fifth and final part of the chapter, I pursue the clinical implications of mentalization theory by linking the high level of mentalization to the concept of "mentalized affectivity" (Jurist, 2006, 2005; Fonagy, Gergely, Jurist, & Target, 2002), and by reflecting on psychoanalytic psychotherapy as concerning the mutual engagement of the patient's and the analyst's mind and self.

WHY MENTALIZATION?

Psychoanalytic developmental theories have placed a special emphasis on motivation and emotions and have had considerably less interest in cognitive aspects of development (Bucci, 1997; Erdelyi, 1985). Stern's (1985) work is a notable exception because of its focus on the cognitive-affective stages that define the development of the self. Past psychoanalytic developmental theories typically have dwelled upon quite specific domains of mental functioning and development, while aiming to fathom subjective experience. The mind in general has not received adequate attention. Fonagy's work has spurred psychoanalysis to contemplate the unfolding of the mind as a mind (Fonagy, 1991; Fonagy, Steele, Moran, Steele, & Higgett, 1993; Fonagy & Target, 1996; Fonagy & Target, *this volume*). Fonagy imports the idea of "mentalization" from the theory of mind literature in developmental psychology (Frith & Happe, 1994; Harris, 1989), where the emphasis is more on cognition; that is, on awareness of thoughts and beliefs rather than desires. In the broadest sense, Fonagy uses the idea of mentalization to capture the process of how the brain becomes a mind, and, more specifically, to delineate the transformative shift that takes place with the ability to experience the mental in terms of representation. Fonagy's interpretation of mentalization remains sensitive to the realm of subjective experience and thus offers a new and valuable way to bring together psychoanalytic and attachment theory, two theories that at first were regarded as incompatible (Diamond, 2004; Eagle, 1995; Fonagy, 2001; Slade, 1999; Steele & Steele, 1998).

Mentalization is the skill that allows one to interpret others' minds, which in turn fosters the ability to read and understand one's own mental states. While mentalization relies upon cognition, according to Fonagy its source lies in the attachment relationship, an affective bond. Secure attachment facilitates the capacity to regulate affects, and, beyond that, the growth of the self and the mind's self-understanding; co-regulation turns into self-regulation. Initially, infants are dependent upon caregivers to help them contain strong negative affects and to promote tolerance for positive affects. As their capacity for affect regulation develops in the second half of the first year of life, the sense of self emerges, which, in turn, renders possible a better capacity for regulation.

Affect regulation relies on discerning the intentions of others and learning to see oneself as a being with its own intentions; thus, as the story goes, it prepares the way for mentalization, which unfolds around the age of 4 years, coinciding with the ability to identify false belief tasks correctly.[1] A "theory of mind" is a step beyond "psychic equivalence," wherein children make the assumption that what exists in their own minds must exist in the world. Play aids the transition to a new understanding: that the mind can shape and interpret what is real/external (Fonagy, 2001; Fonagy et al., 2002; Fonagy & Target, 1996). According to Fonagy et al. (2002), affect regulation is the basis for mentalization, but mentalization then fosters a new, more differentiated kind of affect and self-regulation, such as mentalized affectivity.

As a theory, mentalization offers a powerful tool for integrating ideas from attachment studies and psychoanalysis. Attachment theory has evolved beyond Bowlby's (1969, 1980) original formulation that the goal of attachment is to provide proximity to the caregiver, with the later amendment of the goal of "felt security" (Sroufe, 1996, Sroufe & Waters, 1977). It has transcended Bowlby's "naive realism," the philosophical term for the belief that our minds reflect the world in a direct and unmediated way, in the way that it now construes "internal working models." Main's (Main, Kaplan, & Cassidy, 1985) "move to the level of representation" affirmed that mental representations need to be construed more complexly; the reworking of memory, for example, is identified as altering internal working models. Nevertheless, attachment theory has had a tendency to portray internal working models as cognitive structures, thus failing to grapple with the way affects adhere to cognition (Main, 1991). Psychoanalytic thinkers have provided a richer picture of mental representations as cognitive-affective schemas, which are derived from both the external and internal world (Blatt & Blass, 1996; Loewald, 1962; Sandler & Rosenblatt, 1962).

Fonagy's (Fonagy, 2001; Fonagy et al., 2002) proposal that the goal of attachment is to produce a representational system seems to place it within philosophical idealism—the belief that the way our minds work alters our perception and conception of reality—at the opposite pole from realism. Yet it is more accurate to state that Fonagy's proposal incorporates elements of both realism and idealism, rather than siding with one over the other. For Fonagy, the realm of mental representation reflects Sandler & Rosenblatt's (1962) affectively tinged notion of the "representational world," incorporating both "fantasy" from psychoanalytic theory and "internal working models" from attachment theory. Fonagy's proposal about the goal of attachment is a major step toward mitigating differences that traditionally have divided attachment theory and psychoanalysis and toward synthesizing their respective strengths. His take on the representational system derives from cognitive-affective schemas, but it must also be understood in connection with theory of mind activities, such as social reality-testing and imaginary play.

ATTACHMENT AND MENTALIZATION

Let us turn to examine Fonagy's (Fonagy, 2006; Fonagy & Bateman, 2006; Fonagy & Target, *this volume*) more recent views, as his characterization of the relation between attachment and mentalization has been evolving.

Originally, it was hypothesized that mentalization comes into being through secure attachment: that the very capacity for mentalization is rooted in the attachment relationship (Fonagy, 2001; Fonagy et al., 2002). In Bateman & Fonagy (2004), attachment is portrayed as propelling cognitive development (p. 58), and it is affirmed that mentalization is "greatly facilitated by secure attachment" (p. 72). A key part of this argument includes the claim that in borderline pathology, mentalization is lacking—at times, that mentalization fails, at other times that it shades into a problematic variation, hyperactive mentalization.

In Fonagy & Bateman (2006), their thinking has shifted, and the proposal is made that there is a "loose coupling" between attachment and mentalization. On the one hand, the authors wish to emphasize that attachment and mentalization are not independent of each other. On the other, a "reciprocal relation" is postulated, wherein mentalization can be taken off-line by the activation of the attachment system, and attachment and mentalization are understood in terms of belonging to distinct brain systems. Following Bartels & Zeki (2004), brain system "A" includes the middle prefrontal, inferior parietal, and middle temporal cortices mainly in the right hemisphere, as well as the posterior cingulate cortex. The system "A" functions to integrate cognition and emotions and may contribute to the typology of attachment. The second system, "B," includes the temporal poles, parietotemporal junction, amygdala, and mesial prefrontal cortex. The system "B" is activated with negative emotion, judgments of social trustworthiness, moral judgments, "theory of mind" tasks, and attention to one's own emotions, and underlies our ability to deal with the mental states of others. Most importantly, the system "B" is deactivated by the activation of attachment.

Fonagy & Bateman (2006) acknowledge the potential conflict present between the "positive correlation" linking attachment and mentalization and the fact that they exist in a reciprocal relation. There is nothing contradictory, according to the authors, though, in recognizing that secure attachment promotes the development of mentalization in such a way that the attachment system can be put aside in favor of mentalization. Secure attachment affords a child the opportunity to experiment with mentalization where the stakes are lower than in the real world. As Fonagy (2006) suggests, evolution has selected attachment as the "principal training ground" for the acquisition of mentalization. Indeed, borderlines get into trouble because their attachment systems become activated precisely when they need to be able to mentalize. A significant revision of borderline pathology follows here: it is not so much that borderlines cannot mentalize as that they lose the capacity in particular circumstances: "it is only in the context of intimate relationships that the patient's capacity to depict mental states in others accurately appears to falter" (Fonagy & Bateman, 2006, p. 422).

This qualification in Fonagy's thinking betokens the emergence of a more complex model of mentalization, encompassing a wide range of phenomena. Fonagy (2006) speculates about underlying aspects of mentalization and moves on to present a detailed outline of the evolution of the concept developmentally. One key underlying factor is the notion of "selective attention," which was first introduced by Leslie, Friedman, & German (2004). Another important underlying factor is the capacity to withhold impulsive responses. Fonagy suggests, but does not develop, a two-level system that defines mentalization: a frontal-cortical system that involves declarative representation, and a mirror neuron system that provides a more immediate and direct understanding of others (p. 58). As I will elaborate in the next section, the notion of two levels of mentalization is of crucial significance.

Fonagy (2006) provides a detailed account of the developmental unfolding of mentalization: (a) during the second half of the first year of life, where causal relations begin to connect the agent to the world, although agency is a matter of physical actions and constraints, and mental states are not considered; (b) during the second year of life, where a mentalistic understanding of agency develops, particularly of desires, although the realms of the internal and the external are not clearly delineated (this corresponds to both the psychic equivalence and the pretend mode); (c) during the third to fourth year of life, where representation of epistemic mental states occurs at the same time as the self concept emerges (this corresponds to the time when children pass the false belief task, when "mentalizing abilities take a quantum leap forward"; and (d) during the sixth year, where memories of intentional activities and experiences are organized into a coherent causal-temporal framework, resulting in a temporally extended sense of self. Mistaken beliefs can be identified, mixed emotions are experienced, and social deception (such as "white lies") occurs (pp. 73–74). Fonagy blends the terms "agency," "self," and "mind" here in a seamless way, although questions remain about the interrelation among these concepts.[2]

Gergely & Unoka (Gergely & Unoka, in press, *this volume*) have put forth an original proposal about mentalization, based on recent research findings. They present compelling evidence that mentalization begins earlier in development than had originally been proposed—roughly by 12 months or so. Gergely & Unoka (*this volume*) worry that too much stock has been put in correlational studies linking attachment and mentalization. They point out several factors that have been identified as spurring mindreading as measured by false belief tasks that have "no obvious or demonstrated relation to early measures of infant attachment security" (p. 56) such as having older siblings (Perner, Ruffman, & Leekman, 1994; Ruffman, Perner, Naito, Parkin, & Clements, 1998); language use, specifically the relative frequency and precocity of using complex syntactic complement structures (Aslington & Jenkins, 1999; deVilliers & deVilliers, 2000; deVilliers & Pyers, 2002); and the maturational development of executive function, selective attention, and response inhibition capacities (Leslie, 2000; Leslie et al., 2004; Perner & Lang, 2000). Even the mother's educational level has been linked to better mindreading (Cutting & Dunn, 1999; Meins & Fernyhough, 2002).

Gergely & Unoka (in press) draw attention to new challenges to the theory of mind paradigm from implicit nonverbal versions of false belief experiments that demonstrate mindreading capacities prior to 4 years old. By just around one year old, infants monitor other agents' perceptual access to reality and infer, attribute, and represent the beliefs of others (Onishi & Baillargeon, 2005). Thus, there is reason to question the assumption that false beliefs cannot be discerned, and that mentalization only begins when there is a conclusive turn to a representational theory of mind at 4 years old. Finally, Gergely & Unoka (in press) claim that the growing literature in comparative animal studies ought to make us question the belief that mindreading is a uniquely human activity.

The notion that there is a direct causal and functional link between attachment and mentalization, according to Gergely & Unoka (in press, *this volume*), must be "significantly revised" (p. 58). From their perspective, the implicit and automatic capacity to mentalize about others, as seen in infants, is not a developmental achievement; rather it is "an innate social-cognitive evolutionary adaptation implemented by a specialized and pre-wired mindreading mechanism" (p. 59). Even more to the point, Gergely & Unoka maintain that mentalization ought to be redefined as "separate and unrelated to the function of the attachment system" (p. 59). However, Gergely & Unoka do register their agreement that maladaptive patterns in the infant–parent relationship can play a harmful role in terms of the unfolding of mindreading abilities.

In Gergely & Unoka's (in press) account, attachment is seen as generating a representational world based upon the affective relationship between a child and his or her parents and the capacity for affective self-control. They propose an illuminating distinction between self-to-other and other-to-self representations. In fact, Gergely & Unoka (in press) provide a richly detailed account of the way, during the first year of life, pre-wired basic emotions start to become "visible" to the child by means of the appropriate input from caregivers. This entails linkage of the basic emotions, first, to primary representations, and subsequently, to secondary top-down cognitive appraisals. Gergely & Unoka (in press) add to this narrative that the child benefits from the "natural pedagogy" of the parents' ostensive cueing—the function of which is not merely to forge a self, but to promote initiation into the realm of cultural belief systems. The connection to mentalization occurs in that the quality of second-order cognitive appraisals of emotions must rely on the ability to read and interpret the minds of others. Thus the distinct systems of attachment and mentalization can dovetail, insofar as mentalizing skills are brought to bear on attachment relationships.

Significant differences appear to exist between Fonagy and Gergely's most recent attempts to describe the relation between attachment and mentalization. While Fonagy acknowledges that attachment and mentalization might best be viewed as part of distinct systems, he is more optimistic in his interpretation of the positive correlation between the two and utilizes neuroscientific findings to support his case. Gergely chooses to emphasize the point that attachment and mentalization are part of separate systems. He adheres more to the definition of mentalization as an automatic mechanism that is aimed at understanding and predicting the actions and behaviors of others, a reading that remains closer to the view derived from cognitive psychology. Gergely does concur, however, that mentalization can be modified to include the domain of self-understanding. As I see it, the two views can be compatible insofar as we realize that Gergely is interested in the early biological aspect of mentalization and does not entertain consideration of more complex forms of mentalization, while Fonagy introduces, but has not developed sufficiently, the two levels of mentalization, and seems to be particularly captivated by the more sophisticated level. In the following section, I shall support the idea of differentiating between levels of mentalization by turning to theories of mind, and then I will return to Fonagy and Gergely once again.

THEORIES OF MIND: TWO LEVELS OF MENTALIZATION

It will be helpful to contextualize the meaning of the concept of mentalization by looking at its source in the theory of mind literature from cognitive psychology and philosophy. The distinction between different levels of mentalization has recently become central in the theory of mind literature. As I shall claim, the distinction ought to be incorporated into the psychoanalytic conception of mentalization as well.

Two alternative points of view have been defended in theory of mind: theory-theory and simulation theory (Baron-Cohen, Tager-Flusberg, & Cohen, 2000; Carruthers & Smith, 1996). According to the former, the capacity to interpret the mind of another is based upon formulating a theory of how minds work, which corresponds to our shared beliefs or "folk psychology." Some theory-theory proponents are infatuated with the comparison between what the child does as similar to what scientists do (Gopnik, 1993; Gopnik, Capps, & Meltzoff, 2000). This is controversial, however, and has been criticized as being misleading and undeveloped (Bogdan, 1997; Goldman, 2006).

According to simulationists, the capacity to interpret the mind of another is predicated upon placing oneself in the other person's situation. Simulationists argue that we extrapolate from ourselves in reading others. Mentalization, on this account, relies on our ability to put ourselves in the "mental shoes" of others (Goldman, 2006). Gordon (1996) emphasizes that simulation is a matter of imagination and the suspension of our own reactions. Gordon (1996) also observes that the virtue of the simulationist view is that it is based on "hot cognition," which includes emotions, rather than the "cold cognition," which the theory-theory presumes. A downside of simulationist views is that they seem to presuppose and place a heavy burden on the self-awareness of very young children.

The debate between these two positions continues to the present, and I will not rehearse the arguments in great detail. As already mentioned in the last section, one key new development is the challenge to the lynchpin of the theory-theory position: that caution needs to be exercised in interpreting "false beliefs" experiments based upon switched location tasks, given research that supports an appreciation of earlier mentalizing abilities in children under 4 years old. It should be noted that evidence in support of early mentalization does not mean that there is not an important shift that takes place at 4 to 5 years. What it clearly suggests, however, is that mentalization is not ideally conceived in terms of an either/or, but as a continuum from early development.

In his latest book, *Simulating Minds* (2006), Goldman puts forth what he terms a "hybrid theory" that has elements of both the theory-theory and the simulation perspectives. His theory offers a clear defense of simulation, insofar as he provides a comprehensive analysis of the concept and mounts an argument in support of simulation as a necessary, but insufficient, feature of mentalization. Goldman proposes that simulation relies upon "pretense," an act of imagination in which we aspire to make sense of what it is that the other might be experiencing. A final stage of this process entails "projection"; that is, the attribution of beliefs to the other person. Yet Goldman is willing to concede that some mindreading predictions do not exclusively rely on simulation, but can include theory (p. 174).

Goldman emphasizes that simulation requires us to quarantine our own beliefs for the sake of understanding someone else. The metaphor of quarantine is meant to convey the importance of keeping one's own beliefs separate and the danger of allowing egocentrism to interfere with our judgment, but not the connotation of precaution against disease. Mistakes occur, in this account, because of a failure to quarantine one's own, real point of view (p. 148).

Goldman's account underscores the complexity of mentalization by featuring the distinction between low and high levels. Low mentalization typically concerns detecting emotions, especially facial expressions, and pains. It is relatively simple, primitive, automatic, and largely below consciousness (p. 113). Goldman connects low mentalization to modularity and, in particular, to the neurobiological discovery of mirror neurons. High mentalization involves mental states that are relatively complex, subject to voluntary control, and have some degree of accessibility to consciousness (p. 147). The high level of mentalization requires the use of pretense or enactment imagination; that is, not just conjuring abstractly, but as if the beliefs were real. Interestingly, Goldman connects high mentalization to self-reflection or self-reference, the ability to engage in self-investigation in the context of third-person mentalizing. Goldman notes that we do not yet know much about the neurobiology of high mentalization. High mentalization can be distinguished from low mentalization because of its greater accuracy.

Another philosopher, Stueber (2006), has proposed a distinction between basic and reenactive empathy, which closely resembles the distinction that Goldman makes between low and high mentalization. In the context of defending simulation theory, Stueber contrasts basic empathy, which he sees as a fundamental, perceptual level of interpersonal relations, and reenactive empathy, which requires a richer awareness of context and meaning. Reenactive empathy leads us not just to identify what is going on with another person, but in addition to seek to make it intelligible. Stueber shows a sensitivity to the history of the concept of empathy in thinkers like Lipps, Dilthey, and Collingwood, and he seeks to support what he terms an engaged or "bound" conception of rationality, in opposition to Goldman's defense of disengaged rationality.

The views of Stueber (2006) and Goldman (2006) are, however, largely consistent. The low level of mentalization concerns emotions; the high level concerns emotions as well, but is conditioned by the capacity to regulate and modify them. According to Stueber and Goldman, the high level of mentalization depends upon imagination, a specialized function that allows us to grapple with the complexity of social life. It is important to note that in this reading mentalization is less an online function that primarily governs competitive situations in which we need to know how to act than it is a function that reflects an interior life that is defined by its search for understanding. Emotions are just as important at the high level of mentalization; here they are harnessed to context and meaning. It is this level of mentalization, as we will see in the last part of this chapter, that is particularly relevant for psychotherapy.

Let us consider the two levels of mentalization in relation to Fonagy and Gergely's views. Fonagy (Fonagy, 2006; Fonagy & Target, *this volume*; Gergely & Unoka, *this volume*) has made a similar distinction; moreover, he explicitly affirms the link between the low level of mentalization and mirror neurons (though he does not focus on emotions per se). He has had less to say about the high level of mentalization, which does not seem to be fully accounted for in terms of the sociobiological notion of an "arms race." It would seem that psychotherapy would aim to improve the high level of mentalization, although it is an empirical question whether the low level can be changed (and how this might affect the high level). Gergely's focus (Gergely & Unoka, in press) is on early development, rather than adult treatment; accordingly, his concerns overlap more with the unfolding of the low level of mentalization. However, since Gergely regards early mentalization as primarily cognitive and illustrates how mentalization dovetails with the regulation of emotions, his view does not fit neatly into the first level. (Like his collaborator, Csibra [2007], Gergely questions the view that mirror neurons provide a direct match, and suggests that their working require interpretation). So there are certainly many questions that need to be raised about the two levels and their relation to each other. At this point, it is unclear whether the two levels are categorically different and involve distinct underlying brain systems, or whether the high level of mentalization grows out of the low level. Without further evidence, the best we can conclude now is that the concept of mentalization is even more confusing without any distinction between the two levels.

MENTALIZATION AND ITS DISCONTENTS

The distinction between low and high levels of mentalization ought to be incorporated into the psychoanalytic view and is relevant to all views of mentalization. However, the distinction should not obscure the significant differences that underlie various accounts of mentalization. In this section, therefore, I turn to enumerating and specifying what is at stake in the different views.

The first major issue that distinguishes extant approaches to mentalization is the question of development. Many accounts in the cognitive sciences pay no attention to development. Goldman (2006) points out, for example, that philosophers tend not concern themselves with how mentalization unfolds in development (p. 9). The strong commitment to innateness is one explanation for why both theory-theory advocates and simulationists do not give sufficient attention to the quality of the early relationship (Fonagy et al., 2002). Still, there is a large literature on theory of mind that is developmental but not psychoanalytic. In most of this literature, mentalization is restricted to denote the cognitive ability to read the minds of others. The psychoanalytic, developmental approach to mentalization clearly has more complex aspirations.

First of all, the psychoanalytic, developmental approach to mentalization attends to intersubjectivity: we learn to mentalize from others (caregivers) who already mentalize. Advocates of theory of mind tend to constrict mentalizing to an individual knower who makes predictions about social behavior. Psychoanalysis highlights the interactional context that fosters the emergence of the individual self and mind. This leads us to the second issue. Here, according to the psychoanalytic conception, mentalization comes to have a function that pertains to self-understanding and so is not just about the understanding of others. The infant relies on the mind of the caregiver, and the caregiver serves both to cultivate a unique sense of self and, as Gergely (2007) and Gergely & Csibra (2005, 2006) have emphasized, to teach the infant what it means to belong to culture. Having a self can mean many things, but one thing it certainly refers to is the creation of space for one to be able to mentalize about oneself; that is, both how one is unique (and not like others) and how one has a mind (and thus is like others). A crucial psychoanalytic assumption is that if others mentalize about you and help you to mentalize, it will be a spur to mentalize about yourself.

On a related note, Vygotskians have criticized the theory of mind literature for focusing on the single individual and thus failing to grapple with the force of culture and values, and for examining general social encounters without making further differentiation among different kinds of interaction (Aslington, 1996). The notion of "folk psychology" is invoked in such a way that issues about cultural differences are minimized (Descombes, 2001), and mentalization has not been investigated cross-culturally. It is worth wondering how a paradigm based on general social encounters might be different from one that pertains to the sphere of personal or intimate relationships. As discussed in the last section, there are reasons not to assume that mentalization is predicated upon attachment; thus, it remains a challenge for empirical research to determine the nature of the differences between attachment-related and general social mentalization.

This brings us to the third issue concerning mentalization, as a further implication of the developmental and intersubjective emphasis in psychoanalysis is that mentalization entails emotions. As I have stated, there is a bias in the theory of mind literature toward defining mentalization in terms of cognition, especially among theory-theory proponents. Simulationists do make some room for emotions, without, however, going far enough. Emotions are a necessary feature of how we know others. They do not merely contribute to cognition; they have a more profound and thoroughgoing influence on us. Subjective experience, for example, is permeated with emotions and the struggle to regulate them. I would take this claim further, in fact, arguing that emotional styles are fundamental to the mind.

Emotional style clearly overlaps with attachment style since it is a product of cognitive-affective schemas or representations, plus biogenetic factors, which lead to characteristic and predictable choices and actions.[3] Not only does the term "emotional style" give emotions a central place, but it also accommodates a wide range of styles, thus promising a greater specificity than the categories found in attachment theory. Emotional style is also less pathologizing in that there is a continuum within each category, rather than the presumption of one style (secure) that is deemed healthy and others (insecure, disorganized) that are not.[4] The abstract accounts found in the theory of mind literature ignore emotional styles, just as they ignore the intersubjective, family, and cultural contexts that are intrinsic to mentalization. In the last section of this chapter, I shall return to the topic of emotions and emotional styles as they are manifested in the clinical environment.

The fourth issue about mentalization concerns whether it is, by and large, accurate or not. The theory of mind literature tends to assume that our mindreading capacity, which comes about through evolution, is accurate with exceptions (Nichols & Stich, 2004). The notion of the child as scientist, in particular, suggests that the mentalizer is in pursuit of truth by means of sorting out ideas on the basis of converging evidence. There is an assumption here of first-person authority and objective reality-testing, which obscures the emotional intensity of formative human relationships. Some, like Goldman, wish to challenge the assumption of accuracy by noting that it depends upon the capacity to quarantine one's own mind. However, psychoanalytic views of mentalization take this a step further, emphasizing how often we fail to understand ourselves as well as others (Fonagy, 2006). Our experience of emotions is often aporetic; it is often the case that we do not know what we feel, much less what others feel (Jurist, 2005). The psychoanalytic concept derives, no doubt, from its source in clinical work, a naturalistic context in which people give freer expression to their internal experience, as compared to everyday social life.

One might wonder whether the appreciation of ambiguity and misunderstanding in psychoanalysis is a reflection of its focus on attachment-related mentalization. At first glance this might seem paradoxical, as it makes sense to presume that we would be more confident that we know and understand those with whom we are familiar. At the same time, it makes sense that in situations where the stakes of the relationship are high, and the consequences of problems are correspondingly more emotionally intense (both in terms of pleasure and pain), there might be more sensitivity to the complexities and subtleties of mindreading. The psychoanalytic perspective on mentalization accommodates better and more accurate prediction, but also acknowledges other kinds of experiences, such as being unsure whether one is right and recognizing that one has been or might be mistaken.

The psychoanalytic concept of mentalization connotes not only the ability to read mental states with accuracy, but also the ability to be open-minded. Within psychoanalysis, in other words, the value of mentalization lies in helping us to formulate and hold onto various hypotheses about mental states without necessarily resolving them; this clearly departs from the notion that mentalization produces conclusions or correct inferences. Mentalization, in the psychoanalytic account, includes a disposition to hesitate about one's beliefs, to strive to be inclusive of different beliefs, and to be willing to weigh and attribute value to them. Like the concept of psychological-mindedness, mentalization requires "tolerance of ambiguity," which is distinct from the pursuit of being right (Beitel, Ferrer, & Cecero, 2004). Philosophical sources for this way of thinking about mentalization can be found in "fallibilism," an epistemological perspective that is associated with Peirce (1897), but that is also related to ideas in thinkers ranging from Socrates to Popper. Fallibilism encourages appreciation of the idea that empirical knowledge might need to be revised in light of further observation, and, thus, that what we think we know can turn out to be false. But fallibilism can be distinguished from skepticism in defending knowledge, however tentatively. Mentalizing inspires a kind of humility, with an awareness that further information might alter our beliefs, and that it is always important to remain in touch with how much we do not know.[5]

There is a question of whether mentalization can be equated with moral judgment. Mentalization clearly overlaps to some degree with empathy; not only is one able to know what someone else feels, but one also reveals a capacity to have a regard for that person. For example, Allen (2006) draws attention to the moral quality of mentalization that derives from its connection to empathy, arguing that mentalization is "more than a skill; it is a virtue, a loving act" (p. 23). On the contrary, in the same volume, Fonagy (2006; also see *this volume*) links mentalization to competitive social behavior, analogizing it to an "arms race," in which, presumably, we mentalize in order to strategize and prevail over others. More specifically, Fonagy (2006) maintains that "Possessing the capacity to mentalize neither guarantees that it will be used to serve pro-social ends, nor assumes protection from malign interpersonal influence" (p. 76). Indeed, it is reasonable to speculate that a high-functioning psychopath could be adept at mentalizing and use it for nefarious ends.

There are positions that can be mustered on both sides of this argument. It is difficult not to be troubled by the psychopath's absence of regard for others; yet mentalization does need to be understood in terms of its value in helping us to survive and flourish. It is too limiting to define mentalization as deployed exclusively as a deferral of aggression; at the same time, if we were so benevolently motivated, there might not be much of a need for mentalization. It is most parsimonious to regard mentalization as relevant precisely where we are not sure and do not know what to do; thus conceived, it is germane for both the aspiring saint and the caveman with club in hand. Mentalization is an exciting and illuminating concept, but, as should be apparent at this point, there is much about it that remains uncertain and needs clarification.

MENTALIZED AFFECTIVITY

In this final section, I shall address some of the clinical implications of my discussion of mentalization. The clinical realm is where attachment and mentalization unambiguously come together, where the two levels, and especially the higher level of mentalization, are readily apparent. Clinical work differs from general social interaction in the degree of intimacy that emerges between analyst and patient in a relationship that evolves into an actual attachment relationship and yet is never free of past attachment relationships. Indeed, however intimate the relationship becomes over time, an asymmetry necessarily exists between analyst and patient, no matter how open and revealing the analyst chooses to be. This complex dynamic is precisely why mentalization is a crucial factor in treatment, as the relationship between patient and analyst both is and is not an attachment relationship.

Emotions and emotional style are more exposed in the clinical realm than in everyday life. Emotions emerge, both live and remembered, and it is a crucial function of all psychotherapy to help patients manage and modulate them. A strong argument can be made that the aim of any kind of psychotherapy is to foster better affect regulation. Many kinds of psychopathology can be defined in terms of affect dysregulation (Bradley, 2000; Gross, 1999; Gross & Thompson, 2007, Schore, 2003a; Taylor, Bagby, & Parker, 1997). Yet it can be unsatisfying to affirm the importance of affect regulation without appreciating and qualifying its many meanings (Jurist, 2005).

One significant difference to be noted, for example, lies in the way developmental psychologists and psychoanalysts construe affect regulation. The former understand regulation in terms of limiting of negative affect in the service of socialization, whereas the latter embrace both positive and negative affect; and, significantly, affirm the value of tolerating negative affect and are reluctant to link regulation to the concept of socialization. Valuing the capacity to accept and understand negative affects sets psychoanalysis off from other modalities of treatment as well as from other research models of emotions. Moreover, the stakes are larger in the way psychoanalysis and attachment theory construe regulation: the object of regulation is not simply the affect or emotion, but emotional style, and, ultimately, the self and the mind (Fonagy et al., 2002).

Affect regulation is a complex concept that includes at least two distinct levels. At one level, affect regulation functions as an automatic, procedural process, akin to homeostasis (Hofer, 1990, 1984; Polan & Hofer, 1999; Schore, 2003a, 2003b); at another level, it reflects a developmental achievement that is subject to voluntary control and cognitive appraisal (Fonagy et al., 2002). A parallel can be drawn between the two systems of emotional response that LeDoux (1996) describes, the frontal-cortical and subcortical, and the two levels of mentalization that have been discussed in this paper. Using the term empathy and distinguishing between the phenomenon of emotional contagion and emotions that are mediated by cognition, Preston & deWaal (2002) review brain function and affirm precisely this connection between emotions and theory of mind.

Affect regulation and mentalization are closely related in the clinical sphere, especially the higher levels that are subject to volition, modulation, and control. I have introduced the term *mentalized affectivity* in order to define the capacity to reflect on affect states and to regulate them (Fonagy et al., 2002; Jurist, 2005, 2006). This kind of affect regulation is particularly germane to psychoanalysis and psychoanalytic psychotherapy, as it highlights the difficulty and complexity of knowing others and oneself deeply, and hence marks an area that corresponds to the high level of mentalization.

Mentalized affectivity entails revaluing, not just modulating, affects. Mentalized affectivity captures what is most challenging in adult affect regulation: that new meaning can be created and specified by reflecting upon affective experience. In engaging in such reflection, it is desirable to remain within or to recapture the feeling of that state. The term suggests that this process is not simply a matter of exercising cognitive control over affective states. Mentalized affectivity immerses us in the exploration of how affective experience is mediated by one's emotional style—in other words, how current (and future) affects are experienced through the lens of past experiences, both real and imagined. Some affects might well occur in a pure, universal form without such mediation, but are nevertheless always connected to relationships with others—sometimes in obvious ways, sometimes in ways that are hidden.

Mentalized affectivity enables us to conceptualize the experience of affects as confusing, complex, and fluid. Indeed, there are often affects behind affects: we believe that we feel one thing while we really feel something else or some combination of things. Past history is entangled in our immediate emotional responses—all the more so when there are strong emotions at stake. This implies no devaluation of live affective experience; it only forces us to acknowledge the power of the internalized past. Live, present affects can serve, in fact, as a stimulus for investigating the past, which then may be translated to allow a more profound sense of living in the present. In everyday life and interaction there is not enough time to ponder the implications of the internalized past on the present, but this should not mislead anyone to conclude that the past does not reside in the present.

The concept of mentalized affectivity sharpens what is distinctive about psychoanalytic thinking. Mentalized affectivity challenges us to fathom the meaning(s) of our own and others' affective states. It requires a process of engaging current affective experience in light of one's own representational world. Just as a primary caregiver's understanding facilitates self-understanding in the infant in early development, the analyst plays a crucial role in aiding the patient to accomplish this kind of working through. More specifically, the process entails a differentiated appreciation of the multiple elements of affectivity: identifying, processing, and expressing affects. Each of these three can be delineated into a basic and more complex form: identifying affects into naming and distinguishing them; processing affects into modulating and refining them; and expressing affects into expressing outwardly or inwardly and communicating affects (Jurist, 2005). The inward expression of emotions is particularly important, as it is crucial to know and experience what one feels, regardless of whether one acts on it or not. In the broadest sense, mentalized affectivity aims to preserve and render intelligible the complexity of affective experience.

The value of mentalized affectivity as a concept can be glimpsed in the way it offers an alternative perspective to a model such as "basic emotions," which makes the assumption that affects are short-lived and are accessible to us in a direct and immediate way. In the literature on emotions in psychology and neuroscience there is not enough recognition of how often it is the case that we do not know what we feel and do not know what others feel, especially when it comes to close relationships. Feelings can be elusive, confusing, and contradictory, and this makes reinterpretation of affective experience a human enterprise that is unavoidable and unending.

Psychoanalysts are used to grappling with the range, splendor, and messiness of affects. To some extent, no doubt, psychoanalysts engage in the work of mentalized affectivity with patients, regardless of whether this phenomenon has been named. All treatment entails some movement toward better affect regulation. In the most mundane sense, mentalized affectivity will serve to support symptom relief insofar as it helps patients to strive to have perspectives on affects, and to not automatically act on them. However, mentalized affectivity is also about fathoming oneself in terms of emotional style, and potentially seeking to counterbalance some of one's deeply ingrained natural predilections. This new way of thinking about mentalization is compatible with the overcoming of resistance and the analysis of character defenses. In its highest instantiation, mentalized affectivity is about the creation of meaning; that is, crafting affective experience in a way that incorporates our deepest wishes for ourselves.

There is an aspect of mentalized affectivity that is especially worth pondering in this connection. Beyond the aim of better affect regulation, mentalized affectivity serves to allow the self to flourish. Most analysts would readily agree that a different relationship to the self is at stake in treatment: one knows one's emotions and controls them more adaptively, and one also attains a sense of the parameters of one's own identity. A more ambiguous issue concerns how the analyst helps the patient know his or her own mind. The relation between the self and the mind is not apparent. While they must overlap, for example, in the notion of emotional styles, there must be something distinct between them. The self can be defined in terms of its unique qualities; thus, in psychoanalysis, the bulk of the work concerns the patient's radically individual history that he or she becomes aware of and formulates with the analyst. Moreover, the mind can be defined in terms of its general or universal qualities; that is, what presumably the patient shares with all or at least most others. The analyst has a "pedagogical purpose" (to borrow Gergely's term) in encouraging the patient's investment in understanding the mind, that is, in coming to an understanding of how all minds work. It would take a longer argument to sustain this point, but as I see it there needs to be more acknowledgment of how treatment impacts our understanding of the mind and not just the self.

Ultimately, mentalized affectivity is both a concrete way to measure progress in treatment and an ideal. As it grows to fruition, one can expect to find specific indications of change in the quality of how patients identify, process, and express their feelings, and overall in how they understand their selves and their minds. From this vantage point, mentalized affectivity can be operationalized as a way to measure therapeutic outcome. Yet it is also important to appreciate that mentalized affectivity implies an ideal in which one attains a sense of familiarity as well as a sense of comfort with one's own internal life, as far as these things are possible. Correspondingly, mentalized affectivity will contribute to the further elaboration of one's internal life.

Through mentalized affectivity, affects might be rendered into new and/or subtler shapes; yet, as I have emphasized, affects are not necessarily transformed in their essence. That is, mentalized affectivity can direct us to appreciate new meanings in old affects and, therefore, might not foster the creation of new or different affects. It is fair to claim that an aim of mentalized affectivity is to promote positive affect, but it is also fair to presume that it should help us to be able to tolerate and cope with negative affect. One of the most striking aspects of mentalized affectivity is that it underscores the value of reinterpreting, not just labeling, altering, and acting on, one's affects. Mentalized affectivity enables us to exemplify our humanity by facing up to the complexity of the mind, both yours and mine.

NOTES

1. As Carruthers & Smith (1996) describe it: "The original false-belief task involved a character, Maxi, who places some chocolate in a particular location and then leaves the room; in his absence the chocolate is then moved to another location. The child is then asked where Maxi will look for the chocolate on his return. In order to succeed in this task, the child must understand that Maxi still *thinks* that the chocolate is where he left it—the child must understand that Maxi has a false belief, in fact" (p. 2).

2. Agency is a philosophical term that refers not just to someone who acts, but also to someone who acts freely and well (see Jurist, in press; and Jurist, 2000).

3. Richard Davidson (2000) is developing a neurobiological basis for what he terms "affective styles," defined in terms of reactivity and regulation.

4. It would be a major challenge to provide a detailed account of the entire range of emotional styles. Different styles might be linked to different combinations of defenses. One might begin by making a distinction that is as basic as possible: between human beings who seem to have an easier time with emotions, welcoming direct expression and valuing their potential to affirm connection to others, and those who prefer to keep emotions at a distance and are more comfortable with space between themselves and others. This distinction resembles Balint's (1959) distinction between ocnophils, lovers of closeness, and philobats, lovers of distance. Indeed, this distinction can be utilized to shed light on how philosophers and psychologists have misunderstood the mind; to look at the mind without thinking in terms of emotional styles is itself reflective of a certain kind of style, that is, a philobatic, rather than ocnophil style. This is particularly apparent in the image of the child as scientist postulated by the theory-theory.

5. Peirce (1897), in fact, identified his own version of fallibilism as "contrite." Donna Orange (1995), a philosopher and psychoanalyst, has drawn attention to the relevance of Peirce's notion of fallibilism to psychotherapy.

REFERENCES

Allen, J. (2006). Mentalizing in practice. In J. Allen & P. Fonagy (Eds.), *Handbook of Mentalization-based Treatment*. New York: Wiley.

Aslington, J. W., & Jenkins, J. M. (1999). A longitudinal study of the relation between language and theory-of-mind development. *Developmental Psychology, 35*, 1311–1320.

Aslington, J. W. (1996). What is theoretical about the child's theory of mind?: A Vygotskian view of its development. In P. Carruthers & P. K. Smith (Eds.), *Theories of theories of mind*. Cambridge, UK: Cambridge University Press.

Balint, M. (1959). *Thrills and Regressions*. Madison, CT: International Universities Press.

Baron-Cohen, S., Tager-Flusberg, H., & Cohen, D. J. (Eds.). (2000). *Understanding other minds*. Oxford, UK: Oxford University Press.

Bartels. A,. & Zeki, S. (2004). The neural correlates of maternal and romantic love. *Neuroimage, 212*(3), 1155–1166.

Bateman, A., & Fonagy, P. (2004). *Psychotherapy for borderline personality disorder*. Oxford, UK: Oxford University Press.

Beitel, M., Ferrer, E., & Cecero, J. J. (2004). Psychological mindedness and cognitive style. *Journal of Clinical Psychology, 60*, 567–582.

Bogdan, R. (1997). *Interpreting Minds.* Cambridge, MA: MIT Press

Blatt, S. J., & Blass, R. (1996). Relatedness and self-definition: A dialectical model of personality development. In G. G. Noam & K. W. Fischer (Eds.), *Development and Vulnerabilities in Close Relationships* (pp. 309–338). Hillsdale, NJ: Erlbaum.

Bowlby, J. (1969). *Attachment and loss, Vol. 1. Attachment.* London: Hogarth Press and the Institute of Psycho-Analysis.

Bowlby, J. (1980). *Attachment and loss, Vol. 3. Loss: Sadness and depression.* London: Hogarth Press and the Institute of Psycho-Analysis.

Bradley, S. (2000). *Affect Regulation and the Development of Psychopathology.* New York: Guilford.

Bucci, W. (1997). *Psychoanalysis and Cognitive Science: A Multiple Code Theory.* New York: Guilford.

Carruthers, P., & Smith, P. K. (Eds.). (1996). Introduction. In *Theories of theories of mind.* Cambridge, UK: Cambridge University Press.

Csibra, G. (2007). Action mirroring and action understanding: An alternative account. In P. Haggard, Y. Rosetti, & M. Kawato (Eds.), *Sensorimotor foundations of higher cognition, attention and performance*, XXII. Oxford, UK: Oxford University Press.

Cutting, A. L., & Dunn, J. (1999). Theory of mind, emotion understanding, language, and family background: Individual differences and interrelations. *Child Development, 70*(4), 853–865.

Davidson, R. (2000, November). Affective style, psychopathology, and resilience: Brain mechanisms and plasticity. *American Psychologist, 55*(11), 1196–1214.

Descombes, V. (2001). *The Mind's Provisions: A Critique of Cognitivism.* Princeton, NJ: Princeton University Press.

de Villiers, J. G., & de Villiers, P. (2000). Linguistic determinism and the understanding of false belief. In P. Mitchell & K. Riggs (Eds.), *Children's reasoning and the mind.* Hove, UK: Psychology Press.

de Villiers, J. G., & Pyers, J. E. (2002). Complements to cognition: A longitudinal study of the relationship between complex syntax and false-belief-understanding. *Cognitive Development, 17*, 1037–1060.

Diamond, D. (2004). Attachment disorganization: The reunion of attachment theory and psychoanalysis. *Psychoanalytic Psychology, 21*(2), 271–299.

Eagle, M. (1995). The developmental perspectives of attachment and psychoanalytic theory. In S. Goldberg & R. Muir (Eds.), *Attachment Theory: Social, Developmental, and Clinical Perspectives.* Hillsdale, NJ: Analytic Press.

Edelman, G. (1992). *Bright Air, Brilliant Fire.* New York: Basic Books.

Erdelyi, M. (1985). *Psychoanalysis: Freud's Cognitive Psychology.* New York; W. H. Freeman.

Fonagy, P. (2006). The mentalization-focused approach to social development. In *Handbook of Mentalization-based Treatment.* New York: Wiley.

Fonagy, P. (2001). *Attachment Theory and Psychoanalysis.* New York: Other Press.

Fonagy, P. (1991). Thinking about thinking: Some clinical and theoretical considerations in the treatment of a borderline patient. *International Journal of Psycho-Analysis, 72,* 1–18.

Fonagy, P., & Bateman, A. (2006). Mechanisms of change in mentalization-based treatment of BPD. *Journal of Clinical Psychology, 62*(4), 411–430.

Fonagy, P., Gergely, G., Jurist, E. L., & Target, M. (2002). *Affect Regulation, Mentalization, and the Development of the Self.* New York: Other Press.

Fonagy, P., Steele, H., Moran, G., Steele, M, & Higgitt, A. (1993). Measuring the ghost in the nursery: An empirical study of the relation between parents' mental representations of childhood experiences and their infants' security of attachment. *Journal of the American Psychoanalytic Association, 41,* 957–989.

Fonagy, P., & Target, M. (1996). Playing with reality: I. Theory of mind and the normal development of psychic reality. *International Journal of Psycho-Analysis, 77,* 217–233.

Fonagy, P., & Target, M. (*this volume*). Attachment, trauma, and psychoanalysis: Where psychoanalysis meets neuroscience.

Freud, S. (1895). The project for a scientific psychology. In J. Strachey (Ed.), *Standard edition, 1.* London: Hogarth Press, 1953.

Frith, U., & Happe, F. (1994). Autism: Beyond 'theory of mind.' *Cognition, 50,* 115–132.

Gergely, G. (2007). Learning 'about' versus learning 'from' other minds: Human pedagogy and its implications. In P. Carruthers (Ed.), *The innate mind: Foundations and the future.* Oxford, UK: Oxford University Press.

Gergely, G., & Csibra, G. (2006). Sylvia's recipe: The role of imitation and pedagogy in the transmission of cultural knowledge. In S. Levenson & N. Enfield (Eds.), *Roots of human sociality: Culture, cognition, and human interaction* (pp. 229–255). Oxford, UK: Berg Publishers.

Gergely, G., & Csibra, G. (2005). The social construction of the cultural mind: Imitative learning as a mechanism of human pedagogy. *Interaction Studies, 6*(3), 463–481.

Gergely, G., & Unoka, Z. (in press). Attachment, affect regulation, and mentalization: The developmental origins of the representational affective self. In Sharp, C., Fonagy, P., & Goodyer, I. (Eds.), *Social Cognition and Developmental Psychopathology.* Oxford, UK: Oxford University Press.

Gergely, G., & Unoka, Z. (*this volume*). Attachment and Mentalization in Humans: The Development of the Affective Self.

Goldman, A. (2006). *Simulating minds: The philosophy, psychology, and neuroscience of mindreading.* Oxford, UK: Oxford University Press.

Gopnik, A. (1993). How we know our minds. *Behavioral and Brain Sciences, 16,* 1–14.

Gopnik, A., Capps, L., & Meltzoff, A. (2000). Early theories of mind: What the theory theory can tell us about autism. In S. Baron-Cohen, H. Tager-Flusberg, & D. H. Cohen, (Eds.), *Understanding other minds.* Oxford, UK: Oxford University Press.

Gordon, R. M. (1996). 'Radical' simulationism. In P. Carruthers & P. K. Smith (Eds.), *Theories of theories of mind.* Cambridge, UK: Cambridge University Press.

Gross, J. J., & Thompson, R. (2007). Emotion regulation: Conceptual foundations. In J. J. Gross (Ed.), *Handbook of Emotion Regulation.* New York: Guilford.

Gross, J. J. (1999). Emotion regulation: Past, present and future. *Cognition and Emotion, 13,* 551–573.

Harris, P. (1989). *Children and emotion: The development of psychological understanding.* Oxford, UK: Basil Blackwell.

Hofer, M. (1990). Early symbiotic processes: Hard evidence from a soft place. In R. Glick & S. Bone (Eds.), *Pleasure Beyond the Pleasure Principle.* New Haven, CT: Yale University Press.

Hofer, M. (1984). Relationships as regulators: A psychobiologic perspective on bereavement. *Psychosomatic Medicine, 46,* 183–197.

Jurist, E. L. (in press). Becoming agents: Hegel, Nietzsche, and psychoanalysis. In R. Frie (Ed.), *Psychological Agency: Theory, Practice and Culture.* Cambridge, MA: MIT Press.

Jurist, E. L. (2006). Art and emotion in psychoanalysis. *International Journal of Psycho-Analysis, 87*(5), 1315–1334.

Jurist, E. L. (2005). Mentalized affectivity. *Psychoanalytic Psychology, 22*(3), 426–444.

Jurist, E. L. (2000). *Beyond Hegel and Nietzsche: Philosophy, Culture, and Agency.* Cambridge, MA: MIT Press.

LeDoux, J. E. (1996). *The Emotional Brain: The Mysterious Underpinnings of Emotional Life.* New York: Simon & Schuster.

Leslie, A. M. (2000). 'Theory of mind' as a mechanism of selective attention. In M. S. Gazzaniga (Ed.), *The New Cognitive Neurosciences.* Cambridge, MA: MIT Press.

Leslie, A. M., Friedman, O., & German, T. P. (2004). Core mechanisms in 'theory of mind.' *Trends in Cognitive Sciences, 8,* 528–533.

Loewald, H. (1962). Internalization, separation, mourning, and the superego. Reprinted in Loewald, H., *Papers on Psychoanalysis* (pp. 257–276). New Haven, CT: Yale University Press, 1980.

Main, M. (1991). Metacognitive knowledge, metacognitive monitoring, and singular (coherent) vs. multiple (incoherent) model of attachment: Findings and directions for future research. In: C. M. Parkes, J. Stevenson-Hinde, & P. Marris (Eds.), *Attachment across the life cycle* (pp. 127–159). London: Tavistock/Routledge.

Main, M., Kaplan, N., & Cassidy, J. (1985). Security in infancy, childhood and adulthood: A move to the level of representation. In I. Bretherton & E. Waters (Eds.), *Growing Points of Attachment Theory and Research. Monographs of the Society for Research in Child Development, 50* (Serial 209, 1–2), 66–104.

Meins, E., Fernyhough, C., Wainwright, R., Das Gupta, M., Fradley, E., & Tuckey, M. (2002). Maternal mind-mindedness and attachment security as predictors of theory of mind understanding. *Child Development, 73,* 1715–1726.

Nagel, T. (1979). What does it feel like to be a bat? In *Mortal questions.* Cambridge, UK: Cambridge University Press.

Nichols, S., & Stich, S. (2004). *Mindreading.* Oxford, UK: Clarendon Press.

Onishi, K., & Baillargeon, R. (2005). Do 15-month-old infants understand false beliefs? *Science, 308*(5719), 255–258.

Orange, D. (1995). *Emotional Understanding: Studies in Psychoanalytic Epistemology.* New York: Guilford.

Peirce, C. S. (1897). A Fragment. In *The collected papers of Charles Sanders Peirce,* vol. 1, pp. 13–14.

Perner, J., & Lang, B. (2000). Theory of mind and executive function: Is there a developmental relationship? In S. Baron-Cohen, H. Tager-Flusberg, & D. J. Cohen (Eds.), *Understanding other minds: Perspectives from developmental cognitive neuroscience.* New York: Oxford University Press.

Perner, J., Ruffman, T., & Leekman, S. R. (1994). Theory of mind is contagious: You catch it from your sibs. *Child Development, 65,* 1228–1238.

Polan, H. J., & Hofer, M.A. (1999). Psychobiological origins of attachment and separation responses. In J. Cassidy & P. R. Shaver (Eds.), *Handbook of Attachment: Theory, Research, and Clinical Implications.* New York: Guilford.

Preston, S. D., & deWaal, F.B.M. (2002). Empathy: Its ultimate and proximate bases. *Behavioral and Brain Sciences, 25,* 1–72.

Ruffman, T., Perner, J., Naito, M., Parkin, L., & Clements, W. (1998). Older (but not younger) siblings facilitate false belief understanding. *Developmental Psychology, 34*(1), 161–174.

Sandler, J. (1987). *From Safety to Superego: Selected Papers of Joseph Sandler.* New York: Guilford.

Sandler, J., & Rosenblatt, B. (1962). The representational world. In *From Safety to Superego: Selected Papers of Joseph Sandler* (pp. 58–72). New York: Guilford, 1987.

Schore, A. (2003a). *Affect Dysregulation and Disorders of the Self.* New York: Norton.

Schore, A. (2003b). *Affect Regulation and the Repair of the Self.* New York: Norton.

Searle, J. (1998). *Mind, Language, and Society.* New York: Basic Books.

Slade, A. (1999). Attachment theory and research: Implications for the theory and practice of individual psychotherapy with adults. In J. Cassidy & P. Shaver (Eds.), *Handbook of Attachment: Theory, Research, and Clinical Implications.* New York: Guilford.

Sroufe, L. (1996). *Emotional Development: The Organization of Emotional Life in the Early Years.* New York: Cambridge University Press.

Sroufe, L., & Waters, E. (1977). Attachment as an organizational construct. *Child Development, 48,* 1184–1199.

Steele, H., & Steele, M. (1998). Attachment and psychoanalysis: Time for a reunion. *Social Development, 7*(1), 92–119.

Stern, D. N. (1985). *The Interpersonal World of the Infant.* New York: Basic Books.

Steuber, K. (2006). *Rediscovering Empathy: Agency, Folk Psychology, and the Human Sciences.* Cambridge, MA: MIT Press.

Taylor, G. J., Bagby, R. M., & Parker, J. D. A. (Eds.). (1997). *Disorders of affect regulation.* Cambridge, UK: Cambridge University Press.

Chapter 4

Measuring Mentalization Across Contexts
Links Between Representations of Childhood and Representations of Parenting in an Adoption Sample

Miriam Steele, Jeanne Kaniuk, Jill Hodges,
Kay Asquith, Saul Hillman, and Howard Steele

The concept of representations and the process by which the young infant builds a "representational world" (Sandler & Rosenblatt, 1962) that guides, both consciously and unconsciously, the processing of information from the object world, is perhaps the central feature that connects psychoanalytic formulations with attachment theory and research. Important differences between the two exist, mainly between early psychodynamic formulations focusing more exclusively on intrapsychic interactions and Bowlby's focus on actual interactions between parent and infant, and the jettisoning of drive theory by Bowlby in favor of an ethologically informed control systems view of human motivation (Fonagy, 1999; Steele & Steele, 1999). However, the conviction that we are guided by prototypes of our earliest relationships and modifications of these, or "internal working models" (Bowlby, 1969/1982; Zeanah & Anders, 1987) that shape our expectations of self and other and therefore our behavior, is adhered to not only by attachment theory but also by other variations of psychoanalytic theory. The concept of "mentalization" (Fonagy, Gergely, Jurist,

& Target, 2002), empirically measured by operationalized scales of reflective functioning or RF (Fonagy, Target, Steele, & Steele, 1998) extends our understanding of how representations of the object world set down fundamental ways of thinking and feeling about the self and others. The presence of reflective functioning has been found to critically affect parent–child relationships, where security of attachment in the infant is predicted by high levels of RF in the parent (Fonagy, Steele, Steele, Moran, & Higgitt, 1991). In the world of empirical psychotherapy research, higher incidences of reflective functioning have been linked to improvement in treatment outcomes (Bateman & Fonagy, 2004; Diamond, Stovall-McClough, Clarkin, & Levy, 2003; Fonagy, Steele, Steele, Leigh, Kennedy, et al. 1995; Levy, Kelly, Meehan, Reynoso, Clarkin, et al., 2006) and features of mental health in both parents and their children (Steele & Steele, 2008). This chapter suggests that high levels of RF are also typical of optimal functioning among adoptive parents.

The studies mentioned above utilized the concept of reflective functioning ratings derived from Adult Attachment Interviews (AAIs); that is, from adults speaking *about their past* childhood relationships with attachment figures. There is something uniquely powerful about being asked to produce a narrative in response to the set of 18 childhood-focused questions that comprise the AAI (George, Kaplan, & Main, 1985). For example, the AAI from an obviously verbally fluent trial lawyer, who was one of the participants in the London Parent–Child Project (Steele & Steele, 2005), was assigned a surprisingly low score for RF, because of repeated reliance on disavowal, and a lack of understanding of the nature of mental states. The low RF rating assigned to the narrative this father provided in response to the Adult Attachment Interview foreshadowed his 12-month-old infant's response to him in the Strange Situation assessment where the infant was classified as insecure-avoidant. This chapter explores questions concerning the assessment of reflective functioning in AAIs from adoptive parents, and how this phenomenon possibly links with the assessment of RF in a related domain, namely another interview with the same parent that taps representations not of the adult's distant past, but of the current evolving relationship existing between the adoptive parent and her recently placed child. If such linkage can be demonstrated, then further evidence for the validity of RF ratings derived from AAIs may be found, such that a new and firm ground may be established from which to provide targeted support aimed at supporting adoptive parents.

Arietta Slade (2005) has devoted much attention to studying the possible connection between parents' reflective functioning in discussing their child in the context of the Parent Development Interview (Aber, Slade, Berger, Bresgi, & Kaplan, 1985), an interview that taps parents' representation of their current relationship with their child, and the actual current child–parent relationship as measured by the Strange Situation (Ainsworth, Blehar, Waters, & Wall, 1978). Slade, Grienenberger, Bernbach, Levy, & Locker (2005) in a pilot study provided evidence to suggest that RF regarding one's child may indeed mediate the well-documented link between parents' representations of their childhood (in the AAI) and the child–parent attachment (as observed in the Strange Situation). Fonagy & Target (2005) have correspondingly suggested that the capacity for mentalization, and its expression in reflective functioning manifested during a discussion about being a parent of a particular child in the present, is likely to be the main psychosocial variable mediating the influence of parents' representations of their past upon their child's current attachment. Thus, 10 years after van IJzendoorn (1995) identified the mysterious transmission gap between parents' narratives about the past and the present infant–parent relationship, an end to this mystery has been claimed by Fonagy & Target (2005). That is, now that we have the possibility of measuring reflective functioning in parents' responses to interviews like the Parent Development Interview (Aber et al., 1985), and as Fonagy and Target suggest, vital clues may be gained as to the probable mode of transmitting emotional security from one generation to the next. However, as Slade et al. (2005) point out, "Future research is necessary to assess how closely RF on the AAI and RF on the PDI are linked. . . . It can be assumed that these variables [are] closely correlated but only further research can address this crucial question" (pp. 295–296).

Most of what we know about the links between reflective functioning and parent–child relationships is based on research with biogenetically related parent–child dyads. We wondered whether the same might hold true in an adoption context, and in the case of our study on "Attachment Representations and Adoption Outcome" the question became the following: Does RF as revealed in the AAI of an adoptive parent foreshadow RF in the Parent Development Interview alongside indices of balance and warmth, even in the highly challenging context of parenting a child with a severe and often chronic history of maltreatment?

ATTACHMENT REPRESENTATIONS AND ADOPTION OUTCOME STUDY*

Our study, conducted with Jeanne Kaniuk (Coram Family) and Jill Hodges (Great Ormond Street), represents one of the first to look at intergenerational patterns of attachment in non-biologically linked parents and children. The study highlighted the specific characteristics that each member of the parent–child dyad brings to this new and developing attachment relationship. It was longitudinal in nature, so that the changes in the child, both in terms of their behavior and their thoughts and feelings about attachment relationships could be tracked over time (Hodges, Steele, Hillman, Henderson, & Kaniuk, 2005; Steele, Hodges, Kaniuk, Hillman, & Henderson, 2003). The study's design included administering the Adult Attachment Interview to both prospective adoptive parents before a child was placed with them. Then, within three months of placement, the mothers were administered the Parent Development Interview, along with several questionnaire measures of child behavior problems and indices of parenting stress. The children were assessed using the Story Stem Assessment Profile (Hodges, Steele, Hillman, & Henderson, 2003). This measure of both verbal and nonverbal behavior is aimed at elucidating specific, attachment-relevant aspects of the child's internal world, including representations of self and other that may be reliably rated for the presence of secure, aggressive, disorganized, or avoidant/defensive themes.

Sample

The main sample comprised 58 children who were "late placed," between the ages of 4 and 8 years with a mean of 6 years. These 58 children were adopted by 41 mothers, 25 of whom adopted one child, 15 of whom adopted sibling pairs, and one who adopted a trio of siblings. Of the sample, 43% of children were boys and 85% were white. The children had all suffered serious adversity, including neglect, physical abuse, and sexual abuse. The number

* We are grateful for the generous support of the Sainsbury Family trusts (the Tedworth Charitable Trust and the Glass-House Trust).

of carers they had experienced prior to this adoption ranged from 2 to 18 different placements. Five children were placed with single adopters, and the rest were placed within the context of a married couple. The mean age of the mothers was 40 years. Findings from this study that have been published previously include Hodges et al., 2003; Hodges et al., 2005; Steele et al., 2003; Steele, Henderson, Hodges, Kaniuk, Hillman, & Steele, 2007. The question being reported upon here is whether and how mentalization in the context of the pre-placement Adult Attachment Interview links up with mentalization observed in the series of subsequently administered Parent Development Interviews, and has not previously been reported upon.

The Adult Attachment Interview

The Adult Attachment Interview is structured entirely around the topic of attachment, principally the individual's relationship to their mother and father (and/or to alternative caregivers) during childhood. Interviewees are asked both to describe their relationship with their parents during childhood, and to provide specific memories to support global evaluations. The interviewer asks directly about childhood experiences of rejection, being upset, ill, and hurt, as well as about loss, abuse, and separations. In addition, subjects are asked to offer explanations for their parents' behavior, and to describe the current relationship with their parents as well as the influence they consider their childhood experiences to have had upon their adult personality.

Adult patterns of attachment, identifiable in spoken (recorded and transcribed) responses to the Adult Attachment Interview, refer to different strategies adults rely on when faced with the task of making sense of their childhood relations with parents or caregivers. The signal features of the autonomous strategy are coherence and a strong valuing of attachment. The following is an excerpt from an interview collected from one of the mothers in the sample under study. The pre-placement AAI was ultimately classified autonomous-secure, with evidence for this judgment contained in the fresh, coherent, and genuine speech below:

> I can remember [that he was "caring" yet "at times distant"] because he worked very long hours so mostly I imagine he wasn't 'round but the example is once when I was ill and it

119

was in the middle of the night and it must have been winter. We didn't have any central heating, so it was a really cold house and I just remember him doing this thing of like he'd get the iron and ironed my sheets so the bed would be warm when I laid down in it so in that sense he was kind of like he seemed to know what you wanted and did little things like that it . . . and it felt like you didn't have to tell to do things, so it's the sense in which I felt like he understood me.

The dismissing and preoccupied patterns each represent different forms of insecurity arising out of negative attachment experiences that appear to not have been integrated evenly into the adult's sense of self. The dismissing strategy leads to an incoherent narrative characterized by global statements about a good or normal childhood that cannot be supported by relevant memories. The preoccupied strategy leads to an incoherent narrative characterized by global statements about a difficult childhood that are accompanied by an overabundance of memories and affects from childhood and adulthood, which lead the speaker to express current feelings of anger, or a sense of resignation to difficulties that cannot be overcome. Finally, the unresolved pattern, which may be present in an otherwise dismissing, preoccupied, or autonomous interview, is evident when an adult shows signs of ongoing grief and disorientation concerning some past loss or trauma. Narratives that are assigned a classification of unresolved with respect to loss and/or trauma are most noteworthy for including an excessive attention to detail when discussing loss, or lapses in the monitoring of speech (as when a loss is stated at having occurred at different times, without correction of the contradiction), or lapses in the monitoring of reason (as when a dead loved one is spoken about as actually being alive). AAIs with unresolved mourning have been of great interest ever since they were first shown to be predictive of infant attachment disorganization (Main & Hesse, 1990).

Beyond the 65% of interviews from nonclinical samples that merit the description of organized, integrated, and autonomous–secure, the two insecure patterns noted above reveal difficulties with integrating past negative attachment experiences into a current and balanced state of mind concerning attachment. Some of these interviews err on the side of minimizing past difficulties, with one or both parents (circa 20% of the nonclinical population), and are thus classified as insecure-dismissing; other interviews err on the side of maximizing and becoming entangled with past attachment difficulties and are thus classified as insecure-preoccupied. In the former "dismissing" case, the speaker seems inexorably focused consciously on positive or normal aspects of experience, to the exclusion of what is probably unconsciously recognized as a much more diverse and negative set of actual experiences. In the latter "preoccupied" case, the speaker seems angrily or passively gripped by past relationship difficulties that intrude upon current thoughts about relationships and are accompanied by confusing and difficult-to-control negative feelings. While this pattern is observed only about 15% of the time in nonclinical samples (van IJzendoorn, 1995), the proportion of interview responses fitting this preoccupied pattern swells to over 50% when clinical psychiatric populations have been assessed (van IJzendoorn & Bakermans-Kranenburg, 1996, 2008).

It is a remarkably positive sign when a speaker demonstrates that past trauma has been resolved. Indeed, in the nonclinical population, in cases where childhood experiences have involved trauma, it is not uncommon for the speaker to convey a sense of having moved beyond the fear they felt so often as a child. Additionally, such speakers are capable of progressing toward understanding, though not necessarily forgiving, caregiving figure(s) who once perpetrated abuse against them. In these circumstances, the interview often reveals a robust sense of self, interpersonal awareness, and valuing of attachment, so that one can say the adult who was abused is not likely to become an abuser. Resilience of this kind invariably emerges out of the individual discovering one or more secure bases or refuges beyond the abusive relationship, such as may be provided by an extended family member, a spouse, or a therapist.

In the current study, for the 41 mothers, AAI data was available from 40 (one mother of a pair of siblings was not interviewed). Twenty-nine (73%) of the mothers' interviews were judged autonomous-secure, nine (23%) were judged insecure-dismissing, and 2 (5%) were judged insecure-preoccupied. Of the 40 interviews, 8 (20%) were judged unresolved with respect to past loss or trauma. These eight unresolved interviews were otherwise classified dismissing in four cases, autonomous-secure in two cases, and preoccupied in two cases. This distribution of secure, dismissing, preoccupied, and unresolved mothers is very much in line with samples of nonclinical populations (van IJzendoorn & Bakermans-Kranenbrug, 2008). The first author classified all 40 interviews, without knowledge of the Parent Development Interview. The sixth author independently classified 11 interviews, and there was 100% agreement with the first author on these cases, which included 5 interviews judged unresolved.

The Parent Development Interview

Since the revolutionary development of the Adult Attachment Interview (Main, Kaplan, & Cassidy, 1985), which moved the assessment of attachment from observing infant *behavior* in response to separation and reunion to studying adults' language when *describing and evaluating* childhood experiences of attachment, separation, and loss, several interview protocols have been designed to explore individual differences in the way parents talk, think, and feel about their children. This interest in the representational (or intrapsychic) world of parents has led to an informative set of findings. For example, the Care-giving Parent Interview developed by George & Solomon (1989) focuses on secure base representations (which tap parents' understanding of the child's specific needs and characteristics), goal corrected partnership representations (which tap parents' being able to provide for the child and its needs and yet preserve their own autonomy), and self-perceived competence. A second group of researchers has developed the Working Model of the Child Interview, or WMCI (Zeanah, Benoit, & Barton, 1986), which is directly modeled on the Adult Attachment Interview (AAI). This interview probes for the parents' reactions during pregnancy, the infant's personality, and characteristic features of the relationship as seen by the parent. The coding assesses, among other things, the richness of perceptions, coherence, and care-giving sensitivity. WMCI responses are ultimately placed in one of three distinct classification groups that mirror the secure, dismissing, and preoccupied types identified in AAIs: Balanced, Disengaged, and Distorted classifications. This interview has been used by a range of researchers exploring mothers' representations of their infants in cases of failure to thrive (Benoit, Zeanah, Parker, Nicholson, & Coolbear, 1997) and maternal depression (Wood, Hargreaves, & Marks, 2004), and it has shown impressive associations between those mothers providing balanced interviews and positive features in the mother–infant relationship. Another interview stemming from the approach taken in the AAI, and with promising results, is the Parent Development Interview, developed by Arietta Slade with Larry Aber and their colleagues (Aber, Slade, Berger, Bresgi, & Kaplan, 1985). It is this instrument, in modified form (see below), that we relied on to capture the adoptive parents' representations of their newly placed children.

These various interviews may help explain how it is that the parents' state of mind regarding attachment, with reference to their own attachment history, can predict the quality of their child's attachment behavior toward them. This widely replicated link (e.g., Main, Kaplan, & Cassidy, 1985; Steele, Steele, & Fonagy, 1996; Ward & Carlson, 1995) between parents' interviews *about their past* and the *present* infant–parent relationship has been characterized by the earlier-mentioned term, "transmission gap," because we lack a detailed understanding of *how* parents are transmitting their autonomy/security, or lack thereof (van IJzendoorn, 1995). This question is being investigated by several research teams (see Oppenheim, Goldsmith, & Koren-Karie, 2004) and a likely answer lies, at least in part, with investigating the thoughts, feelings, and the more global representations parents form and maintain regarding their children. Slade (2005) points out that the advantage of Parent Development Interviews is their focus on an "ongoing, developing 'live' relationship as opposed to a prior memorialized relationship. It is believed that a parent's capacity to describe and contain complex mental states within the context of a relationship that is full of current feeling (not all of which is positive) is particularly crucial for a range of later developments in the child" (p. 293).

A primary interest in our study was in assessing the capacity for mentalizing, as evidenced in the Adult Attachment Interview, and in exploring possible links with the capacity for mentalizing in the Parent Development Interview. In our sample of adoptive parents this was assessed across three different time points: at early placement, and at 1 and 2 years following the initiation of a new parent–child relationship. Slade et al. (2005) demonstrated that Adult Attachment Interview classifications of Secure-Autonomous, Dismissing, Preoccupied, and Unresolved correlated with Parent Development Interview ratings of Reflective Functioning conducted with parents of 10-month-olds. Our study differs not only in terms of the nongenetic link between adoptive parent and older (4- to 8-year-old) child, but also in that we were able to compare Reflective Functioning measured in one domain (the

Adult Attachment Interview) with Reflective Functioning measured in another (the Parent Development Interview). While the key feature of being able to mentalize is being assessed in both, the current study, by using two very different catalysts to uncover this capacity, has the potential to reveal features of mentalization that link representations of past childhood experiences with representations of the current parent–child relationship, in cases where the child has no genetic link to the parent. The latter detail is significant because the children in our study who are the focus of the parents' PDI responses are unique in several ways as compared to age-matched peers. Firstly, these are relatively new placements, so especially for the first interview the adoptive parent has only been with the child for a relatively short period of time, namely 3 months or less. Secondly, these children, by virtue of their adverse histories, are more likely to present with an array of challenging behaviors that are associated with their experiences of maltreatment and changes in caregivers.

With these considerations in mind, we were aware of the need to adjust the questions of the Parent Development Interview, designed for birth parents of toddlers, so that they could match up with the probable experiences of the adoptive parents in our sample. With Kay Henderson leading this endeavor, we slightly modified the set of PDI questions to take account of the distinctive experiences of our sample, and subsequently changed the original coding manual (Henderson, Steele, & Hillman, 2001). The Parent Development Interview protocol (Aber et al., 1985), with our slight modifications, asks the parent about the following: what the child was like when they first arrived; a scenario when they did, and did not, click with the child during the last week; five adjectives that describe the child with accompanying examples/incidents for each; and from what do they derive the most, and least, amount of pleasure in the relationship.

The coding is organized around features relating to how parents see themselves in the role of parent, their representation of the child, and then several codes originally developed by Zeanah, Benoit, & Barton (1986), which include assessing the richness of the parent's perceptions, and the global characteristics of the narrative such as the central construct of coherence. We also borrowed from, and adapted to the special context of adoption, PDI coding guidelines initially formulated by Slade, Aber, Fiorello, DeSear, Meyer, Cohen, et al. (1994), ending up with a PDI manual especially suited to adoptive parents (Henderson, Steele, & Hillman, 2001). We coded the criteria according to a 4-point scale with operational definitions and anchored points, with scores of 1 generally indicating paucity of a construct and 4 indicating high degrees. We included a scale for rating reflective functioning and added other variables of special interest to our sample. One such code is "level of child focus." Here we sought to capture the extent of interest in the individual child among the possibly complex motivations behind pursuing the adoption. That is, adoptive parents might have pursued adoption to facilitate a particular child's development and to satisfy a wish to become a family, or to help consolidate a troubled marital relationship, or fulfill some narcissistic wish to be a parent that is not grounded in a realistic understanding of this prospect, or in a loving appreciation for the individual child adopted. Another important dimension included specifically for this sample concerns both the level of, and satisfaction with, emotional support. Given the extensive knowledge we now have of the intense challenges these children bring to their new families (Brodzinsky, 1987; Quinton, Rushton, Dance, & Mayes, 1998; Triseliotis & Russell, 1984), we were convinced that this would be a key issue to explore. We were especially interested to explore whether parents with a high capacity for mentalization in the AAI would, as we expected, be most willing to expose their need for social support, as contrasted with those with lower mentalizing capacities who we expected would be given to defensiveness around this topic through which their (understandable) vulnerability may be exposed. We predicted that we would find a "mid-range" or "Goldilocks" model (Beebe, 2000; Kaitz & Maytal, 2005) similar to the one constructed by infant researchers studying affect and attachment, who found that the most positive predictors of later attachment security were scores of vocal rhythm and gaze patterns in the middle of the range of scores, with too much or too little tracking being linked with insecurity. Here we expected that a certain amount of disclosure of needing support would be a good thing, with too little or a denial of needing help, or an exaggerated description of needing extensive support conveying more worrying features.

Results

The results will be presented in two sections. The first is a qualitative section that will include verbatim examples from an adoptive mother's PDI responses. In the second, we will present data linking the RF scale coded from the Adult Attachment Interviews with features of the PDI codes.

Qualitative results

At one end of the spectrum, we met with a number of adoptive mothers who were able to convey their understanding of their child in a rich and reflective way. Consider this adoptive mother's account of what has changed over the first year since the child was placed with her family:

> Sarah displays quite a high degree of confidence in her ability to do things, whereas when she first moved in she didn't have any confidence that she could do anything really and I mean even something like doing a picture, which she wouldn't even start, because it might be wrong. Her teacher told me the other day, that despite Sarah being very agile and usually loving PE [physical education], for two weeks in a row, she doesn't want to do PE anymore, you try and think of a reason why but I couldn't. So I talked to her about it and she said it's because, there's one boy in her group who is a bit of a terror and that when they were supposed to do an exercise to get a ball into a square or something, he had spoiled it and let the group down. When I asked her what happened next, she said she just went away and I said well you could have said to him that you don't like what you're doing and she said no 'cos he said nasty things to me before so she's quite clear about what she does to sort of get herself away from people she doesn't like that make her feel bad and that you know, that could potentially be quite a problem, she can miss out on good things, but in a way it's her solution for sorting out people she doesn't like.

Later in this same interview, when asked what her child is like, the mother said:

> I am really careful not just to go overboard for everything that has some sort of value so I'll say "Ooh I really like that cat in the

picture" and she'll say "You just say those things to make me happy" or she says all the time "People just say they like me because they don't want to upset me it's not like they really do," and so it's like you know she's got a worldview and she's not going to change it easily. Obviously it is much better that she can talk about it but she's a real perfectionist, she demands a lot of herself. If she writes something wrong I mean we got her a blackboard to help practice her spelling because if she gets it wrong, she can just easily erase it, because for her just seeing she's got it wrong is really painful to her.

This example conveys that this mother is able to put herself in her daughter's shoes, modulate her own responses when interacting with her, and put her child's needs at the forefront in creatively supplying the easily erasable black-board, thus showing a high level of child focus.

At the other end of the spectrum were some mothers who showed high levels of hostility and despair. For example, one mother, when asked to describe her newly adopted son, said the following in a very disparaging tone:

Tom is a little charmer. You know, I mean when people look at him, you know, they see what appears to be a happy little child. He's far from being a happy little child. He needs statementing [special educational help provided by statutory services]. The previous borough got out of that. Hopefully the borough that we're in will do that for him. But just say, you know, the worst scenario and, you know, he didn't do very well at school and that, he could probably get by in life because of his charm. Once he got to the stage where he could use it to his own good, whereas at the moment he's not able to reason or anything like that.

Quantitative results

Results consist of a Table (see below) that displays significant correlations observed between reflective functioning in the pre-placement AAIs and aspects of the Parent Development Interviews, as collected three months, one year, and two years later. A consistent pattern of associations emerges based on these comparisons between adoptive mothers' mentalization regarding their attachment history in the AAI and some of the 27 individual rating scales (Henderson, Steele, & Hillman, 2001) applied to the PDI narratives concerning the mothers' currently evolving attachment relationship with their children. Given the large number of PDI scales, the statistically informed reader will wonder if we took account of chance findings arising from so many tests (27 at each time period and 81 in total). Given 81 tests, one could expect 4 or 5 results to appear significant when in fact they are due to nothing more than chance. Against this metric, Table 1 looks impressive since not 5, but 20 significant correlations are shown, 6 from the post-placement interview, 9 from the one-year interview, and 5 from the two-year interview. Moreover, these significant results are all in the anticipated direction, contributing to a meaningful picture concerning the influence of mentalization about one's attachment history, at once long ago and familiar, upon thinking and feeling about the present parent–child relationship, which is a new, more or less rewarding, and challenging one.

Table 1 shows that reflective functioning (RF) in the AAI conducted prior to placement correlated positively three months later with coherence, warmth, extent of child focus, being able to reflect on the new relationship with the adopted child, and richness, as evident in the PDI. At the same time, RF in the AAI correlated positively with the mother reporting that the child was prone to show mothering behavior toward the mother, a widely reported phenomenon in late-placed children wishing to secure the good will of the parent and ward off any further abandonment. That is, mothers with high RF in the AAI were more likely to notice and report this pattern than mothers with low RF.

Table 1 also reveals a large number of ways in which RF in the pre-placement AAI foreshadowed thinking and feeling about the new adoptive relationship more than one year later. For example, mothers with high RF at the outset of the new relationship were more likely one year later to acknowledge the need for emotional and social support, and more free to acknowledge unsatisfying aspects of the parenting experience. At the same time, in contrast again to mothers with low RF originally, the higher RF mothers were more likely to report showing physical affection toward their children, to maintain a focus on the strengths and difficulties their child faces,

Table 1

ADOPTIVE MOTHERS' REFLECTIVE FUNCTIONING IN THE AAI

*Correlated with her thoughts and feelings about her adopted child
in the Parent Development Interview (PDI),
3 months into placement, one year and two years into the adoption*

3 months into placement (n = 56)	RF in the AAI
PDI scales:	
Coherence	.27*
Warmth	.28*
Reports being mothered by child	.30*
Child focus	.33*
RF re relationship with child	.34*
Richness	.49***
One year into placement (n = 55)	
Need for support	.28*
Satisfaction	.29*
Shows physical affection	.31*
Child focus	.32*
Richness	.32*
Knowledge of attachment	.32*
Confidence	.36**
RF re relationship with child	.36**
Description of relationship	.40**
Warmth	.44***
Two years into placement (n = 54)	
Coherence	.29*
Richness	.33**
Reports being mothered by child	.36**
Need for support	.40**
Child seen as overfriendly	.50***

Note: All tests 2-tailed, * p < .05, ** p < .01, *** p < .001; after Bonferroni correction only those correlations significant at the p < .001 level remain significant and to describe their experience of their children with rich detail. Interestingly, despite being in touch with the less satisfying aspects of their situation, and noting the need for support, these high RF mothers had greater confidence (than mothers with low RF) and were better able to be reflective about the relationship with their child or children. They showed an impressive ability to describe their children and their relationship with them ($r = .40$) and most strikingly, in comparison to low RF mothers, they showed significantly greater warmth ($r = .44$, $p < .001$).

Finally, Table 1 points to significant links observed between RF in the pre-placement AAI and features of the Parent Development Interviews collected more than two years later. Here what stands out is not only that RF predicted the positive qualities of coherence and richness, but also that RF linked up with three signs of persisting difficulties, namely: (a) reports that the child engages in mothering (role reversed) behavior; (b) depictions of the child as being overfriendly; and, (c) the acknowledgment on the high RF mother's part of a need for support.

After imposing the conservative step of Bonferroni correction upon the 81 correlations computed, three of these results remained as highly robust associations to be considered significant PDI correlates of RF in the AAI, with one from each of the three time periods studied. From the three-month, one-year, and two-year follow-up these were, respectively, richness of the narrative, warmth evident toward the child, and acknowledgment of the child showing overfriendly behavior.

DISCUSSION

Our discussion here will pertain to the long-term positive influence of reflective functioning concerning one's childhood, as assessed in the AAI, upon one's thoughts and feelings about being the adoptive mother of a late-placed, previously maltreated child, as assessed in the PDI. As well, attention is given to the particular constellation of PDI codes, not RF per se, that correlated most strongly with RF in the AAI. Here we will focus on the PDI codes for warmth, richness, and awareness of the child's propensity toward overfriendliness.

With RF as measured in the AAI, we appear to have arrived at an operational measure of mentalization that yields a powerful and long-term prediction as to who will thrive in the parenting role. With the presently reported results, we see that even in the most challenging of parenting tasks, that is, adopting a previously maltreated child in the early school-aged years, RF foreshadows adaptation, thoughtfulness, and a flexible awareness of the self as parent, as well as of the child, together with an ability to acknowledge the difficulties, and yet show confidence in the parenting task, and a robust warmth toward the child. Interestingly, Main (1991), while writing about a capacity that prompted the development of the concept of RF (Steele & Steele, 2008), a capacity she termed "metacognitive monitoring," commented that metacognition entails the ability to move back and forth between maintaining a coherent dialogue with the interviewer and accessing one's own memories, including ones that may in some cases be painful and upsetting (Main, 1991). This capacity to hold in mind and share upsetting experiences without becoming upset was clearly shown by those adoptive mothers in the current sample who presented in the pre-placement AAI with high RF and then showed later in their PDIs that they could maintain a coherent, rich narrative about their parenting experience without minimizing the difficulties. Thus, their PDIs both contained signs of warmth as well as an awareness of their own need for support, and showed an appreciation for the child's tendency at times to display overfriendly behavior toward strangers, or mothering behavior toward the parent(s). Overfriendly and mothering behaviors are well-known consequences of early deprivation, and have been widely documented (Bengtsgard & Bohlin, 2001; O'Connor, Bredenkamp, & Rutter, 1999; Zeanah, Smyke, & Dumitrescu, 2002).

The fact that mothers with high RF were more likely to mention these difficulties than mothers with low RF is likely to be a result of the high RF mothers' nondefensiveness. Correspondingly, this high RF group showed openness toward seeking advice and help. In other words, high RF *about the past* appears to signal the ability to seek out an attachment figure even as it also implies the ability to embrace the task of serving as one, as indicated by the high warmth ratings given to the high RF group.

The capacity for thinking in a reflective way about the past, which appears to fuel organized thought and behavior in the present, can also be found in *observations* of mentalizing parents as they engage with their children. For example, in the "Co-Construction" task (Steele, Hodges, Kaniuk, Steele, D'Agostino, Blom, et al., 2007) we developed initially for use in the longitudinal adoption study, one mother was asked to engage her newly placed, previously maltreated son for five minutes, building with blocks. She sat attentively, focused primarily on her son, and then secondarily on the task of block building. As his excited affect began to gain momentum and he clapped his hands loudly with a block in each hand and an increasingly aggressive stance, mother, with ease, moved the escalating interaction toward calmer middle ground by carefully asking him whether he remembered how they listened to the marching band over the weekend. Her mentalizing capacity allowed her, in the moment, deftly to move back and forth in terms of carefully monitoring where things are right now while at the same time having a foot in the door as to where things might be headed.

Clearly, the overwhelming conclusion from the current report is that mentalizing *in the present about the current* parent–child relationship, even when it is as new and challenging as a late-adoptive placement, is foreshadowed in meaningful ways by a parent's mentalizing about their own early childhood relationships. This AAI to PDI link merits much exploration in order to approach an understanding of the full set of factors involved in this apparent stability in mentalization across important relationship contexts. To some extent, this was achieved in the current work because of the large range of PDI codes deployed. Had we relied on an overall summary score for RF in the PDI we would not have been able to isolate the unique factors of richness, warmth, and being able to see the child as overfriendly that emerged from inspection of the multiple significant correlations observed between RF in the AAI and distinct but overlapping PDI results.

In conclusion, the AAI and PDI deserve to be used together in much further research and clinical work, as they hold out great promise in opening up for careful study the representational worlds of parents hoping for (and deserving of) support for the positive influence they can have on the children they love. The following quote from one of the mothers describes well the positive outcome that the intervention of adoption can have in facilitating adaptive and reflective functioning in previously maltreated adopted children:

Lisa is really very interested in what's going on very close to her and in people's heads as well, I mean she was walking along the street yesterday and she said to me, "Sometimes I think it's funny

Mummy, I think that, it's like our brains are connected, 'cos you think something and I think it," and she's really interested and she'll ask how you feel or she'll say "I expect someone was feeling so and so."

REFERENCES

Aber, L., Slade, A., Berger, B., Bresgi, I., & Kaplan, M. (1985). The Parent Development Interview. Unpublished protocol. The City University of New York.

Ainsworth, M., Blehar, M., Waters, E., & Wall, S. (1978). *Patterns of Attachment: A Psychological Study of the Strange Situation.* Hillsdale, NJ: Erlbaum.

Bateman, A., & Fonagy, P. (2004). *Psychotherapy for borderline personality disorder: Mentalization-based treatment.* Oxford, UK: Oxford University Press.

Beebe, B. (2000). Co-constructing mother–infant distress. *Psychoanalytic Inquiry, 20,* 421–400.

Benoit, D., Zeanah, D. H., Parker, K. C. H., Nicholson, E., & Coolbear, J. (1997). 'Working Models of the Child Interview': Infant clinical status related to maternal perceptions. *Infant Mental Health Journal, 18*(1), 107–121.

Bengtsgard, K., & Bohlin, G. (2001). Social inhibition and overfriendliness: Two-year follow-up and observational validation. *Journal of Clinical Child Psychology, 30,* 364–375.

Bowlby, J. (1969/1982). *Attachment and loss: Vol. 1. Attachment.* London: Hogarth Press and the Institute of Psychoanalysis.

Brodzinsky, D. M. (1987). Adjustment to adoption: A psychological perspective. *Clinical Psychology Review, 7,* 25–47.

Diamond, D., Stovall-McClough, C., Clarkin, J. F., & Levy, K. N. (2003). Patient–therapist attachment in the treatment of borderline personality disorder. *Bulletin of the Menninger Clinic, 67*(3), 224–257.

Fonagy, P. (1999). Psychoanalytic theory from the viewpoint of attachment theory and research. In J. Cassidy & P. Shaver (Eds.), *Handbook of Attachment: Theory, Research, and Clinical Applications* (pp. 595–624). New York: Guilford.

Fonagy, P., Gergely, G., Jurist, E., & Target, M. (2002). *Affect Regulation, Mentalization, and the Development of the Self.* New York: Other Press.

Fonagy, P., Steele, M., Steele, H., Leigh, T., Kennedy, R., Mattoon, G., & Target, M. (1995). Attachment, the reflective self, and borderline states: The predictive specificity of the Adult Attachment Interview and pathological emotional development. In

S. Goldberg, R. Muir, & J. Kerr (Eds.), *Attachment Theory: Social, Developmental, and Clinical Perspectives* (pp. 233–279). Hillsdale, NJ: Analytic Press.

Fonagy, P., Steele, M., Steele, H., Moran, G., & Higgitt, A. (1991). The capacity for understanding mental states: The reflective self in parent and child and its significance for security of attachment. *Infant Mental Health Journal, 13*, 200–217.

Fonagy, P., & Target, M. (2005). Bridging the transmission gap: An end to an important mystery of attachment research. *Attachment & Human Development, 7*, 333–343.

Fonagy, P., Target, M., Steele, H., & Steele, M. (1998). Reflective Functioning Coding Manual. Unpublished document, University College, London.

George, C., Kaplan, N., & Main, M. (1985). Adult Attachment Interview (2nd ed.). Unpublished manuscript, University of California at Berkeley.

George, C., & Solomon, J. (1989). Internal working models of caregiving and security of attachment at age six. *Infant Mental Health Journal, 10*(3), 222–238.

Henderson, K., Steele, M., & Hillman, S. (2001). Experience of Parenting Coding Manual. Unpublished manuscript, Anna Freud Centre, London.

Hodges, J., Steele, M., Hillman, S., Henderson, K., & Kaniuk, J. (2003). Changes in attachment representations over the first year of adoptive placement: Narratives of maltreated children. *Clinical Child Psychology and Psychiatry, 8*, 351–367.

Hodges, J., Steele, M., Hillman, S., Henderson, K., & and Kaniuk, J. (2005). Change and continuity in mental representations of attachment after adoption. In D. M. Brodzinsky & J. Palacios (Eds.), *Psychological Issues in Adoption: Research and Practice*. Westport, CT: Praeger Publishers.

Kaitz, M., & Maytal, H. (2005). Interactions between anxious mothers and their infants: An integration of theory and research findings. *Infant Mental Health Journal, 26*, 570–597.

Levy, K. N., Kelly, K. M., Meehan, K. B., Reynoso, J. S., Clarkin, J. F., Lenzenweger, M. F., & Kernberg, O. F. (2006). Change in attachment and reflective function in the treatment of borderline personality disorder with transference focused psychotherapy. *Journal of Consulting and Clinical Psychology, 74*, 1027–1040.

Main, M. (1991). Metacognitive knowledge, metacognitive monitoring, and singular (coherent) vs. multiple (incoherent) model of attachment: Findings and directions for further research. In C. M. Parkes, J. Stevenson-Hinde, & P. Marris (Eds.), *Attachment across the life cycle* (pp. 127–159). London: Routledge.

Main, M., & Hesse, E. (1990). Parents' unresolved traumatic experiences are related to infant disorganized attachment status: Is frightened and/or frightening parental behavior the linking mechanism? In M. T. Greenberg, D. Cicchetti, & E. M. Cummings (Eds.), *Attachment in the Preschool Years: Theory, Research, and Intervention* (pp. 161–182). Chicago: University of Chicago Press.

Main, M., Kaplan, N., & Cassidy, J. (1985). Security in infancy, childhood, and adulthood: A move to the level of representation. In I. Bretherton & E. Waters (Eds.), *Growing Points of Attachment Theory and Research. Monographs of the Society for Research in Child Development, 50* (1-2, Serial No. 209), 66–104.

O'Connor, T. G., Bredenkamp, D., & Rutter, M. (1999). Attachment disturbances and disorders in children exposed to early severe deprivation. *Infant Mental Health Journal, 30,* 10–29.

Oppenheim, D., Goldsmith, D., & Koren-Karie, N.(2004). Maternal insightfulness and preschoolers' emotion and behaviour problems: Reciprocal influences in a therapeutic preschool program. *Infant Mental Health Journal, 25,* 352–367.

Quinton, D., Rushton, A., Dance, C., & Mayes, D. (1998). *Joining New Families: A Study of Adoption and Fostering in Middle Childhood.* New York and Chichester, UK: Wiley.

Sandler, J., & Rosenblatt, B. (1962). The concept of the representational world. *Psychoanalytic study of the child, 17,* 128–188.

Slade, A. (2005). Parental reflective functioning: An introduction. *Attachment and Human Development, 5,* 269–281.

Slade, A., Aber, J. L., Fiorello, J., DeSear, P., Meyer, J., Cohen, L. J., & Wallon, S. (1994). *Parent Development Interview Coding System.* New York: City University of New York.

Slade, A., Grienenberger, J., Bernbach, E., Levy, D., & Locker, A. (2005). Maternal reflective functioning, attachment, and the transmission gap: A preliminary study. *Attachment and Human Development, 7,* 283–298.

Slade, A., Belsky, J., Aber, J. L., & Phelps, J. (1999). Maternal representations of their relationship with their toddlers: Links to adult attachment and observed mothering. *Developmental Psychology, 35,* 611–619.

Steele, H., & Steele, M. (1999). Psychoanalytic views about development. In D. Messer & S. Millar (Eds.), *Exploring developmental psychology* (pp. 263–283). London: Francis Arnold.

Steele, H., & Steele, M. (2005). Understanding and resolving emotional conflict: The London Parent Child Project. In K. Grossmann, K. Grossmann, & E. Waters (Eds.), *Attachment from Infant to Adulthood: The Major Longitudinal Studies.* New York: Guilford.

Steele, H., & Steele, M. (2008). On the origins of reflective functioning. In F. Busch (Ed.), *Mentalization: Theoretical Considerations, Research Findings, and Clinical Implications.* NY: Analytic Press.

Steele, H., Steele, M., & Fonagy, P. (1996). Associations among attachment classifications of mothers, fathers, and their infants: Evidence for a relationship-specific perspective. *Child Development, 67,* 541–555.

Steele, M., Hodges, J., Kaniuk, J., Hillman, S., & Henderson, K. (2003). Attachment representations in newly adopted maltreated children and their adoptive parents: Implications for placement and support. *Journal of Child Psychotherapy, 29,* 187–205.

Steele, M., Henderson, K., Hodges, J., Kaniuk, J., Hillman, S., & Steele, H. (2007). In the best interests of the late placed child: A report from the Attachment Representations and Adoption Outcome Study. In L. Mayes, P. Fonagy, & M. Target (Eds.), *Developmental Science and Psychoanalysis* (pp. 159–182). London: Karnac.

Steele, M., Hodges, J., Kaniuk, J., Steele, H., D'Agostino, D., Blom, I., Hillman, S., & Henderson, K. (2007). Intervening with maltreated children and their adoptive parents: Identifying attachment facilitating behavior. In D. Oppenheim & D. Goldsmith (eds.), *Clinical Applications of Attachment Theory.* New York: Guilford.

Triseliotis, J., & Russell, J. (1984). *Hard to place: The outcome of adoption and residential care.* London: Heinemann.

van IJzendoorn, M. H. (1995). Adult attachment representations, parental responsiveness, and infant attachment: A meta-analysis on the predictive validity of the Adult Attachment Interview. *Psychological Bulletin, 117,* 382–403.

van IJzendoorn, M. H., & Bakermans-Kranenbrug, M. J. (1996). Attachment representations in mothers, fathers, adolescents, and clinical groups: A meta-analytic search for normative data. *Journal of Consulting and Clinical Psychology, 64*(1), 8–21.

van IJzendoorn, M. H., & Bakermans-Kranenbrug, M. J. (2008). The distribution of adult attachment representations in clinical groups: Meta-analytic search for patterns of attachment. In H. Steele & M. Steele (Eds.), *Clinical Applications of the Adult Attachment Interview* (pp. 69–96). New York: Guilford Press.

Ward, M. J., & Carlson, E. A. (1995). Associations among adult attachment representations, maternal sensitivity, and infant mother attachment in a sample of adolescent mothers. *Child Development, 66*(1), 69–79.

Wood, B. L., Hargreaves, E., & Marks, M. N. (2004). Using the working model of the child interview to assess postnatally depressed mothers' internal representation of their infants: A brief report. *Journal of Reproductive and Infant Psychology, 22*(1), 41–44.

Zeanah, C., Benoit, D., & Barton, M. (1986). Working model of the child interview. Unpublished manuscript, Brown University Program in Medicine, Providence, Rhode Island.

Zeanah, C., & Anders, T. (1987). Subjectivity in parent–infant relationships: A discussion of internal working models. *Infant Mental Health Journal, 6,* 237–250.

Zeanah, C., Smyke, A., & Dumitrescu, A. (2002). Attachment disturbances in young children. II: Indiscriminate behavior and institutional care. *Journal of the American Academy of Child & Adolescent Psychiatry, 41*(8): 983–989.

Part II

MENTALIZATION IN CLINICAL AND NEUROSCIENCE RESEARCH

Chapter 5

Mentalization-Based Treatment of Borderline Personality Disorder

Peter Fonagy and Anthony Bateman

Mentalization is the capacity to make sense of each other and ourselves, both implicitly and explicitly, in terms of subjective states and mental processes. Understanding the behavior of others in terms of their likely thoughts, feelings, wishes, and desires is a major developmental achievement that originates in the context of the attachment relationship. This chapter will outline the concept of mentalization as applied to borderline personality disorder (BPD), it will consider the changing views of BPD as a severe and enduring personality disorder, and it will argue that a focus on mentalization as a core component of treatment provides the best chance of successful outcome. The reason for this is not simply because a focus on mentalization addresses the central problem of the patient, but also because it reduces the likelihood of causing harm to a patient who may be particularly sensitive to psychotherapeutic intervention.

ATTACHMENT AND MENTALIZATION

As our understanding of the relationship between brain development and early psychosocial experience increases, we can see that the evolutionary role of the attachment relationship goes far beyond giving physical protection to the human infant. In our view, the major selective advantage conferred by attachment to humans is the opportunity to develop social intelligence through proximity to concerned adults. Our understanding both of others and of ourselves critically depends on whether, as infants, our own mental states have been adequately understood by caring, nonthreatening adults. A baby's experience of himself as having a mind or self is not a genetic given; it evolves from infancy through childhood, and its development critically depends upon interaction with more mature minds, assuming these are benign, reflective, and sufficiently attuned.

The quality of a child's primary attachment relationship was shown to predict mentalization by a number of—but not all—studies (e.g., Fonagy & Target, 1997; Harris, 1999; Meins, Fernyhough, Russell, & Clark-Carter, 1998; Ontai & Thompson, 2002; Raikes & Thompson, 2006; Steele, Steele, Croft, & Fonagy, 1999; Symons, 2004; Thompson, 2000). This relationship is more likely to be observed when investigating emotion understanding rather than theory of mind; in at least two studies, the child's Internal Working Model (IWM) of their primary attachment relationship was shown to correlate with emotion understanding (de Rosnay & Harris, 2002; Fonagy, Redfern, & Charman, 1997). More pertinent to the current set of hypotheses, it is quite likely that family dynamics mediate the relationship between attachment and mentalization, probably via the coherence and mentalizing nature of the general discourse in the home (e.g., Dunn, 1996; Dunn, Brown, Somkowski, Telsa, & Youngblade, 1991; Nelson, 2005; Ruffman, Slade, & Crowe, 2002). Consequently there is ample opportunity for the development of mentalization to be disrupted.

Our premise is that individuals with BPD have histories of insecure and disorganized attachment, leading to an unstable or reduced mentalizing capacity. There is limited but suggestive evidence in support of this theory: two longitudinal studies following children from infancy to early adulthood have found associations between insecure attachment in early childhood and BPD symptoms on follow-up (Lyons-Ruth, Yellin, Melnick, & Atwood, 2005; Sroufe, Egeland, Carlson, & Collins, 2005). Furthermore, Levy (2005) recently reviewed the growing literature on the relationship of BPD and attachment; to date, nine studies have examined attachment patterns with patients diagnosed with BPD using the best available assessment of adult attachment, the Adult Attachment Interview (AAI); two further studies have used rating scales, and over a dozen have used self-report measures. BPD is strongly associated with insecure attachment (6–8%), and there are indications of disorganization (unresolved and cannot classify categories of attachment) in interviews, and fearful, avoidant, and preoccupied attachment in questionnaire studies (Levy, 2005). Summarizing across several studies, early insecurity was found to be a relatively stable characteristic of the individual with BPD (94%), particularly in conjunction with subsequent negative life events (Hamilton, 2000; Waters, Merrick, Treboux, Crowell, & Albersheim, 2000; Weinfield, Sroufe, & Egeland, 2000). Given the evidence for the continuity of attachment from early childhood, at least in adverse environments the extent to which childhood attachment may affect mentalization may be relevant to the development of BPD.

Individuals with BPD are "normal" mentalizers except in the context of attachment relationships. In these contexts, a failure to mentalize can become apparent in a number of ways. Usually, mentalization (a psychological self-narrative) maintains an agentive sense of self (Fonagy & Target, 1997). Temporary failure of mentalization is invariably associated with changes in the phenomenology of the self. In the face of negative affect, individuals with BPD struggle to experience themselves as authors of their actions, leading not only to a sense of a temporally diffused identity (Kernberg, 1983), but also to experiences of inauthenticity, incoherence, and emptiness; an inability to make commitments; disturbances of body image; and gender dysphoria (Akhtar, 1992)—all of which are borne out by factor-analytic studies of data from clinically experienced informants for adult (Wilkinson-Ryan & Westen, 2000) and adolescent patients (Betan & Westen, 2005). In such states, BPD patients tend to misread minds, both their own and those of others. Work from Drew Westen's laboratory has consistently demonstrated that patients with BPD represent others' internal states with less complexity and differentiation than patients with other disorders such as major depression (Baker, Silk, Westen, Nigg, & Lohr, 1992; Westen, Lohr, Silk, Gold, & Kerber, 1990). In our view, any treatment of BPD must, to be successful, have mentalization as its focus, or at the very least stimulate development of mentalizing as an epiphenomenon.

MENTALIZATION DEFICIT MODEL OF BORDERLINE PERSONALITY DISORDER

We have discussed our developmental model of BPD in detail elsewhere (Bateman & Fonagy, 2004; Fonagy, Gergely, Jurist, & Target, 2002; Fonagy, Target, Gergely, Allen, & Bateman, 2003). The model centers around the development of the social affiliative system, which we consider to drive many higher-order social cognitive functions that in turn underpin interpersonal interactions, specifically in the attachment context. Four of these cognitive functions are of primary importance: affect representation and, related to this, affect regulation; attentional control, which also has strong links to the regulation of affect; the dual arousal system involved in maintaining an appropriate balance between mental functions undertaken by the anterior and posterior portions of the brain; and mentalization, a system for interpersonal understanding within the attachment context. Since these capacities evolve in the context of the primary caregiving relationships experienced by the child, they are vulnerable to extremes of environmental deficiency, including severe neglect, psychological or physical abuse, childhood molestation, and other forms of maltreatment.

We assume that to achieve normal self-experience the infant requires his emotional signals to be accurately or contingently mirrored by an attachment figure. This enables the infant to internalize the representation of the parent's reflection of his experience and thus generate a representational system for internal states (a kind of social biofeedback system) (Gergely & Watson, 1996). The mirroring must be "marked" (i.e., exaggerated or slightly distorted) if the infant is to understand the caregiver's display as part of his emotional experience rather than an expression of hers. There is evidence to suggest that the absence of marked contingent mirroring is associated with the later development of disorganized attachment (Gergely, Koós, & Watson, 2002; Koós & Gergely, 2001). Infants with disorganized attachment exhibit behaviors like freezing (dissociation) and self-harm, and go on to develop oppositional and highly controlling behavioral tendencies in middle childhood.

We also suggest that when a child cannot develop a representation of his own experience through the caregiver's mirroring interactions, he internalizes the image of the caregiver as part of his self-representation (Winnicott, 1956). We have called this discontinuity within the self the "alien self." We understand the controlling behavior of children with a history of disorganized attachment as the persistence of a pattern analogous to projective identification, where the experience of incoherence within the self is reduced through externalization (Kochanska, Coy, & Murray, 2001; Solomon, George, & Dejong, 1995). The intense need for the caregiver, which is characteristic of separation anxiety in middle childhood and which is also associated with disorganized attachment, does not simply reflect an insecure attachment relationship, but also results from the need for a vehicle (the caregiver) to contain the alien part of the self and through which the alien part of the self can be externalized.

The experience of fragmentation within the self-structure can be reduced by the concurrent development of mentalization and associated capacities for affect representation, affect regulation, and attentional control, which we assume are in place normally to control, obscure, or limit the potential for a regression toward a much more primitive form of subjectivity. This form of subjectivity is dominated by modes of representing internal states and distinguishing between internal and external that are observable in the mental functioning of young children. Our central thesis is that these primitive processes, in combination with the profound disorganization of self-structure, explain many facets of borderline personality functioning. The phenomenology of BPD is the consequence of: (a) the attachment-related inhibition of mentalization; (b) the reemergence of modes of experiencing internal reality that antedate the developmental emergence of mentalization; and (c) the constant pressure for projective identification and the reexternalization of the self-destructive alien self. Individuals with BPD tend to misread minds, both their own and those of others, when emotionally aroused. As their relationship with another person moves into the sphere of attachment, the intensification of the relationship means that their ability to think about the mental state of the other can rapidly disappear. When this happens, pre-mentalistic modes of organizing subjectivity emerge, and these have the power to disorganize the attachment relationships and to destroy the coherence of self-experience generated by the narrative that normal mentalization provides.

In this way, mentalization gives way to psychic equivalence, which clinicians normally consider under the heading of "concreteness of thought": that is, a state of mind in which no alternative perspectives are possible.

There is a suspension of the experience of "as if," and everything appears to be "for real." This can add drama as well as risk to interpersonal experience, and the exaggerated reaction of patients is justified by the seriousness with which they suddenly experience their own and others' thoughts and feelings. The consequent vivid and bizarre quality of subjective experience can appear as "quasi-psychotic" symptoms (Zanarini, Gunderson, & Frankenburg, 1990), and is reminiscent of the physically compelling memories associated with post-traumatic stress disorder (PTSD) (Morrison, Frame, & Larkin, 2003).

Conversely, thoughts and feelings can come to be dissociated almost to the point of near meaninglessness. In these states, patients can discuss experiences without contextualizing them in any kind of physical or material reality. Several studies using Rorschach, TAT, and other narrative methods have provided evidence of hyper-complex representations of the mental states of others, which are often malevolent and idiosyncratically elaborated (Stuart et al., 1990; Westen, Lohr et al., 1990; Westen, Ludolph, Lerner, Ruffins, & Wiss, 1990). Attempting psychotherapy with patients who are in this mode can lead the therapist to lengthy but inconsequential discussions of internal experiences that have no link to genuine experiences. Dissociation is now a component of one of the diagnostic criteria of BPD.

Finally, early modes of conceptualizing action in terms of that which is apparent can come to dominate motivation. Within this mode there is a primacy of the physical, and experience is only felt to be valid when its consequences are apparent to all. Affection, for example, is only deemed true when accompanied by physical expression.

The most disruptive feature of borderline cognition is the apparently unstoppable tendency to create experiences within the other that feel unacceptable in the self. Externalization of the alien self is desirable for the child with a disorganized attachment because it is too terrifying to internalize the frightening parent. This externalization is a matter of life and death for the traumatized individual who has internalized the abuser as part of the self. The alternative to projective identification is the destruction of the self in a teleological mode, that is, physically, by self-harm and suicide. Suicide and self-harm can also serve to create a terrified alien self in the other—be that a therapist, friend, or parent—who subsequently becomes the vehicle for what is emotionally unbearable. The need for this other can become overwhelming, and an adhesive and addictive pseudo-attachment to this individual can develop.

Our model does not attribute a central role to trauma. Many patients with BPD did not experience sexual or physical abuse (Paris, 2004), and so an etiological model must also explain the development of BPD for non-traumatized individuals. Given the high prevalence of maltreatment in the history of individuals with BPD, it is easy to lose sight of what may be the critical causal contextual variables. Evidence suggests that contextual factors such as caregiver response to the disclosure of the abuse may be more important than sexual and physical abuse per se in long-term outcome (Horwitz, Widom, McLaughlin, & White, 2001). Numerous aspects of a family environment that involves maltreatment might undermine the robust development of the child's mentalization, including family chaos, disrupted attachments, multiple caregivers, parental neglect, alcoholism, and affective instability among the family members. A child's level of mental state understanding (particularly emotion understanding) is closely linked to the extent that emotions are openly discussed in the mother–child dyad. Other relevant features of the emotional climate within the family (e.g., Cassidy, Parke, Butkovsky, & Braungart, 1992) are likely to be disrupted by maltreatment, especially the child's opportunity to engage in pretend play, which also greatly facilitates the emergence of mentalization (Harris, de Rosnay, & Pons, 2005; Jenkins & Astington, 2000; Taylor et al., 1998; Youngblade & Dunn, 1995).

Thus, the mentalization-based approach predicts that *it is less the fact of maltreatment than a family environment that discourages coherent discourse concerning mental states that is likely to predispose the child to BPD.* In line with this, a number of studies point to the importance of neglect, low parental involvement, and emotional maltreatment rather than the presence of physical and sexual abuse as the critical predictors of BPD (Johnson et al., 2001; Ludolph et al., 1990). In our formulation, we consider parental emotional under-involvement with children as most likely to impair the appropriate development of social cognition. We consider that the impact of trauma is most likely to be felt as part of a more general failure, through neglect, rejection, excessive control, and unsupportiveness, to consider the child's perspective. However, we believe that aggression and cruelty directly focused on the child will, if present, often have specific effects in addition to the nonspecific influences referred to above. In individuals who have been made vulnerable by early inadequate mirroring and disorganized attachment to highly stressful psychosocial experiences in an attachment context, trauma can play a key role both in shaping the pathology of BPD and in causing it directly by undermining the capacity for mentalization. This may be due to: (a) the defensive inhibition of the capacity to think about others' malevolent thoughts and feelings about the self; (b) early excessive stress that may distort the functioning of arousal mechanisms inhibiting orbito-frontal cortical (mentalizing) activity at far lower levels of risk than would be normally the case (Arnsten, 1998); and/or (c) chronic arousal of the attachment system (Bartels & Zeki, 2000, 2004). Any trauma arouses the attachment system, but in the case of attachment trauma, in seeking proximity to the traumatizing attachment figure as a consequence of trauma, the child may naturally be further traumatized. The prolonged activation of the attachment system may be an additional problem as the arousal of attachment may have specific inhibitory consequences for mentalization in addition to those that might be expected as a consequence of increased emotional arousal.

We see the capacity to mentalize as that which has the power to hold back modes of primitive mental functioning in those who are subjected to traumatic experience but who suffer little or no adverse effects. It makes conceptual sense, therefore, that mentalizing should be a focus for therapeutic intervention if we are to help borderline patients bring primitive modes of mental functioning under better regulation and control. But, before we discuss treatment, it is necessary to understand the longitudinal course of BPD, because it is against this background that treatment is applied and potentially can provide great benefit or induce considerable harm.

THE COURSE OF BORDERLINE PERSONALITY DISORDER

Early follow-up studies of BPD highlighted the inexorable nature of the "disease," talking of "burnt out" borderlines and hinting less at recovery than at a disease process that runs a long-term course (e.g., Stone, 1990). Skepticism about the usefulness of treatment with this population was justified by the intensity and incomprehensibility of the emotional pain patients suffered, the often dramatic self-mutilation, and the degree of ambivalence in interpersonal relationships, which was considered unintelligible.

However, two carefully designed and fully powered prospective studies have highlighted the inappropriateness of these pessimistic attitudes that condemned individuals with severe BPD to the margins of even generous health care systems (Shea et al., 2004; Zanarini, Frankenburg, Hennen, & Silk, 2003). The majority of BPD patients experience a substantial reduction in their symptoms far sooner than previously assumed. After six years, 75% of patients diagnosed with BPD severe enough to require hospitalization achieve remission by standardized diagnostic criteria (Cohen, Crawford, Johnson, & Kasen, 2006; Skodol et al., 2006; Zanarini et al., 2003; Zanarini, Frankenburg, Hennen, Reich, & Silk, 2006). Patients with BPD *can* undergo remission—a concept previously used solely in the context of Axis I pathology. A remission rate of about 50% occurs by four years, and the remission is steady (10–15% per year). Recurrences are rare, perhaps no more than 10% over six years. This contrasts with the natural course of many Axis I disorders, such as affective disorder, where improvement may be more rapid but recurrences are common. In the Collaborative Depression Study, 30% of patients had not recovered at one year, 19% at two years and 12% at five years (Keller et al., 1992).

While improvements in BPD patients are substantial, it is symptoms such as impulsivity and associated self-mutilation and suicidality—as opposed to affective symptoms or social functioning—that show dramatic change. The dramatic symptoms recede, but abandonment concerns, a sense of emptiness, relationship problems, and vulnerability to depression are likely to remain present in at least half the patients. When dramatic improvements occur, they sometimes occur quickly, quite often associated with relief from severely stressful situations (Gunderson et al., 2003). It seems that certain co-morbidities undermine the likelihood of improvement (Zanarini, Frankenburg, Hennen, Reich, & Silk, 2004), and the persistence of substance use disorders decreases the likelihood of remission, suggesting that the latter must be treated as well.

THE REALITY OF IATROGENIC HARM

Given that the vast majority of cases of BPD naturally resolve within six years, why have clinicians across the globe traditionally agreed about the treatment-resistant character of the disorder? As we have argued elsewhere

(Fonagy & Bateman, 2006a), one possible conclusion may be that some psychosocial treatments that are still practiced, and which may have been practiced more commonly in the past, may impede the borderline patient's capacity to recover due to the natural cycle of the disorder and/or advantageous changes in social circumstances. In Michael Stone's (1990) classic follow-up of patients treated nearly 40 years ago, only a 66% recovery rate was achieved in 20 years (four times longer than reported in more recent studies). While it is possible that greater awareness of diagnosis has changed thresholds and allowed less-severe cases to enter these follow-along studies, it seems unlikely that the nature of the disorder has changed or that treatments have become that much more effective. The known efficacy of pharmacological agents, new and old, cannot account for this difference (Tyrer & Bateman, 2004), and evidence-based psychosocial treatments are not widely available. It is, sadly, far more likely therefore that the apparent improvement in the course of the disorder is accounted for not by improvements in treatment but by harmful treatments being offered less frequently. This change itself is possibly more a consequence of the changing pattern of health care, particularly in the United States (Lambert, Bergin, & Garfield, 2004), than a recognition by clinicians of the possibility of iatrogenic deterioration and an avoidance of damaging side-effects. As part of the regular scrutiny of side-effects, pharmacological studies routinely explore the potential harm that a well-intentioned treatment may cause. In the case of psychosocial treatments, we all too readily assume that such treatments are at worst inert and unlikely to do harm. This may indeed be the case for most disorders where psychotherapy is used as part of a care plan, but not universally so.

In fact, there may be particular disorders where psychological therapy represents a significant *risk* to the patient. Whatever the mechanisms of therapeutic change, traditional psychotherapeutic approaches depend for their effectiveness on the individual's capacity to consider their experience of their own mental state alongside its re-presentation by the psychotherapist. The appreciation of the difference between one's own experience of one's mind and that presented by another person is a key element. It is the integration of one's current experience of mind with the alternative view presented by the psychotherapist that must be the foundation for a change process. The capacity to mentalize, to understand behavior in terms of its associated mental states in self and other (Bateman & Fonagy, 2004; Fonagy et al., 2002), is essential to this integration.

While most people without major psychological problems are in a relatively strong position to utilize the alternative perspective presented by the psychological therapist, individuals who have a very poor appreciation of their own and others' perception of mind are unlikely to benefit from traditional (particularly insight-oriented) psychological therapies. We have argued that individuals with BPD have an impoverished model of their own and others' mental function, and we have accumulated some evidence to support this view (Bateman & Fonagy, 2004). They have schematic, rigid, and sometimes extreme views that make them susceptible to powerful emotional storms and apparently impulsive actions, and that create profound problems of behavioral regulation, including affect regulation. The weaker an individual's sense of their own subjectivity, the more difficult it is for them to compare the validity of their own perception of the way their mind works with that of a "mind expert." When presented with a coherent and perhaps even accurate view of mental function in the context of psychotherapy, they are not able to compare the picture offered to them with a self-generated model; all too often, they may uncritically accept alternative perspectives or reject them wholesale. Even focusing on how the patient feels can have its dangers. A person who has little capacity to discern the subjective state associated with anger can benefit neither from being told that they are feeling angry nor from an explanation of the underlying cause of that anger. Such an effort addresses nothing that is known or that can be integrated. It can only be accepted as true or rejected outright, but in neither case is it helpful. In the context of feelings of attachment to the therapist, the dissonance between the patient's inner experience and the perspective given by the therapist leads to bewilderment, which in turn leads to instability as the patient attempts to integrate the different views and experiences. Unsurprisingly, this results in more, rather than less, mental and behavioral disturbance.

The problem is compounded by the fact that attachment and mentalization are loosely coupled systems existing in a state of partial exclusivity (Fonagy & Bateman, 2006b; Fonagy & Target, *this volume*). Whilst mentalization has its roots in the sense of being understood by an attachment figure, it is also, for those individuals whose problem is fundamentally one of attachment (Gunderson, 1996), more challenging to maintain in the context of an attachment relationship (e.g., the relationship with the therapist). Recent intriguing neuroscientific findings have highlighted how the activation of the attachment system tends temporarily to inhibit or decouple the normal adult's capacity to mentalize (Bartels & Zeki, 2004). We have proposed, on the basis of both research findings and clinical observations, that individuals with BPD have hyperactive attachment systems as a result of their history and/or biological predisposition (Fonagy & Bateman, in press). This may account for their compromised mentalizing capacity.

MENTALIZING AS THE KEY TO SUCCESSFUL TREATMENT

It follows from the evidence outlined above that the recovery of the capacity to mentalize in the context of attachment relationships must be a primary objective of all psychosocial treatments for BPD. But we suggest that patients with BPD are particularly vulnerable to suffering side effects from psychotherapeutic treatments that activate the attachment system. Yet without activation of the attachment system borderline patients will never develop a capacity to function psychologically in the context of interpersonal relationships. This seeming impasse lies at the core of their problems. The psychiatrist or other mental health professional must tread a precarious path between stimulating a patient's attachment and involvement with treatment while also helping him to maintain mentalization. Treatment will only be effective to the extent that it is able to enhance the patient's mentalizing capacities without generating too many negative iatrogenic effects as it stimulates the attachment system. Following this principle, we developed a treatment that focuses on mentalization and then subjected that treatment to research scrutiny.

RESEARCH EVIDENCE FOR TREATMENT FOCUSING ON MENTALIZING

Our research into mentalization based treatment (MBT) demonstrates the need to take into account the validity of both internal and external evidence in order to assess the generalizability of the treatment method. On the positive side, the program was initially developed and implemented by a team of generically trained mental health professionals who have an interest in psychoanalytically orientated psychotherapy rather than by highly trained personnel within a university research department. Secondly, the research took place within a normal clinical setting and in a locality and health-care system in which patients were unlikely to be able to obtain treatment elsewhere; the latter enabled the effective tracing of patients within the service and the accurate collection of clinical and service utilization data. Thirdly, patients were treated at only two local hospitals for medical emergencies such as self-harm, enabling us to obtain highly accurate data of episodes of self-harm and suicide attempts requiring medical intervention. On the negative side, the program was complex, leading to difficulty in identifying the effective ingredients, if any. However, the program was also designed so that it could be dismantled at a later date to determine the therapeutic components.

Our initial task in setting up the treatment program was to review the literature, to consider the evidence for effective interventions, and to match those to the skills within the team. From the evidence discussed above, we concluded that treatments shown to be effective with BPD had certain common features. They tended: (a) to be well-structured; (b) to devote considerable effort to the enhancing of compliance; (c) to be clearly focused, whether that focus was on a problem behavior such as self-harm or on an aspect of interpersonal relationship patterns; (d) to be theoretically highly coherent to both therapist and patient, sometimes deliberately omitting information incompatible with the theory; (e) to be relatively long-term; (f) to encourage a powerful attachment relationship between therapist and patient, enabling the therapist to adopt a relatively active rather than a passive stance; and (g) to be well integrated with other services available to the patient. While some of these features may be specifically characteristic of a successful research study rather than a successful therapy, we concluded that the manner in which treatment protocols were constructed and delivered was probably as important in the success of treatment as the quality of the theory underlying the interventions.

With these general features in mind, we developed a program of treatment and organized a research program to test the effectiveness of the intervention. From the outset it was clear that this was to be "effectiveness research" rather than "efficacy research"—we would investigate the outcome of BPD treated by generically trained but nonspecialist practitioners within a normal clinical setting. In this way, the treatment was more likely to be translatable to other services without extensive and expensive additional training of personnel.

Our own evidence base remains small as far as treatment outcome is concerned; yet replication studies are under way, and an increasing number of practitioners are using mentalization techniques in treatment, such that more information will become available soon. Our original randomized controlled trial (RCT) of treatment of BPD in a partial hospital program offering individual and group psychoanalytic psychotherapy (Bateman & Fonagy, 1999, 2001) showed significant and enduring changes in mood states and interpersonal functioning associated with an 18-month program. The benefits, relative to treatment as usual (TAU), were large (number needed to treat stood at around two) and were observed to increase during the follow-up period of 18 months, rather than staying level, as with dialectical behavior therapy (DBT).

Forty-four patients who participated in the original study were assessed at three-monthly intervals after completion of the earlier trial. Outcome measures included frequency of suicide attempts and acts of self-harm, number and duration of inpatient admissions, service utilization, and self-report measures of depression, anxiety, general symptom distress, interpersonal function, and social adjustment. Data analysis used repeated measures analysis of covariance and non-parametric tests of trend. Patients who had received partial hospitalization treatment not only maintained their substantial gains but also showed a statistically significant continued improvement on most measures, in contrast to the control group of patients, which showed only limited change during the same period. This suggests that "rehabilitative" changes had developed, enabling patients to negotiate the stresses and strains of everyday life without resorting to former ways of coping such as self-harm.

The health-care utilization of all participating patients was assessed using information from case notes and service providers (Bateman & Fonagy, 2003). Costs of psychiatric, pharmacological, and emergency room (ER) treatment were compared 6 months prior to treatment, during the 18-month treatment, and 18 months after treatment as a follow-up. There were no differences between the groups in the costs of service utilization during pre-treatment and treatment. The additional cost of day hospital treatment was offset by less psychiatric inpatient care and reduced ER treatment. The trend toward decreasing costs in the experimental group during the 18 months after treatment and before follow-up was not apparent in the control group, suggesting that day hospital treatment for BPD is no more expensive than general psychiatric care and shows considerable cost savings after treatment.

The effective components of this complex treatment program remain unclear, although the common feature of all the different treatment elements was mentalization. Patients received a range of treatments along with group and individual therapy, including psychodrama and other expressive therapies, along with some psycho-education early in treatment. To determine whether the focus on mentalizing is a key component and to see if a more modest program may be effective in a less-severe group of borderline patients, we are currently undertaking an RCT of only individual and group psychotherapy offered in an outpatient program. Results are not yet available. Nevertheless we have defined those interventions that we believe are likely to enhance mentalizing, packaging them within a structured program.

MENTALIZATION-BASED TREATMENT OF BPD

MBT aims to develop a therapeutic process in which the mind of the patient becomes the focus of treatment. The objective is for the patient to find out more about how he thinks and feels about himself and others, how this dictates his responses, and how "errors" in his understanding of himself and others lead to actions that are attempts to retain stability and to make sense of incomprehensible feelings. It is not for the therapist to "tell" the patient about how he feels, what he thinks, how he should behave, and what are the underlying reasons, be they conscious or unconscious in origin, for his difficulties. We believe that any therapeutic approach that moves toward "knowing" how a patient "is," how he should behave and think, and "why he is like he is," is likely to be harmful. The therapist has to ensure that he retains an approach that focuses on the mind of the patient as he is experiencing himself and others at any given moment. In an attempt to capture the stance that gives the therapist the best chance of achieving mentalizing goals, we have differentiated between a mentalizing, an inquisitive, and a "not-knowing" stance. This latter stance is not synonymous with having no knowledge. The term "not-knowing" is an attempt to convey how mental states are opaque and how the therapist can have no more idea of what is in the patient's mind than the patient himself. When the therapist offers the patient a perspective that differs from the ptient's own views, this should be verbalized and explored in relation to the patient's alternative perspective with no assumption being made about whose viewpoint has greater validity. The task is to determine the mental processes that have led to alternative viewpoints and to consider each perspective in relation to the other, accepting the coexistence of diverse outlooks. Where differences are clear and cannot initially be resolved, they should be identified, stated, and accepted until resolution seems possible. The mentalizing stance requires the therapist to own up to his own anti-mentalizing errors, which are treated as opportunities to learn more about feelings and experiences (or: "How was it that I did that at that time?"). The therapist must articulate what has happened in order to model honesty and courage but above all to demonstrate that he is continually reflecting on what goes on in his mind and on what he does in relation to the patient, which is a central component of mentalizing itself.

Some therapy techniques are actively avoided in MBT. Firstly, we suggest that therapists avoid allowing excessive free association, a technique possibly more useful for neurotic patients. Secondly, we do not encourage active fantasy about the therapist. The use of fantasy and free association is not a major aspect of MBT because the development of insight is not one of its primary aims. Working with fantasy is a technique used in insight-orientated therapy as a way of understanding unconscious thinking. MBT is more concerned with preconscious and conscious aspects of mental function within the interpersonal domain. Fantasy itself is too distant from reality, and we do not therefore encourage elaboration of the patient's fantasies about the therapist because it is likely to be iatrogenic and to encourage dissociation rather than to increase elaborated representations linked to reality. Alternatively, fantasy experienced in psychic equivalence mode may be experienced as real, losing its as-if quality. Thirdly, recognizing that patients operate in psychic equivalence mode also implies that their understanding is characterized by a conviction about being right, and this makes entering into Socratic debates mostly unhelpful. Fourth, patients commonly assume that they know what the therapist is thinking, and this is to be accepted initially, for problems will arise if the therapist claims primacy for introspection, as for example if he says that he knows his own mind better than the patient, which will lead to fruitless debate. Fifth, and in contrast to many therapies that actively withhold self-disclosure, we suggest that tactful disclosure about what the therapist is feeling is essential if the patient is to discover his own state of mind by contrasting it with the therapist's. Finally, we discourage too much identification of patterns, as it might reduce the development of the patient's ability to seek his own understanding. We emphasize the therapist's role in fostering the development of the available mental resources in order to deal with recurrent patterns of behavior and relationships, rather than in identifying of these patterns themselves. Clinically, this emphasis is nontrivial. Mentalizing therapists do not get involved in discussing the structure or nature of the relationship that the patient brings, but focus more on the patient's capacity to think about the relationship. For example, the MBT therapist addresses the rigidity of schematic representations or roles rather than the roles or schemas themselves; the MBT therapist tries to enhance and facilitate flexibility and to generate alternative perspectives. We suspect that this process may be one effective component of a number of psychotherapeutic approaches; while work in therapy is ostensibly focused more on the actual roles, it is the action of teasing out these roles, rather than the understandings that are teased out, that the patient arrives at as a consequence of the work, that is crucial. From a mentalizing perspective, the problem lies in the capacity to process roles and experiences when they are activated within specific contexts.

The trajectory of MBT has three main phases. Each phase has a distinct aim and harnesses specific processes. The overall aim of the initial phase is the assessment of mentalizing capacities and personality function and the engagement of the patient in treatment. Specific processes include giving a diagnosis, providing psycho-education, establishing a hierarchy of therapeutic aims, stabilizing social and behavioral problems, reviewing medication, and defining a crisis pathway. During the middle phase, the aim of all the active therapeutic work is to stimulate an ever-increasing mentalizing ability. In the final phase, preparation is made for ending intensive treatment. This requires the therapist to focus on the feelings of loss associated with ending treatment and on how to maintain gains that have been made, as well as to develop, in conjunction with the patient, an appropriate follow-up program tailored to his particular needs.

There are two variants of MBT. The first is a day hospital program, which patients attend initially on a five-day-per-week basis. This program is a combination of individual and group psychotherapy focusing on implicit mentalizing processes, and expressive therapies promoting skills in explicit mentalizing. The exact structure and content of each group is less important than the interrelationship of the different aspects of the program, the working relationship between the different therapists, the continuity of themes between the groups, and the consistency with which the treatment is applied over a period of time. Such nonspecific aspects probably form the key to effective treatment, and the specificity of the therapeutic activities remains to be determined. Integration within the program is achieved through our focus on mentalizing. All groups have an overall aim of increasing mentalizing and doing so within a framework that encourages exploration of minds by minds, even if the route to this goal is via explicit techniques such as artwork and writing. The maximum length of time in this program is 24 months.

Entrance to the day hospital program requires the patient to show at least some of a number of features, including high risk to self or others, inadequate social support, repeated hospital admissions interfering with adaptations to everyday living, unstable housing, substance misuse, and fragmented mentalizing. Patients who show some capacity for everyday living and who have stable social support and accommodation are more likely to be treated through the second adaptation of MBT, which is an intensive outpatient (IOP) program, particularly if their mentalizing processes are characterized only by vulnerability in close emotional relationships. At present there is no agreed measure of severity of personality disorder, and so it remains impossible to assign individuals to one program or the other according to a score on a recognized instrument. The primary considerations are risk and instability of social circumstances.

The 18-month intensive outpatient treatment consists of weekly individual sessions lasting 50 minutes and group sessions lasting 90 minutes. As in the day hospital program, the group therapist is different from the individual therapist. The requirements placed on patients are more onerous than those placed on day hospital patients, because participants are less chaotic and have better mentalizing abilities, as well as some capacity for attentional and affective control. The two aspects of the program, namely the group and individual sessions, are not divisible, and frequent absence from one leads to discussion about continuation in treatment. It is not our policy simply to discharge someone because of nonattendance, but if someone does not attend one aspect of the program then this is discussed with him in the next session he does attend, be it an individual or a group session. Patients are told at the beginning of treatment that persistent and prolonged absence from any aspect of the program will lead to discharge to our low-maintenance outpatient clinic for further consideration of treatment. Return to the program remains possible after this, but only following further work on the underlying anxieties.

This more rigorous stance about attendance is taken because many patients find the individual session more acceptable than the group session and attend the former and not the latter. The patient may apparently have accepted the inevitability of group work in the assessment interviews, yet have kept secret that he has only done so to access individual therapy. This must be addressed as soon as treatment starts. Borderline patients have a reduced capacity to keep themselves in mind or to recognize that others have them in mind when listening to the problems of others. To some degree, this accounts for their anxiety about groups and their oscillations between over- and under-involvement with others. As they become involved with someone else's problems, they lose themselves in their own mind and in the mind of the other, and when they do so they begin to feel alone and self-less, which in turn leads to rapid distancing from the other person in order to save themselves.

After the first few sessions and after discussion with the treatment team, the individual therapist makes an initial formulation, which is given in written form to the patient. The purpose of the formulation of the patient's problems is to place feelings and behavior within an individual context and to commence the development of a coherent interpersonal and developmental narrative. Frequently, borderline patients have at their disposal only an incoherent narrative that makes little sense to them, leaving them unable to explain their personality development with any lucidity. They become schematic and categorical, linking specific events with explicit problems. The development of the formulation is the beginning of helping the patient to understand himself by exploring his personal story. Any formulation must be jointly developed and must be understandable to patient, therapist, and team alike. It is written down as a working hypothesis rather than as a veridical truth established by a therapist, and it is reviewed throughout the treatment program. In the formulation, the initial goals should be clearly stated and linked to those aspects of treatment that will enable the patient to attain them. There should be a brief summary of the joint understanding that has developed, with a focus on the underlying causes of the patient's problems in terms of mentalizing, the patient's development, and their current function. The formulation should also include longer-term goals in terms of the patient's social and interpersonal adjustment, areas that are likely to be important indicators of improved mentalizing.

All patients in the partial hospital program and in IOP attend a review with the whole treatment team every three months. The group therapist, the individual therapist, the psychiatrist, and other relevant mental health professionals meet with the patient to discuss progress, problems, and other aspects of treatment. Having practitioners meeting together with the patient ensures not only that the views of everyone are taken into account and integrated into a coherent set of ideas, but also that mentalizing as manifested through the discussion of the different viewpoints is modeled as a constructive activity that furthers understanding. These regular reviews lead to a reformulation that can then form the basis of ongoing treatment.

The hard work for the patient takes place in the middle phase. For the therapist, this phase may appear easier because by the time the initial phase has been negotiated many of the crises will have subsided, the level of engagement in treatment will be clear, the patient's motivation may have increased, and the capacity to work within individual and group therapy may be more pronounced. In addition, the therapist may have a better understanding of the patient's overall difficulties and so have a more robust image of him in mind, while the patient has also become aware of the therapist's foibles and ways of working. For other patients, the treatment trajectory may continue to be disrupted, and a primary task of the therapist is to repair ruptures in the therapeutic alliance and to sustain their own and the patient's motivation while maintaining a focus on mentalizing.

Although, as we have seen, borderline patients naturally improve over time, the improvement is primarily in impulsive behavior and symptoms of affective instability. Complex interpersonal interaction, intricate negotiation of difficult social situations, and interaction with systems may be less responsive to treatment. The borderline patient who no longer self-harms may still lead a life severely curtailed by his inability to form constructive relationships with others. Patients remain incapacitated in how they live their lives unless they develop constructive ways of interacting with others. The focus of the final phase is on the interpersonal and social aspects of functioning, along with integrating and consolidating earlier work, as long as the symptomatic and behavioral problems are well controlled.

The final phase starts at the 12-month point when the patient has a further 6 months' treatment. In keeping with the principles of dynamic therapy, we consider the ending of treatment and associated separation responses to be highly significant in the consolidation of gains made during therapy. Inadequate negotiation by the patient of the experience of leaving (and, incidentally, inadequate processing of the ending on the part of the therapist) may provoke in the patient a reemergence of earlier ways of managing feelings and a concomitant decrease in mentalizing capacities. The consequence is a reduction in social and interpersonal function.

Responsibility for developing a coherent follow-up program and for negotiating further treatment is given to the patient and individual therapist. No specific follow-up program is now routinely offered. Most patients ask for further follow-up. Some patients may have had a career over many years of interacting with mental health services; to leave this behind requires a massive change in lifestyle, which may not be fully embedded by the end of 18 months. For the severe personality-disordered patient who has had many years of failed treatments, multiple hospital admissions, and inadequate social stability, it is unlikely that it will be possible or acceptable for them to walk away from services never to return after 18 months, irrespective of the success of the treatment. Most patients require further support as they adapt to a new life. Many patients choose intermittent follow-up appointments rather than further formal psychotherapy. This is organized within the treatment team. Senior practitioners who have known the patient and who are known to the patient offer weekly, individual 30-minute appointments for four to six weeks. During follow-up appointments, the therapist continues to use mentalizing techniques, exploring the underlying mental states of the patient and discussing how understanding themselves and others can lead to a resolution of problems, to the reconciliation of differences, and to the management of problematic interpersonal areas and intimate relationships. The follow-up contract is flexible and the patient can request an additional appointment if there is an emotional problem that cannot easily be managed. But, in general, the trajectory over follow-up is toward an increase in the time between appointments over a six-month period to encourage greater patient responsibility. How long a patient is seen in this manner depends on both the therapist and patient, and should be agreed between them. Some patients elect to be discharged relatively early during follow-up on the grounds that they may call and request an appointment at any time in the future. Other patients prefer to have a further appointment arranged many months in advance, for this provides them with adequate assurance that the therapist will continue to have them in mind, giving them greater confidence and self-reliance to negotiate the stresses and strains of everyday life.

The principal aims of MBT are familiar: to reinstate mentalizing at the point at which it is lost, to stabilize mentalizing in the context of an attachment relationship, to minimize the likelihood of adverse effects, and to allow the patient to discover himself and others through a mind considering a mind. Careful focus on the patient's current state of mind will achieve these aims. As one patient said: "Before I did all this, it never even occurred to me that what I did or thought had any effect on anyone else. Sometimes I still think that life was better then because sometimes I don't like what other people think. But it does make life more interesting."

CONCLUSION

All moderately effective current therapies for BPD are able to present a view of the internal world of the patient that is stable, coherent, can be clearly perceived, and that may be adopted as the reflective part of the self (the self-image of the patient's mind). In other words, it is possible to argue that all these therapies stimulate attachment to the therapist while asking the patient to evaluate accuracy of statements concerning mind states in self and others. It is the combination of these two treatment components that is probably most helpful in enabling the person to retain a mentalized understanding of intrapsychic experiences even in the context of a relatively intense relationship. Their effectiveness lies in creating structures that enable the balancing of attachment and mentalizing components. Both need attention and careful planning if the treatment is to be delivered as intended, not least because of the client group's propensity for treatment-defeating behavior. Focusing solely on cognition or the environment does not satisfy the patient who feels uniquely vulnerable in intimate interpersonal relationships. Focusing exclusively on such relationships risks aggravating problems of mentalization and undermines the possibility of change driven by self-reflection.

REFERENCES

Akhtar, S. (1992). *Broken Structures: Severe Personality Disorders and Their Treatment.* Northvale, NJ: Jason Aronson.

Arnsten, A.F.T. (1998). The biology of being frazzled. *Science, 280,* 1711–1712.

Baker, L., Silk, K. R., Westen, D., Nigg, J. T., & Lohr, N. E. (1992). Malevolence, splitting, and parental ratings by borderlines. *Journal of Nervous and Mental Disease, 180*(4), 258–264.

Bartels, A., & Zeki, S. (2000). The neural basis of romantic love. *Neuroreport, 11*(17), 3829–3834.

Bartels, A., & Zeki, S. (2004). The neural correlates of maternal and romantic love. *Neuroimage, 21*(3), 1155–1166.

Bateman, A. W., & Fonagy, P. (1999). The effectiveness of partial hospitalization in the treatment of borderline personality disorder: A randomised controlled trial. *American Journal of Psychiatry, 156,* 1563–1569.

Bateman, A. W., & Fonagy, P. (2001). Treatment of borderline personality disorder with psychoanalytically oriented partial hospitalization: An 18-month follow-up. *American Journal of Psychiatry, 158*(1), 36–42.

Bateman, A. W., & Fonagy, P. (2003). Health service utilization costs for borderline personality disorder patients treated with psychoanalytically oriented partial hospitalization versus general psychiatric care. *American Journal of Psychiatry, 160*(1), 169–171.

Bateman, A. W., & Fonagy, P. (2004). *Psychotherapy for borderline personality disorder: Mentalization-based treatment.* Oxford, UK: Oxford University Press.

Betan, E., & Westen, D. (2005). Identity disturbance in adolescents with personality pathology. Unpublished manuscript, Emory University, Atlanta, Georgia.

Cassidy, J., Parke, R. D., Butkovsky, L., & Braungart, J. M. (1992). Family-peer connections: The roles of emotional expressiveness within the family and children's understanding of emotion. *Child Development, 63*(3), 603–618.

Cohen, P., Crawford, T. N., Johnson, J. G., & Kasen, S. (2006). The Children in the Community Study of developmental course of personality disorder. *Journal of Personality Disorders, 19*(5), 466–486.

de Rosnay, M., & Harris, P. L. (2002). Individual differences in children's understanding of emotion: The roles of attachment and language. *Attachment and Human Development, 4*(1), 39–54.

Dunn, J. (1996). The Emanuel Miller Memorial Lecture 1995. Children's relationships: Bridging the divide between cognitive and social development. *Journal of Child Psychology and Psychiatry, 37*, 507–518.

Dunn, J., Brown, J., Somkowski, C., Telsa, C., & Youngblade, L. (1991). Young children's understanding of other people's feelings and beliefs: Individual differences and their antecedents. *Child Development, 62*, 1352–1366.

Fonagy, P., & Bateman, A. (2006a). Progress in the treatment of borderline personality disorder. *British Journal of Psychiatry, 188*, 1–3.

Fonagy, P., & Bateman, A. (in press). Mechanisms of change in mentalisation based therapy with BPD. *Journal of Clinical Psychology*.

Fonagy, P., & Bateman, A. W. (2006b). Mechanisms of change in mentalization-based treatment of BPD. *Journal of Clinical Psychology, 62*(4), 411–430.

Fonagy, P., Gergely, G., Jurist, E., & Target, M. (2002). *Affect Regulation, Mentalization, and the Development of the Self*. New York: Other Press.

Fonagy, P., Redfern, S., & Charman, T. (1997). The relationship between belief-desire reasoning and a projective measure of attachment security (SAT). *British Journal of Developmental Psychology, 15*, 51–61.

Fonagy, P., & Target, M. (1997). Attachment and reflective function: Their role in self-organization. *Development and Psychopathology, 9*, 679–700.

Fonagy, P., Target, M., Gergely, G., Allen, J. G., & Bateman, A. (2003). The developmental roots of borderline personality disorder in early attachment relationships: A theory and some evidence. *Psychoanalytic Inquiry, 23*, 412–459.

Gergely, G., Koós, O., & Watson, J. S. (2002). Contingency perception and the role of contingent parental reactivity in early socio-emotional development [Perception causale et role des comportements imitatifs des parents dans le développement socio-émotionnel précoce]. In J. Nadel & J. Decety (Eds.), *Imiter pour découvrir l'human: Psychologie, neurobiology, robotique et philosophie de l'esprit* (pp. 59–82). Paris: Presses Universitaires de France.

Gergely, G., & Watson, J. (1996). The social biofeedback model of parental affect-mirroring. *International Journal of Psycho-Analysis, 77*, 1181–1212.

Gunderson, J. G. (1996). The borderline patient's intolerance of aloneness: Insecure attachments and therapist availability. *American Journal of Psychiatry, 153*(6), 752–758.

Gunderson, J. G., Bender, D., Sanislow, C., Yen, S., Rettew, J. B., Dolan-Sewell, R., et al. (2003). Plausibility and possible determinants of sudden "remissions" in borderline patients. *Psychiatry, 66*(2), 111–119.

Hamilton, C. E. (2000). Continuity and discontinuity of attachment from infancy through adolescence. *Child Development, 71*(3), 690–694.

Harris, P. L. (1999). Individual differences in understanding emotions: The role of attachment status and emotional discourse. *Attachment and Human Development, 1*(3), 307–324.

Harris, P. L., de Rosnay, M., & Pons, F. (2005). Language and children's understanding of mental states. *Current Directions in Psychological Science, 14*(2), 69–73.

Horwitz, A. V., Widom, C. S., McLaughlin, J., & White, H. R. (2001). The impact of childhood abuse and neglect on adult mental health: A prospective study. *Journal of Health and Social Behavior, 42*(2), 184–201.

Jenkins, J. M., & Astington, J. W. (2000). Theory of mind and social behavior: Causal models tested in a longitudinal study. *Merrill-Palmer Quarterly, 46*, 203–220.

Johnson, J. G., Cohen, P., Smailes, E., Skodol, A., Brown, J., & Oldham, J. (2001). Childhood verbal abuse and risk for personality disorders during adolescence and early adulthood. *Comprehensive Psychiatry, 42*, 16–23.

Keller, M. B., Lavori, P. W., Mueller, T. I., Endicott, J., Coryell, W., Hirschfeld, R. M., et al. (1992). Time to recovery, chronicity, and levels of psychopathology in major depression. A 5-year prospective follow-up of 431 subjects. *Archives of General Psychiatry, 49*, 809–816.

Kernberg, O. F. (1983). Object relations theory and character analysis. *Journal of the American Psychoanalytic Association, 31*, 247–271.

Kochanska, G., Coy, K. C., & Murray, K. T. (2001). The development of self-regulation in the first four years of life. *Child Development, 72*(4), 1091–1111.

Koós, O., & Gergely, G. (2001). A contingency-based approach to the etiology of 'disorganized' attachment: The 'flickering switch' hypothesis. *Bulletin of the Menninger Clinic, 65*(3), 397–410.

Lambert, M., Bergin, A. E., & Garfield, S. (2004). Introduction and historical overview. In M. Lambert (Ed.), *Bergin and Garfield's Handbook of Psychotherapy and Behavior Change* (pp. 3–15). New York: Wiley.

Levy, K. N. (2005). The implications of attachment theory and research for understanding borderline personality disorder. *Development and Psychopathology, 17*(4), 959–986.

Ludolph, P. S., Westen, D., Misle, B., Jackson, A., Wixom, J., & Wiss, F. C. (1990). The borderline diagnosis in adolescents: Symptoms and developmental history. *American Journal of Psychiatry, 147*(4), 470–476.

Lyons-Ruth, K., Yellin, C., Melnick, S., & Atwood, G. (2005). Expanding the concept of unresolved mental states: Hostile/helpless states of mind on the Adult Attachment Interview are associated with disrupted mother-infant communication and infant disorganization. *Development and Psychopathology, 17*(1), 1–23.

Meins, E., Fernyhough, C., Russell, J., & Clark-Carter, D. (1998). Security of attachment as a predictor of symbolic and mentalising abilities: A longitudinal study. *Social Development, 7,* 1–24.

Morrison, A. P., Frame, L., & Larkin, W. (2003). Relationships between trauma and psychosis: A review and integration. *British Journal of Clinical Psychology, 42,* 331–353.

Nelson, K. (2005). Language pathways into the community of minds. In J. W. Astington & J. A. Baird (Eds.), *Why language matters for theory of mind* (pp. 26–49). Oxford, UK: Oxford University Press.

Ontai, L. L., & Thompson, R. A. (2002). Patterns of attachment and maternal discourse effects on children's emotion understanding from 3 to 5 years of age. *Social Development, 11*(4), 433–450.

Paris, J. (2004). Sociocultural factors in the treatment of personality disorders. In W. J. Livesley (Ed.), *Handbook of Personality Disorders: Theory and Practice* (pp. 135–147). New York: Wiley.

Raikes, H. A., & Thompson, R. A. (2006). Family emotional climate, attachment security, and young children's emotion knowledge in a high-risk sample. *British Journal of Developmental Psychology, 24*(1), 89–104.

Ruffman, T., Slade, L., & Crowe, E. (2002). The relation between children's and mothers' mental state language and theory-of-mind understanding. *Child Development, 73,* 734–751.

Shea, M. T., Stout, R. L., Yen, S., Pagano, M. E., Skodol, A. E., Morey, L. C., et al. (2004). Associations in the course of personality disorders and Axis I disorders over time. *Journal of Abnormal Psychology, 113*(4), 499–508.

Skodol, A. E., Gunderson, J., Shea, M. T., McGlashan, T., Morey, L. C., Sanislow, C., et al. (2006). The Collaborative Longitudinal Personality Disorders Study (CLPS): Overview and implications. *Journal of Personality Disorders, 19*(5), 487–504.

Solomon, J., George, C., & Dejong, A. (1995). Children classified as controlling at age six: Evidence of disorganized representational strategies and aggression at home and at school. *Development and Psychopathology, 7,* 447–463.

Sroufe, L. A., Egeland, B., Carlson, E., & Collins, W. A. (2005). *The Development of the Person: The Minnesota Study of Risk and Adaptation from Birth to Adulthood.* New York: Guilford.

Steele, M., Steele, H., Croft, C., & Fonagy, P. (1999). Infant-mother attachment at one year predicts children's understanding of mixed emotions at 6 years. *Social Development, 8,* 161–178.

Stone, M. H. (1990). *The Fate of Borderline Patients: Successful Outcome and Psychiatric Practice.* New York: Guilford.

Stuart, J., Westen, D., Lohr, N. E., Benjamin, J., Becker, S., & Vorus, N. (1990). Object relations in borderlines, depressives, and normals: An examination of human responses on the Rorschach. *Journal of Personality Assessment, 55,* 296–318.

Symons, D. K. (2004). Mental state discourse, theory of mind, and the internalization of self-other understanding. *Developmental Review, 24,* 159–188.

Taylor, S. F., Liberson, I., Fig, L. M., Decker, L. R., Minoshima, S., & Koeppe, R. A. (1998). The effect of emotional content on visual recognition memory: A PET activation study. *Neuroimage, 8,* 188–197.

Thompson, R. A. (2000). The legacy of early attachments. *Child Development, 71,* 145–152.

Tyrer, P., & Bateman, A. (2004). Drug treatments for personality disorders. *Advances in Psychiatric Treatment, 10,* 389–398.

Waters, E., Merrick, S. K., Treboux, D., Crowell, J., & Albersheim, L. (2000). Attachment security from infancy to early adulthood: A 20-year longitudinal study. *Child Development, 71*(3), 684–689.

Weinfield, N., Sroufe, L. A., & Egeland, B. (2000). Attachment from infancy to early adulthood in a high risk sample: Continuity, discontinuity and their correlates. *Child Development, 71*(3), 695–702.

Westen, D., Lohr, N., Silk, K., Gold, L., & Kerber, K. (1990). Object relations and social cognition in borderlines, major depressives, and normals: A TAT analysis. *Psychological Assessment: A Journal of Consulting and Clinical Psychology, 2,* 355–364.

Westen, D., Ludolph, P., Lerner, H., Ruffins, S., & Wiss, F. C. (1990). Object relations in borderline adolescents. *Journal of the American Academy of Child and Adolescent Psychiatry, 29,* 338–348.

Wilkinson-Ryan, T., & Westen, D. (2000). Identity disturbance in borderline personality disorder: An empirical investigation. *American Journal of Psychiatry, 157*(4), 528–541.

Winnicott, D. W. (1956). Mirror role of mother and family in child development. In D. W. Winnicott (Ed.), *Playing and reality* (pp. 111–118). London: Tavistock.

Youngblade, L., & Dunn, J. (1995). Individual differences in young children's pretend play with mother and sibling: Links to relationships and understanding of other people's feelings and beliefs. *Child Development, 66,* 1472–1492.

Zanarini, M., Gunderson, J. G., & Frankenburg, F. R. (1990). Discriminating borderline personality disorder from other Axis II disorders. *American Journal of Psychiatry, 147,* 161–167.

Zanarini, M. C., Frankenburg, F. R., Hennen, J., Reich, D. B., & Silk, K. R. (2004). Axis I comorbidity in patients with borderline personality disorder: 6-year follow-up and prediction of time to remission. *American Journal of Psychiatry, 161*(11), 2108–2114.

Zanarini, M. C., Frankenburg, F. R., Hennen, J., Reich, D. B., & Silk, K. R. (2006). The McLean Study of Adult Development (MSAD): Overview and implications of the first six years of prospective follow-up. *Journal of Personality Disorders, 19*(5), 505–523.

Zanarini, M. C., Frankenburg, F. R., Hennen, J., & Silk, K. R. (2003). The longitudinal course of borderline psychopathology: 6-year prospective follow-up of the phenomenology of borderline personality disorder. *American Journal of Psychiatry, 160*(2), 274–283.

Chapter 6

Mentalization and Attachment in Borderline Patients in Transference Focused Psychotherapy

Otto F. Kernberg, Diana Diamond, Frank E. Yeomans,
John F. Clarkin, and Kenneth N. Levy

INTRODUCTION

Mentalization, or the capacity to think in terms of intentional mental states of self and other, is at the basis of human interpretive capacities, and as such it has been identified as both a major goal of treatment and a key mechanism of change in psychodynamic psychotherapy with borderline patients (Bateman & Fonagy, 2004a, 2004b; Levy, Clarkin, et al., 2006; Yeomans, Clarkin, Diamond, & Levy, in press). More specifically, mentalization refers to recognition that the mind is representational in nature, and that "what is in the mind is in the mind, and reflects knowledge of one's own and the other's mental states" (Bateman & Fonagy, 2004b, p. 36). Fonagy and his colleagues (Fonagy, Gergely, Jurist, & Target, 2002) have linked mentalization to an Interpersonal Interpretive Mechanism (IIM), which is a fundamental aspect of the evolutionary selective advantage of the attachment behavioral system. This mechanism, which involves the capacity for psychological interpretation—that is, the ability to make sense of the beliefs and desires that motivate human behavior, to distinguish psychological states of self and other, to create meanings, and to enrich symbolic thinking—is thought to be deficient in patients with severe personality disorders. These theoretical formulations are supported by an impressive body of developmental and clinical research (Fonagy et al., 2002) that suggests that deficits in mentalization—which are developed in the context of insecure attachment relationships, often characterized by early unresolved trauma—is an enduring characteristic of borderline pathology (Fonagy et al., 2002). The development of the capacity for mentalization in the context of a secure attachment relationship with the therapist, leading to increased coherence, integration, and modulation in the representational world, has become the hallmark of psychodynamic approaches to treatment of severe personality disorders (Bateman & Fonagy, 2004a; Fonagy, 1999; Kernberg, 2004a). In this paper we will review and critique the concept of mentalization as it is applied to the theory and treatment of patients with severe personality disorders from the vantage point of object relations theory, particularly Kernberg's object relations model.

Finding the most effective methods of treating this group of patients, who are characterized by chronic suicidal and parasuicidal behaviors; identity diffusion; dissociative states that may or may not be linked to early trauma (Paris, 1994); chaotic, unstable interpersonal relationships; affective volatility and impulsivity; impaired occupational functioning; and overutilization of health services (see Clarkin, Foelsch, Levy, Hull, Delaney, & Kernberg, 2001), has become increasingly important as borderline patients have become more prevalent among both inpatient and outpatient groups. Patients with borderline personality disorder now characterize 1–4% of the general population, 10–15% of psychiatric outpatients, and up to 20% of psychiatric inpatients (Lenzenweger, Loranger, Korfine, & Neff, 1997; Paris, 1999; Torgersen, Kringlen, & Cramer, 2001; Weissman, 1993). In keeping with the increased emphasis on the development and implementation of empirically validated treatments, investigations of borderline patients and their treatment have moved beyond theoretical elaborations about the nature of the pathology itself to the development of evidence-based treatment approaches that can be manualized and assessed for efficacy and outcome.

In the psychodynamic realm, the two major manualized treatments for BPD are Transference Focused Psychotherapy (TFP, Clarkin, Yeomans, & Kernberg, 1999, 2006) based on Kernberg's (1984) object relations model, and Mentalization Based Treatment (MBT, Bateman & Fonagy, 2004a), based on Fonagy and colleagues' (Fonagy et al., 2002) developmental theory of mentalization, which integrates philosophy (theory of mind), ego psychology, and attachment theory. In the cognitive behavioral realm the major approach is Linehan's (1993) Dialectical Behavior Therapy (DBT), which integrates cognitive behavioral theory with dialectical philosophy and Buddhist principles of mindfulness. All three groups have developed theoretically consistent, evidence-based, comprehensive treatment programs for BPD that have demonstrated efficacy in reducing symptomatology, service utilization, and suicidality in borderline patients (Bateman & Fonagy, 1999, 2001, 2003, 2004a; Clarkin & Levy, 2003; Levy, Meehan, et al., 2006; Linehan, Armstrong, Suarez, Allmon, & Heard, 1991; Linehan, Kanter, & Comtois, 1993, Linehan et al., 2006).

Bateman and Fonagy (2004b) have proposed that all effective treatments for BPD are built, in part, on implicit and explicit mentalization, with the former referring to the largely unconscious, procedural mental activity that has its roots in nonverbal mirroring transactions, and the latter referring to relatively conscious intentional reflective processes involved in contemplating the mental states of self and others (Allen, 2003). The concept of mentalization has been operationalized in the Reflective Function (RF) scale (Fonagy, Target, Steele, & Steele, 1997), an attachment-based measure of mentalization, which provides us with a tool to evaluate changes in the capacity to think in mental-state terms over the course of treatment (Diamond, Stovall-McClough, Clarkin, & Levy, 2003; Levy, Meehan, et al., 2006). To date, however, TFP is the only therapeutic modality that has been empirically associated with improvements in the capacity for mentalization as assessed by increases in RF ratings over the course of one year of treatment (Levy, Meehan, et al., 2006; see summary of research below).

In previous publications, we delineated the specific treatment techniques that we believe lead to improvements in the capacity for mentalization for borderline patients in TFP, with a focus on the role of the treatment frame and on the techniques of clarification, confrontation, and particularly interpretation (Levy, Clarkin, et al., 2006). In this paper we will discuss more fully our interpretive approach and its relationship to implicit and explicit mentalization. We first delineate some of the points of contact and divergence between TFP and MBT, and provide a more detailed overview of TFP and its theoretical foundations. Next we summarize recent research findings from three studies on the efficacy of TFP, which examine changes in attachment status, reflective function, and symptomatology in borderline patients over the course of one-year, twice-weekly TFP treatment. Finally, we present case material to illustrate our general outcome data, as well as data on reflective functioning (RF) as a mechanism of change in TFP, and discuss how our research and clinical investigations have led to an expansion of the concept of mentalization.

MBT AND TFP: COMMON GROUND AND CONTROVERSIES

The concept of mentalization as developed by Fonagy and colleagues, which emphasizes the cognitive aspects of the structuralization of the representational world, is complementary to the object relations foundations of TFP (Kernberg, 2004a). Improvements in the capacity for mentalization are thought by both approaches to go hand in hand with the capacity to develop fuller and more elaborated representations of the self and internal objects (Fonagy, 1999; Kernberg, 2004a). As Fonagy (1999) has observed, "enhanced reflective capacity allows patients to integrate split off parts of the self and create representations with complex thoughts, mixed emotions and differentiated desires" (p. 16). Further, the perspectives of TFP and MBT converge around the idea that changes in mentalization are catalyzed through the here-and-now experiences with the therapist rather than through excavation and exploration of past experiences. However, there are fundamental differences between the two approaches in the following areas: (a) the etiology of borderline disorders; (b) the centrality of affect; (c) the type and function of interpretation; and (d) the nature of the internal world.

THE ETIOLOGY OF BORDERLINE PATHOLOGY

Fonagy and his colleagues have made fundamental contributions to understanding borderline psychopathology by linking it with insecure attachment, and by articulating the basic mechanisms of early parent–infant interactions, including contingent marked mirroring in infancy, pretend play in early childhood, and talk about mental states in later childhood—

all of which are thought to consolidate the development of secure attachment relationships, setting the foundation for mentalization (Allen, 2003). Our research investigations, along with those of Fonagy and colleagues, suggest that the majority of borderline patients are characterized by insecure and/or disorganized states of mind with respect to attachment, with the latter involving lack of resolution of early traumatic experiences (Diamond et al., 2003; Fonagy et al., 1996; Levy, Meehan, et al., 2006. According to Fonagy and colleagues, borderline patients inhibit their capacity to comprehend the mental states, motivations, wishes, feelings, and thoughts that govern behavior—their own and that of others—either (a) as a defensive reaction to severe chronic abuse and/or neglect, which protects them from contemplating the frightening and heinous intentions of those who abused them; or (b) as a deficit resulting from early pathogenic, unmarked, and noncontingent interactions in which the caregiver either fails to accurately and empathically recognize the child's mental states, or imposes her own mental states on those of the child. In either case the child is left with a legacy of overwhelming unmentalized psychic experiences and/or boundary confusion (Fonagy et al., 2002). As a result of either scenario, the individual shuts down the capacity to think in multifaceted or complex ways about the mental states of self and other, and instead splits the internal world into rigidly idealized and persecutory sectors.

These formulations advance our understanding of the etiology of borderline disorders in expanding the role of trauma into the realm of problematic early attachment relationships. There are now a number of studies that have shown that early attachment traumata and especially physical, psychological, and sexual abuse, are significantly more prevalent in patients with severe personality disorders than in patients with milder personality pathology or the general population (Paris, 1994). However, there is also increasing evidence that irregularities of the neurochemical and neurohormonal systems function as inborn dispositions to levels of intensity, rhythm, and threshold for affective response, and particularly to negative affect, leading to aggressive and uncontrolled behavior (Kernberg, 2004a; Stone, 1993). Our model of borderline pathology posits a dynamic interaction of temperament—especially a preponderance of negative affect over positive affect and low, effortful control—with the absence of a coherent sense of self and others, under the influence of an insecure working model of attachment (Depue & Lenzenweger, 2005; Clarkin & Posner, 2005; Posner et al., 2003). While we take into account the etiological role of trauma, including trauma deriving from insecure/disorganized attachment, the emphasis of our treatment is on the ways in which trauma contributes to configuring the internal representational world. Fonagy and colleagues acknowledge that, for borderline patients, representations of self and others are imbued with rageful or idealizing affects that are not amenable either to reflection or modulation (Fonagy, 1999). Although these researchers highlight the contributions of deficits in affect regulation, they tend to play down the centrality of negative affect and difficulties with its regulation—which they attribute almost solely to deficits in mentalization—to the etiology of borderline disorders. (We will expand on our understanding of the etiology of BPD below.)

THE CENTRALITY OF AFFECT

In our view, mentalization encompasses not only a set of cognitive functions, such as representing and reasoning about beliefs and desires of self and others, but also the capacity to represent and regulate affects, to signify the subjective aspects of affects, and to connect affects with their representational roots. Kernberg's (2004a) object relations model offers a comprehensive theory of the development of the capacity to symbolize and regulate affect, and of the complex processes through which the concepts of self and other evolve out of early affective experiences. These are all crucial aspects of the process of mentalization that have been perhaps under-theorized given the emphasis on mentalization as a set of cognitive skills and processes linked to theory of mind. In emphasizing the affective roots of mentalization we are contributing to a trend to propel the concept of mentalization (and the theory of mind with which it is linked) beyond the cognitive sphere into the affective realm by focusing on how young children's efforts to manage and comprehend the feelings of self and others provide pathways to understanding of mental states (Carpendale & Lewis, 2004; Fonagy, in press; Gergely & Unoka, in press; Thompson, Laible, & Ontai, 2003). However, despite this recent emphasis on the role of affect activation and modulation in the development of mentalization, the focus of Fonagy and colleagues is on the immediate interpersonal processes that are at the basis of mentalizing capacities, rather than on the building up of complex object relationships that structure and modulate affect activation and hence contribute to mentalization. The one exception to this trend is the work of Jurist (Fonagy et al., 2002; Jurist, 2005) on "mentalized affectivity," which integrates Kernberg's object relations theory with the theory of mentalization. Jurist (2005) defines mentalized affectivity as an "exploration of how our affective experience is mediated by the representational world—in other words how current (and future) affects are experienced through the lens of past experiences, both real and imagined" (p. 429). Thus, mentalized affectivity involves the capacity to recognize, understand, and regulate the self's affective states.

Kernberg's object relations model sees affects as the primary psychophysiological dispositions that are activated by early bodily experiences in the context of the development of object relations. Affects become linked with self and object representations in elementary dyads as highly pleasurable and unpleasurable experiences accrue in the course of early development, and come to form in their supraordinate organization the building blocks for libidinal and aggressive drives, while the representation of self and objects eventually evolves into the more complex tripartite structure (ego, id, and superego). In Kernberg's view, then, primitive affects constitute a primary motivational system that integrates cognitive appraisal of the momentary experiences of gratification or frustration with the subjective experience of pleasure or unpleasure in the context of particular object relations. Affects, which are activated by crucial and distinctive patterns of facial expressions in early mirroring exchanges between infant and caregiver that serve a communicative function (Kernberg, 2004a), thus include a cognitive component, as well as a subjective component of pleasure and unpleasure, along with psychomotor activation and neurovegetative discharge phenomena. Thus, the early activation of affects in the context of the mother–infant relationship serves simultaneously to trigger and consolidate the attachment behavioral system and to build up the internalized world of object relations, so that these two spheres are inevitably linked although not synonymous. Further, the early affective exchanges set the foundation for mentalization since in the course of development each momentary activation of a dyadic relation between self and object contributes to and is then confronted by a more permanent integrated view of self and others against which the momentary state can be evaluated.

From an object relations perspective, then, affects are the primary vehicles that give rise to primary representations (Kernberg, 2004a; Sandler & Sandler, 1998). The movement from primary to secondary representations involves a cognitive framing of affect that contributes to the building up of self and object representations. Through the process of marked and contingent mirroring transactions, which facilitate affect regulation and shape the infant's experience of internal and external reality, primary representations are transformed into secondary representations characterized by more realistic models of self and significant others that are gradually consolidated into a stable, overarching concept of self and object. In the treatment of severely disturbed patients, interpretation contributes to a move from primary to secondary representations, with a concomitant modulation and integration of affective states. In Bion's (1962, 1967, 1970) terms, interpretation functions as "an apparatus for thinking" that serves the purpose of transforming "beta elements" into "alpha elements." The object relations approach in TFP involves working directly with affect through interpretation as it is mobilized in the transference. By contrast, Bateman & Fonagy (2004a) believe that mentalization is most likely to be enhanced when affect is quiescent, and when the attachment behavioral system with its associated affects is not activated.

INTERPRETATIVE ACTIVITY AND MENTALIZATION

The focus on interpretation differentiates TFP from both MBT and the cognitive behavioral approach of Linehan (1993). Bateman (Bateman & Fonagy 2004a, 2004b) has proposed that interpretation is at the heart of all psychodynamic treatments for borderline patients. However, he and his colleagues have stipulated that even in interpretive therapies such as TFP, the mutative factor in the treatment is not the specific content of interpretations, but the process of engaging the patient in the contemplation of his or her own mental states and those of the therapist. Furthermore, MBT advises against interpretation except in advanced stages of therapy.

Although we agree that the focus on mental states in the context of an attachment relationship with the therapist is a fundamental aspect of psychodynamic treatment with borderline patients (Bateman & Fonagy, 2004a; Kernberg, 2004a), TFP does not limit its focus to improving mentalization as defined by Bateman and Fonagy (2004a). Rather, our interpretive approach focuses first on clarifying and understanding the conscious mental states experienced in the moment and moves gradually toward the exploration of mental states that are split off, denied, and/or repressed. We now turn to a more detailed explication of TFP to further clarify the relationship between our conceptualizations of BPD and of the roles of interpretation, affect, and mentalization in TFP treatment.

TRANSFERENCE FOCUSED PSYCHOTHERAPY (TFP)

TFP is based on an understanding of borderline personality that combines psychoanalytic (object relations) concepts of the structural organization of personality, especially the concept of the split internal world and identity diffusion (Kernberg, 1984, 2004b, 2006), and ideas of interaction between behavior and neurobiological variables, as delineated above. TFP is based on the idea that early affective experiences are cumulatively internalized in the course of development, and become established in the psychological structure as "object relations dyads"—units that combine a specific representation of the self in relation to a specific representation of the other linked by a specific affect. These dyads are not exact, accurate representations of early experience, but rather reflect the complex mesh of fantasy, drive, affect, wishes, and conflicts that are evoked in interactions with primary attachment figures in early development, as well as the activation of defenses and their adaptive or distorting influence (Diamond & Blatt, 1994; Kernberg, 1980, 2004a).

In borderline individuals, as development proceeds, these separate dyads do not become integrated into unified or mature concepts of self and of others, as is the case in normal psychological development. Instead, dyads associated with sharply divergent affects (e.g., idealized and persecutory) exist in polarized and chaotic relation to one another, and determine the lack of continuity of the borderline patient's subjective experience of self and others. Furthermore, different dyads may be closer to conscious awareness than others, so that, for example, aggressively laden dyads may form a defensive configuration to protect the individual from awareness of more loving, gratifying representations of self and other, or vice versa.

While the patient has little conscious awareness of this split internal world, this structure underlies the symptoms of borderline personality such as chaos in interpersonal relations, emotional lability, black-and-white thinking, inchoate anger, contradictory behaviors, and proneness to lapses in reality testing.

TFP focuses on the transference because the patient lives out his or her predominant object relations dyads in the transference, as in other relationships. For the borderline patient, splitting leads to instability of the internal world, with chaotic alternating identifications with positive and negative, and idealized and persecutory representations or sectors of experience. The core tasks in TFP are to establish a stable relational context, to identify the patient's predominant internal object relations dyads, and to help him or her observe, modulate, and integrate the split sectors of experience into unified coherent representations of self and other. The therapist's task is to listen to the three channels of communication—the verbal, nonverbal, and countertranferential—and first translate enactments and somatization (nonverbal channels through which borderline patients typically find affective expression without conscious awareness) into the corresponding affects, and then elaborate self and object representations that underlie the affect. As treatment proceeds, these dominant object relations are identified, and the roles of self and object are observed to repeat and reverse multiple times, as well as to appear alongside other dyads.

Hence, as treatment proceeds multiple sets of split-off object relations dyads that are derived from a number of behavioral systems emerge in the transference. These dyads' impulsive or defensive functions must be systematically interpreted in order to be worked through. The combination of understanding and affective experience in the therapy leads to the modulation and integration of the split-off persecutory and gratifying representations, and the creation of an integrated identity and experience of others. By interpreting how the patient is experiencing the interaction at any given moment, and how the patient oscillates between identifying with the self and object aspects of the dyad, the therapist also introduces the observing third. Close monitoring of the countertransference, along with consistent attention to the multiple transference manifestations, fosters a split in the therapist in that one part of the therapist is a full participant in the affective maelstrom of the transference–countertransference relationship while the other part functions as a third, observing presence.

The nature and content of the interpretive process in TFP depends not only on the patient's stage of treatment, but also on his or her individual characteristics, including attachment status and capacity for mentalization, as well on the dynamics of the particular patient–therapist dyad. In the early stages of treatment, clarification and confrontation of split-off self and object representations predominate. The technique of clarification consists of the therapist's inviting the patient to expand his representation of present feeling states or other material, with the goal of becoming more aware of self states and the perceptions of the other in the moment. After clarification of the patient's appreciation of the experience of self and other in the moment, the therapist uses the technique of confrontation to bring attention to contradictions or inconsistencies in the patient's communication. These may be either within the patient's verbal communication, comparing what he expressed at two different points in time, or between the verbal and nonverbal channels of communication at one moment in time. The therapist engages the patient in reflecting on these inconsistencies.

The formulations of Fonagy and colleagues have led us to expand our conceptualization and application of the technique of clarification. For example, in the case of patients who present with psychic deadness and severe affective constriction, or with severe history of trauma, a prolonged phase focusing on the identification, differentiation, and exploration of affect at the verbal and nonverbal level may be necessary. These techniques set the stage for early interpretations that deal with material that is generally conscious or preconscious, with interpretation of unconscious material coming into play only when the patient shows the capacity to make use of it.

TFP thus involves a stepwise interpretive process in which the therapist moves gradually from clarification and confrontation in the early stages to increasingly complex and multifaceted interpretations in the later stages. In the first phase of the interpretative process, interventions tend to be therapist- or analyst-centered (Steiner, 2002) in that they function to identify and articulate the patient's often polarized and inchoate experience of the therapist at any given moment, without exploring it. Such therapist-centered interpretations function to provide cognitive containment for primitive affects that may be elicited as archaic split object relations are activated in the transference. The second phase involves identification of the dominant object relational dyads that are activated in the transference relationship, and of the role reversals that occur as the patient alternately identifies with the self and object aspects of the particular object relation. The concept of the patient ultimately identifying with the entire object relationship rather than just one pole of it is central to TFP. The third phase involves the integration of the split-off, idealized, and persecutory sectors of experience as they emerge in the here-and-now of the transference, and interpretation of how consciously held and prominent object relational dyads may defend against split-off material represented by other dyads (e.g., the aggression-laden dyads defending against gratifying or libidinal dyads). Finally, in the fourth stage object relational dyads and primitive defensive operations that emerge in the transference are linked to unconscious motivations, conflicts, and anxieties, and/or are placed in the context of past relationships. The interpretative process outlined above is epigenetic in nature, but involves repeated cycles involving different levels of interpretation adjusted to the patient's progress toward integration or movement away from it.

Although we believe that the more complex and advanced interpretations are an essential ingredient for integration of the internal world and the resolution of identity diffusion, we also hold to the idea that interpretation of any sort for borderline patients whose primary defense is splitting must deal with conscious self-states that are experienced sequentially in a fragmented way or dissociated. It is only in the later stages of treatment, when the patient's primitive defenses have shifted to more mature ones, and in the context of a more consolidated identity, that interpretation deals with assumed unconscious states and motivations. The focus on unconscious meanings in the here-and-now in the arena of the transference follows Sandler & Sandler's (1987) idea that analysis of "the present unconscious" provides a route to the unconscious template reflecting "the past unconscious." That interpretations of split-off material are made primarily as this material emerges in the arena of the transference insures that they will have immediate affective resonance and that the treatment will not be derailed into intellectual speculation or pseudo-collaboration on the part of the patient. Through systematic attention to the transference, there is a "gradual transformation of pathological character patterns into an emotional experience and self reflection in the transference" (Kernberg, 2004a, p. 126). The therapist's interpretation of the patient's direct affective experience of the therapeutic relationship is viewed as the route to increased integration of the representational world, to the shift from insecure to secure attachment, and to improvements in the capacity for mentalization.

Our interpretative approach is based on the idea that the symbolic function is not totally deficient in borderline patients, most of whom have preserved reality testing and the capacity for abstraction under most circumstances, and are thus able to symbolize except under conditions of intense affect, when symbolization may deteriorate defensively. In our view, symbolization is a cognitive function that does not depend on object relations alone although it is certainly fostered by it. These formulations differ somewhat from those of Fonagy and colleagues, who have hypothesized that borderline patients are inherently deficient in the capacity for symbolization as well as mentalization, and that they therefore are not amenable to an interpretive approach until late in the treatment. According to Fonagy and colleagues, the thinking of borderline patients remains either concrete, functional, and overly attuned to external reality with little capacity to elaborate a separate internal world (psychic equivalence), or, most often, sequestered in a mode of idiosyncratic fantasy (the pretend mode) leading in extreme forms to a sphere of dissociated experience and thinking (Target & Fonagy, 1996). While such formulations enhance our understanding of the developmental underpinnings of borderline disorders, they do not take into account that, even for borderline patients, the fantasy world in the transitional state may be in fact intensely invested emotionally, and that this enlivens rather than deadens the therapeutic interactions.

The question has been raised about whether interpretations of self-object affect dyads as they are mobilized in the transference are beyond the reflective capacities of borderline patients through the initial and mid phases of treatment (Bateman & Fonagy, 2004b; Gabbard, 2006; Gabbard, Horwitz, Allen, Frieswyk, Newsom, et al., 1994). One concern is that if the therapist talks about complex mental states in interpretive work before the later stages of treatment, there will be a pseudo-agreement on the part of the patient without insight or scrutiny; mentalization may appear to improve but it does not lead to changes in behavior or in external relationships. We view such a therapeutic process as the result of badly formulated or poorly timed interpretations. While there are certainly individual differences in the ways borderline patients respond to interpretations at different stages of the treatment— which necessitate a flexible, stepwise interpretative approach as outlined above—our research investigations have shown substantial improvements in borderline patients' capacity for mentalization (as measured by the RF scale), as well as in psychosocial functioning and symptomatology, in the interpretive climate of TFP (see summary of research below).

In TFP the therapist's interpretations of self-object affect dyads as they are activated and expressed in the transference in frequent role reversals are designed to present patients with split-off experiences as they emerge in the transferential situation, leading to increased tolerance of contradictory affects and identifications and an expanded capacity to take mulitiple and diverse perspectives on self and others, and in this way help the patient to acquire a deeper sense of mental states of self and others. This in turn makes the patient more capable of making use of transitional phenomena or transitional modes of relatedness in which internal and external experience are both linked and differentiated. It is important to note that Fonagy and Target (1996) have stipulated that psychoanalytically oriented treatment and psychoanalytic interpretation take place in the pretend mode: "Psychoanalysis is in many respects a 'pretend' experience. Play is essential to it, just as it is essential to our psychoanalytic model of the developing mind. Analyst and patient discuss fantasies, feelings and ideas they 'know' at the same time to be false" (p. 459). While this statement applies to psychoanalytic treatment, it is also in our view applicable to the psychoanalytic psychotherapy of borderline patients, who—in the interpretive climate of TFP—develop, in conjunction with the capacity for mentalization, a tolerance of fantasy and the opening of the transitional space that enables them to understand and play with interpersonal distortions as they emerge in the transference (Clarkin, Yeomans, & Kernberg, 2006).

INTERPRETIVE ACTIVITY AND THE ALIEN SELF

The object relations approach in TFP also has implications for understanding Fonagy and colleagues' (Fonagy et al., 2002) concept of the alien self, defined as an "internalized other" that is "unconnected to the structures of the constitutional self" (Fonagy et al., 2002, p. 358). The alien self represents a self-state that develops in situations when the caregiver's mirroring is neither contingent nor marked, but rather represents the imposition of his or her own self-states onto the child. In such situations, instead of developing a second-order or symbolic representation of his or her own affective states, the child internalizes an alien representation that does not correspond to the constitutional self, is experienced as persecutory, and that thus must be repeatedly externalized or projected onto others in the interest of self stabilization.

From our point of view, what Fonagy calls the alien self is really a composite structure consisting of a highly fantastic, primitive self and a correspondent object representation. In the language of TFP, the alien self is conceptualized as a split-off object relation of a highly negative sort, which coexists with an opposite, highly positive object relation representing a defensive and covering attitude of idealization. In other words, we think the "alien self" concept encapsulates a specific relationship framed by a particular affect state. This alien object relation is split off and activated not just as an alien self, but as an alien self relating to an alien object or bad internal object. The patient will alternatively identify with both while projecting the corresponding other onto the therapist. Thus, transference evokes not just an alien self, but an alien object relation with a constituent self and self representations controlled and distorted by severely negative affect. In our view, it is typical for borderline patients to alternately behave as the alien self, or see the therapist as an alien self; whether they enact it or project it, they are in a complementary role. Through our technique, which fosters the bringing together of split-off experiences, the alien self and its corresponding objects are transformed into self, and respectively, object representations that can be integrated with their opposite. This permits the modulation of affect, particularly the mastery and sublimation of aggressive affects, and the strengthening of cognitive functions, including the beginning of reflective function. (See case illustration for an example.)

In contrast, Fonagy and colleagues stipulate that the emotional truth and valence of the alien self, as an element that colonizes rather than is part of the patient's internal world, must be acknowledged and accepted by the therapist who is in the position of carrying this projection. Accordingly, the therapist's task is to gently question the patient's misperception of the therapist in ways that clarify and validate the perception, while offering an alternative view of the therapist's intentions in the interests of containing and ultimately dissolving the alien self. We agree that clarification of the alien self—or rather, of the object relation that it represents—is the first step. However, in our view, if one tries to dissolve the alien self through containment and other supportive techniques with the assumption that improved mentalization will move the patient beyond it, then one may be neglecting the splitting mechanisms that underlie and characterize the alien self and that may in fact drive conflict into a deeper, less-accessible level.

Finally, according to Fonagy and colleagues, in borderline patients who have experienced trauma, the interpretation of the transference may actually stimulate states of arousal (in both the prefrontal and posterior cortical and subcortical systems) such that the individual shuts down mentalization in the face of increased activation of attachment via the transference. In such cases, interpretations are thought to range from being useless to harmful (Bateman & Fonagy, 2004a). We agree that in such situations—as always—interpretations must be tailored to the patient's capacity to work with them productively. However, the work of LeDoux (1996, 2002) points to the importance of interpretation for the ultimate resolution of trauma. There is neurophysiological evidence that the emotional charge associated with experiences, stored subcortically, cannot change without cortical involvement (LeDoux, 1996, 2002); therefore, a therapy that uses the transference and thus brings such implicit structures into play in an emotionally meaningful way, and utilizes cortical techniques such as transference interpretations, seems not only desirable but arguably a critical component of therapeutic action in the context of trauma.

RESEARCH INVESTIGATIONS

In developing an object relations outpatient treatment for patients with borderline personality disorder, we have systematically followed the steps of treatment development (Kazdin, 2001), including (a) describing the treatment in a manual; (b) investigating the impact of the therapeutic approach on a small group of patients; (c) comparing the clinical progression of these individual treatments to a comparison group that received treatment as usual in the clinic; and finally (d) comparing TFP to other plausible treatments for these patients over a one-year period. For several years we videotaped sessions with borderline patients conducted by senior clinicians in our group, and gradually developed our principles of treatment that are explicated in a treatment manual (Clarkin, Yeomans, & Kernberg, 1999, 2006). This process of developing and refining the manual, along with the initial empirical investigations, has been has been delineated in detail elsewhere (Clarkin, Levy, & Schiavi, 2005).

Encouraged by the positive results of our initial studies of TFP (Clarkin et al., 2001; Levy, Clarkin, Foelsch, & Kernberg, 2004), which showed large effect sizes, we embarked upon a randomized clinical trial (RCT) of TFP (Clarkin, Levy, Lenzenweger, & Kernberg, 2004, 2007), in which borderline patients were randomly assigned to one-year ambulatory treatment with TFP, DBT, or a psychodynamic supportive treatment. This RCT of psychotherapy of BPD patients, which was funded by the Borderline Research Foundation (O. Kernberg and J. Clarkin, Co-PIs) and NIMH (K. Levy, PI), is unique in a number of ways. Perhaps most importantly, we examined not only symptom change, emphasized in most studies, but also changes in the organization of the personality as reflected in such domains as mentalization (reflective functioning) and identity.

Preliminary results indicate that patients in all three treatments showed significant clinical change in many domains at the end of one year of treatment, including diminution of depression and anxiety and improved psychosocial or interpersonal functioning (Clarkin, Levy, Lenzenweger, & Kernberg, 2007). Patients in both TFP and DBT fared significantly better in the domain of suicidality, while only patients in TFP showed a marked diminution of factors related to aggression such as impulsivity and verbal and direct assault (Clarkin et al., 2007).

We were also interested in examining the mechanisms of change; that is, how does TFP bring about change, as compared to the other treatments? For these investigations, we used the reflective functioning score (RF), an attachment-based index of mentalization obtained from the Adult Attachment Interview (AAI, George, Kaplan, & Main, 1998) given prior to and after one year of treatment for patients in all treatment conditions. The AAI

(George, Kaplan, & Main, 1998) is a semistructured interview designed to assess the individual's state of mind with respect to early attachment relationships and experiences. It provides an index to attachment representations of self and others. Interviews are classified into one of five attachment categories: secure, preoccupied, dismissing, unresolved for loss and trauma, and cannot classify (Main & Goldwyn, 1998). Interviews are also rated for Reflective Function (Fonagy et al., 1997) on the 11-point RF scale, which ranges from −1, or active repudiation or bizarre formulations of mental states, to 9, or the formulation of unusual, highly elaborated, original, and multifaceted depictions of mental states of self and others, with a midpoint of 5, which shows a clear, explicit (if somewhat ordinary) capacity to think in mental state terms. After one year of treatment, RF increased significantly in a positive direction for the patients in the TFP group, but did not change for patients either in the DBT or the supportive treatment groups (Levy, Meehan et al., 2006). In addition, patients in all three groups improved in the coherence of their narratives about early attachment experiences on the AAI, although the TFP group improved the most, with scores after one year in the near average range (Main & Goldwyn, 1998). We will now turn from this global picture of overall group effects to examine specific clinical aspects of one case.

CLINICAL ILLUSTRATION OF IMPROVEMENT IN MENTALIZATION: THE CASE OF SARA

Sara, a single, unemployed Asian-American woman, started TFP at age 36 after many years in other treatments. Her condition had worsened to the point where she spent the six months prior to beginning TFP isolated in her apartment, lying in bed with chronic suicidal ideation, binge eating, and only rarely bathing. Sara was the middle of three daughters in an upper middle class family. Although Sara described her father as emotionally absent and preoccupied with his legal career, she also experienced him as obsessed with his children's educational performance to the point of abusing them verbally and sometimes physically if they did not perform up to expectations. She described her mother as an emotionally unstable woman whose frequent panic attacks made her unable to consistently care for her children. The patient dropped out of college and then held a series of jobs, but was repeatedly fired because of interpersonal difficulties that often involved her perception of others as hostile or negative toward her. She stopped working when news of her belligerent character kept her from being hired. The patient understood her conflictual relations with others as the result solely of racial discrimination. She had no history of sexual relations except for one occasion when a man she had dated three times began to make love to her. She panicked, stopped the interaction before intercourse, and later brought formal rape charges against him. Sara had a limited history of overt self-destructiveness, cutting herself superficially on occasion, but had persistent wishes to kill herself. She had had three psychiatric hospitalizations and had been diagnosed with bipolar disorder. She had been on many medications, all of which were discontinued during the first year of TFP.

In the research evaluation, she met criteria not only for borderline personality disorder, but also for narcissistic and avoidant personality disorders on the International Personality Disorders Examination (IPDE, Loranger, 1999; Loranger, Sartorius, Andreoli, & Berger, 1994), and she met SCID-I (First, Gibbon, Spitzer, & Williams, 1996) criteria for current dysthymia. Her reflective functioning (RF) score prior to the initiation of treatment was minus one (−1), indicating that she actively repudiated any consideration of mental states of self and other, and showed cognitive disorganization and confusion in the face of questions designed to elicit reflection on mental states. In the few instances in which she spoke in RF terms, she gave unintegrated and bizarre responses. On the Adult Attachment Interview (AAI) she showed contradictory and inconsistent states of mind with respect to attachment, shifting chaotically between dismissive devaluation of early attachment figures, and angry preoccupation with parental objects with whom she was emotionally entangled, leading to an attachment classification of Cannot Classify, with mixed Preoccupied and Dismissing states of mind (CC/E2/D2). Finally on the Inventory of Personality Organization (IPO) (Lenzenweger, Clarkin, Kernberg, & Foelsch, 2001), she scored very high on identity diffusion, and high on primitive defenses, compromised reality testing, and aggression.

From the first session, Sara's interactions with her therapist were characterized by a nonstop monologue that blocked his participation in the therapy. If he tried to speak, she spoke over him. His first interventions consisted of clarification of this self-state. In the initial sessions, he directed her attention to this behavior, offered a description of it, and wondered with her what might motivate this way of interacting, which appeared designed to exert control over him. Sara tearfully responded that if she did not control him, he would leave. Such interventions brought into focus a dyad—that of the abandoner and the abandonee, with the abandonee trying to prevent abandonment by controlling the other. It was only after repeated clarification of this dynamic in the context of the therapeutic relationship that Sara was able to sort out the feelings of anger and fear of abandonment that fueled her controlling behavior and begin to question her view of the therapist. With a clearer articulation of her experience of self and other, she began to occasionally notice that, while she chronically complained of others treating her harshly and rejecting her, she could treat others, including her therapist, in a similar way; this was the beginning of understanding her projection of aggressive affects within her, as the process became apparent in observing the oscillations of a dyad involving a harsh critic and the object of the criticism. So, in the initial phases of therapy Sara became able first to articulate how she saw the therapist, to consider that he might have a different state of mind than that which she attributed to him, and then to recognize that she could behave in the way she had experienced him behaving.

In a session that took place six months into the first year of treatment, Sara initially presented with a similar defensive structure, but was able more quickly to reflect on the interaction and consider other perspectives. She began by stating that she had been feeling suicidal and had taken a minor overdose. As the therapist tried to understand the affect and the fantasied relationship motivating her suicidal gesture, Sara said: "My wanting to kill myself has nothing to do with your going away." (The therapist was leaving for a week.) The therapist pointed out that Sara had made this connection herself and that it may be humiliating to care so much about him when she felt he did not care about her.

She replied: "You say the same thing to every one of your patients! I'm not like all of them!"

Therapist: "You feel like you're one on an assembly line."

Sara: [with sudden change of affect, from angry to sad]: "I don't feel that I deserve to be here . . . I don't know [patient covers her face with her hands]. I just feel badly that I have to walk around with other human beings. I just don't feel like . . ."

Therapist: "I think you don't want me to see you in the longing that you feel. You don't mind if I see you in your anger and your rejection of me. You don't want me to see the longing, because you think I'll just use that to humiliate you, by rejecting, by turning away from you."

The therapist then suggested that her fear of rejection could explain the off-putting way in which she interacted: she might induce rejection to feel she controlled it.

Sara: "You mean because I think that rejection is inevitable I try to confirm it, like by dressing this way? I just feel like the tragedy of everything, of all of this, is that I have help available . . . You're actually working with me . . ."

The oscillation or alternative distribution of the roles of the dyad noted above must be differentiated from the split between opposite dyads carrying polarized affective charges. The final step of interpretation consists in linking of the dissociated positive and negative transferences, leading to an integration of the mutually split-off idealized and persecutory segments of experience with the corresponding resolution of identity diffusion. As Sara shifted from her discussion of wanting to kill herself to what she was feeling toward her therapist, she moved from a dyad imbued with negative affect that served defensive purposes (the harsh critical object rejecting the helpless unworthy self) to a dyad imbued with positive affect. She continued "I guess there's a longing in a way, 'cause I did come on time, I didn't really want to come, but I do long to come here, in a way, I guess I do. And it's not the same thing between seeing Dr. Smith and you. I'm more attached to you than I was to him. . . . I like you more. . . . I remember this boy in high school. There weren't many Asian-American students there. . . . I was one of the only ones. . . . I never thought he'd speak to me. One day . . ."

Her questioning and relinquishment of her chronic defensive belligerent stance toward others can be understood in relation to Sara's having begun to "take back" and metabolize the negative affects she had consistently projected onto others, which in turn allowed her to experience other more positive and nuanced states of mind with regard to herself and the therapist. Her therapist's approach was to ask her to reflect on these shifting states as they played out between them. Thus, the therapeutic work focused on clarifying which part of her experience belonged to the other person and which part to her self, ultimately expanding her capacity to experience a range of mental states with respect to self and therapist.

In her external life, Sara's complaints of mistreatment decreased. She reported less anxiety and more positive interactions in her volunteer work setting, where she was offered a paid position. With regard to intimate and sexual relations, in the period of time when Sara was still utilizing primitive defense mechanisms—omnipotent control and projective identification— she was attracted to a narcissistic, unavailable man into whom she had deposited her critical judgmental part. An erotic transference emerged fitfully during the first year of treatment, first in moments of seductive posture and only rarely verbalized. Her mention of sexual feelings alternated between shame and a sense of danger. In the course of treatment, as she progressed in taking back projected anger and hostility, she started a relationship with and eventually married (after three years of therapy) a more appropriate loving and empathic man.

The work described so far took place mostly in the first year of therapy. It is interesting to look more closely at the AAI that was given at admission and at the one given after this year of TFP. As mentioned previously, on the AAI, Sara advanced from a reflective functioning score of minus one (−1), to a score of 6, which indicates not only the capacity to form stable and multifaceted mental models of the minds of self and other, but also some flashes of complex and original thinking about mental states of self and others. A comparison of Sara's responses to the AAI question *"How do you think your childhood experiences have affected your adult personality?"* at time 1 and time 2 illustrate the dramatic increase in her capacity for mentalization and coherence. At time 1, she gave a response that began with some explicit references to mental states in that she wondered what she would have been like if she had had parents who assured her that "nothing bad was going to happen," but became increasingly bizarre, incoherent, and even shocking— a hallmark of deficient RF—as she veered off into describing a movie she saw as a child with her father in which a woman is tricked and raped.

> I think that if somebody had been in my room, put me to sleep, and assured me that there was nothing bad going to happen, I think a lot of this stuff would have gone all right, I don't think I would be talking about all of this . . . My dad and I, we went to

a movie once . . . and it was a movie about this woman. . . . and um, the woman that I remembered upset me a lot. And I was about, maybe third or fourth grade then. It was about this woman—she's married, and she goes to this party, and um, her friend—and her husband doesn't come with her to the party. And her friend says, well you know, [you] like this guy, he'll take [you] home . . . He doesn't exactly take her home. He rapes her.

After one year of TFP, Sara responds to the questions with a multifaceted, coherent response that not only explores the impact of her parents' behaviors on her mental states, but also shows recognition of the role her own mental state might have had on her choices and behavior.

Oh my God, my adult personality. . . . I really don't buy that argument that . . . I was born overly sensitive I don't think so. . . . Not when I can remember experiences as far back as like 3 years old and my parents not being there. . . . They didn't take an interest in us. . . . I didn't live up to my potential . . . so I may have had dreams and wishes and I had the potential to do it but I just couldn't do it like now . . . certainly my life is so much better now. . . . I regret the fact that I'm 37 and I only found this program at 36 . . .

This response shows the development of a stable coherent model of the mind of self and parents along with a transactional perspective on mental states—that is, the way in which her mental states were shaped not only by biological predisposition but by her reactions to the parent's mental states and behaviors.

While the patient's reflective functioning went from −1 to +6 as rated in the AAI after one year of TFP, the therapist reported variability in her capacity for mentalizing in the therapy sessions. His clinical impression was that the patient was more capable of reflection in situations of stability, but would regress to unreflective thinking under the influence of primitive defense mechanisms in threatening situations. Sara's reflective capacities faltered when sexual feelings arose in sessions. She often directed seductive looks or gestures toward her therapist without any capacity to talk about the meaning of her nonverbal behavior. Periodically she would burst out with a comment that he wanted to force her to talk about sex. When he wondered about this impression, she either referred to her experience with the man she had accused of rape, an accusation she began to question, or talked about her own sexually aggressive behavior toward her sister when they were prepubertal. It was only after the emergence and working through of an erotic transference that she was able to integrate loving and sexual feelings.

AN EXPANDED VIEW OF MENTALIZATION

Detailed examination of our clinical process and outcome data has led us to identify three phases in the development of mentalization. In this section we present a theoretical model that links these three phases to the interpretive process that characterizes TFP. In our view, mentalization is a process whereby, sequentially, the individual develops (a) the capacity to know that he or she has a mind that is like another; (b) the capacity to think about the other in mental state terms and to recognize one's own mental states in the mental states of the other; and (c) the capacity to observe his or her own mind as if it is another mind, which involves placing mental states of self and other in a wider historical and temporal context where understanding in the moment is linked to a broader set of integrated positive and negative representations of self and others. Working independently, Semerari and colleagues (Semerari et al., 2003) identified three phases in the attainment of mentalizing capacities including (1) understanding one's own mind; (2) understanding the mind of the other; and (3) mastery of mental states. Each of these levels of mentalization is reflected in the level and aim of the interpretative activity of the therapist in TFP and in the progression of changes in object relations and ego and superego development that occur in TFP treatment.

The first phase of mentalization involves the capacity to cognitively frame mental states out of diffuse psychic experience. The capacity to cognitively clarify mental states in one's own mind develops in early life via the child's experience of congruent, marked interactions. In the therapeutic situation, the first step in the development of the capacity for mentalization involves helping the patient to understand her own state of mind, through identifying initially how she sees the therapist, a process that is referred to in TFP as tolerating the confusion and clarification. It is also important for the therapist to introduce the idea that it is possible that he or she may have a different state of mind than that which the patient attributes to him or her. The patient's realization that her perception of the therapist does not necessarily correspond to what is in the therapist's mind enables her to learn that there is a discrepancy between her own mind and that of the other. Thus, the therapeutic task involves helping the patient to accurately identify the affect that is being experienced in the immediate interaction with the therapist, and to recognize that these polarized affects are linked to specific representations of self in interaction with others. In borderline patients, this understanding can transform an action powered by an unarticulated and split-off affect into an understanding of self and other in the momentary experience so that the patient can tolerate and modify the affect without the need to discharge it immediately into action. In our case illustration, for example, Sara's coming to awareness of her relentless attempts to control the interaction with the therapist, and the way that this represented an avoidance of split-off fear and rage linked to an object relational dyad of a powerless, devalued self in interaction with a controlling, rejecting object, epitomizes the first level of mentalization.

At the second level of mentalization, the patient recognizes that he or she experiences the therapist in quite disparate and even opposite ways that cannot be reconciled. Further, the patient realizes that some of her mental states regarding the therapist correspond to states that she had previously perceived in the therapist, while the therapist is perceived as experiencing a state akin to what the patient formerly experienced. This involves the recognition that aspects that she attributed to the object actually represent aspects of the self. At this stage the awareness of the alternation or interchange of roles within the same object relational constellation is crucial. The therapeutic task at this phase is to help the patient to understand and tolerate the double identification with self and object representations, through interpretation of the many repetitions and reversals of specific object relational dyads as they emerge in the transferential relationship, and to interpret the splitting of the libidinal from the aggressive aspects of self as represented by different dyads. The patient's alternation between identification with self and object representations of a particular dyad infused with a particular affect leads to an expanded understanding of the mind of the other as well as her own mind in that it enables her to recognize that her mind is representational in nature; that is, that her experience of self and others is shaped in part by myriad mental models of self in relation to others. In the case illustration, interpretation of Sara's attempt to omnipotently control the supposed rejecting other led to an awareness of rejecting and critical elements in herself, and this identification with both poles of the dyad enabled her to take back the projection, clearing the way for more libidinally charged gratifying experience of the self in relation to the therapist to emerge, and for integration of her disparate experiences of self and object.

The process of identifying the various self-object-affect clusters or dyads that emerge in relation to the therapist in TFP, along with increased awareness of and tolerance for identifications with both aspects of each dyad, leads to increasing integration of the representational world and a concomitant modulation of affective experience, which sets the stage for the third phase in the development of mentalization. This stage involves the capacity to integrate and modulate the positive and negative segments of experience, which occurs when the patient recognizes that he or she experiences loving and aggressive feelings toward the same person, and that these contradictory states correspond to divisions in his or her own internal world (Klein, 1946, 1957). The recognition that the individual can have completely opposite feelings toward the same person—feelings that he or she may have previously attributed to that person—enables the individual to feel a sense of responsibility over aggressive or negative feelings or states, instead of having to project them. This leads to the development of a sense of concern about the object that the individual wants to preserve.

The emergence of the sense of concern and of responsibility for others sets the stage for the development of superego functions. Insofar as the superego derives from the awareness of the effects of the internalized prohibitions and demands of others, it consists of mental states. The capacity to connect disparate mental states with each other and with their historical antecedents enables one to understand how mental states that derive from the demands and prohibitions of others can be compared with other states. Mental states that involve awareness of parental prohibitions and strictures are recognized as only one set of mental states among others. This recognition in turn expands conscious awareness and tolerance of mental states that might engender conflict. Mentalization thus leads to improved functioning in the sexual realm, in that it enables one to recognize that states linked to intense passion and/or erotic excitement are transient heightened mental states in which one experiences reality differently, while the capacity to correctly identify—and identify with—the mental states of the other, enhances sexual passion.

Sara provides an example of a patient with excessively persecutory and prohibitive superego elements accompanied by a severe inhibition in sexual functioning, which was significantly modified in the course of treatment. At the beginning of treatment she represented all sexual relationships, when she allowed herself to think of them, in the most primitive form—that of exploiter and exploited. As her reflective capacities improved in the course of treatment, this patient was able to establish and sustain a fully intimate emotional erotic relationship in which tenderness and sexuality were integrated. The progress in this area paralleled her integrating projected aggressive elements of herself, but with a delay. Even after she was able to understand the relation between her fear of verbal attacks from others and the capacity she discovered in herself for angry criticism and rejection, sexual feelings remained a source of anxiety. Her anxiety was related not only to the aggressive elements that her sexual feelings carried, but also to her fear of lack of control; she worried that sexual feelings would lead to uncontrolled promiscuity. Sara anticipated condemnation each time these came up, and a lengthy and intermittent period of interpretation of her fear of her desires and their imagined consequences eventually led to her ability to enjoy sex and sexual fantasies.

As mentioned above, clinical observation, as in the case of Sara, suggests that RF is variable across different self and object representations that may be evoked in response to the activation of different behavioral systems. It may be that the attachment relationship between patient and therapist is well consolidated in the early to mid phases of treatment, leading to a substantial increase in mentalization, but if later what emerges in the transference is a recapitulation of an eroticized or seductive relationship with an early attachment figure, or aggression, then mentalization may decrease. Different levels of mentalization thus may be activated in response to the activation of different behavioral systems (e.g., attachment and sexuality). In our case illustration, the patient's capacity for reflective function was noted by the therapist to be variable through the later stages of treatment; it diminished markedly when an erotic transference developed, even though her RF improved significantly in the context of a discussion of early attachment experiences on the AAI at one year.

SUMMARY AND CONCLUSION

Our research and clinical findings suggest that after one year of TFP, borderline patients show significant improvement in their capacity for mentalization (as indicated by increases in RF ratings described above), an improvement in their capacity to create a coherent autobiographical narrative (as indicated by the increase in coherence subscale scores of the AAI), and a decrease on measures of aggression (Clarkin et al., 2007; Levy, Meehan, et al., 2006). That these gains occurred primarily in the interpretive climate of TFP, and not in either DBT or supportive psychodynamic psychotherapy (STP)—one of which (STP) also used psychodynamic techniques (but not interpretation)—suggests that the described improvement in RF may be in part a result of specific techniques in TFP not present in the other treatments. Our hypothesis is that the improvements in the complexity and integration of the Reflective Function scores are a result in part of the interpretative process that is unique to TFP. In this process, the therapist moves from defining the dominant object relations, identifying role reversals between self and object poles of the object relational dyads as they occur in the transference, and confronting splitting of idealized from persecutory aspects of self in different dyads, to then offering a hypothesis about why it occurs and gradually linking these primitive defensive operations to unconscious wishes, fears, and motivations. This interpretive process leads to the gradual integration of disparate, split-off self and object representations into an overarching stable concept of the self and objects. We propose that the consolidation of identity in turn fosters mentalization in that it provides a stable and consistent working model of self and others against which momentary mental states, even those that are affect- or drive-laden, can be assessed and evaluated.

Further investigation of other factors in the treatment that might account for gains in RF will have to be conducted before we can definitely link the improvement in RF to the increasingly complex interpretive focus that is unique to our treatment. In support of our formulations are the recent investigations of Høglend and colleagues (Høglend et al., 2006), which showed that transference interpretations were more helpful for patients with more severe pathology of object relations. Ultimately, however, as Gabbard (2006), Blatt (1992), and others have pointed out, the challenge is to refine our understanding of the particular characteristics that might make patients more or less amenable to different therapeutic approaches.

Our use of the RF measure to assess mechanisms of change in TFP has made us more aware of the strengths and limitations of the instrument at both the theoretical and empirical level. Our research and clinical investigations suggest that mentalization is a complex and multistaged process that involves transformations in cognitive and affective ego and superego structures. In particular, our findings on improvements in mentalization in TFP lend support to the idea that a focus on the identification, articulation, and regulation of affect, and the ways that it is linked to specific constellations of self and object representations, is a significant catalyst for understanding mental states. In our view, the development of the capacity for mentalization, along with the development of secure attachment with which it is linked, are cumulative processes that reflect the building up, modulation, and integration of object relations. These complex processes, particularly the affective components of RF that cannot be disconnected from object relationships, are not necessarily captured by one reflective function global rating. Thus, the RF scale as it is now constituted reduces to one numerical score a complex array of variables. In addition, mentalization may fluctuate markedly within the same individual as different behavioral systems are evoked in individual maturation, in different interpersonal contexts, and at different stages in treatment. As Fonagy (Fonagy et al., 2002) and others have noted (Diamond et al., 2003; Yeomans et al., in press), borderline patients can be reflective under certain circumstances and not under others. It is not clear that the AAI interview, from which the RF rating is derived, captures or addresses the situations and issues that are particularly difficult for the individual patient, and that may lead to lapses in mentalization. The above formulations are offered in the interests of advancing the fruitful dialogue between MBT and TFP, two psychodynamic perspectives on borderline pathology and its treatment that continue to enrich and enhance each other. An honest assessment and exploration of points of contact and divergence can only lead to increased precision in our treatment approaches and their theoretical underpinnings.

ACKNOWLEDGMENTS

The research presented in this article was supported by grants from the National Endowment of Mental Health (Grant No. MH53705, John F. Clarkin, P.I., Kenneth N. Levy, P.I.); the NIMH (Grant No. R21MH53705-01, John Clarkin, P.I.); The International Psychoanalytical Association's Research Advisory Board (Grant No. 75159-00 01, Diana Diamond, P.I, Kenneth N. Levy, Co-P.I.); the Research Foundation of the City of New York (RF-CUNY Research Fund, Grant No. 6269-1-0031, Diana Diamond, P.I.); and the Kohler-Stifung Foundation of Munich (Kenneth N. Levy, P.I.; Diana Diamond, Otto Kernberg, and Pamela Foelsch, Co-PIs). We gratefully acknowledge the contributions of our colleagues in the Personality Disorders Institute at Weill Medical College of Cornell University, including Ann Appelbaum, Eve Caligor, Monica Carsky, Jill Delaney, Pamela Foelsch, Kay Haran, James Hull, and Michael Stone.

REFERENCES

Allen, J. (2003). Mentalizing. *Bulletin of the Menninger Clinic, 67,* 91–112.

Bateman, A., & Fonagy, P. (1999). Effectiveness of partial hospitalization in the treatment of borderline personality disorder: A randomized controlled trial. *American Journal of Psychiatry,* 156, 1563–1569.

Bateman, A., & Fonagy, P. (2001). Treatment of borderline personality disorder with psychoanalytically oriented partial hospitalization: An 18 month follow-up. *American Journal of Psychiatry, 158,* 36–42.

Bateman, A., & Fonagy, P. (2003). The development of an attachment-based treatment program for borderline personality disorder. *Bulletin of the Menninger Clinic, 67,* 187–211.

Bateman, A., & Fonagy, P. (2004a). *Psychotherapy for borderline personality disorder: Mentalization-based treatment.* New York: Oxford University Press.

Bateman, A., & Fonagy, P. (2004b). Mentalization-based treatment of BPD. *Journal of Personality Disorders, 18*(1), 36–51.

Bion, W. R. (1962). A theory of thinking. *International Journal of Psycho-Analysis, 43*, 306–310.

Bion, W. R. (1967). *Second Thoughts.* London: Karnac.

Bion, W. R. (1970). *Attention and Interpretation.* London: Tavistock.

Blatt, S. J. (1992). The differential effect of psychotherapy and psychoanalysis on anaclitic and introjective patients: The Menninger Psychotherapy Research Project revisited. *Journal of the American Psychoanalytic Association, 40*, 691–724.

Carpendale, J. M., and Lewis, C. (2004). Constructing an understanding of mind: The development of children's social understanding within social interaction. *Behavioral and Brain Sciences, 27*, 79–151.

Clarkin, J. F., Foelsch, P. A., Levy, K. N., Hull, J. W., Delaney, J. C., & Kernberg, O. F. (2001). The development of a psychoanalytic treatment for patients with borderline personality disorder: A preliminary study of behavioral change. *Journal of Personality Disorders, 15*, 487–495.

Clarkin, J. F., & Levy, K. N. (2003). A psychodynamic treatment for severe personality disorders: Issues in treatment development. *Psychoanalytic Inquiry, 23*(2), 248–267.

Clarkin, J. F., Levy, K. N., Lenzenweger, M. F., & Kernberg, O. F. (2004). The Personality Disorders Institute/Borderline Personality Disorder Research Foundation randomized control trial for borderline personality disorder: Rationale, methods, and patient characteristics. *Journal of Personality Disorders, 18*(1), 52–72.

Clarkin, J. F., & Posner, M. (2005). Defining the mechanisms of borderline personality disorder. *Psychopathology, 38*, 56–63.

Clarkin, J. F., Levy, K. N., & Schiavi, J. M. (2005). Transference focused psychotherapy: Development of a psychodynamic treatment for severe personality disorders. *Clinical Neuroscience Research, 4*, 379–386.

Clarkin, J. F., Yeomans, F., & Kernberg, O .S. (1999). *Transference-focused Psychodynamic Therapy for Borderline Personality Disorder Patients.* New York: Wiley.

Clarkin, J. F., Yeomans, F., & Kernberg, O. F. (2006). *Psychotherapy for borderline personality: Focusing on object relations.* Washington, DC: American Psychiatric Publishing.

Clarkin, J. F., Levy, K. N., Lenzenweger, M. F., & Kernberg, O. F. (2007). Evaluating three treatments for borderline personality disorder: A multiwave study. *American Journal of Psychiatry, 164*, 1–8.

Depue, R. A., & Lenzenweger, M. F. (2005). A neurobehavioral dimensional model of personality disturbance. In M. Lenzenweger & J. F. Clarkin (Eds.), *Major Theories of Personality Disorder* (2nd ed., pp. 391–453). New York: Guilford.

Diamond, D. & Blatt, S. J. (1994). Internal working models of attachment and psychoanalytic theories of the representational world: A comparison and critique. In M. Sperling & W. Berman (Eds.), *Attachment in Adults: Clinical and Developmental Perspectives* (pp. 72–97). New York: Guilford.

Diamond, D., Stovall-McClough, C., Clarkin, J. F., & Levy, K. N. (2003). Patient–therapist attachment in the treatment of borderline personality disorder. *Bulletin of the Menninger Clinic, 67*(3):224–257.

First, M. B., Gibbon, M., Spitzer, R. L., & Williams, J. B. W. (1996). User's guide for the Structured Clinical Interview for DSM-IV Axis I Research Version (SCID-1), version 2.0. New York: New York State Psychiatric Institute, Biometrics Research.

Fonagy, P. (1999, April). The process of change and the change of processes: What can change in a "good analysis." Keynote Address to the Spring Meeting of Division 39 of the American Psychological Association, New York.

Fonagy, P. (in press). The mentalization approach to social development. In F. Busch (Ed.). *Mentalization: Theoretical Considerations, Research Findings, and Clinical Implications.* New York: Analytic Press.

Fonagy, P., Leigh, T., Steele, M., Steele, H., Kennedy, R., Mattoon, G., Target, M., & Gerber, A. (1996). The relation of attachment status, psychiatric classification and response to psychotherapy. *Journal of Consulting and Clinical Psychology, 64,* 2–31.

Fonagy, P., & Target, M. (1996). Playing with reality: I. Theory of mind and the normal development of psychic reality. *International Journal of Psycho-Analysis, 77,* 217–233.

Fonagy, P., Target, M., Steele, H., & Steele, M. (1997). Reflective Functioning Manual: Version 5. For application to Adult Attachment Interviews. London: University College.

Fonagy, P., Gergely, G., Jurist, E. L., & Target, M. (2002). *Affect Regulation, Mentalization, and the Development of the Self.* New York: Other Press.

Gabbard, G. O. (2006) When is transference work useful in dynamic psychotherapy? *American Journal of Psychiatry, 163,* 1667–1669.

Gabbard, G. O., Horwitz, L., Allen, J. G., Frieswyk, S., Newsom, G., et al. (1994). Transference interpretation in the psychotherapy of borderline patients: A high-risk, high-gain phenomenon. *Harvard Review of Psychiatry, 2,* 59–69.

George, C., Kaplan, N., & Main, M. (1998). The Berkeley Adult Attachment Interview. Unpublished manuscript, Department of Psychology, University of California, Berkeley.

Gergely, G., & Unoka, Z. (in press). The development of the unreflective self. In F. Busch (Ed.), *Mentalization: Theoretical Considerations, Research Findings, and Clinical Implications.* New York: Analytic Press.

Høglend, P., Amlo, S., Marble, A., Bøgwald, K., Sørbye, Ø., Cosgrove Sjaastad, M., & Heyerdahl, O. (2006). Analysis of the patient–therapist relationship in dynamic psychotherapy: An experimental study of transference interpretations. *American Journal of Psychiatry, 163,* 1739–1746.

Jurist, E. (2005). Mentalized affectivity. *Psychoanalytic Psychology, 22*(3):426–444.

Kazdin, A. E. (2001). Bridging the enormous gaps of theory with therapy research and practice. *Journal of Clinical Child Psychology, 30,* 9–66.

Kernberg, O. F. (1980). *Internal World and External Reality: Object Relations Theory Applied.* New York: Jason Aronson.

Kernberg, O. (1984). *Severe Personality Disorders: Psychotherapeutic Strategies.* New Haven, CT: Yale University Press.

Kernberg, O. (2004a). *Aggressivity, Narcissism, and Self Destructiveness in the Psychotherapeutic Relationship: New Developments in the Psychopathology and Psychotherapy of Severe Personality Disorders.* New Haven, CT: Yale University Press.

Kernberg, O. F. (2004b). Borderline personality disorder and borderline personality organization: Psychopathology and psychotherapy. In J. Magnavita (Ed.), *Handbook of Personality Disorders: Theory and Practice* (pp. 92–119). Hoboken, NJ: Wiley.

Kernberg, O. F. (2006). Recent findings and clinical implications. *Psychoanalytic Quarterly, 75,* 969–1004.

Klein, M. (1946). Notes on some schizoid mechanisms. In J. Riviere (Ed.), *Developments in Psychoanalysis* (pp. 311–338). London: Hogarth Press, 1952.

Klein, M. (1957). *Envy and Gratitude.* New York: Basic Books.

LeDoux, J. E. (1996). *The Emotional Brain.* New York: Simon and Schuster.

LeDoux, J. E. (2002). *Synaptic Self: How Our Brains Become Who We Are.* New York: Viking.

Lenzenweger, M. F., Clarkin, J. F., Kernberg, O. F., & Foelsch, P. A. (2001). The Inventory of Personality Organization: Psychometric properties, factorial composition, and criterion relations, with affect, aggressive dyscontrol, psychosis-proneness, and self domains in a nonclinical sample. *Psychological Assessment, 13,* 577–591.

Levy, K. N., Clarkin, J. F., Foelsch, P. A., & Kernberg, O. F. (2004). Transference-focused psychotherapy for patients diagnosed with borderline personality disorder: A comparison with a treatment-as-usual cohort. Manuscript in review.

Levy, K. N., Clarkin, J. F., Yeomans, F. E., Scott, L. N., Wasserman, R. H., & Kernberg, O. F. (2006). The mechanisms of change in the treatment of borderline personality disorder with transference focused psychotherapy. *Journal of Clinical Psychology, 62,* 481–501.

Levy, K. N., Meehan, K. B., Kelly, K. M., Reynoso, J. S., Clarkin, J. F., Lenzenweger, M. F., & Kernberg, O. F. (2006). Change in attachment and reflective function in the treatment of borderline personality disorder with transference focused psychotherapy. *Journal of Consulting and Clinical Psychology, 74,* 1027–1040.

Linehan, M. M. (1993). *Cognitive-behavioral Treatment of Borderline Personality Disorder.* New York: Guilford.

Linehan, M. M., Armstrong, H. E., Suarez, A., Allmon, D., & Heard, H. L. (1991). Cognitive-behavioral treatment of chronically parasuicidal borderline patients. *Archives of General Psychiatry, 48,* 1060–1064.

Linehan, M. M., Comtois, K. A., Murray, A. M., Brown, M. Z., Gallup, R. J., et al. (2006). Two-year randomized controlled trial and follow-up of dialectical behavior therapy vs. therapy by experts for suicidal behaviors and borderline personality disorder. *Archives of General Psychiatry, 63,* 757–766.

Linehan, M. M., Kanter, J. W., & Comtois, K. A. (1999). Dialectical behavior therapy for borderline personality disorder: Efficacy, specificity, and cost effectiveness. In D. S. Janowsky (Ed.), *Psychotherapy indications and outcomes* (pp. 93–118). Washington, DC: American Psychiatric Association.

Loranger, A. (1999). *International Personality Disorder Examination (IPDE) manual.* Odessa, FL: Psychological Assessment Resources, Inc.

Lenzenweger, M. F., Loranger, A. W., Korfine, L., & Neff, C. (1997). Detecting personality disorders in a nonclinical population: Application of a 2-stage procedure for case identification. *Archives of General Psychiatry, 54,* 345–351.

Loranger, A. W., Sartorius, N., Andreoli, A., & Berger, P. (1994). The international personality disorder examination: The World Health Organization/Alcohol, Drug Abuse, and Mental Health Administration international pilot study of personality disorders. *Archives of General Psychiatry, 51,* 215.

Main, M., & Goldwyn, R. (1998). Adult attachment scoring and classifications system. Unpublished scoring manual. Department of Psychology, University of California, Berkeley.

Paris, J. (1994). *Borderline Personality Disorder.* Washington DC: American Psychiatric Press.

Paris, J. (1999). Borderline Personality Disorder. In T. Millon, P. H. Blaney, & R. D. Davis (Eds.), *Oxford Textbook of Psychopathology* (pp. 625–652). New York: Oxford University Press.

Posner, M. I., Rothbart, M. K., Vizueta, N., Thomas, K. M., Levy, K. N., Fossella, J., et al. (2003). An approach to the psychobiology of personality disorders. *Development and Psychopathology, 15,* 1093–1106.

Sandler, J., & Sandler, A. (1987). The past unconscious, the present unconscious, and the vicissitudes of guilt. *International Journal of Psycho-Analysis, 8,* 331–341.

Sandler, J., & Sandler, A. (1998). *Internal Objects Revisited.* Madison, CT: International Universities Press.

Semerari, A., Carcione, A., Dimaggio, G., Falcone, M., Nicolo, G., Procacci, M., et al. (2003). How to evaluate metacognitive functioning in psychotherapy? The Metacognition Assessment Scale and its applications. *Clinical Psychology and Psychotherapy, 10,* 238–261.

Steiner, J. (2002). *Psychic retreats.* London: Brunner Routledge.

Stone, M. (1994). Etiology of borderline personality disorder: Psychobiological factors contributing to an underlying irritability. In J. Paris (Ed.), *Borderline Personality Disorder* (pp. 87–102). Washington, DC: American Psychiatric Press.

Target, M., & Fonagy, P. (1996). Playing with reality. II: The development of psychic reality from a theoretical perspective. *International Journal of Psycho-Analysis, 77,* 459–479.

Torgersen, S., Kringlen, E., & Cramer, V. (2001). The prevalence of personality disorders in a community sample. *Archives of General Psychiatry, 58,* 590–596.

Thompson, R. A., Laible, D. J., & Ontai. L. L. (2003). Early understanding of emotion, morality, and the self: Developing a working model. In R. V. Kail (Ed.), *Advances in Child Development and Behavior,* vol. 31. Academic Press.

Weissman, M. M. (1993). The epidemiology of personality disorders: A 1990 update. *Journal of Personality Disorders, 7*(Suppl.), 44–62.

Yeomans, F. E., Clarkin, J. F., Diamond, D., & Levy, K. N. (in press). An object relations treatment of borderline patients with reflective functioning as a mechanism of change. *Psychoanalytic Inquiry.*

Chapter 7

A Neurobiological Perspective on Mentalizing and Internal Object Relations in Traumatized Borderline Patients

Glen Gabbard, Lisa Miller, and Melissa Martinez

Patients with borderline personality disorder (BPD) have long been recognized as creating extraordinary challenges for the clinicians who treat them (Bateman & Fonagy, 2004; Gabbard & Wilkinson, 1994; Gunderson, 2001). One of the major reasons for the treatment difficulty encountered is the repetition of patterns of relationships established in childhood and recreated in the therapeutic dyad. Moreover, problems with mentalizing make it difficult for patients to reflect on these patterns. Using splitting and projective identification as principal defense mechanisms (Kernberg, 1975), patients with borderline personality disorder divide their internal world into a constellation of malevolent persecutors and idealized nurturers. These intrapsychic representations are then characteristically attributed to those with whom they form attachment relationships, such as treaters, lovers, friends, or coworkers. These recreations of internal object relationships are accompanied by extraordinary affective intensity. Those involved with someone with BPD often feel that the patient has gotten under their skin to the point where they feel coercively transformed by the patient. A therapist may feel, for example, "I'm not acting like myself" when treating a borderline patient (Gabbard & Wilkinson, 1994).

Many psychodynamic theories of etiology and pathogenesis have been advanced to explain the origins of these problematic relationships, including separation issues (Kernberg, 1975; Mahler, Pine & Bergman, 1975; Masterson & Rinsley, 1975), failure to develop a soothing internal object (Adler, 1985), and insecure modes of attachment that lead to a defect in the ability to mentalize (Bateman & Fonagy, 2004). These psychodynamic hypotheses have now been supplemented by a burgeoning literature based in neurobiology so that an integration of psychodynamic and neuroscience perspectives is within our grasp in the understanding of borderline personality disorder. We would be naive to think that neurobiology *explains* the intricacies of the unconscious internal world of borderline patients. However, data from neurobiology supplement findings from psychodynamic psychotherapy and help us understand possible mechanisms of therapeutic action in psychotherapeutic work. Neurobiology and psychoanalytic theory use different languages but mutually inform one another (Gabbard, 2005a). This examination of the interface of these two levels of explanation is an example of what Kendler (2001) has called "explanatory dualism." While this type of dualism acknowledges that the mind is the activity of the brain rather than a separate substance, it also underscores the fact that there are two different ways of knowing or understanding that require two different levels of explanation.

Borderline personality disorder has a multifactorial etiology (Zanarini & Frankenburg, 1997). In this effort at bridging neurobiology and psychodynamic thinking, we are reviewing a literature on a subgroup of female patients with borderline personality disorder who experienced early abuse and neglect. Prospective research (Johnson, Cohen, Brown, Smailes, & Bernstein, 1999) has clearly linked borderline symptoms in adults to childhood sexual abuse and neglect. However, significant numbers of borderline patients do not have such histories in the many retrospective studies that have been conducted. Here we will restrict our review to the role that early neglect and abuse play in the development of borderline personality disorder and link it to both neurobiology and internal object relations.

HYPERREACTIVITY OF THE HPA AXIS

One consequence of early interpersonal trauma with parents or caregivers is that borderline patients may have a persistent hypervigilance because they need to scan the environment for the possibility of others who may have malevolent intentions toward them. Neurobiological findings are confirming these sequelae of developmental trauma. Rinne et al. (2002) studied 39 female BPD patients who were given combined dexamethasone/corticotropin releasing hormone (CRH) tests using 11 healthy subjects as controls. Twenty-four of these women had histories of sustained childhood abuse. Fifteen of them had no histories of sustained childhood abuse. When they examined the results, the chronically abused BPD patients had significantly enhanced ACTH and cortisol responses to the dexamethasone/CRH challenge compared with non-abused subjects. In addition, there were no significant differences between non-abused BPD subjects and normal controls. They concluded that a history of sustained childhood abuse is associated with hyperresponsiveness of ACTH release. Their findings suggest that this hyperreactive physiological state is relevant to this subgroup of borderline patients but not necessarily to those who lack such histories. Sustained childhood abuse appears to increase the CRH receptors' sensitivity.

Knowledge of the hyperresponsiveness of the HPA axis fits well with our understanding of the pattern of internal object relationships in borderline personality disorder. Because we understand that internal object relationships are created through building blocks of self-representations, object representations, and affects linking the two, we can infer that an anxious and hypervigilant affect state would be linked to a perception of others as persecuting and the self as victimized (Gabbard, 2005b). Hence there is an expectation of malevolence in the environment, and the borderline patient may misread the intentions of others as persecuting in a way that creates repetitive conflict with others. States of arousal undermine the capacity to accurately mentalize the internal states of others. Hypervigilant misperceptions appear to be related to amygdala hyperactivity, and a review of recent research in that area is illuminating.

THE ROLE OF THE AMYGDALA

One function of the amygdala is to increase vigilance and to facilitate an individual's evaluation of the potential for novel or ambiguous situations (Donegan et al., 2003). A functional MRI study (Herpertz et al., 2001) comparing six female BPD patients with six female control subjects found that the amygdala on both sides of the borderline patients' brains showed enhanced activation compared to the control group. The investigators concluded that the perceptual cortex in a borderline patient may be modulated through the amygdala in such a way that attention to emotionally relevant environmental stimuli is increased.

Two different studies (Donegan et al., 2003; Wagner & Linehan, 1999) examined how borderline patients react to standard presentations of faces compared to control subjects. In one study (Herpertz et al., 2001), borderline patients showed significantly greater left amygdalar activation to facial expressions of emotion compared with normal control subjects. Of even greater importance, though, was the tendency for borderline subjects, in contrast to controls, to attribute negative attributes to neutral faces. Faces that were without expression were regarded as threatening, untrustworthy, and possibly plotting to do something nefarious. A hyperactive amygdala may be involved in the predisposition to be hypervigilant and overreactive to relatively benign emotional expressions. This misreading of neutral facial expressions is clearly related to the transference misreadings that occur in psychotherapy of borderline patients and in the recreation of "bad object" experiences in the lives of borderline patients. It is also connected to the common observation of therapists that the usual professional boundaries and therapeutic neutrality are experienced by BPD patients as cruel and withholding (Gabbard & Wilkinson, 1994).

As Donegan et al. (2003) point out, the perception of threat may actually elicit reactions in others that confirm what is being projected. When the therapist, for example, feels falsely accused, he or she may react with irritation, which may subsequently elicit higher levels of amygdalar activity. This form of projective identification is a common experience that therapists report in the treatment of borderline patients.

> A 24-year-old female borderline patient began a session by complaining about the therapist's upcoming vacation. She said to the therapist, "You generally give me over a month's advance notice when you are going to be gone, and this time you told me only two weeks ahead. You know how difficult your vacations are for me. Why did you wait so long to let me know?" The therapist, feeling on the defensive, replied by saying, "I

don't think I always give you at least a month's notice." The patient became more insistent: "Oh, yes, you do. I keep track of these things." The therapist then responded, "Well, I'm not sure that's true, but it's possible I wanted to avoid the reaction I usually get from you when I say I have to take a vacation." The patient felt hurt and said to the therapist, "See? You *did* delay in letting me know because you want to avoid how I feel. I'm sorry if my feelings of neediness were too much for you."

In this vignette, the therapist appears to put off announcing vacation as a way of avoiding the emotional outburst she expects from the patient. Inadvertently, however, she confirms the patient's sense that she is malevolent by not taking into account the patient's need for greater notice and also confirms the patient's view of herself as in some way noxious.

Studies using magnetic resonance imaging techniques with borderline patients and controls have demonstrated reduced hippocampal and amygdalar volumes in BPD versus those of control groups (Driessen et al., 2000; Schmahl, Elzinga, et al., 2003; Tebartz van Elst et al., 2003). While the role of stress/trauma in reducing hippocampal volume has been observed in many studies, the exact relationship between early trauma and the decreased volumes in the amygdala is unclear. Genetic factors may be at work as well. Hariri et al. (2002) found that normal individuals with one or two copies of the short allele of the serotonin transporter (5-HTT) promoter gene demonstrate greater amygdalar neuronal activity in response to fearful stimuli compared to individuals homozygous for the long allele. Further research on 5-HTT status in borderline patients would be helpful to explore this hypothesis.

THE PREFRONTAL CORTEX: "TOP DOWN" REGULATION

The foregoing focus on such subcortical structures as the amygdala only partly addresses the clinical phenomena associated with BPD. The regulatory functions of cortical structures must be taken into account as well. Our emphasis on the amygdala and HPA axis examines borderline object relations from a perspective described in the literature as "bottom up" (reflexive) regulation (Berston, Sarter, & Cacioppo, 2003). Consideration of "top down" regulation by the prefrontal cortex is equally important in understanding the interpersonal difficulties and affective dysregulation seen in patients with borderline personality disorder (Herpertz et al., 2001).

Both the medial prefrontal cortex and the orbital prefrontal cortex have direct, reciprocal connections with areas of the brain that are crucial to emotion, and both have an inhibiting effect on the amygdala (Hariri, Mattay, Tessitore, Fera, & Weinberger, 2003; LeDoux, 2002; Rausch, Shin, & Wright, 2003). The dorsolateral prefrontal cortex also appears to exert a modulatory influence upon the amygdala indirectly via its direct connections with the medial and orbital prefrontal cortices (Hariri et al., 2003; LeDoux, 2002).

Investigators postulate that dual brain pathology involving increased activity in the amygdala and decreased activity in the prefrontal regions may be central to understanding borderline phenomena. In two studies (Lyoo, Han, & Cho, 1998; Tebartz van Elst et al., 2003), reductions in medial and orbital frontal lobe volumes have been noted in the brains of borderline patients. Of particular interest in the fMRI study by Tebartz van Elst et al. was that the left orbitofrontal volumes correlated significantly with amygdala volumes. Hence the weakening of prefrontal inhibitory controls may actually contribute to the hyperreactivity of the amygdala. This combination may be related to the common clinical situation where a borderline patient cannot seem to "control" or "shut off" intense emotional responses.

THE PREFRONTAL CORTEX AND MENTALIZATION

The prefrontal cortex is crucial for mentalization, or the ability to assign separate mental states to self and others in order to explain and predict behavior (Gallagher et al., 2000). A securely attached caregiver passes on secure attachment and the capacity to mentalize to the infant. The caregiver ascribes mental states to the child, treats the child as someone with agency, and helps the child to create internal working models. The end result is that a child can read the expression on another's face and know what that person is feeling without extensive conscious effort to figure out the meaning of the facial expression. Research has linked BPD patients with insecure attachment (Alexander et al., 1998; Allen, 2001; Patrick, Hobson, Castle, Howard, & Maughan, 1994; Stalker & Davies, 1995). The failure to resolve trauma appears to distinguish the BPD group from others. Early childhood trauma leads to defensive withdrawal from the mental world on the part of the victim. Hence some patients with borderline personality disorder who have had severe trauma cope with the abuse by avoiding reflection on the content of the caregiver's mind. This defensive shutdown may be needed to avoid thinking about the caregiver as a malevolent individual or the self as deserving of abuse. It may also prohibit resolution of abusive experiences (Fonagy, 2001).

Imaging studies suggest that mentalization involves a network of different, functionally related brain regions working in concert (Baron-Cohen et al., 1999; Calarge, Andreasen, & O'Leary, 2003; Frith & Frith, 1999; Gallagher et al., 2000). Such brain structures appear to include orbital (Grezes, Frith, & Passingham, 2004; Ramnani & Miall, 2004) and medial prefrontal regions (Abu-Akel, 2003; Gallagher et al., 2000; Grezes, Frith, & Passingham, 2004; Ramnani & Miall, 2004; Frith & Frith, 1999, 2003; Gallagher & Frith, 2003), mirror neurons originating in the premotor cortex (Abu-Akel, 2003; Grezes, Frith, & Passingham, 2004; Ramnani & Miall, 2004), temporal lobe structures, including the temporal poles (Frith & Frith, 2003; Gallagher & Frith, 2003) and amygdala (Abu-Akel, 2003; Baron-Cohen et al., 1999; Fine, Lumsden, & Blair, 2001), temporo-parietal regions, including the superior temporal sulcus (Abu-Akel, 2003; Grezes, Frith, & Passingham, 2004; Ramnani & Miall, 2004; Frith & Frith, 2003; Gallagher et al., 2000; Gallagher & Frith, 2003) and fusiform gyrus (Gallagher et al., 2000), and the cerebellum (Abu-Akel, 2003; Calarge, Andreasen, & O'Leary, 2003). Of these structures, functional neuroimaging studies most consistently demonstrate activation of the medial prefrontal cortex during mentalization tasks (Gallagher et al., 2000; Abu-Akel, 2003; Frith & Frith, 2003). As noted above, neuroimaging studies of borderline patients demonstrate abnormalities in many of these brain regions, including the medial prefrontal cortex, the orbital prefrontal cortex, and amygdala. Theories involving simulation and internalized self/object representations suggest ways in which these structures may work together in the process of mentalization.

SIMULATION THEORY AND MENTALIZATION

Current evidence supports the notion that mentalization relies, in part, upon internal simulations of the perceived emotions and mental states of others (Abu-Akel, 2003; Adolphs, 2002; Grezes, Frith, & Passingham, 2004; Ramnani & Miall, 2004). This hypothesis is strengthened by studies that demonstrate that imitating facial expressions of others induces the emotional content of those expressions in the imitator (Adolphs, Damasio, Tranei, Cooper, & Damasio, 2000).

Mirror neurons in the premotor cortex appear to automatically trigger unconscious internal simulations of the observed behaviors of others so that the observer may reconstruct their mental states and emotions (Abu-Akel, 2003; Adolphs, 2001; Grezes, Frith, & Passingham, 2004). Mirror neurons are activated by *either* performance of goal-directed behaviors, like grasping or frowning, *or* observation of them in others (Adolphs, 2001; Buccino, Binkofski, & Riggio, 2004; Gallese, 2003; Grezes, Frith, & Passingham, 2004; Hari et al., 1998; Tai, Scherfler, Brooks, Sawamoto, & Castiello, 2004). Gallese (2003) hypothesizes that a broad array of "mirror matching mechanisms" are present in the human brain that enable intersubjective communication and attribution of intentionality.

For example, representations of the frowning facial expression of another person may register in the superior temporal sulcus and fusiform gyrus of the observer (Abu-Akel, 2003; Adolphs, 2002). Nonconscious, temporo-parietal representations of the frowning facial expression may activate mirror neurons in the premotor cortex (Abu-Akel, 2003; Adolphs, 2002), which appear to automatically trigger unconscious simulations of frowning in the observer (Grezes, Frith, & Passingham, 2004; Ramnani & Miall, 2004; Tai et al., 2004). Simulations of frowning are believed to trigger the associated feeling and mental states (e.g., anger) (Abu-Akel, 2003).

Research suggests that conscious discernment of feeling states of self and others relies on the encoding of such *feeling state representations* in two areas of the right somatosensory cortex known as the insula and SSII (Adolphs, 2001; Damasio, 2003; Damasio et al., 2000; Critchley, Mathias, & Dolan, 2001; Singer et al., 2004). The SSII and insular regions appear to be important in generating nonconscious neural representations of feeling states associated with different emotions (Adolphs et al., 2000; Damasio et al., 2000). Investigators propose that the medial prefrontal cortex reads the neural representations of self and other feeling states conveyed by SSII and insular regions (Damasio et al., 2000; Singer et al., 2004). This observation is relevant to the role of the medial prefrontal cortex (e.g., anterior cingulate cortex and paracingulate gyrus) in conscious attention to emotional states of the self and others (Devinsky, Morrell, & Vogt, 1995; Stuss & Knight, 2002).

INTERNALIZED SELF/OBJECT REPRESENTATIONS AND MENTALIZATION

The amygdala, with reciprocal connections to both the sensory cortices and the prefrontal cortices, may also participate in the generation of internalized mental state representations of both the self and others (Abu-Akel, 2003; Schore, 1997, 2003). Nonconscious representations of self and others in parieto-temporal regions, such as the superior temporal sulcus and fusiform gyrus, are matched up with self and other representations based on prior experience, and are in turn linked with the orbital prefrontal cortex by affects generated by the amygdala based on prior learning (Schore, 1997, 2003). An important function of the orbital prefrontal cortex, relevant to mentalizing capacity, is to decode the reward and punishment value of emotions and behaviors of self and others (Kringelbach & Rolls, 2004; Rolls, 2004; Soloff et al., 2003). It is also involved both in the learning of these values and in the *reversal* of that learning. The orbitofrontal cortex is particularly responsive to facial emotional expressions, and is important in attachment processes (Schore, 1997).

These functions of the orbital prefrontal cortex are critical to the ability to predict the intentions and motives of others, and to the impact of one's behaviors upon the mental states of others (Abu-Akel, 2003; Kringelbach & Rolls, 2004; Schore, 1997). Schore contends that these self and other representations conveyed to the orbital prefrontal cortex, along with their associatively linked affects (conveyed from the amygdalae to the orbital prefrontal cortex), are integrated in the orbital prefrontal cortex as internalized object relations—that is "a self-representation, an object representation, and a linking affect state" (pp. 822, 854).

ABNORMALITIES OF THE PREFRONTAL CORTEX IN PATIENTS WITH BPD

Understanding how the prefrontal cortex regulates affect states via direct inhibitory modulation, and via mechanisms involving mentalization, may shed light on the dysfunctional affect regulation seen in patients with borderline personality disorder. Functional neuroimaging studies of BPD patients demonstrate abnormalities in regions of the medial and orbital prefrontal cortex (Soloff et al., 2003; Schmahl, Elzinga et al., 2003). Dysfunction of these prefrontal regions may be associated with reduced prefrontal serotonergic function (Soloff et al., 2003), but the etiology is unknown. As noted previously, a recent structural imaging study showed significantly reduced volumes of the medial and orbital prefrontal cortex in patients with BPD (Tebartz van Elst et al., 2003). These prefrontal abnormalities may correlate with impaired recognition of emotional states of self and others, feelings of psychic emptiness, an urge to self-mutilate, emotional affect dysregulation, and the impulsivity so commonly seen in patients with BPD (Tebartz van Elst et al., 2003; Soloff et al., 2003). Medial prefrontal cortical dysfunction induced by transcranial magnetic stimulation has been associated with lengthening of reaction times to pictures of angry expressions in normal subjects (Adolphs, 2002), supporting the concept that the medial prefrontal cortex is important to the shutting off of negative affect states (Schmahl, Elzinga, et al., 2003).

Simulation theory may partially explain impaired mentalization in borderline patients. The generation of internal simulations of perceived emotions and mental states of others in traumatized BPD patients relies upon neural networks in which abusive self and object representations are encoded. Additionally, the proposed dual brain pathology of prefrontal cortex and limbic circuits (Tebartz van Elst et al., 2003) may further contribute to conditioning of negative affect states to self and other representations, also leading to negative interpretive biases such as those described in reaction to neutral faces by Donegan et al. (2003).

The centrality of separation anxiety and abandonment themes in patients with BPD has also been studied using positron emission tomography imaging (PET) by Schmahl et al. (2003). These investigators studied 20 women with a history of childhood sexual abuse and 20 controls while they listened to scripts describing neutral and personal abandonment events. These investigators noted that, similar to rhesus monkeys exposed to maternal separation, the BPD women exposed to memories of abandonment showed evidence of increased activation of the right dorsolateral prefrontal cortex. Hence the investigators postulate that stress associated with maternal separation activates the same prefrontal brain regions as memories of childhood abandonment in these patients. They also propose that the reduced right medial prefrontal activation may reflect the inability, in BPD patients, to shut down negative emotions.

Our discussion of the role of prefrontal cortex and amygdalar abnormalities in BPD patients highlights important considerations involving regions of aberrant activation in functional neuroimaging studies. For example, when we see increased or decreased activation of the amygdala in functional neuroimaging studies, there are multiple possibilities to consider other than that the amygdala is intrinsically abnormal. For example, distorted self-object neural representations may activate a normally functioning amygdala. Alternatively, aberrant amygdalar activation may be related to dysfunction in another brain region, such as a hypofunctioning prefrontal cortex; or the problem may lie in diffuse systems that interact with widespread brain regions including the prefrontal cortex and amygdala, such as the serotonergic system.

Most of our attention up to this point has been directed to the prefrontal cortex and the amygdala. However, learning from experience involves structures that encode memory, notably the hippocampus. We now turn to these considerations and their influence on the repetition of problematic object relations.

IMPAIRMENTS IN MEMORY RELATED TO HIPPOCAMPAL ABNORMALITIES

The relationships of BPD patients are characterized by a repetitive quality suggesting that these patients have difficulty learning from experiences. Could there be a disturbance in memory that contributes to this difficulty? As the studies summarized up to this point have illustrated, hippocampal abnormalities are commonly noted in BPD. The hippocampus is involved in the formation and retrieval of implicit and explicit memories. Whereas implicit memories are activated unconsciously, explicit memories are activated consciously (Solms & Turnbull, 2002). The neural networks created in the process of forming and retrieving memories are dependent upon which cells are stimulated. In other words, "cells that fire together, wire together" (Hebb, 1949).

The four stages involved in forming and accessing memories include encoding, consolidation, storage, and retrieval. When new information is acquired, it is initially encoded. With time, this information is consolidated and stored. The process of consolidation involves "entrenching" memories into deeper and deeper levels of storage. When necessary, this information is retrieved for further use (Solms & Turnbull, 2002).

Among the multiple hormones and neurotransmitters involved in the formation of memories, glucocorticoids appear to play a preeminent role. Numerous studies suggest that increased levels of glucocorticoids can impair or enhance the formation of memories, depending on the content of the memory, the duration of exposure to elevated glucocorticoid levels, and the temporal relationship between exposure to elevated glucocorticoid levels and the item to be learned (McGaugh & Roozendaal, 2002). Whereas acute increases in glucocorticoid exposure can enhance memory consolidation, they can also impair memory encoding and retrieval. This effect on memory occurs through direct impairment of a process called long-term potentiation (Grossman, Buschsbaum, & Yehuda, 2002).

In long-term potentiation (LTP), receptors are activated and a cascade of events is initiated that eventually results in the strengthening of synaptic connections between neurons. These synaptic connections are essential for the encoding, consolidation, storage, and retrieval of memories. Changes in systemic glucocorticoid levels can interfere acutely with the process of LTP (Grossman, Buschsbaum, & Yehuda, 2002), and thus interfere with the process of forming memories. Hence, borderline patients who have experienced early childhood trauma and have a hyperreactive HPA axis, leading to elevated systemic glucocorticoid levels, may have difficulty forming and retrieving declarative memories.

Elevated glucocorticoid levels can affect the physical structures involved in memory formation and retrieval as well. Sustained exposure to elevated glucocorticoid levels leads to neuronal degeneration in the CA3 hippocampal region in vervet monkeys and rats (McEwen & Magarinos, 2001; McKittrick et al., 2002; Sapolsky, Uno, Rebert, & Finch, 1990). Increased endogenous glucocorticoid production resulting from stressful conditions causes dendritic pruning in animals (McKittrick et al, 2002; Watanabe, Gould, & McEwen, 1992). Therefore, the possibility exists that patients with a history of early life trauma, which could result in alterations of endogenous glucocorticoid levels due to stress, might subsequently suffer from memory impairments and structural damage to the hippocampus (Bremner et al., 1997; Gabbard, 2005a; Stein, Koverola, Hanna, Torchia, & McClarty, 1997).

As noted above, patients with a history of BPD and early life trauma have smaller hippocampal and amygdalar volumes than those without a history of BPD (Driessen et al., 2000; Schmahl, Elzinga, et al., 2003; Tebartz van Elst et al., 2003). These decreased volumes could be due to multiple etiologies such as neuronal cell death, neuronal atrophy, inhibited neurogenesis, or dendritic pruning (Grossman, Buschsbaum, & Yehuda, 2002), possibly related to elevated glucocorticoid levels. Stress connected with childhood trauma and neglect may induce elevations of cortisol and decreased levels of brain-derived neurotrophic factor (BDNF). Exposure to elevated glucocorticoid levels may contribute to excitotoxicity and subsequent neuronal cell death, while lower levels of BDNF may result in decreased neurogenesis (Schmahl, Elzinga, et al., 2003).

However, this correlation between BPD and smaller hippocampal and amygdalar volumes does not definitively prove a traumatic cause. While it is possible that these smaller volumes could result from damage occurring over time, which subsequently results in the development of BPD, it is also possible that people with smaller hippocampal and/or amygdalar volumes may be more predisposed to having this disorder. Frodl et al. (2004) found that smaller hippocampal volumes are associated with the long variant of the serotonin transporter polymorphism in major depression, suggesting the possibility that patients with BPD may also have a genetic predisposition to smaller hippocampal volumes.

In any case, patients with BPD appear to have specific memory impairments. Smaller hippocampal and temporal lobe size have been associated with poorer memory performance regardless of diagnosis (Grossman et al., 2002). Stevens, Burkhardt, Hautzinger, Schwarz, & Unckel (2004) compared 22 female subjects with BPD to 25 matched controls on tests of working memory and perception. The BPD subjects suffered from impairments in working memory and perceptual speed when compared with the controls. Impaired nonverbal executive functioning and nonverbal memory have been noted in patients with BPD when compared to controls as well (Dinn et al., 2004).

Neural networks that survive the pruning that occurs during development serve as templates, or models, around which all later memories are organized. These networks are called trunk circuits, and are activated on a regular basis even if the events that created them in the first place are not consciously recalled (Solms & Turnbull, 2002). In fact, access to memories created during childhood may not be possible as the brain functions differently during different stages of development (Solms & Turnbull, 2002). In addition, traumatic memories may not be encoded in a form that leaves them accessible to subsequent conscious recall due to the hippocampal dysfunction occurring during the traumatic event (Solms & Turnbull, 2002), such as impairment of the LTP process.

Perception of reality is based on what one has learned about the world. In other words, it is based on what is remembered. Reality is constructed based on expectations of what it "should" be, which are based on our memories. One example of this is the blind spot, the location in the retina where the optic nerve enters and exits the eye. Because there are not receptors in this specific area, there is a "hole" in one's vision. This hole, however, does not interfere with one's perception of the world as this region is "filled in" with what one expects to see (Solms & Turnbull, 2002).

Patients with borderline personality disorder, like everyone else, thus perceive others in accordance with the internalized models contained in their trunk circuits. The memory that informs expectations may be both explicit, or conscious, and implicit, or unconscious. The "how to" of relatedness is encoded early in life in implicit procedural memory as a set of unconscious internal object relationships of self, others, and affect states connecting them (Westen & Gabbard, 2002). These internalized models of relationships are played out again and again in a manner that often seems obligatory. In a psychotherapeutic setting, borderline patients often enact these patterns without being able to articulate them in a way that makes them understandable in light of previous experience.

These patterns are also repeated outside of the therapy, and one of the greatest challenges in the therapy is trying to help the borderline patient reflect on the meaning of the patterns and learn from them. Patients often actively resist connections of this sort. A therapist said to a female borderline patient who had a long series of unhappy relationships that the man she was now dating was similar to the previous man she dated, who ended up neglecting her and cheating on her. The patient responded with great intensity and told the therapist in no uncertain terms, "I don't want to talk

about him. He's in the past. I don't ever want to think about him again."
This type of temporal splitting (Gabbard, 2005b), in which the patient actively keeps apart past object relationships and present object relationships,
may contribute to the tendency for borderline patients not to learn from
previous experience. What we are also suggesting is that anatomical changes
in the hippocampus may be linked to difficulties in remembering specifics
of past relationships that are requisite to process the potential for repeating
past relationship patterns.

As stated earlier, the borderline patient may need to choose a partner
who seems like a good receptacle for the terrifying parts of the self. Alternatively, these patients may need to transform the romantic partner into a
"bad object" through projective identification as a way of externalizing an
abusive internal object so that someone else must be in control of frightening impulses (Gabbard, 2005b). The obligatory nature of the repetition of
these patterns can be understood through a mechanism of getting another
person to "own" aspects of the borderline patient.

> A 29-year-old borderline patient came to conjoint therapy with
> her husband because of chronic arguments and fights that stopped
> just short of physical altercations. In the course of the therapy, the
> husband of the patient made a poignant statement illustrating the
> extent to which he felt transformed by the patient's behavior: "I
> keep telling her over and over again, I am *not* your abusive father.
> I don't want to hurt you, hit you, or be mean to you. But it's like
> no matter what I do, she sees me as somehow mistreating her. I'm
> at a loss as to what to do. I feel like giving up."

This vignette illustrates that while borderline patients may unconsciously
select partners who are suitable templates for transformation into abusive
objects, they also may transform others into a figure that fits their expectations of reality based on past experience. As noted previously, amygdalar
hyperactivity in association with reduced cortical regulation may cause them
to misconstrue facial expressions or behavior in a way that overreads malevolence in benign actions. Through projective identification, they may
nudge the partner into confirming the expectations derived from the past.

REWARD CIRCUITS

Therapists often wonder why such maladaptive relationships are so compelling to the borderline patient. Another mechanism may involve reward circuitry. In his studies of addiction, Insel (2003) has suggested that social attachment or pair-bonding may have circuitry in common with addictive disorders. Dopamine release in the nucleus accumbens is associated with both reward and addictive behaviors. Studies of pair-bonding in mammals suggest that a dopamine agonist can induce partner preferences. Research has even shown that a partner preference could be facilitated with a D2 agonist infused directly into the nucleus accumbens. A D2 antagonist infused in the same location blocks development of a partner preference in the presence of mating (Insel, 2003). We might hypothesize that the familiar relationships experienced by borderline patients are in some way soothing because they tap into circuitry that releases dopamine and functions like the gratification of an addiction.

Projections from the amygdala to the nucleus accumbens may also be involved in mediating amygdalar effects on memory consolidation. If memories and attachment are associated with reward, then the task of weakening old circuits becomes daunting. BPD patients may be neurochemically rewarded for activating old circuits and old internalized objects.

FMRI studies have shown that both romantic and maternal love activate regions of reward circuitry, as well as regions specific to each kind of attachment (Bartels & Zeki, 2004). While this reward circuitry is activated the brain regions associated with negative emotions and the evaluation of others' emotions and intentions are deactivated. This pattern of activation and deactivation encourages attachment without the critical assessment of others, and may contribute to the repeated strong attachments borderline patients develop with abusive others. In other words, the capacity to mentalize is deactivated when the patient falls in love.

CONCLUDING COMMENTS

In this communication we have outlined a number of neurobiological correlates with the object relationship patterns of patients diagnosed with borderline personality disorder. A hyperreactive HPA axis may be associated with heightened perception of threat in the environment. Excessive amygdalar activity appears to contribute to the misinterpretation of neutral faces as potentially malevolent. This "bottom up" regulation appears to be supplemented by impaired "top down" regulation from the prefrontal cortex due to decreased volume and hypoactivity of that region. Abnormalities of the prefrontal cortex may also influence impaired mentalization in patients with borderline psychopathology. Hippocampal abnormalities may be relevant to the problems these patients have in learning from previous relationships and applying that knowledge to current relationships. Finally, reward circuitry associated with the nucleus accumbens and dopamine may make the patterns tenaciously resistant to treatment. The elucidation of neurobiological underpinnings helps us understand the tenacity with which these patterns are maintained and the need for extended psychotherapeutic and pharmacologic intervention to alter these patterns. Indeed, one of the implications of this understanding is that extended psychotherapeutic intervention is necessary to see substantial changes in these relational patterns.

Another implication is that selective serotonin reuptake inhibitors (SSRIs) may be useful as an adjunct to psychotherapy. Because serotonin has an inhibitory effect on behavior, the impulsivity characteristic of borderline patients may in part relate to this altered serotonergic activity (Siever & Davis, 1991). Moreover, Rinne and colleagues (Rinne et al., 2003) found that one of the SSRIs, fluvoxamine, reduced the hyperreactivity of the HPA axis in borderline patients. Hence SSRIs may facilitate psychotherapy by reducing "affective noise" such as hypervigilant anxiety, intense anger, or dysphoria that interferes with mentalizing (Gabbard, 2005a).

Several other implications for psychotherapy derive from this understanding. Much of dynamic psychotherapy links past patterns with current patterns. If hippocampal dysfunction and/or damage is present, then formation and retrieval of memories become more challenging. Moreover, representations of object relationships are not "things" stored in memory, but connections among nodes of a network that have been activated together for many years (Gabbard & Westen, 2003). These potentials for reactivation exist in a heightened state of potential, and a great deal of time is necessary to weaken links between nodes in this network that have fired together for a long time. What we call structural change in psychotherapy involves a relative deactivation of problematic links in activated networks and an increased activation of new, more adaptive connections. By the strengthening of the new and more adaptive circuits combined with the weakening activation of old circuits, the newer circuits ultimately override the old circuits. Working in parallel with this change in circuitry is an increased capacity for conscious self-reflection and mentalization that allows the patient to override unconscious patterns once they are recognized (Gabbard & Westen, 2003). The challenge of overriding old patterns when they have an addiction-like appeal to the patient is a formidable one, and further research on these mechanisms is badly needed.

REFERENCES

Abu-Akel, A. (2003). A neurobiological mapping of theory of mind. *Brain Research. Brain Research Reviews, 43*, 29–40.

Adler, G. (1985). *Borderline Psychopathology and Its Treatment.* New York: Jason Aronson.

Adolphs, R. (2001). The neurobiology of social cognition. *Current Opinions in Neurobiology, 11*, 231–239.

Adolphs, R. (2002). Neural systems for recognizing emotion. *Current Opinions in Neurobiology, 12*, 169–177.

Adolphs, R., Damasio, H., Tranei, D., Cooper, G., & Damasio, A. R. (2000). A role for somatosensory cortices in the role of visual recognition of emotions as revealed by 3-dimensional lesion mapping. *Journal of Neuroscience, 20*, 2683–2690.

Alexander, P. C., Anderson, C. L., Brand, B., Schaeffer, C. M., Grelling, B. Z., & Kretz, L. (1998). Adult attachment and long-term effects in survivors of incest. *Journal of Child Abuse & Neglect, 22*, 45–61.

Allen, J. G. (2001). *Traumatic Relationships and Serious Mental Disorders.* New York: Wiley.

Baron-Cohen, S., Ring, H. A., Wheelwright, S., Bullmore, E. T., Brammer, M. J., Simmons, A., et al. (1999). Social intelligence in the normal and autistic brain: An fMRI study. *European Journal of Neuroscience, 11*, 1891–1898.

Bartels, A., & Zeki, S. (2004). The neural correlates of maternal and romantic love. *Neuroimage, 21*, 1155–1166.

Bateman, A., & Fonagy, P. (2004). *Psychotherapy for Borderline Personality Disorder: Mentalization-based Treatment.* New York: Oxford University Press.

Berston, G. G., Sarter, M., & Cacioppo, J. T. (2003). Ascending visceral regulation of cortical affective information processing. *European Journal of Neurology, 18,* 2103–2109.

Bremner, J. D., Randall, P., Vermetten, E., Staib, L., Bronen, R. A., Mazure, C., et al. (1997). Magnetic resonance imaging based measurement of hippocampal volume in posttraumatic stress disorder related to childhood physical and sexual abuse—A preliminary report. *Biological Psychiatry, 41,* 23–32.

Buccino, G., Binkofski, F., & Riggio, L. (2004). The mirror neuron system and action recognition. *Brain and Language, 89,* 370–376

Calarge, C., Andreasen, N. C., & O'Leary, D. S. (2003). Visualizing how one brain understands another: A PET study of theory of mind. *American Journal of Psychiatry, 160,* 1954–1964.

Critchley, H. D., Mathias, C. J., & Dolan, R. J. (2001). Neuroanatomical basis for first- and second order representations of bodily states. *Nature Neuroscience, 4,* 207–212.

Damasio, A. (2003). *Looking for Spinoza: Joy, Sorrow, and the Feeling Brain* (1st ed.). New York: Harcourt.

Damasio, A. R., Grabowski, T. J., Bechara, A., Damasio, H., Ponto, L. L. B., Parvizi, J., et al. (2000). Subcortical and cortical brain activity during the feeling of self-generated emotions. *Nature Neuroscience, 3,* 1049–1056.

Devinsky, O., Morrell, M. J., & Vogt, B. A. (1995). Contributions of anterior cingulate cortex to behavior. *Brain, 118,* 279–306.

Dinn, W. M., Harris, C. L., Aycicegi, A., Greene, P. B., Kirkley, S. M., & Reilly, C. (2004). Neurocognitive functioning in borderline personality disorder. *Progress in Neuropsychopharmacology and Biological Psychiatry, 28,* 329–341.

Donegan, N. H., Sanislow, C. A., Blumberg, H. P., Fulbright, R. K., Lacadie, C., Skudlarski, P., et al. (2003). Amygdala hyperreactivity in borderline personality disorder: Implications for emotional dysregulation. *Biological Psychiatry, 54,* 1284–1293.

Driessen, M., Herrmann, J., Stahl, K., Zwaan, M., Meier, S., Hill, A., et al. (2000). Magnetic resonance imaging volumes of the hippocampus and the amygdala in women with borderline personality disorder and early traumatization. *Archives of General Psychiatry, 57,* 1115–1122.

Fine, C., Lumsden, J., & Blair, R. J. R. (2001). Dissociation between 'theory of mind' and executive functions in a patient with early left amygdala damage. *Brain, 124,* 287–298.

Fonagy, P. (2001). *Attachment Theory and Psychoanalysis.* New York: Other Press.

Frith, C. D., & Frith, U. (1999). Interacting minds—A biological basis. *Science, 286,* 1692–1695.

Frith, U., & Frith, C. D. (2003). Development and neurophysiology of mentalizing. *Philosophical Transactions of the Royal Society of London, 358,* 459–473.

Frodl, T., Meisenzahl, E. M., Zill, P., Baghai, T., Rujescu, D., Leinsinger, G., et al. (2004). Reduced hippocampal volumes associated with the long variant of the serotonin transporter polymorphism in major depression. *Archives of General Psychiatry, 61*, 177–183.

Gabbard, G. O. (2005a). *Psychodynamic Psychiatry in Clinical Practice* (4th ed.). Washington, DC: American Psychiatric Press.

Gabbard, G. O. (2005b) Mind, brain, and personality disorders. *American Journal of Psychiatry, 162*, 648–655.

Gabbard, G. O., & Westen, D. (2003). Rethinking therapeutic action. *International Journal of Psycho-Analysis, 84*, 823–841.

Gabbard, G. O., & Wilkinson, S. (1994). *Management of Countertransference with Borderline Patients*. Washington, DC: American Psychiatric Press.

Gallagher, H. L., & Frith, C.D. (2003). Functional imaging of "theory of mind." *Trends in Cognitive Science, 7*, 77–83.

Gallagher, H. L., Happe, F., Brunswick, N., Fletcher, P. C., Frith, U., & Frith, C. D. (2000). Reading the mind in cartoons and stories: An fMRI study of "theory of mind" in verbal and nonverbal tasks. *Neuropsychologia, 38*, 1121.

Gallese, V. (2003). The roots of empathy: The shared manifold hypothesis and the neural basis of intersubjectivity. *Psychopathology, 36*, 171–180.

Grezes, J., Frith, C. D., & Passingham, R. E. (2004). Inferring false beliefs from the actions of oneself and others: An fMRI study. *Neuroimage, 21*, 744–750.

Grossman, R., Buschsbaum, M. S., & Yehuda, R. (2002). Neuroimaging studies in post-traumatic stress disorder. *Psychiatric Clinics in North America, 25*, 317–340.

Gunderson, J. G. (2001). *Borderline Personality Disorder: A Clinical Guide*. Washington, DC: American Psychiatric Press.

Hari, R., Forss, N., Avikainen, S., Kirveskari, E., Salenius, S., & Rizzolatti, G. (1998). Activation of human primary motor cortex during action observation: A neuromagnetic study. *Proceedings of the National Academy of Sciences, 95*, 15061–15065.

Hariri, A. R., Mattay, V. S., Tessitore, A., Fera, F., & Weinberger, D. R. (2003). Neocortical modulation of the amygdala response to fearful stimuli. *Biological Psychiatry, 53*, 494–501.

Hariri, A. R., Mattay, V. S., Tessitore, A., Kolachana, B., Fera, F., Goldman, D., et al. (2002). Serotonin transporter genetic variation and the response of the human amygdala. *Science, 297*, 400–403.

Hebb, D. O. (1949). *Organization and Behavior*. New York: Wiley.

Herpertz, S. C., Dietrich, T. M., Wenning, B., Krings, T., Erberich, S. G., Willmes, K., et al. (2001). Evidence of abnormal amygdala functioning in borderline personality disorder: A functional MRI study. *Biological Psychiatry, 50*, 292–298.

Insel, T. R. (2003). Is social attachment an addictive disorder? *Physiology & Behavior, 79*, 351–357.

Johnson, J. G., Cohen, P., Brown, J., Smailes, E. M., & Bernstein, D. P. (1999). Childhood maltreatment increases risk for personality disorders during early adulthood. *Archives of General Psychiatry, 56,* 600–606.

Kendler, K. S. (2001). A psychiatric dialogue on the mind and body problem. *American Journal of Psychiatry, 158,* 989–1000.

Kernberg, O. F. (1975). *Borderline Conditions and Pathological Narcissism.* New York: Jason Aronson.

Kringelbach, M. L., & Rolls, E. T. (2004). The functional neuroanatomy of the human orbitofrontal cortex: Evidence from neuroimaging and neuropsychology. *Progress in Neurobiology, 72,* 341–372.

LeDoux, J. (2002). *Synaptic Self: How Our Brains Become Who We Are.* New York: Penguin Putnam.

Lyoo, I. K., Han, M. H., & Cho, D. Y. (1998). A brain MRI study in subjects with borderline personality disorder. *Journal of Affective Disorders, 50,* 235–243.

Mahler, M. S., Pine, F., & Bergman, A. (1975). *The Psychological Birth of the Human Infant: Symbiosis and Individuation.* New York: Basic Books.

Masterson, J. F., & Rinsley, D. B. (1975). The borderline syndrome: The role of the mother in the genesis and psychic structure of the borderline personality. *International Journal of Psycho-Analysis, 56,* 163–177.

McEwen, B. S., & Magarinos, A. M. (2001). Stress and hippocampal plasticity: Implications for the pathophysiology of affective disorders. *Human Psychopharmacology, 16,* S7–S19.

McGaugh, J. L., & Roozendaal, B. (2002). Role of adrenal hormones in forming lasting memories in the brain. *Current Opinions in Neurobiology, 12,* 2005–2010.

McKittrick, C. R., Magarinos, A. M., Blanchard, D. C., Blanchard, R. J., McEwen, B. S., & Sakai, R. R. (2002). Chronic social stress reduces dendritic arbors in CA3 of hippocampus and decreases binding to serotonin transporter sites. *Synapse, 36,* 85–94.

Patrick, M., Hobson, R. P., Castle, D., Howard, R., & Maughan, B. (1994). Personality disorder and the mental representation of early experience. *Developmental Psychopathology, 6,* 375–388.

Ramnani, N., & Miall, R. C. (2004). A system in the human brain for predicting the actions of others. *Natural Neuroscience, 7,* 85–90.

Rausch, S. L., Shin, L. M., & Wright, C. I. (2003). Neuroimaging studies of amygdala function in anxiety disorders. *Annals of the New York Academy of Sciences, 985,* 389–410.

Rinne, T., de Kloet, E. R., Wouters, L., Goekoop, J. G., de Rijk, R. H., & van den Brink, W. (2003). Fluvoxamine reduces responsiveness of HPA axis in adult female BPD patients with a history of sustained childhood abuse. *Neuropsychopharmacology, 28*(126), 132.

Rinne, T., de Kloet, E. R., Wouters, L., Goekoop, J. G., DeRijk, R. H., & van den Brink, W. (2002). Hyperresponsiveness of hypothalamic-pituitary-adrenal axis to combined dexamethasone/corticotropin-releasing hormone challenge in female borderline personality disorder subjects with a history of sustained childhood abuse. *Biological Psychiatry, 52,* 1102–1112.

Rolls, E. T. (2004). The functions of the orbitofrontal cortex. *Brain and Cognition, 55,* 11–29.

Sapolsky, R. N., Uno, H., Rebert, C. S., & Finch, C. E. (1990). Hippocampal damage associated with prolonged glucocorticoid exposure in primates. *Journal of Neuroscience, 10,* 2897–2902.

Schmahl, C. G., Elzinga, B. M., Vermetten, E., Sanislow, C., McGlashan, T. H., & Bremner, J. D. (2003). Neural correlates of memories of abandonment in women with and without borderline personality disorder. *Biological Psychiatry, 54,* 142–151.

Schore, A. (1997). A century after Freud's project: Is a rapprochement between psychoanalysis and neurobiology at hand? *Journal of the American Psychoanalytic Association, 45,* 808–840.

Schore, A. N. (2003). *Affect Regulation in the Repair of the Self.* New York: Norton.

Siever, L. J., & Davis, K. L. (1991). A psychobiological perspective on the personality disorders. *American Journal of Psychiatry, 148,* 1647–1658.

Singer, T., Seymour, B., O'Doherty, J., Kaube, H., Dolan, R. J., & Frith, C. D. (2004). Empathy for pain involves the affective but not sensory components of pain. *Science, 303,* 1157–1162.

Solms, M., & Turnbull, O. (2002). *The Brain and the Inner World: An Introduction to the Neuroscience of Subjective Experience.* New York: Other Press.

Soloff, P. H., Meltzer, C. C., Becker, C., Greer, P. J., Kelly, T. M., & Constantine, D. (2003). Impulsivity and prefrontal hypometabolism in borderline personality disorder. *Psychiatry Research, 123,* 153–163.

Stalker, C. A., & Davies, F. (1995). Attachment organization and adaptation in sexually abused women. *Canadian Journal of Psychiatry, 40,* 234–240.

Stein, M. B., Koverola, C., Hanna, C., Torchia, M. G., & McClarty, B. (1997). Hippocampal volume in women victimized by childhood sexual abuse. *Psychological Medicine, 27,* 951–959.

Stevens, A., Burkhardt, M., Hautzinger, M., Schwarz, J., & Unckel, C. (2004). Borderline personality disorder: Impaired visual perception and working memory [Abstract]. *Psychiatry Research, 125,* 257–267.

Stuss, D., & Knight, R. (2002). *Principles of Frontal Lobe Function.* New York: Oxford University Press.

Tai, Y. F., Scherfler, C., Brooks, D. J., Sawamoto, N., & Castiello, U. (2004). The human premotor cortex is "mirror" only for biological actions. *Current Biology, 14,* 117–120.

Tebartz van Elst, L., Hesslinger, B., Thiel, T., Geiger, E., Haegele, K., Lemieux, L., et al. (2003). Frontolimbic brain abnormalities in patients with borderline personality disorder: A volumetric magnetic resonance imaging study. *Biological Psychiatry, 54,* 163–171.

Wagner, A. W., & Linehan, M. M. (1999). Facial expression recognition ability among women with borderline personality disorder: Implications for emotion regulation? *Journal of Personality Disorders, 13,* 329–344.

Watanabe, Y., Gould, E., & McEwen, B. S. (1992). Stress induces atrophy of apical dendrites of hippocampal CA3 pyramidal neurons. *Brain Research, 588,* 341–345.

Westen, D., & Gabbard, G. O. (2002). Developments in cognitive neuroscience, II. Implications for the concept of transference. *Journal of the American Psychiatric Association, 50,* 99–113.

Zanarini, M. C., & Frankenburg, F. R. (1997). Pathways to the development of borderline personality disorder. *Journal of Personality Disorders, 11,* 93–104.

Chapter 8

Changes in the Representation of Self and Significant Others in the Treatment Process

Links Between Representation, Internalization, and Mentalization[1]

Sidney J. Blatt, John S. Auerbach, and Rebecca Smith Behrends

Considerable emphasis has been placed in recent years on the development of a concept of mind—that is, on the recognition that one has a mind that is unique and is distinct from those of others. This maturational achievement is rooted in the development of self and object constancy (e.g., Blatt, 1995) and the capacity for reflexive self-awareness (see Auerbach, 1993; Bach, 1985, 1994; Broucek, 1991). The concept of mind is, furthermore, crucial to the development of a capacity for mentalization in the treatment process—the ability to reflect on thoughts and feelings, both one's own and those of others, and to recognize them as mental states that motivate behavior. Central to this effort have been the research and theoretical formulations of Fonagy, Target, and their colleagues (Fonagy, Steele, Steele, Moran, & Higgitt, 1991; Fonagy, Target, Steele, & Steele, 1998) using the Adult Attachment Interview (AAI; George, Kaplan, & Main, 1985) to assess Reflective Function (RF), an operational definition of mentalization. Alternatively, the concept of mind has been studied through the investigation of the development of mental representations or cognitive-affective schemas of self and significant others. These investigations have evaluated

Rorschach responses (e.g., Blatt, Brenneis, Schimek, & Glick, 1976; Mayman, 1967; Urist, 1977), Thematic Apperception Test (TAT) stories (e.g., Westen, 1991a), and spontaneous descriptions of self and significant others (Object Relations Inventory [ORI]; Blatt, Wein, Chevron, & Quinlan, 1979; Blatt, Chevron, Quinlan, & Wein, 1981; Diamond, Blatt, Stayner, & Kaslow, 1991). The report in this chapter is based on research using the ORI to study changes in the thematic content and structural organization of descriptions of self and significant others during long-term intensive psychodynamically oriented inpatient treatment of seriously disturbed, treatment-resistant adolescents and young adults.

The evaluation of RF is usually made from a very rich data base gathered as part of the extensive AAI. Reflective Function is assessed on an 11-point continuum from negative reflective functioning to full or exceptional reflective function. Individuals at the bottom of the scale either actively resist thinking about mental states or think about mental states in an unintegrated, bizarre, or inappropriate way. Individuals toward the top of the continuum display an organized, consistent, complex, often surprising understanding of the motivations that guide their own actions and those of others. The ORI, in contrast, is used with a more restricted database, the spontaneous descriptions given by individuals in response to the simple request to "describe" themselves, as well as specified significant others (e.g., mother, father, therapist) and an unspecified significant other (e.g., Harpaz-Rotem & Blatt, 2005). Blatt and colleagues (e.g., Blatt, Chevron, Quinlan, Schaffer, & Wein, 1988; Blatt, Schaffer, Bers, & Quinlan, 1992; Diamond et al., 1991) have developed methods for systematically assessing the thematic content and structural organization of these brief descriptions. These methods include, most prominently, the complex multidimensional Differentiation-Relatedness (D-R) Scale, which assesses the degree to which the figure is differentiated and described in relationship with others. The D-R scale will be described in detail in a later section of this paper, but in general, it is a 10-point scale on which to rate increasing articulation and stabilization of the concept of the object and increasing appreciation of mutual, empathically attuned relatedness expressed in individuals' descriptions of self and of their significant others.

The Differentiation-Relatedness (D-R) Scale and the RF Scale are complementary efforts at assessing the degree of psychological differentiation and the capacity for interpersonal relatedness, but they derive from different theoretical orientations and from a different research literature (Auerbach & Blatt, 2002; Blatt & Auerbach, 2003). The RF Scale derives in large part from the research literature on attachment and the developmental achievement of a concept of mind and was designed to be used with the AAI. The D-R scale, in contrast, has its origins in psychoanalytic developmental theories like those of Mahler (e.g., Mahler, Pine, & Bergman, 1975) and D. N. Stern (1985), and in the theoretical work of Blatt and colleagues (e.g., Blatt, 2006, 2008; Blatt & Blass, 1990, 1996; Blatt & Shichman, 1983) on the dialectic of relatedness and self-definition in personality development and psychopathology.

THE PROCESS OF INTERNALIZATION IN PSYCHOLOGICAL DEVELOPMENT

The study of both reflective function and of self and other mental representations is consistent with the increased emphasis in psychoanalysis on relational conceptualizations of the self and the mind (e.g., Aron, 1996; Auerbach & Blatt, 1996, 2001, 2002; Behrends & Blatt, 1985; Benjamin, 1995; Blatt, 2006, 2008; Blatt & Blass, 1990, 1996; Bromberg, 1998; Mitchell, 1988, 2000; Ogden, 1994; D. B. Stern, 1997). Both conceptualizations assume the importance in development of the internalization of aspects of significant relationships with caregiving others.

Internalization is a fundamental mechanism by which psychological development occurs throughout life, as well as in the therapeutic process. Behrends and Blatt (1985) identified two components in the internalization process. The first component is a gratifying relationship or an attachment, as initially established through mother–infant interactive regulation, with the resulting affective bond between baby and caregiver serving as a necessary condition for internalization (e.g., Beebe & Lachmann, 1994; Beebe, Lachmann, & Jaffe, 1997; Gergely & Watson, 1996; Jaffe, Beebe, Feldstein, Crown, & Jasnow, 2001; D. N. Stern, 1985; Tronick, 1989). Inevitable, progressive, minute losses of aspects of this gratifying relationship also appear to be essential, however, for internalization and for consequent self–object differentiation and individuation, as well as for the development of mental representations. Thus, the second component of the internalization process is some disruption of the attachment or gratifying relationship.

If the disruption is not too sudden or extensive and does not exceed adaptive capacities, the normal infant manages these losses in the mother–infant relationship through processes of internalization. Alternatively, internalization can be described as resulting from cycles of match, disruption, and repair, or from a middle range of coordinated interpersonal timing in affective transactions between infant and caregiver (Beebe & Lachmann, 1994, 2002; Gergely & Watson, 1996; Jaffe et al., 2001; D. N. Stern, 1985), such that the infant comes to experience his or her caregiver as a secure base from which to explore the world and to individuate (see Ainsworth, 1967, 1969; Bowlby, 1977, 1979, 1988b).

Behrends and Blatt (1985) chose the term *gratifying involvement* to describe the first phase of the internalization process, in which a relationship provides certain fundamental needs and creates an impetus to do for oneself what one has originally relied on the other to provide. Gratifying involvement signifies that individuals experience relationships in terms of certain basic psychological needs. The nature of what constitutes a gratifying involvement changes with maturation. The gratifying involvements of adulthood, for example, occur in the context of relationships that not only offer closeness and intimacy but also encourage individuation and autonomy by respecting differences and tolerating expressions of disagreement and even anger. A gratifying involvement with others, at any level, enables the person to function with a degree of coherence and integrity that would not otherwise be possible. Gratifying involvement refers to a relationship with a significant other in which the individual's phase-appropriate psychological needs are met. Even though the needs that relationships provide change in form and complexity with development, a gratifying involvement with, or an attachment to, another person appears to be an essential precondition for internalization at every developmental level.

The prototype of the second step in the internalization process is the inevitable disruption of mother–infant affective matching or mirroring. Borrowing a term from George Klein (1976), Behrends and Blatt (1985) called these developmental crises *experienced incompatibilities*. Klein originally used this term to describe experiences in which the integrity of a person's identity or self-structure was threatened in some fashion through experiences such as conflicting aims, developmental crises, traumas, or life circumstances—threats that provoked a sense of limitation or dissociation of the self. Behrends and Blatt (1985) extended this concept to place more emphasis on disruptions within a relational matrix in which a previously established relationship no longer meets the needs of at least one of the participants. Experienced incompatibility can take many forms, including object loss, deprivation of function, intrapsychic conflict, conflict between one's own wishes and the demands and limitations of the environment, and maturational change. The concept of experienced incompatibility, because it is not restricted to object loss alone, provides an expanded conceptualization of the various cleavages, rifts, and discontinuities in interpersonal relations that can instigate the process of internalization at any level (Behrends & Blatt, 1985).

An experienced incompatibility may occur either consciously or unconsciously, symbolically or presymbolically.[2] Experienced incompatibility can come about for a variety of reasons, including the possibility that the other person either no longer wants to or is no longer able to gratify one's needs. Incompatibility may occur when one of the individuals, in his or her own right, feels ready to move the relationship to a more mature or less mature level. If the disruption in the relationship is not too sudden or severe, the individual can preserve psychologically significant aspects of the previous gratifying involvement or attachment by making them part of himself or herself. And this internalization results in changes in the content and structural organization of representations of the self and significant others, and of their relationship. If the disruption in the relationship is premature, the individual may not be prepared to appropriate adaptive functions of the relationship and thus may be forced to resort to other, less successful, means of adaptation (i.e., the experience of anxiety and the formation of symptoms, or the development of some form of pathological mourning) to the loss of gratifying involvement.

Internalization, Mentalization, and Intersubjectivity

In this regard, the view that experienced incompatibility in the context of an emotionally significant relationship leads to representational growth is also consistent with the basic propositions in intersubjectivity theory, which hold that children become independent subjects only if they are recognized as such (i.e., as beings with minds, wills, and feelings of their own) by their caregivers (Benjamin, 1990, 1995; Fonagy et al., 1995; Fonagy, Gergely, Jurist, & Target, 2002; Ogden, 1994; Winnicott, 1982) and that sensitive caregivers do this from the moment of birth, long before an infant has intentionality, feelings of bodily cohesion, self-reflexivity, and language—in short, long before the emergence of mentalization and other psychological capacities that are essential to human subjectivity.

Intersubjectivity theory further holds, however, that a child becomes an independent subject only if he or she in turn recognizes the independent subjectivity—in more familiar language, the autonomy and separateness—of his or her caregiver. In other words, the term *intersubjectivity* refers not only to an interpersonal situation in which parents regard their children as independent subjects, but also to a psychological capacity (i.e., the ability to appreciate another's independent subjectivity) that emerges developmentally from this interpersonal matrix. This cognitive-affective capacity enables a child in turn to come to understand his or her parent's mind. It is this mutual recognition, by caregiver and child, of each other's mental states, that ultimately constitutes the intersubjective situation. In other words, intersubjectivity as an interpersonal interaction—in Aron's (1996) phrase, a meeting of minds—and intersubjectivity as a psychological capacity are deeply intertwined concepts. The former constitutes the transactional matrix from which the latter emerges, much as the dialectic of gratifying involvement and experienced incompatibility, another way of describing this meeting of minds, constitutes the transactional substrate of internalization. It must be understood that this intersubjectivity, this meeting of minds, is fraught with psychological peril and should be not be considered a psychoanalytic bromide. Any true meeting of minds, on this perspective, always involves the possibility of abandonment, separation, rejection, or loss—or, concomitantly, of attempts at omnipotent control to forestall these painful outcomes. Nevertheless, the appropriation of important functions provided by a significant interpersonal relationship is a primary basis for the development of psychological structures and organization that make possible more differentiated and integrated representations of self and significant others, especially of their minds (i.e., their feelings, wishes, fears, and intentions; e.g., Loewald, 1962).

Internalization, the Relational Matrix, and Psychological Growth

Representations of the other and the self are revised and modified throughout development, with these revisions enabling individuals to think of themselves and others in a more differentiated and integrated fashion and to relate to others in more mature ways. These new levels of internalization can provide a richer and more complex psychological matrix that can then serve as a new substrate for subsequent internalization and psychological growth. Thus, episodes of gratifying involvement (relatedness) and of experienced incompatibility (separation) are the crucial factors in development, with these events and their meanings in the person's life both transforming and being transformed by developmental processes. And with increased psychological development, internalizations can come about when the elements of gratifying involvement and experienced incompatibility exist on a purely subjective level, without overt observable activities.

The individual, in an attempt to preserve psychologically significant aspects of the relationship, gradually transforms those functions that the relationship had previously provided into his or her own enduring self-generative functions and characteristics (Behrends & Blatt, 1985). Psychologically significant dimensions of the relationship, both gratifying and nongratifying, and including both conscious and unconscious feelings and attitudes in the responses of significant others to aspects of the self that are experienced in the relationship, are internalized. Thus, for example, hostile introjects (conscious and unconscious destructive elements in the relationship) may be made part of oneself because they are intimately tied to some aspect of the relationship that was gratifying. Alternatively, as Fairbairn (1952), for example, noted, individuals can remain attached to bad object relations, especially to exciting, even harmful, seductive aspects of them, to avoid experiences of abandonment and aloneness.

On the basis of these developmental considerations, *internalization* can be defined as those processes that occur when individuals seek to recover lost or disrupted regulatory, gratifying interactions with others, which may have been either real or fantasized, by appropriating those interactions, transforming them into their own, enduring, self-generated functions and characteristics (Behrends & Blatt, 1985). The establishment of a gratifying involvement and the subsequent experience of an incompatibility in the context of psychologically significant relationships constitute the fundamental under-lying mechanisms of the internalization process, with this process in turn resulting in increased psychological differentiation and individuation. Psychological growth occurs as these elemental steps are repeated, again and again, over the course of the entire life cycle, in the form of a "hierarchical spirality" (Werner, 1948). At various levels of psychological development, the mechanisms of this process remain the same even though they are manifest in new forms and in new contexts and result in increasingly greater psychological differentiation and higher levels of organization. The internalization process, and the increased psychological individuation that results from it, is basic to all developmental periods and to the development of more mature representations of self and significant others.

REPRESENTATIONS OF SELF AND SIGNIFICANT OTHERS

Mental representation is a central theoretical construct in psychoanalysis, in cognitive science, and in developmental and social psychology. According to psychoanalysis and cognitive developmental psychology, children transform interactions with primary caregivers into cognitive-affective schemas of self and other, and these schemas regulate and direct a wide range of subsequent behavior, especially in interpersonal relationships (e.g., Ainsworth, 1969, 1983; Beebe & Lachmann, 2002; Blatt, 1991, 1995; Blatt & Lerner, 1983; Bowlby, 1973, 1982, 1977, 1979, 1988b; Fonagy et al., 1995; Lichtenberg, 1983; Mahler, Pine, & Bergman, 1975; Main, Kaplan, & Cassidy, 1985; Piaget, 1954; Sandler & Rosenblatt, 1962; D. N. Stern, 1985). Formulations and findings from psychoanalytic object-relations theory and from attachment theory are thus consistent with the recent focus in developmental psychology, cognitive science, information processing, and social cognition with respect to the role of relational schemas of self and others as heuristic prototypes that provide the basis for social interaction and interpersonal behavior (e.g., Anderson, 1983; Auerbach, 1993; Brewer & Nakamura, 1984; Fiske & Taylor, 1984; Gardner, 1985; Horowitz, 1988; Mandler, 1988; Markus, 1977; Nelson & Gruendel, 1987; Westen, 1991b). On the other hand, both psychoanalysis and attachment theory differ from cognitive psychology, cognitive science, and even much of academic developmental psychology in that these latter disciplines study mainly the representation of affectively neutral objects, whereas for both psychoanalysis and attachment theory the primary focus is on the mental representation of emotionally charged relationships (Blatt, 1974, 1983, 1995).

According to both attachment theory and psychoanalysis, therefore, cognitive-affective schemas or representations of these emotionally significant relationships develop through the internalization of aspects of early transactions between self and significant others. Attachment theory assumes that, during the first 18 months of life, the child establishes mental representations or *internal working models* (IWMs) of attachment relationships (see Bowlby, 1973, 1980, 1982)—"a set of conscious and unconscious rules for the organization of information relevant to attachment and for obtaining or limiting access to that information, that is, to information regarding attachment-related experiences, feelings and ideations" (Main et al., 1985, p. 67). The affective (or libidinal) bond between infant and caretaker established during the first year of life evolves into a "secure base" (Ainsworth, 1967, 1969; Bowlby, 1988b) that enables the child to leave the mother in order to explore more fully the world beyond the primary relationship with her. Presymbolic representations of the affective bond in the first year of life (Beebe & Lachmann, 1994) are transformed in the second year into symbolic representations with object permanence and object constancy (Blatt, 1995). These cognitive-affective schemas provide templates that maintain the continuity of interpersonal behavior from infancy into childhood, adolescence, and adulthood. As Main et al. (1985) noted, the internal working model of attachment established by the end of the first year of life functions as a "template of previously unrecognized strength" (p. 94) that is "related not only to individual patterns in nonverbal behavior, but also to patterns of language and structures of mind" (p. 67). As Bowlby (1988b) similarly observed,

> The working models a child builds of his mother and her ways of communicating and behaving towards him, and a comparable model of his father, together with the complementary models of himself in interactions with each, are being built by a child during the first few years of his life and, it is postulated, soon become established as influential cognitive structures. (p. 130)

The patterns of secure, insecure avoidant, and insecure preoccupied attachment establish fundamental cognitive-affective schemas that form the basis for normal and deviant behavior in adolescence and adulthood.

Both psychoanalytic and attachment theorists stress that the appropriation of early, affectively charged interactions with caregivers results in the formation of representations of self and others, and of their actual and potential relationships (Beebe & Lachmann, 1994, 2002; Blatt, 1974; Blatt, Wild, & Ritzler, 1975; Bowlby, 1982, 1988b; Kernberg, 1966, 1976, 1990; Kohut, 1971; Mahler et al., 1975; Behrends & Blatt, 1985; Bretherton, 1987; Loewald, 1962; D. N. Stern, 1985; Zeneah & Anders, 1987). Consistent, positive, affective experiences between child and attachment figures lead to relatively integrated and differentiated internal working models of attachment relationships, in which stable attributes of the attachment relationship become elaborated and consolidated. New experiences over succeeding years and developmental periods are integrated into earlier mental representations and eventuate in advances over prior stages, such as the development of object and self constancy and of symbolic activity more generally. Overwhelming fluctuations, inconsistencies, disruptions, and negative experiences in caretaking interactions, however, can lead to less differentiated, integrated, and consolidated representational schemas that are organized with a more limited potential for psychological development as individuals attempt to establish a sense of security in distorted and maladaptive ways (Blatt, 1995).

Differentiation-Relatedness in Mental Representation

Blatt and colleagues (e.g., Blatt et al., 1979, 1988; Blatt, Bers, & Schaffer, 1992; Diamond et al., 1991) developed procedures to assess aspects of mental representations by evaluating the structural organization and thematic content of spontaneous descriptions of self and significant others. Using concepts from psychoanalytic and cognitive developmental theories, they constructed methods for assessing the degree of differentiation and interpersonal relatedness (Diamond et al., 1991) of these descriptions.

Drawing from theoretical formulations and clinical observations about very early processes of boundary articulation (Blatt & Wild, 1976; Blatt et al., 1975; Jacobson, 1964; Kernberg, 1975, 1976), processes of separation-individuation (Coonerty, 1986; Mahler et al., 1975), the formation of the sense of self and the development of intersubjectivity (D. N. Stern, 1985), and the interplay between the development of self-definition and increasingly mature levels of interpersonal relatedness (Blatt & Shichman, 1983; Blatt & Blass, 1990, 1996), Diamond and colleagues (1991) constructed a 10-point scale to assess the degree of differentiation and relatedness in descriptions of self and significant others. The Differentiation-Relatedness (D-R) Scale identifies the following 10 points:

1. A lack of basic differentiation between self and others (Levels 1 and 2);
2. The use of mirroring (Level 3), self–other idealization or denigration (Level 4), and an oscillation between polarized negative and positive attributes (Level 5), as maneuvers to establish and consolidate or stabilize representations;
3. An emergent differentiated, constant, and integrated representation of self and other, with increasing tolerance for complexity and ambiguity (Levels 6 and 7);
4. Representations of self and others as empathically interrelated (Level 8);
5. Representations of self and other in reciprocal and mutually facilitating interactions (Level 9); and
6. Reflectively constructed integrated representations of self and others in reciprocal relationships (Level 10).

This scale is based on the assumption that psychological development moves toward the emergence of a consolidated, integrated, and individuated sense of self-definition and empathically attuned mutual relatedness with significant others (Aron, 1996; Benjamin, 1995; Blatt, 1991, 1995, 2006, 2008; Blatt & Blass, 1990, 1996; Blatt & Shichman, 1983; Jordan, 1986; Miller, 1984; Mitchell, 1988; D. N. Stern, 1985; Surrey, 1985). Differentiation (separation) and relatedness, in this model, are interactive dimensions that unfold throughout development. The dialectical interaction between these two developmental dimensions facilitates the emergence and consolidation of increasingly mature levels of both self-organization and reciprocally attuned empathic relatedness. The scale assumes that, with psychological development, representations of self and other become increasingly differentiated and integrated and also begin to reflect an increased appreciation of interpersonal relatedness.

As regards the dimension of differentiation, the scale reflects, at the lowest levels, the compromise of boundaries with regard to basic body awareness, emotions, and thoughts. The next scale levels reflect a unitary, unmodulated view of self and of the other as extensions of each other or as mirrored images (i.e., images in which aspects of self and other are identical). At an intermediate level of differentiation, representations are organized around a unitary idealization or denigration of self or other (i.e., around an exaggerated sense of the goodness or badness of the figure described). At the next level, these exaggerated aspects of self and other alternate in a juxtaposition of polarized (i.e., all-good or all-bad) extremes. Later scale levels of differentiation reflect an increased capacity to integrate disparate aspects of self and other and an increased tolerance for ambivalence and ambiguity (Kernberg, 1977).

As regards the dimension of relatedness, the D-R Scale assesses the progression toward empathically attuned mutuality and reciprocity in complex interpersonal relationships. At lower levels, the sense of relatedness in representations may involve being overwhelmed or controlled by the other (e.g., trying to resist the onslaught of an other who is experienced as bad and destructive). At increasingly higher levels, relatedness may be expressed primarily in parallel interactions, in expressions of cooperation and collaboration, in understanding the other's perspective, or in expressions of empathically attuned mutuality (Blatt & Blass, 1990, 1996). At the highest levels, descriptions will reflect a sense of one's participation in complex relational matrices that determine perceptions, attributions, and the constructions of meaning.

Research on Differentiation-Relatedness

Levy, Blatt, & Shaver (1998), for example, assessing the structural organization of descriptions of significant others (mother and father) in young adults, found significant differences, as measured by the D-R Scale, in descriptions of parents by individuals with different attachment styles. The descriptions by insecurely attached individuals were less cohesive, differentiated, and integrated than were those of securely attached persons. Secure attachment appeared to involve more stable, consistent, and integrated representations of significant others and the ability to differentiate more fully from one's parents while still maintaining a sense of relatedness. Insecurely attached individuals, both Dismissive Avoidant and Preoccupied (or Anxious Ambivalent), gave less differentiated, one-sided, unidimensional descriptions of their parents as punitive, malevolent, and lacking in warmth, or as highly idealized. These individuals had a rigid categorization of their parents either as extremely negative or as idealized caregivers.

The D-R Scale was also used to study changes in significant-figure descriptions in severely disturbed adolescent and young adult inpatients in long-term, psychoanalytically oriented treatment. Changes in D-R in descriptions of self and of significant figures were positively correlated with changes in level of psychosocial functioning, as independently measured on the Global Assessment Scale (GAS; Endicott, Spitzer, Fleiss, & Cohen, 1976), rated from detailed case reports. The mean D-R score increased from a predominance of polarization and splitting (Level 5) to an emergent object constancy (Level 6). In addition, patients who showed the greatest clinical improvement initially described their therapists in a manner that was already approaching the emergence of object constancy, while those who were to show less improvement started at the level of polarization and splitting in describing their therapists (Blatt, Auerbach, & Aryan, 1998). And at discharge, those patients with greater therapeutic change had a consolidation of object constancy (D-R Level 7) in their therapist descriptions, whereas patients with less improvement had just achieved the emergence of object constancy (D-R Level 6). To be sure, the patients remained some distance from fully mature object relations and object representations, but the development of the capacity to tolerate ambivalent feelings about significant objects should be viewed as an important and necessary step on the way to this more mature level of interpersonal relatedness. Vermote (2005), evaluating changes in D-R scores over a nine-month inpatient treatment program of patients with personality disorders, also found a highly significant increase in the D-R scores at termination, an increase that was sustained in a follow-up evaluation conducted one year after the termination of treatment.

These findings by Vermote (2005) and by Blatt et al. (1996, 1998) of significant increases in D-R score in intensive inpatient treatment of seriously disturbed patients are consistent with recent conclusions by Sandell

(2005) that successful psychodynamic treatment results in the appropriation of "inner soothing objects" that can be helpful in dealing with subsequent stressful life events. These findings suggest that internalization plays a central role in the treatment process through growth in the differentiation and relatedness of self- and object representations.

INTERNALIZATION, INTERSUBJECTIVITY, AND MENTALIZATION IN THE THERAPEUTIC PROCESS

The processes of gratifying involvement (interpersonal relatedness) and experienced incompatibility (separation and individuation) are therefore central to psychological growth not only in normal development but also in the psychotherapy. Although significant differences exist between the sequences of change that occur in normal development and in long-term, intensive treatment, the fundamental mechanisms of psychological growth may be the same. As in normal development, an oscillation between relatedness and separation, between gratifying involvement and experienced incompatibility, is central to the therapeutic process. Psychoanalysis is conducted in what Stone (1961) described as a state of "intimate separation" (pp. 89, 91) or "deprivation in intimacy" (p. 105). The mutative power of long-term intensive psychotherapy appears to derive from the ongoing tension between closeness and distance, between attachment and separation, between gratifying involvement and experienced incompatibility. Gratification, according to Stone, must not be totally lost in the frustrations of analysis; the analyst's "physicianly concerns" must be combined with the analyst's deprivations of the patient if the analytic process is to develop and flourish. To extend Stone's argument, repeated sequences of gratifying involvement and experienced incompatibility are basic to the internalization that is necessary for therapeutic change (Blatt & Behrends, 1987).

Gratifying involvement or attachment occurs in various ways in long-term intensive treatment. By remaining relatively nonjudgmental and dispassionate while simultaneously concerned and compassionate (see Coveleyn & Luyten, 2005), the therapist creates a context in which the patient is able to experience various forms of gratifying involvement in the transference at different developmental levels. Gratifying involvement in long-term treatment evolves from the patient's feeling respected and understood and finding the therapist accepting, empathic, and capable of assuming the patient's frame of reference (Rogers, 1951), and it grows as patient and therapist together give voice to the multiplicity of subtle feelings, emotions, and thoughts that occur within the therapeutic hour. The patient develops feelings of affection by repeatedly experiencing the therapist as a caring, perceptive person. Interpretations, if accurate, well-timed, and tactfully stated, can be experienced as an expression of the therapist's concern and understanding (Modell, 1976). Interpretations convey not only ideas and observations but also the therapist's emotional attitudes toward the patient (Rycroft, 1956). Accurate interpretations enable patients to achieve the sense that they can make contact with others, that they are able to communicate, and that their feelings and experiences have a logic and a coherence that can be understood and accepted by another person (Atwood & Stolorow, 1980; Blatt & Erlich, 1982; Fonagy & Target, 2005; Rycroft, 1956). Both the quality of the therapeutic relationship and the sensitivity of interpretations contribute to the creation of a "holding environment" (Modell, 1976; Winnicott, 1960).

Indeed, as Winnicott (1982) stated, "Psychotherapy is not making clever and apt interpretations; by and large it is a long-term giving back what the patient brings. It is a complex derivative of the [maternal] face that reflects back what there is to be seen" (p. 117). Similarly, Bromberg (1998) observes, "For characterological growth to occur the patient must be able to see himself through the eyes of the analyst as an ongoing aspect of feeling himself validated and understood in the terms he sees himself" (p. 149). Indeed, specifically noting the parallels between childhood and psychotherapeutic experiences in being recognized as having one's subjectivity and mentalization, Fonagy and Target (2005) write, "Patients experience an intense hunger for understanding the ways that minds function; they learn this not so much from specific comments of the analyst but rather through the observation of the analyst's developing a coherent model of their minds—through the experience of a mind's having their minds in mind" (p. 208). It is further noted that, per intersubjectivity theory, one of the consequences of the therapist's having the patient's mind in mind is that the patient comes to recognize the independent subjectivity of the therapist— that is, to recognize the therapist not only as object of one's wishes and fears but also as having wishes and fears of his or her own. In many ways, then, the shared affective experiences in treatment are similar in basic form to the affective communication between child and caregiver that are so vital to psychological development, and interpretations produce their effects in large part because they are situated in these relational, intersubjective processes. As the empirical psychotherapy literature (e.g., Blatt & Zuroff, 2005; Krupnick et al., 1996; Norcross, 2002; Wampold, 2001; Zuroff & Blatt, 2006) suggests, the therapeutic alliance is more important than therapeutic technique in producing therapeutic outcomes, but it must also be understood that therapeutic technique, in the form of accurate, empathic interpretations, is essential to the beneficial unfolding of the therapeutic relationship (Blatt, 2008).

The degree and form of attachment (gratifying involvement) and separation (experienced incompatibility) that fosters psychological development also depends upon the developmental level and personality organization of the patient. As the patient's level of functioning changes, even within a single hour, it is expressed in fluctuations of the therapeutic relationship that may call for different types of interventions—in the direction of facilitating either separation or gratifying involvement. The therapist can respond appropriately to the patient's developmental needs or can be too frustrating—either by prematurely demanding a degree or type of differentiation that exceeds the patient's capacity for internalization or by thwarting appropriate strivings for separation and independence. As a result of the therapist's interpreting accurately the various forms of gratifying involvements and incompatibilities, attachments and separations, as they are expressed in the therapeutic relationship, patients increasingly experience the therapist and themselves in new ways, thereby providing greater opportunity for the appropriation of aspects of a more mature therapeutic relationship and of more differentiated and integrated schemas of self and of interpersonal relations. As a consequence of interpretation and working through, the therapeutic relationship moves toward more mature forms of relatedness in which needs are satisfied on increasingly higher levels and in the self's becoming more differentiated and integrated. As Loewald (1960) noted, "The satisfaction involved in the analytic interaction is a sublimated one, in increasing degree as the analysis progresses" (p. 239).

Interpretation and insight lead to the capacity to revise, even relinquish, disruptive (pathological) internalizations—that is, conceptions of self and of others that limit openness to new experiences and thwart possibilities for the development of new aspects of the self and new dimensions of interpersonal relatedness (Blatt & Erlich, 1982). Revising or relinquishing pathological aspects of internalizations creates the opportunity to achieve new internalizations that facilitate more mature functioning. New internalizations derive in part from interpretation and insight and in part through experiences in the therapeutic relationship. As Loewald (1960) stated, the resumption of ego development in the therapeutic process "is contingent on the relationship with a new object, the analyst" (p. 221). Internalization occurs in therapy in essentially the same way and through the same basic process that internalization takes place in normal development: through a hierarchical spirality of gratifying involvements and experienced incompatibilities, of attachments and separations, within an interpersonal relationship, and with this dialectic leading to the capacity for more mature forms of relatedness and a more integrated sense of self.

INTERNALIZATION AND THE THERAPEUTIC RELATIONSHIP

These formulations of the mutative forces in the treatment process do not necessarily suggest any alteration of basic therapeutic technique. But further understanding of the mechanisms of therapeutic action can be gained by considering both the gratifying and depriving aspects of interpretation and the therapeutic relationship. The patient continually oscillates between seeking gratifying involvement with the therapist and experiencing incompatibilities with this gratifying involvement in its current form. The oscillation between gratification and incompatibilities, between attachments and separations, enables the patient eventually to appropriate crucial aspects of the therapeutic relationship, with this internalization facilitating movement toward progressively higher and more mature forms of interpersonal relatedness and self-definition. As Loewald (1960) stated, "The analyst relates to the patient in tune with the shifting levels of development manifested by the patient at different times but always from the viewpoint of potential growth" (p. 230); see also Gedo & Goldberg (1973). Loewald (1960) also noted that "Mature object relations are not characterized by a sameness of relatedness but by an optimal range of relatedness and by the ability to relate to different objects according to their particular levels of maturity" (p. 230). A mature relationship combines the gratification of intimate union with the recognition and enhancement of separateness and personal or self development of both members of the relationship (Schafer, 1959).

A previously thwarted developmental process is reinitiated in therapy by a relative neutrality that allows the patient to construct the therapist in ways that meet the patient's needs. As the therapist comes to know the patient's needs within the therapeutic relationship, the therapist interprets these needs in a way and at a pace that the patient can tolerate and work with effectively. Interpretations in this sense constitute a disruption or frustration of the gratifying involvement of the therapeutic relationship, and this disruption encourages the patient to begin to assume for himself or herself aspects of the psychological functions that he or she previously depended upon the therapist to provide. Interpretations enable the patient to recognize the nature of his or her gratifying involvement with or attachment to the therapist and to experience a sense of incompatibility with less-mature types of involvement. Pathological introjects expressed in the therapeutic relationship are eventually replaced by more stable and autonomous identifications with aspects of the therapeutic process (Meissner, 1979). The patient's appropriation of significant aspects and functions of the therapeutic relationship is consistent with Freud's (1921) observation that "In the individual's mental life someone else is invariably involved, as a model, as an object, as a helper, as an opponent" (p. 69).

Experienced incompatibility can take many forms in therapy besides interpretation, such as interruptions of the cadence of hours because of the absence of the therapist or patient, failures in communication and empathy, or the patient's own increasing dissatisfaction with his or her level of functioning. It is important to stress that experienced incompatibility is not only externally imposed by the therapist through interpretations or by events such as the therapist's absence, but can also originate with the patient, who may become increasingly dissatisfied with a particular level of gratifying involvement or a particular form of attachment. These experienced incompatibilities propel patient and therapist to reestablish the gratifying involvement of the therapeutic relationship in a new form. This redefinition of the self and recasting of the relationship sometimes occurs in bold and dramatic form. Often, however, this process is subtle and even imperceptible as it occurs from moment to moment (Behrends & Blatt, 1985).

Interpretations are generally conceptualized as a major form of confrontation or experienced incompatibility. But it is important to stress that for an interpretation to be truly mutative, it must embody both a gratifying involvement (the patient's feeling understood) and an experienced incompatibility (the confrontation by the therapist of transference wishes rooted in pathological object relations). The timing, tact, and tone of the intervention, as well as the quality of the therapeutic relationship, influence its therapeutic effectiveness. In this sense, interpretations and the therapeutic relationship are inextricably intertwined and are interdependent (Blatt & Behrends, 1987).

Interpretations implicitly encourage the patient to seek a real object—the empathic and concerned therapist in a relationship that has evolved with the patient's emerging sense of self. Relinquishing dysfunctional or pathologic forms of gratification or attachment (including masochistic ones) requires the patient and the therapist to try to reestablish the gratifying involvement on a new level. Following an experienced incompatibility, the patient tries to restore a somewhat revised attachment to or a gratifying relationship with the therapist. Much as when the mother is absent and the child struggles to form some sense of connection to her in her absence, the patient struggles to establish a fuller sense of the therapist and of himself or herself in the therapeutic relationship. The patient, having appropriated a significant aspect of the therapeutic relationship, will revise his or her sense of self and begin to relate to the therapist in a more mature way. Likewise, the therapist will feel the need to move to a new level of therapeutic involvement and interpretation. The next series of interpretations, if accurate, empathically stated, and well timed, should lead to the next level of attachment or gratifying involvement, and it in turn will be disrupted by an experienced incompatibility that fosters yet a new level of internalization and development of a new sense of self (Blatt & Behrends, 1987).

Internalization occurs throughout the therapy, but it is particularly central for both the patient and the therapist in the termination phase. With termination, the ultimate experienced incompatibility in therapy, the patient must carry on the therapeutic work alone, with the initial task of working through the difficult process of mourning. In termination, a fundamental uncertainty always remains for both patient and therapist. Neither can be absolutely certain of the outcome because appropriation of the therapeutic relationship and a consolidation of the sense of self can only reach its fullest extent subsequent to formal termination. The therapist, however, feels confident about termination when he or she has established a well-consolidated and stable representation of the patient as being able to conduct the therapeutic dialogue in his or her own right. And the patient feels confident about termination when he or she has established a mentalized and well-consolidated and stable representation of the therapist and of his or her independent subjectivity.

Thus, therapeutic progress appears to occur through the same mechanisms and in a way similar to normal psychological development. Therapeutic change occurs as a developmental sequence that can be characterized as a constantly evolving process of attachment and separation–individuation, of evolving levels of interpersonal relatedness and self-definition that derive from gratifying involvement, experienced incompatibility, and internalization. Patients gradually come to experience the therapist and themselves as separate objects, increasingly free of distortion by narcissistic needs or projections from past relationships. Union and separation, relatedness and self-definition, are fundamental and universal psychological needs and experiences that occur repeatedly in the course of psychological growth and development (see also Nacht, 1964). The degree and form of union and separation, of gratifying involvement and experienced incompatibility that fosters individuation and the capacity for interpersonal relatedness, depends upon the developmental level of the patient. This will vary at different points in the therapeutic process as the patient moves to new developmental levels. As the patient's level of functioning undergoes changes, even within a single hour, it is expressed in fluctuations—in the direction either of greater separation or of gratifying involvement. But reunion, safety, and security, as well as separation and mastery, are fundamental to psychological development, and both are essential for the therapeutic process.

A CLINICAL EXAMPLE

The clinical and theoretical formulations discussed thus far suggest that therapeutic change, especially in the treatment of seriously disturbed patients, involves three fundamental processes:

1. Relinquishing, revising, or transforming disruptive (pathological) aspects of internalizations as they are experienced in the transference;
2. Becoming available to internalize more adaptive, self-enhancing relationships, particularly the therapeutic relationship;
3. Constructing a more coherent self-definition, and the emergence of a capacity for mutual, reciprocal interpersonal relatedness[3].

Descriptions of self and significant others (mother and therapist) provided by a seriously disturbed early adolescent girl every 6 months during long-term (18 months) intensive inpatient treatment, including three times weekly psychodynamically oriented psychotherapy, demonstrate the processes through which this young woman began to revise a destructive psychotic maternal introject and to construct a more coherent and adaptive self-definition or identity.

Allison,[4] a single white 13-year-old female, was admitted for a third psychiatric hospitalization with a diagnosis of a severe psychotic depression with serious substance abuse, including IV heroin, a seriously distorted body image (anorexia), suicidal impulses, and marked paranoid trends with mixed histrionic and compulsive features in a borderline personality disorder. During her one and a half years of intensive, comprehensive inpatient treatment, Allison's GAS scores rose from 22 ("needs some supervision to prevent hurting self or others") at admission, to 43 ("serious symptoms or impairments that obviously require treatment or attention") at discharge. Independent periodic reports of Allison's treatment over the 19 months of hospitalization indicated that her self-esteem improved noticeably, including taking pride in her womanly body. She became less vulnerable to psychotic decompensation and was more capable of using relationships to get through personal crises. She was also able to realize that her intense involvement with drugs was a substitute for the nurturance she felt she could not obtain in other ways. Although considered by staff to be still vulnerable to psychotic regression, Allison was discharged to a residential facility because her parents could not afford to continue intensive treatment. To delineate the ways in which Allison changed in the course of treatment, we present and discuss her descriptions of mother, self, and therapist, collected at admission to the hospital and every six months thereafter until discharge. These descriptions are presented in Tables 1, 2, and 3.

Table 1

DESCRIPTIONS OF THERAPIST

Admission

Sweet, supportive, trusting, and caring.

6 Months

I can't describe her because I don't know her. Seems to care about me. That's it.

1 Year

I don't know her. I won't do it. I don't like her. Unaware, without knowing it. Has too much faith in me. [Refused inquiry.]

Discharge

I'm trying to think of a word. Tactful in approaching subjects. That wasn't the word I was thinking of—not blunt—can say things in a better fashion. She can put things in a better way that doesn't sound so intimidating or so cruel. She's sweet, generous and has high morals. She's a nice person. Has high standards.

Table 2

DESCRIPTIONS OF MOTHER

Admission

Worried, aggressive, unhappy, and lonely.
Inquiry: [Anything else?] No.

6 Months

Neurotic, irregular, stubborn, caring, overwhelming, cold. That's it.
Inquiry: [Neurotic?] She's crazy. She's very edgy. The slightest thing may set her off. [Irregular?] Not consistent. Too moody. [Stubborn?] Won't budge on something she believes is right. Won't listen to reason. [Caring?] She means well. [Overwhelming?] Overbearing. [Cold?] She can turn herself off and be cold.

1 Year

I don't want to do this . . . she means well. Tries hard to be understanding. Overprotective. Suspicious. Alone. Insomniac. No, don't write that please. Cross it out. That's it. Oh yeah curly hair, bleached. Tweezed eyebrows. Bad skin.

Inquiry: [Means well?] Good intentions. [Understanding?] Self-explanatory. But has little concept of what my problems really are. [Overprotective?] Restricting of freedom. [Suspicious?] Untrusting. [Alone?] Doesn't really confide in anybody, I don't think.

Discharge

She's sweet, caring, opinionated. She tries hard, works hard. Sometimes overbearing. She's about 5 feet 5 inches, say 120 pounds, curly hair, not much on top, sort of flat-chested. Stubborn.

Inquiry: [Overbearing?] Sometimes she's just too much for me— all these qualities are too much for me. She doesn't like to give in.

Table 3

DESCRIPTIONS OF SELF

Admission

Depends on how I'm feeling. Sometimes I'm outgoing but other times I'm withdrawn. I don't know.

Inquiry: [What else?] I don't want to describe myself. [Why?] 'Cause I get upset when I do. [Can you tell me what upsets you?] I'm either too conceited or too modest to answer something like this.

6 Months

I can't describe myself. You describe me. It's hard. No, it's easy. Vulnerable. Hurt. Lonely. Sort of happy. Getting more confident. No—please write gaining confidence. Considerate.

Inquiry: [Vulnerable?] I can easily be hurt. [Hurt?] Can't say more. [Lonely?] I'm suffering from lack of caring. I'm not cared about the way I'd like to be. [Considerate?] Care about others' feelings.

1 Year

Depressed, suspicious, alone, manipulative, musical, artistic, sensitive, hopeless. Drug abuser, sympathetic. Can be friendly. Opinionated, withdrawn, angry, chain smoker. Can be humorous. That's it.

Inquiry: [Depressed?] I don't enjoy life. [Suspicious?] Don't trust people easily. [Sensitive?] I take things personally. [Hopeless?] I'm a failure. I'll never make it. Doomed to be depressed. [Sympathetic?] Self-explanatory. [Opinionated?] I form my own opinions. [Withdrawn?] Keep to myself. [Angry?] Lots of hidden rage. Someday it will come out.

Discharge

Lonely, insecure. Hiding behind a facade. Have sense. Abnormal opinions. One of my abnormal opinions is that people who want to kill themselves should be allowed to kill themselves—and I wasn't referring to myself either. Mature—can be mature—haven't really acted it during the psych testing. I sort of fooled around. Should have more confidence.

Revising and Relinquishing Distorted and Disruptive Introjects

Initially at admission to the hospital, Allison described her therapist in positive, idealized terms ("Sweet, supportive, trusting, and caring") that were remarkable because they indicated that Allison, unlike most severely impaired adolescents, was able to think about the therapist as a potentially caring figure and therefore about significant others in mentalized terms—that is, in terms of thoughts and feelings. Nevertheless, this emotionally positive description of the therapist became somewhat more realistic at 6 months. The idealized adjectives at admission were now omitted, and Allison expressed some reservations about her therapist's feelings about her ("I can't describe her because I don't know her. She *seems* to care about me. That's it"). Allison's description of her therapist at one year indicated that the therapeutic relationship had shifted dramatically from the idealization at admission. She now said that she did not like her therapist and refused to describe her ("I don't know her. I won't do it. I don't like her. Unaware, without knowing it. Has too much faith in me"). These changes in the descriptions, while showing that Allison could still think about her therapist's possible mental states, indicated burgeoning intense hostile feelings that were, at least partly, an expression of the emergence of an intense negative, psychotic, maternal transference.

Early in treatment, the therapist described Allison as "very needy," as desperately hoping that her female therapist would become her wished-for, idealized mother who would care for and nurture her. Allison reacted to rescheduled therapy hours and to the therapist's vacation with feelings of rejection and anger, becoming psychotic at times in response to these perceived losses.

The independently prepared treatment review at one year indicated that, in the therapist's view, an intense psychotic, negative maternal transference had gradually developed during the previous six months. Toward the end of the first year of therapy, Allison began to express in very concrete ways intense wishes that the therapist become a literal mothering figure. She made attempts to hug the therapist, and at one point she asked to sit on the therapist's lap. Allison perceived as a rejection her therapist's request that Allison not enact but put into words her wishes for the therapist to become a mothering figure. Subsequently, Allison reported being tormented by hallucinations in which her mother's disembodied arms were chasing her with tweezers. Allison became increasingly critical, oppositional, hostile, and sadistic toward the therapist. On one occasion, Allison had to be restrained to control her homicidal impulses to stab the therapist with a pair of scissors, and for a period of time Allison discontinued her therapy sessions. The therapist viewed this transient psychotic transference as deriving in part from the emergence of very painful paranoid feelings—specifically, a belief that her mother wanted to kill her. Prior to hospitalization, for example, Allison often slept with a knife under her pillow to protect herself from her mother, who wandered around the house at night because of insomnia. As this psychotic transference was enacted and worked through in the treatment, Allison began to feel closer to her therapist, and eventually to her mother. In contrast to her refusal to describe her therapist at one year, at termination, after 19 months of treatment, Allison described her therapist in positive terms, emphasizing her relatedness with the therapist, especially their sharing of feelings, thoughts, and enriching experiences ("Tactful. . . . Sweet, generous, and has high morals. She's a nice person. Has high standards"). Quite clearly, Allison's ability to mentalize self and therapist, although present at the beginning of her treatment, had grown considerably by the time of her discharge from the hospital. Indeed, her therapist reported that, in her final therapy session, Allison stated, "I think you probably made the right decision by not letting me sit on your lap. I would have felt good, like I was sitting on my mother's lap, but I also think I would have had sexual feelings. It would have been confusing for me."

Resolution of a psychotic maternal introject was indicated not only by this marked transformation in Allison's descriptions of her therapist, but also by revisions in Allison's descriptions of her mother from an initial markedly negative and dysphoric description at admission ("Worried, aggressive, unhappy, and lonely") to a characterization of mother after one year of treatment that contrasted grotesque qualities ("Suspicious, alone, insomniac, . . . curly bleached hair, tweezed eyebrows, bad skin") with a brief statement about mother's "good intentions" of trying "hard to be understanding." This attempt by Allison to understand her mother's mental states—her thoughts and feelings—is particularly impressive in this context because of the pressure of persecutory material that nearly overwhelms Allison's ability to keep positive aspects of her mother in mind. Nevertheless, through the therapeutic process, this initial effort, at one year, to modulate the frightening, grotesque, destructive image of the mother into a more balanced, qualified, and differentiated representation became even more differentiated at termination. Allison described her mother in more reality-based physical terms ("She's about 5 feet, 5 inches, say 120 pounds, curly hair, not much on top, sort of flat-chested") that implied her mother's limited ability to meet Allison's fundamental needs for maternal care. On the other hand, in an integration of modulated positive and negative terms, she portrayed her mother as having some capacity and interest in providing for her ("She's sweet, caring, opinionated. She tries hard, works hard. Sometimes overbearing, . . . Stubborn").

Internalization and the Construction of a Coherent Identity or Self-Definition

Equally impressive was the process through which Allison attempted to construct a more coherent identity. It is important to note in this regard that describing oneself is a significantly more complex process than describing another because the self-description requires an integration of both self as subject and self as object. Insofar as it is a self-reflexive structure, in which subjective and objective views on the self are integrated (see, e.g., Auerbach, 1993; Auerbach & Blatt, 1997, 2001; Bach, 1985, 1994; Broucek, 1991;

Damon & Hart, 1988; Harter, 1999; Modell, 1993), the self-description is crucial to the process of mentalization, as well as to psychic growth more generally (see Auerbach & Blatt, 1996, 1997, 2001, 2002). At admission, therefore, Allison's self-description, while basically negative in tone, contained perplexing polarities that suggested a beginning capacity to recognize contradictory aspects of herself and the realization that her feelings about herself were highly dependent on her affect state ("Depends on how I'm feeling. Sometimes I'm outgoing but other times I'm withdrawn. I don't know. I don't want to describe myself because I get upset when I do. I'm either too conceited or too modest to answer something like this"). Even though her description was fragmented, poorly integrated, and organized around only rudimentary positive and negative elements, the distinctions suggested a capacity for developing more subtle differentiations and for recognizing her need to integrate these disparate qualities.

At six months, Allison described herself with adjectives similar to those she used to describe her mother at admission. Although her self-description continued to comprise generally contradictory images, it was no longer based solely on the juxtaposition of polarized attributes. Despite expressions of narcissistic vulnerability, she now expressed a sense of hope and optimism— in her words, a sense of confidence ("Vulnerable, hurt. Lonely, sort of happy, getting more confident—no, please write gaining more confidence, considerate"). This exchange around Allison's concern about the precision of her verbalizations conveyed, in word and deed, her self-reflectivity, her subtle grasp of mental states, and her increased self-esteem, as well as her ability to form a working relationship with the examiner.

Allison's self-description at one year indicated a movement toward a more differentiated, unified, and coherent sense of self. The self-description contained several alternations between juxtaposed series, first of negative and then of positive attributes, ending with a more positive conditional note ("Depressed, suspicious, alone, manipulative, musical, artistic, sensitive, hopeless. Drug abuser, sympathetic. Can be friendly. Opinionated, withdrawn, angry, chain smoker. Can be humorous. That's it"). Although some of the adjectives reflected her continuing identification with her mother's dysphoria, Allison's increased acknowledgment of these painful affects was an important part of her increasing self-cohesion. Her growing capacity for self-reflection and mentalization and her attempts to share painful feelings and thoughts with another paralleled her increased empathic appreciation of her parents. As a consequence of this greater empathy, she now viewed herself as "sensitive" and "sympathetic."

Depressive themes evident in Allison's self-description at one year were continued in her self-description at discharge, but they were less pervasive and intense. Her concern about suicide also indicated her continuing dysphoria, although she was now able to modulate this concern through intellectualization. But primary among the changes at discharge was Allison's increased capacity for self-reflection and mentalization. Allison had finally begun to think of herself in a formal operational mode, in which she was concerned about abstract moral principles.

A comparison of Allison's self-descriptions with her descriptions of her therapist calls our attention to a very important mechanism in her construction of a coherent identity as an essential aspect of her therapeutic progress. It is noteworthy that Allison's description of her therapist at discharge emphasizes the very same capacity in the therapist that Allison had enacted in her self-description at six months when she told the examiner to revise her statement, "getting more confident," to the more adroit phrase, "gaining confidence." Allison again displayed this interest in verbal precision in her description of her therapist at termination as she sought to select appropriate words and phrases to communicate her appreciation of the therapist's verbal facility to say things in ways that are not intimidating or cruel. ("I'm trying to think of a word—tactful in approaching subjects. That wasn't the word I was thinking of—not blunt—can say things in a better fashion. She can put things in a better way that doesn't sound so intimidating or so cruel"). Similarly, Allison's recognition of her therapist's high moral standards ("She's sweet, generous, and has high morals; she's a nice person, has high standards") parallels Allison's formulations of her own ethical beliefs and principles, specifically about suicide, with these ethical concerns again indicating the growth in Allison's capacity for mentalization.

Adaptive Projective Identification

This clinical example suggests that some patients may not only internalize and take as their own aspects of the therapeutic activities, attitudes, and functions of the therapist as part of the process of therapeutic change, but may also actively seek to identify and construct in their therapist qualities that derive from or meet some of their own needs, the development of which had previously been thwarted by their psychological disturbances and conflicts (Blatt et al., 1996). With the resolution of more pathological introjects earlier in the treatment process, some patients may then seek to take as their own qualities that they have long sought to acquire for themselves and have now identified or constructed in the therapist. In this regard, as intersubjectivity theory suggests, internalization and growth in mentalization are situated in an interpersonal matrix and are set in motion, within the therapeutic situation, by a meeting of minds. We have termed this process, by which patients seek and find in their therapists their own partially internalized psychological strengths, *adaptive projective identification* (Blatt et al., 1996). We have some concerns about terminology, however, and have thought that the process is more accurately described as a form of transitional object relatedness—that is, an attempt to remain connected to caregiving figures while becoming separate, to use a relationship to differentiate as well as to become oneself (Auerbach & Blatt, 2001, 2002).

Thus, intensive psychodynamic treatment appears to have therapeutic effect through the internalization of new psychic structures, revised representations of self and others and of their actual and potential interactions, that emerge in the relationship with the therapist. Disturbed internalizations that limit and impair functioning are relinquished, revised, and replaced by the internalization of more differentiated psychic structures organized around a new object—the therapist (McLaughlin, 1981). Powerful disruptive internalizations are projected onto the therapist early in the treatment process, and as these pathological transferences are resolved in the therapeutic relationship, patients begin to construct more adaptive interpersonal schemas. These more adaptive psychic structures are eventually appropriated in a more consolidated way through identification. In the therapeutic relationship, patients discover qualities of their therapist that they eventually take on as their own because these qualities are congruent with their own fundamental needs, goals, aspirations, and capacities. These new, more adaptive representational structures are based not only on the qualities of the therapist and aspects of the therapeutic process but also on the patient's perceptions and constructions of the therapist, on understandings that derive in part from preexisting adaptive partial introjects that the patient has long sought to express but was unable to sustain because of distorting pathological identifications, because of traumatic anxieties about accepting strengths and competences as part of the self. Patients, therefore, are active agents who seek in the therapeutic relationship to construct and identify with personally meaningful and functionally significant aspects of the therapist that they must first find and experience in a significant attachment or need-gratifying relationship as properties and characteristics of another before they can more fully appropriate these functions for themselves. This process of finding disavowed positive aspects of the self in the therapist and in the therapeutic relationship is a prime example of mentalization and internalization. Once these functions are experienced within the therapeutic relationship, patients can begin to make these functions their own and become less reliant on others to provide these functions for them (Blatt & Behrends, 1987). In so doing, patients become more accepting of the separateness of both their own minds and the mind of their therapists, while valuing the relational context that allows this separateness to emerge. This complex process of externalization and internalization, of adaptive projective identification, of appropriating in a more adaptive form aspects of the self that have been unexpressed or even disavowed, is often prompted by the recognition of the eventual loss of the object. The acknowledgment and acceptance of the object's separateness, in this case, the therapist, results in the formation of more integrated psychic structures—more adaptive interpersonal schemas, more differentiated and integrated representations of self and of significant others in interpersonal relationships characterized by greater mutuality and reciprocity.

NOTES

1. This paper derives from and integrates and extends earlier contributions, including Auerbach & Blatt, 1996, 2001, 2002; Behrends & Blatt, 1985; Blatt, 2006, 2008; Blatt & Auerbach, 2001, 2003; Blatt & Behrends, 1987; Blatt, Stayner, Auerbach, & Behrends, 1996.

2. In a psychologically mature individual, these experiences of gratifying involvement, experienced incompatibility, and internalization may occur through fantasized engagement with another person, a set of ideals, works of art, or values.

3. We describe this process as a linear sequence primarily for ease of communication, but we want to stress that this process usually occurs as a series of hierarchically organized synergistic interactions, even within a single treatment session as well as throughout the treatment process.

4. Allison's ORI protocol, her descriptions of self and of mother, father, therapist, and a significant other, have been discussed in prior reports (Auerbach & Blatt, 1996, 2001; Blatt, Stayner, Auerbach, & Behrends, 1996; Diamond, Kaslow, Coonerty, & Blatt, 1990; Gruen & Blatt, 1990) in which she was called "Patient A."

REFERENCES

Ainsworth, M. D. S. (1967). *Infancy in Uganda: Infant Care and the Growth of Love*. Baltimore, MD: Johns Hopkins University Press.

Ainsworth, M. D. S. (1969). Object relations, dependency, and attachment: A theoretical review of the mother-infant relationship. *Developmental Psychology, 40*, 969–1025.

Anderson, J. R. (1983). *The Architecture of Cognition*. Cambridge, MA: Harvard University Press.

Aron, L. (1996). *A Meetings of Minds: Mutuality in Psychoanalysis*. Hillsdale, NJ: Analytic Press.

Atwood, G. E., & Stolorow, R. D. (1980). Psychoanalytic concepts and the representational world. *Psychoanalytic Contemporary Thought, 3*, 267–290.

Auerbach, J. S. (1993). The origins of narcissism and narcissistic personality disorder: A theoretical and empirical reformulation. In J. M. Masling & R. F. Bornstein (Eds.), *Empirical Studies of Psychoanalytic Theories: Vol. 4. Psychoanalytic Perspectives on Psychopathology* (pp. 43–110). Washington, DC: American Psychological Association.

Auerbach, J. S., & Blatt, S. J. (1996). Self-representation in severe psychopathology: The role of reflexive self-awareness. *Psychoanalytic Psychology, 13*, 297–341.

Auerbach, J. S., & Blatt, S. J. (1997). Impairment of self-representation in schizophrenia: The roles of boundary articulation and self-reflexivity. *Bulletin of the Menninger Clinic, 61*, 297–316.

Auerbach, J. S., & Blatt, S. J. (2001). Self-reflexivity, intersubjectivity, and therapeutic change. *Psychoanalytic Psychology, 18*, 427–450.

Auerbach, J. S., & Blatt, S. J. (2002). The concept of mind: A developmental analysis. In R. Lasky (Ed.), *Symbolization and Desymbolization: Essays in Honor of Norbert Freedman* (pp. 75–117). New York: Other Press.

Bach, S. (1985). *Narcissistic States and the Therapeutic Process*. New York: Jason Aronson.

Bach, S. (1994). *The Language of Perversion and the Language of Love*. Northvale, NJ: Jason Aronson.

Beebe, B., & Lachmann, F. M. (1994). Representation and internalization in infancy: Three principles of saliency. *Psychoanalytic Psychology, 11*, 127–165.

Beebe, B., & Lachmann, F. M. (2002). *Infant Research and Adult Treatment: Co-constructing Interactions*. Hillsdale, NJ: Analytic Press.

Beebe, B., Lachman, F., & Jaffe, J. (1997). Mother–infant interaction structures and pre-symbolic self- and object representations. *Psychoanalytic Dialogues, 7*, 133–182.

Behrends, R. S., & Blatt, S. J. (1985). Internalization and psychological development through-out the life cycle. *Psychoanalytic Study of the Child, 40*, 11–39.

Benjamin, J. (1990). An outline of intersubjectivity: The development of recognition. *Psychoanalytic Psychology, 7*, 33–46.

Benjamin, J. (1995). *Like Subjects, Love Objects: Essays on Recognition and Sexual Differences*. New Haven, CT: Yale University Press.

Blatt, S. J. (1974). Levels of object representation in anaclitic and introjective depression. *Psychoanalytic Study of the Child, 29*, 107–157.

Blatt, S. J. (1983). Narcissism and egocentrism as concepts in individual and cultural development. *Psychoanalysis and Contemporary Thought, 6*, 291–303.

Blatt, S. J. (1991). A cognitive morphology of psychopathology. *Journal of Nervous and Mental Disease, 179*, 449–458.

Blatt, S. J. (1995). Representational structures in psychopathology. In D. Cicchetti & S. Toth (Eds.), *Rochester Symposium on Developmental Psychopathology: Vol. 6. Emotion, Cognition, and Representation* (pp. 1–33). Rochester, NY: University of Rochester Press.

Blatt, S. J. (2006). A fundamental polarity in psychoanalysis: Implications for personality development, psychopathology and the therapeutic process. *Psychoanalytic Inquiry, 26*, 492–518.

Blatt, S. J. (2008). *Polarities of Experience: Relatedness and Self-definition in Personality Development, Psychopathology, and the Therapeutic Process*. Washington, DC: American Psychological Association.

Blatt, S. J., & Auerbach, J. S. (2001). Mental representation, severe psychopathology, and the therapeutic process. *Journal of the American Psychoanalytic Association, 49*, 113–159.

Blatt, S. J., & Auerbach, J. S. (2003). Psychodynamic measures of therapeutic change. *Psychoanalytic Inquiry, 23*, 268–307.

Blatt, S. J., Auerbach, J. S., & Aryan, M. (1998). Representational structures and the therapeutic process. In R. F. Bornstein & J. M. Masling (Eds.), *Empirical Studies of Psychoanalytic Theories: Vol. 8. Empirical Investigations of the Therapeutic Hour* (pp. 63–107). Washington, DC: American Psychological Association.

Blatt, S. J., & Behrends, R. S. (1987). Internalization, separation-individuation, and the nature of therapeutic action. *International Journal of Psycho-Analysis, 68,* 279–297.

Blatt, S. J., Bers, S. A., & Schaffer, C. (1992). *The Assessment of Self.* Unpublished research manual, Yale University.

Blatt, S. J., & Blass, R. B. (1990). Attachment and separateness: A dialectic model of the products and processes of psychological development. *Psychoanalytic Study of the Child, 45,* 107–127.

Blatt, S. J., & Blass, R. (1996). Relatedness and self definition: A dialectic model of personality development. In G. G. Noam & K. W. Fischer (Eds.), *Development and Vulnerabilities in Close Relationships* (pp. 309–338). Hillsdale, NJ: Erlbaum.

Blatt, S. J., Brenneis, C. B., Schimek, J., & Glick, M. (1976). A Developmental Analysis of the Concept of the Object on the Rorschach. Unpublished research manual, Yale University.

Blatt, S. J., Chevron, E. S., Quinlan, D. M., & Wein, S. (1981). The Assessment of Qualitative and Structural Dimensions of Object Representations. Unpublished research manual, Yale University.

Blatt, S. J., Chevron, E. S., Quinlan, D. M., Schaffer, C. E., & Wein, S. (1988). The Assessment of Qualitative and Structural Dimensions of Object Representations (Rev. ed.). Unpublished research manual, Yale University.

Blatt, S. J., & Erlich, H. S. (1982). Levels of resistance in the psychotherapeutic process. In P. Wachtel (Ed.), *Resistance: Psychodynamic and Behavioral Approaches* (pp. 69–91). New York: Plenum.

Blatt, S. J., & Lerner, H. D. (1983). Investigations in the psychoanalytic theory of object relations and object representation. In J. Masling (Ed.), *Empirical Studies of Psychoanalytic Theories,* (Vol. 1, pp. 189–249). Hillsdale, NJ: Analytic Press.

Blatt, S. J., Schaffer, C. E., Bers, S. A., & Quinlan, D. M. (1992). Psychometric properties of the Adolescent Depressive Experiences Questionnaire. *Journal of Personality Assessment, 59,* 82–98.

Blatt, S. J., & Shichman, S. (1983). Two primary configurations of psychopathology. *Psychoanalysis and Contemporary Thought, 6,* 187–254.

Blatt, S. J., Stayner, D., Auerbach, J., & Behrends, R. S. (1996). Change in object and self representations in long-term, intensive, inpatient treatment of seriously disturbed adolescents and young adults. *Psychiatry: Interpersonal and Biological Processes, 59,* 82–107.

Blatt, S. J., Wein, S. J., Chevron, E. S., & Quinlan, D. M. (1979). Parental representations and depression in normal young adults. *Journal of Abnormal Psychology, 88,* 388–397.

Blatt, S. J., & Wild, C. M. (1976). *Schizophrenia: A Developmental Analysis.* New York: Academic Press.

Blatt, S. J., Wild, C., & Ritzler, B. A. (1975). Disturbances in object representation in schizophrenia. *Psychoanalysis and Contemporary Science, 4,* 235–288.

Blatt, S. J., & Zuroff, D. C. (2005). Empirical evaluation of the assumptions in identifying evidence based treatments in mental health. *Clinical Psychology Review, 25,* 459–486.

Bowlby, J. (1973). *Attachment and Loss, Vol. 2. Separation, Anxiety, and Anger.* New York: Basic Books.

Bowlby, J. (1977). The making and breaking of affectional bonds: 1. Etiology and psychopathology in light of attachment theory. *British Journal of Psychiatry, 130,* 201–210.

Bowlby, J. (1979). *The Making and Breaking of Affectional Bonds.* New York: Tavistock.

Bowlby, J. (1980). *Attachment and Loss: Vol. 3. Loss: Sadness and Depression.* New York: Basic Books.

Bowlby, J. (1982). *Attachment and Loss: Vol. 1. Attachment.* (2nd ed.). New York: Basic Books. (Original work published 1969, New York: Basic Books)

Bowlby, J. (1982). *Attachment and Loss: Vol. 3. Loss.* New York: Basic Books.

Bowlby, J. (1988a). Developmental psychology comes of age. *American Journal of Psychiatry, 145,* 1–10.

Bowlby, J. (1988b). *A secure base: Clinical applications of attachment theory.* London: Routledge & Kegan Paul.

Bretherton, I. (1987). Security, communication, and internal working models. In J. Osofsky (Ed.), *Handbook of Infant Development* (pp. 1061–1100). New York: Wiley.

Brewer, W. F., & Nakamura, G. V. (1984). The nature and function of schemas. In R. S. Wyer & T. K. Srull (Eds.), *Handbook of Social Cognition,* (Vol. 1, pp. 119–160). Hillsdale, NJ: Erlbaum.

Bromberg, P. M. (1998). *Standing in the Spaces: Essays on Clinical Process, Trauma, and Dissociation.* Hillsdale, NJ: Analytic Press.

Broucek, F. J. (1991). *Shame and the Self.* New York: Guilford.

Coonerty, S. (1986). An exploration of separation-individuation themes in borderline personality disorder. *Journal of Personality Assessment, 50,* 501–511.

Corveleyn, J., & Luyten, P. (2005). Psychodynamic psychologies and religion: Past, present, and future. In R. F. Paloutzian & C. L. Park (Eds.), *Handbook of the Psychology of Religion and Spirituality* (pp. 80–100). New York: Guilford.

Damon, W., & Hart, D. (1988). *Self-understanding in Childhood and Adolescence.* Cambridge, UK: Cambridge University Press.

Diamond, D., Blatt, S. J., Stayner, D., & Kaslow, N. (1991). Self-other Differentiation of Object Representations. Unpublished research manual, Yale University.

Diamond, D., Kaslow, N., Coonerty, S., & Blatt, S. J. (1990). Change in separation-individuation and intersubjectivity in long-term treatment. *Psychoanalytic Psychology*, *7*, 363–397.

Endicott, J., Spitzer, R. L., Fleiss, J. L., & Cohen, J. (1976). The Global Assessment Scale: A procedure for measuring overall severity of psychiatric disturbance. *Archives of General Psychiatry*, *33*, 766–771.

Fairbairn, W. R. D. (1952). *Psychoanalytic studies of the personality*. London: Routledge & Kegan Paul.

Fiske, S. T., & Taylor, S. E. (1984). *Social Cognition* (2nd ed.). New York: Random House.

Fonagy, P., Gergely, G., Jurist, E. L., & Target, M. (2002). *Affect Regulation, Mentalization, and the Development of the Self*. New York: Other Press.

Fonagy, P., Steele, M., Steele, H., Leigh, T., Kennedy, R., Mattoon, G., & Target, M. (1995). Attachment, the reflective self, and borderline states: The predictive specificity of the Adult Attachment Interview and pathological emotional development. In S. Goldberg, R. Muir, & J. Kerr (Eds.), *Attachment Theory: Social, Developmental, and Clinical Perspectives* (pp. 233–278). Hillsdale, NJ: Analytic Press.

Fonagy, P., Steele, M., Steele, H., Moran, G. S., & Higgitt, A. C. (1991). The capacity for understanding mental states: The reflective self in parent and child and its significance for security of attachment. *Infant Mental Health Journal*, *12*, 201–218.

Fonagy, P., & Target, M. (2005). Some reflections on the therapeutic action of psychoanalytic therapy. In J. S. Auerbach, K. N. Levy, & C. E. Schaffer (Eds.), *Relatedness, self-definition, and mental representation: Essays in honor of Sidney J. Blatt* (pp. 191–212). London: Routledge.

Fonagy, P., Target, M., Steele, H., & Steele, M. (1998). Reflective-functioning manual, version 5, for application to Adult Attachment Interviews. Unpublished research manual, Sub-Department of Clinical Health Psychology, University College London.

Freud, S. (1921). Group psychology and the analysis of the ego. In J. Strachey (Ed. and Trans.), *The standard edition of the complete psychological works of Sigmund Freud*, *18*, 69–143. London: Hogarth Press, 1957.

Gardner, H. (1985). *The Mind's New Science: A History of the Cognitive Revolution*. New York: Basic Books.

Gedo, J. E., & Goldberg, A. (1973). *Models of the Mind: A Psychoanalytic Theory*. Chicago: University of Chicago Press.

George, C., Kaplan, N., & Main, M. (1985). *The Berkeley Adult Attachment Interview*. Unpublished manuscript, Department of Psychology, University of California, Berkeley.

Gergely, G., & Watson, J. S. (1996). The social biofeedback theory of parental affect-mirroring: The development of emotional self-awareness and self-control in infancy. *International Journal of Psycho-Analysis*, *77*, 1181–1212.

Gruen, R. J., & Blatt, S. J. (1990). Change in self-and object representation during long-term dynamically oriented treatment. *Psychoanalytic Psychology*, 7, 399–422.

Harpaz-Rotem, I., & Blatt, S. J. (2005). Changes in representations of a self designated significant other in long term intensive inpatient treatment of seriously disturbed adolescents and young adults. *Psychiatry—Interpersonal and Biological Processes*, 68, 266–282.

Harter, S. (1999). *The Construction of the Self: A Developmental Perspective*. New York: Guilford.

Horowitz, M. J. (1988). *Introduction to Psychodynamics: A New Synthesis*. New York: Basic Books.

Jacobson, E. (1964). *The Self and the Object World*. New York: International Universities Press.

Jaffe, J., Beebe, B., Feldstein, S., Crown, C. L, & Jasnow, M. D. (2001). *Rhythms of Dialogue in Infancy. Monographs of the Society for Research in Child Development*, 66(2, Serial No. 265). Boston: Blackwell.

Jordan, J. V. (1986). The meaning of mutuality. *Work in Progress*, 23. Wellesley, MA: The Stone Center.

Kernberg, O. F. (1966). Structural derivatives of object relationships. *International Journal of Psycho-Analysis*, 47, 236–253.

Kernberg, O. F. (1975). *Borderline Conditions and Pathological Narcissism*. New York: Jason Aronson.

Kernberg, O. F. (1976). *Object Relations Theory and Clinical Psychoanalysis*. New York: Jason Aronson.

Kernberg, O. F. (1977). Boundaries and structure in love relations. *Journal of the American Psychoanalytic Association*, 25, 81–114.

Kernberg, O. (1990). New perspectives in psychoanalytic affect theory. In R. Plutchik & H. Kellerman (Eds.), *Emotion, Psychopathology, and Psychotherapy* (pp. 115–131). San Diego, CA: Academic Press.

Kohut, H. (1971). *The Analysis of the Self: A Systematic Approach to the Psychoanalytic Treatment of Narcissistic Personality Disorders*. New York: International Universities Press.

Klein, G. S. (1976). *Psychoanalytic Theory: An Exploration of Essentials*. New York: International Universities Press.

Krupnick, J. L., Sotsky, S. M., Simmens, S., Moyer, J., Elkin, I., Watkins, J., & Pilkonis, P. A. (1996). The role of the therapeutic alliance in psychotherapy and pharmacotherapy outcome: Findings in the NIMH Treatment of Depression Collaborative Research Program. *Journal of Consulting and Clinical Psychology*, 64, 532–539.

Levy, K. N., Blatt, S. J., & Shaver, P. R. (1998). Attachment style and mental representation in young adults. *Journal of Personality and Social Psychology*, 74, 407–419.

Lichtenberg, J. D. (1983). *Psychoanalysis and Infant Research*. Hillsdale, NJ: Analytic Press.

Loewald, H. W. (1960). On the therapeutic action of psychoanalysis. *International Journal of Psycho-Analysis, 41*, 16–33.

Loewald, H. W. (1962). Internalization, separation, mourning, and the superego. *Psychoanalytic Quarterly, 31*, 483–504.

Mahler, M. S., Pine, F., & Bergman, A. (1975). *The Psychological Birth of the Human Infant: Symbiosis and Individuation*. New York: Basic Books.

Main, M., Kaplan, N., & Cassidy, J. (1985). Security in infancy, childhood and adulthood: A move to the level of representation. In I. Bretherton & E. Waters (Eds.), *Growing Points in Attachment Theory and Research. Monographs of the Society for Research in Child Development, 50*, (1 & 2, Serial No. 209), 66–104.

Mandler, J. M. (1988). How to build a baby: On the development of an accessible representational system. *Cognitive Development, 3*, 113–136.

Markus, H. (1977). Self-schemata and processing information about self. *Journal of Personality and Social Psychology, 35*, 63–78.

Mayman, M. (1967). Object-representations and object-relationships in Rorschach responses. *Journal of Projective Techniques and Personality Assessment, 31*, 17–24.

McLaughlin, J. T. (1981). Transference, psychic reality, and countertransference. *Psychoanalytic Quarterly, 50*, 637–664.

Meissner, W. A. (1979). Internalization and object relations. *Journal of the American Psychological Association, 27*, 345–360.

Miller, J. B. (1984). *Toward a New Psychology of Women*. Boston, MA: Beacon Press.

Mitchell, S. A. (1988). *Relational Concepts in Psychoanalysis: An Integration*. Cambridge: Harvard University Press.

Mitchell, S. A. (2000). *Relationality: From Attachment to Intersubjectivity*. Hillsdale, NJ: Analytic Press.

Modell, A. H. (1976). The holding environment and the therapeutic action of psychoanalysis. *Journal of the American Psychoanalytic Association, 24*, 285–308.

Modell, A. H. (1993). *The Private Self*. Cambridge, MA: Harvard University Press.

Nacht, S. (1962). Panel on the curative factors in psychoanalysis. *International Journal of Psycho-Analysis, 43*, 206–211.

Nacht, S. (1964). Silence as an integrative function. *International Journal of Psycho-Analysis, 45*, 299–300.

Nelson, K., & Gruendel, J. (1987). Generalized event representations: Basic building blocks of cognitive development. In M. Lamb & A. L. Brown (Eds.), *Advances in Developmental Psychology* (Vol. 1, pp. 131–158). Hillsdale, NJ: Erlbaum.

Norcross, J. (2002). *Psychotherapy Relationships That Work: Therapist Contributions and Responsiveness to Patients*. New York: Oxford University Press.

Ogden, T. H. (1994). *Subjects of Analysis*. Northvale, NJ: Jason Aronson.

Piaget, J. (1954). *The Construction of Reality in the Child* (M. Cook, Trans.). New York: Basic Books. Originally published as *La construction du réel chez l'enfant* (Neuchâtel, Paris: Delachaux & Niestlé, 1937).

Rogers, C. R. (1951). *Client-centered Therapy*. Boston: Houghton Mifflin.

Rycroft, C. (1956). The nature and function of the analyst's communication to the patient. *International Journal of Psycho-Analysis, 37,* 469–472.

Sandler, J., & Rosenblatt, B. (1962). The concept of the representational world. *Psychoanalytic Study of the Child, 17,* 128–145.

Sandell, R. (2005). Learning from the patients through research. Paper presented at the 18th conference of the European Psychoanalytical Federation. Villanova, Portugal.

Schafer, R. (1959). Generative empathy in the treatment situation. *Psychoanalytical Quarterly, 20,* 342–372.

Stern, D. B. (1997). *Unformulated Experience: From Dissociation to Imagination in Psychoanalysis.* Hillsdale, NJ: Analytic Press.

Stern, D. N. (1985). *The Interpersonal World of the Infant: A View from Psychoanalysis and Developmental Psychology.* New York: Basic Books.

Stone, L. (1961). *The Psychoanalytic Situation: An Examination of Its Development and Essential Nature.* New York: International Universities Press.

Surrey, J. L. (1985). Self-in-relation: A theory of women's development. Unpublished manuscript, Stone Center for Developmental Services and Studies, Wellesley College, Wellesley, MA.

Tronick, E. (1989). Emotions and emotional communication. *American Psychologist, 44,* 112–119.

Urist, J. (1977). The Rorschach test and the assessment of object relations. *Journal of Personality Assessment, 41,* 3–9.

Vermote, R. (2005). *Touching inner change.* Unpublished dissertation. Katholieke Universiteit, Leuven, Belgium.

Wampold, B. E. (2001). *The Great Psychotherapy Debate: Models, Methods, and Findings.* Mahwah, NJ: Erlbaum.

Werner, H. (1948). *Comparative Psychology of Mental Development.* New York: International Universities Press.

Westen, D. (1991a). Clinical assessment of object relations using the TAT. *Journal of Personality Assessment, 56,* 56–74.

Westen, D. (1991b). Social cognition and object relations. *Psychological Bulletin, 109,* 429–455.

Winnicott, D. W. (1960). The theory of the parent–infant relationship. *International Journal of Psycho-Analysis, 41,* 585–595.

Winnicott, D. W. (1982). *Playing and Reality.* London: Routledge. (Original work published 1972, New York: Basic Books; London: Tavistock)

Zeanah, C. H., & Anders, T. F. (1987). Subjectivity in parent–infant relationships: A discussion of internal working models. *Infant Mental Health Journal, 8,* 237–250.

Zuroff, D. C., & Blatt, S. J. (2006). The therapeutic relationship in the brief treatment of depression: Contributions to clinical improvement and enhanced adaptive capacities. *Journal of Consulting and Clinical Psychology, 47,* 130–140.

Chapter 9

Parent–Infant Attachment Systems
Neural Circuits and Early-Life Programming

James E. Swain, Prakash Thomas, James F. Leckman, and Linda C. Mayes

INTRODUCTION

In this chapter we will consider a number of *parental* factors underlying the development of parent–infant attachment. A consideration of the complex psychological, neurological, and biological aspects of parenting seems especially apropos for this volume, as its quality is thought to be intrinsic to the child's developing capacities for internalization, representation, and—ultimately—mentalization. Parenthood is a stage in life, a personal choice, a psychological transition, a psychobiological condition, a cultural creation, a necessity for the species, and a state of mind. For some, the word conjures up memories of the past; for others, the anticipated and desired; and for many, an idealization. The multiplicity of these characterizations underscores how the real and imagined roles of parents are woven through our developmental and psychological landscape. Much of the study of parenting has focused on how parents care for their infants and young children; less often has it focused on how adults become parents, how they make the normative psychological (and necessarily biological) adjustments to pregnancy and the birth of their child, and develop necessary empathy and caretaking thoughts and behaviors.

This chapter focuses initially on changing states of mind adults experience as they become parents and the caretaking behaviors these new states of mind engender. We begin by presenting an empirical line of work on parental preoccupation (Winnicott, 1960) that addresses this classical and clinically relevant psychoanalytic construct, which implicitly refers to the changing states of mind inherent in new parenthood. Next, we consider recent advances in our understanding of the genetic, epigenetic, and neurobiological substrates of maternal behavior in model mammalian species and their potential relevance for understanding risk and resiliency. For example, some of the studies reviewed suggest that aspects of maternal behavior are nongenomically transmitted from one generation to the next and that the nature of the maternal care received in infancy may program aspects of infants' responses to stress later in life and have enduring consequences in their approach to the world (Francis, Diorio, Liu, & Meaney, 1999; Ladd et al., 2000; Ladd, Huot, Thrivikraman, Nemeroff, & Plotsky, 2004). If similar mechanisms are at work in human populations, they may provide a basis for successful early-intervention programs (Eckenrode et al., 2000; Olds et al., 1999) and may deepen our understanding of why some individuals are more vulnerable, or conversely more resilient, to certain forms of psychopathology (Werner, 1996, 2004). Further, these studies of the intergenerational transmission of parenting behaviors are very relevant to psychoanalytic developmental theories regarding the internalization of parenting experiences and the clinical appreciation of the enduring power of these representations.

EARLY PARENTAL LOVE

For the most part, empirical studies of the early parent–child relationship have been child centered. Most reports have focused on the development of attachment behaviors in the child and on the moment-to-moment observable, behavioral functioning of the parent–infant dyad. These points of focus have revealed the highly specialized nature of parental verbal and nonverbal behaviors with very young infants, and the importance of early synchrony and reciprocity in parent–child interactions, as well as the critical impact of early experiences on the child's subsequent attachment behaviors toward the parent—and in subsequent intimate relationships (Anderson,

Vietze, & Dodecki, 1997; Bornstein, 1995; Dunn, 1977; Leckman et al., 2004; Stem, 1974; Trevarthan, 1979). These studies underscore the potential negative impact of early parental deprivation and neglect on the development of socialization capacities in the child. Moreover, they emphasize the importance of parental marital adjustment, self-esteem, and social supports for the successful adaptation to parenting a newborn (Egeland & Sroufe, 1981). However, relatively neglected in these lines of research have been the thoughts of parents regarding their roles, the significance and meaning of the infant in their lives, and how these thoughts influence their behaviors toward, and ultimately their enduring relationship to, their child.

In 1956 Donald Winnicott, a pediatrician and psychoanalyst, drew attention to "primary maternal preoccupation." He described this state as "almost an illness" that a mother must experience and recover from in order to create and sustain an environment that can meet the physical and psychological needs of her infant (Winnicott, 1956). He speculated that this special state began toward the end of the pregnancy and continued through the first months of the infant's life. He likened it to a withdrawn or dissociated state which, in the absence of pregnancy and a newborn, would resemble a mental illness of acute onset. In this period, mothers are deeply focused on the infant to the apparent conscious exclusion of all else; this preoccupation heightens their ability to anticipate the infant's needs, learn his or her unique signals, and over time to develop a sense of the infant as an individual. Winnicott emphasizes the crucial importance of such a stage for the infant's self-development and the developmental consequences for infants when mothers are unable to tolerate such a level of intense preoccupation. Although this concept has been incorporated into subsequent clinical formulations of disordered mother–infant interactions, it has received relatively little scientific attention, especially in considerations of the normative developmental trajectory of parenting (Benoit, Parker, & Zeanah, 1997; Feldman, Weller, Leckman, Kuint, & Eidelman, 1999; Leckman et al., 1999; Zeanah et al., 1993; Zeanah, Scheeringa, & Boris, 1994).

Introducing a notion similar to that of primary maternal preoccupation, others have suggested that, for both mothers and fathers, there is an initial critical period of "engrossment" with the infant in which all other concerns and realities assume a lesser role in day-to-day life (Greenberg & Morris, 1974).

In a prospective longitudinal study of 82 parents, we have documented the course of early preoccupations and found that they peak around the time of delivery (Leckman et al., 1999). Although fathers and mothers displayed a similar time course, the degree of preoccupation was significantly less for the fathers in our study. For example, at two weeks after delivery, mothers of normal infants, on average, reported spending nearly 14 hours per day focused exclusively on the infant, while fathers reported spending approximately half that amount of time (Leckman et al., 1999).

The mental content of these preoccupations includes thoughts of reciprocity and unity with the infant, as well as thoughts about the perfection of the infant. For example, we found that 73% of the mothers and 66% of the fathers reported having the thought that their baby was "perfect" at 3 months of age (Leckman et al., 1999). These idealizing thoughts may be especially important in the establishment of resiliency and the perception of self efficacy.

These parental preoccupations also include anxious intrusive thoughts about the infant. In a longitudinal study of 120 couples during their first pregnancy and in the six months after birth, women reported increasing levels of worry toward the end of their pregnancy and 25 to 30% described being preoccupied with worries about caring for the infant postpartum (Entwisle & Doering, 1981). Immediately before and after birth this figure may be substantially higher. In our study, we found that 95% of the mothers and 80% of the fathers had such recurrent thoughts about the possibility of something bad happening to their baby at 8 months of gestation. In the weeks following delivery this percentage declined only slightly to 80% and 73% for mothers and fathers, respectively, and at three months these figures were unchanged (Leckman et al., 1999). After delivery and on returning home, the concerns most frequently cited were about feeding the baby, about the baby's crying, one's adequacy as a new parent, and thoughts about the infant's well-being (Leckman et al., 1999). Conditions such as these are more commonly reported among parents of very sick preterm infants, infants with serious congenital disorders or malformations, or infants with serious birth complications (Leckman et al., 1999).

Less commonly, intrusive thoughts of injuring the child beset the new mother (or father); these thoughts can in turn lead to postpartum obsessive-compulsive disorder or depression or both (Brockington, 2004).

Parents also endorse fantasies or worries that they may in some way inadvertently harm their infant, for example by dropping the baby; or, in a time of exhaustion or frustration, more actively ignoring or injuring the baby. Naturally, such persistent worries, even those of harming the infant, are commonly observed among parents of, for example, preterm infants or infants with serious birth complications or congenital disorders or malformations (Bidder, Crowe, & Gray, 1974; Minde, Shosenberg, Thompson, & Marton, 1983). Among many mental health clinicians, such worries are often taken as concerning clues of potential disturbances in early parent–infant attachment. But normative studies suggest that in late pregnancy and in the first months after delivery, these preoccupations with more negative, anxiety-provoking content are common and normative. It is their persistence beyond the first three to six months that may signal difficulties in the parent–infant relationship.

Nursing and feeding are the parental behaviors that are perhaps most associated with a new infant. Women describe breastfeeding as a uniquely close, very physical, and at times sensual experience, and one that brings a particular unity between the mother and her infant (Sichel, Cohen, Dimmock, & Rosenbaum, 1993). In some instances, mothers appear not to experience breastfeeding as an interpersonal event but rather as a moment when they and the infant are joined as one. Grooming and dressing behaviors carry a special valence inasmuch as they permit closeness between parent and infant and are times for close inspection of the details of the infant's body and appearance.

Even before the child is born, parents preoccupy themselves with creating a safe, clean, and secure environment for the infant. Major cleaning and renovation projects are commonplace as the human form of nest building unfolds. After birth, unimpeded access and safety are among parents' uppermost concerns. Safety issues include the cleanliness of the infant and the infant's immediate environment, taking extra care not to drop the infant, as well as protection from potential external threats. Parents also report feeling compelled to these actions and anxious if prevented from accomplishing them even though they recognize that their behaviors may be extreme, exaggerated, or even unwarranted (e.g., that the baby is safe, the room and clothes thoroughly clean and warm). Community and cultural rituals (baby showers, baptism) not only mark the infant's arrival into a larger community but also have an element of safeguarding and protective actions. After birth, this same sense of heightened responsibility leads parents to check on the baby frequently, even at times when they know the baby is fine (Leckman et al., 1999).

Similarly, preoccupation with the baby's physical perfection is given behavioral voice not only in the already mentioned detailed reveries about the details of his body and appearance but also in the choice of clothes that may have special meanings. Parents often choose clothing that indicates their wishes and fantasies for their child or that bears a special relationship to their family, such as the clothes they wore as an infant, or clothing made by one or more grandparents. Again, in and of themselves, these behaviors are not unusual in the commonality but they are part and parcel of the intense state of preoccupation characterizing the first months after a baby is born. These behavioral sets lessen in intensity after the first six months when, we might say, the baby is safe and, if all has gone well, has a firm place in the parents' psychological structure.

Viewed from an evolutionary perspective, it seems nearly self-evident that the behavioral repertoires associated with early parenting skills would be subject to intense selective pressure (Clutton-Brock, 1991; Feygin, Swain, & Leckman, 2006). For one's genes to self-replicate, sexual intimacy must occur and the progeny of such unions must survive. Pregnancy and the early years of an infant's life are fraught with mortal dangers. Indeed, it has only been during the past century that infant mortality rates have fallen from over 100/1,000 live births in 1900 to about 10/1,000 in 1984 (Corsini & Viazzo, 1997). It is little wonder then, that a specific state of heightened sensitivity on the part of new parents would be evolutionarily conserved.

It is worth noting that becoming a new parent often comes at high physiological and mental cost. Most concretely, for nursing mothers there is the need to increase their caloric intake as well as to remain well hydrated. However, the birth of a child often leads the parent(s) to reevaluate what is important in life. Caregiving is just one of several competing motivational systems for parents. They must also consider the needs of the other children in the family, their occupational duties, the needs of the marital relationship, and the demands of the larger social group so that the advent of a new infant involves an adjustment in the parent's hedonic homeostasis as they establish lasting reciprocal social bonds and make room in their inner lives for a new family member (Hrdy, 2000).

Finally, too much or too little primary parental preoccupation may be problematic. Just as too much can lead to obsessive-compulsive-like states, too little parental preoccupation may set the stage for abuse or neglect in vulnerable, high-risk families (Eckenrode et al., 2000). One condition that has been repeatedly associated with disrupted mother–infant attachment and poses a risk for children's development across life is maternal postpartum depression (Field et al., 1988; Goodman & Gotlib, 1999). In terms of primary parental preoccupation, depressed mothers reported lower levels of preoccupations, particularly the aspect relating to the building of a meaningful relationship with the infant, such as interacting with the infant in a special way, calling him or her by a nickname, imagining the infant's future, or idealizing the child (Leckman et al., 1999). These data suggest that the function impaired by depression is the behavioral and mental investment in forming a relationship with the new infant.

What are the potential relationships between mentalization and a mother's capacity to invest in, or become preoccupied with her baby? There are a number of possible answers to this question. Is the capacity to reflect on one's own and others' mental states and to see mental states as key to understanding one's own and others' behavior a necessary precursor to normative parental preoccupation? Alternatively, does the level of parental preoccupation or investment provide the mental substrate for adults' redirecting their mentalization capacities toward their infant, in essence making room in their minds for a new person who is completely dependent upon them? In this alternative model, the more intense the state of early preoccupation, the more reflective a parent may be regarding her infant's emotional states and needs. Or as a third possibility, are these capacities for mentalization and preoccupation orthogonal to one another? That is, is the state of being preoccupied about the infant functionally equivalent to a diminishment in mentalizing, in effect a temporary suspension of reflective thinking, in order to totally and unreservedly focus on the infant's needs? In this formulation, more effective mentalization about the infant is neither a by-product nor a corollary of early preoccupation. There has, to date, been little to no empirical work bringing together individual differences in either adult or parental mentalization abilities with differences in the intensity of early parental preoccupation. Nor have there been studies relating individual differences in parental preoccupation to differences in parental attachment configurations. From a host of early-intervention studies, it appears that intervention efforts are most successful with parents who demonstrate greater investment in their infant—a hint that at least some shift in priorities or mental focus is essential for the transition to parenthood. However, early investment as a construct may relate as much to an ability to shift focus to the infant as it does to being reflective about the relation between one's own and others' mental states and behaviors. Although not mutually exclusive, the capacity to attend to the newborn child and the capacity to mentalize may occupy different developmental trajectories that call for further empirical investigation.

In the next section we will describe a neurobiological basis for the shift in priorities required for successful parenting; in particular, we will consider the role of oxytocin and other hormones in promoting the initiation and maintenance of maternal behavior. In addition, parenting behaviors, once under way, must endure the stress of competing personal, relational, and familial demands. Simply put, the new mother must subordinate her imminent hunger to feed her crying infant, not to mention the demands of other children and her partner. No wonder, then, that the neural groups associated with maternal behavior are also associated with the neurobehavioral response to stress.

NEURAL CIRCUITRY OF MATERNAL BEHAVIOR

Although the central nervous system events that accompany parental care in humans are largely unknown, it is likely that there is a substantial degree of conservation across mammalian species (Fleming, Steiner, & Corter, 1997). Classical lesion studies done in rodent model systems (rats, mice, and voles) have implicated the medial preoptic area (MPOA) of the hypothalamus, the ventral part of the bed nucleus of the stria terminalis (BNST), and the lateral septum (LS) as regions pivotal for regulation of pup-directed maternal behavior (Leckman & Herman, 2002; Numan & Insel, 2003). Estrogen, prolactin, and oxytocin can act on the MPOA to promote maternal behavior. Oxytocin is primarily synthesized in the magnocellular secretory neurons of two hypothalamic nuclei, the paraventricular (PVN) and the supraoptic (SON) nuclei. The PVN and SON project to the posterior pituitary gland. Pituitary release of oxytocin into the bloodstream results in milk ejection during nursing and uterine contraction during labor. It has also been shown that oxytocin fibers, which arise from parvocellular neurons in the PVN, project to areas of the limbic system, including the amygdala, BNST, and LS (Numan & Insel, 2003).

There are several reports that oxytocin facilitates maternal behavior (sensitization) in estrogen-primed nulliparous female rats. Intracerebroventricular (ICV) administration of oxytocin in virgin female rats induces full maternal behavior within minutes (Pedersen & Prange, 1979). Conversely, central injection of an oxytocin antagonist, or a lesion of oxytocin-producing cells in the PVN, suppresses the onset of maternal behavior in postpartum female rats (Insel & Harbaugh, 1989; van Leengoed, Kerker, & Swanson, 1987). However, these manipulations have no effect on maternal behavior in animals permitted several days of postpartum mothering. This result suggests that oxytocin plays an important role in facilitating the onset, rather than the maintenance, of maternal attachment to pups (Fleming, Vaccarino, Tambosso, & Chee, 1979).

Brain areas that may inhibit maternal behavior in rats have also been identified (Sheehan, Cirrito, Numan, & Numan, 2000). For example, the vomeronasal and primary olfactory systems have been identified as brain regions that mediate avoidance behavior in virgin female rats exposed to the odor cues of pups (Fleming, Vaccarino, & Luebke, 1980).

Ascending dopaminergic and noradrenergic systems associated with reward pathways also appear to play a crucial role in facilitating maternal behavior (Koob & Le Moal, 1997). For example, rat dams given micro-infusions of the neurotoxin 6-hydroxydopamine (6-OHDA) in the ventral tegmental area (VTA) to destroy catecholaminergic neurons during lactation showed a persistent deficit in pup retrieval but were not impaired with respect to nursing, nest building, or maternal aggression (Hansen, Harthon, Wallin, Lofberg, & Svensson, 1991). There also appears to be an important interaction between dopaminergic neurons and oxytocin pathways. Specifically, pup retrieval and assuming a nursing posture over pups were blocked in parturient dams by infusions of an oxytocin antagonist into either the VTA or MPOA (Pedersen, Caldwell, Walker, Ayers, & Mason,

1994). Furthermore, infant cues appear to trigger dopamine release in the nucleus accumbens, which mediates reward states for specific behaviors (Champagne et al., 2004).

In summary, the initiation and maintenance of maternal behavior involves a specific neural circuit. With pregnancy or with repeated exposure to pups, structural and molecular changes occur. These involve specific limbic, hypothalamic, and midbrain regions that adapt to the many demands of maternal care, amounting to an adjustment of hedonic homeostasis.

Remarkably, many of the same cell groups implicated in determining maternal behavior are also in control of ingestive (eating and drinking) behavior, and thermoregulatory (energy homeostasis) and social (defensive and sexual) behaviors, as well as general exploratory or foraging behaviors (with locomotor and orienting components) that are required for obtaining any particular goal. Many of these same structures are also intimately involved in stress responses. Swanson has conceptualized this set of limbic, hypothalamic, and midbrain nuclei as being the "behavioral control column" that is voluntarily regulated by cerebral projections (Swanson, 2000). Consistent with this formulation, it is readily apparent that motherhood presents a major homeostatic challenge within each of these behavioral control columns.

While information about these circuits in humans and other primate species is sparse, the available data are consistent with the same circuitry being involved (Fleming, O'Day, & Kraemer, 1999). For example, Fleming and coworkers have found that first-time mothers with high levels of circulating cortisol were better able to identify their own infant's odors. In these same primiparous mothers, the level of affectionate contact with the infant (affectionate burping, stroking, poking, and hugging) by the mother was associated with higher levels of salivary cortisol (Fleming, Steiner, & Corter, 1997). Both of these findings support the hypothesis that our stress response systems are adaptively activated during the period of heightened maternal sensitivity surrounding the birth of a new infant.

PARENT-INFANT NEUROIMAGING STUDIES

In this section, we present data on the brain basis of human maternal behavior and thoughts, using the high resolution and noninvasive technique of functional magnetic resonance imaging (fMRI). This is a brain imaging technique that assays brain activity by measuring blood oxygenation. The differences between oxygenated and deoxygenated hemoglobin provide characteristic magnetic signals that are detected by scanners positioned around the head of each subject, and the signals are localized to millimeter resolution. An important caveat throughout the interpretation of fMRI studies is that brain activity measurements represent an integration of activity over blocks of several seconds; thus, information regarding brain regions activated by salient infant cues reflect an average across a block of time rather than a picture of activations linked specifically to the moment a stimulus is introduced. In these studies, auditory and visual baby and control stimuli are presented to parents during these blocks of time. Brain activity may then be measured and compared between periods of attending to different stimuli to generate maps of the brain indicating brain activity that is implicated in one set of thoughts versus another. For example, comparison of brain activity during a baby cry versus control noise experience may yield significant differences in certain brain regions that may then be said to relate to the experience of a baby cry, and so to the associated parenting thoughts and behaviors as well (Squire & Stein, 2003; Swain, Lorberbaum, Kose, & Strathearn, 2007).

We begin with a brief orientation to plausible parenting brain circuits. We will then detail the parental brain imaging experiments that are relevant to the study of the parental side of attachment and the developing capacity to care for and think about the child.

Based on the animal studies of parenting behaviors reviewed in previous sections, we expect that human parenting brain responses should include motivation circuits of the midbrain and basal forebrain, emotion control circuits involving the amygdala and other limbic regions, and sensation-driven emotion and decision-making thalamocingulate circuits. In humans, we would also expect that regions involved in the appraisal of parenting context and memory would require hippocampal and parahippocampal circuits.

Importantly, we would also expect higher order emotion and cognition areas to facilitate parental empathy and caregiving for the infant; these same regions might be implicated in mentalizing processes. Empathy in general requires forming a model of another's mind that predicts their behavior and influences emotions (Baron-Cohen & Wheelwright, 2004), that is, a capacity for mentalizing. Parental empathy toward an infant would require the understanding and predicting of one's infant's mental states and behaviors as well as the experiencing of appropriate emotions. Candidate brain circuits that could support parental empathy include a variety of cortical regions, including the inferior frontal, premotor, insular, temporoparietal, and cingulate cortices (Decety & Grezes, 2006; Saxe, 2006).

Related to these issues are investigations of the biological bases of human attachment; in these studies, brain activity can be measured during tasks designed to activate the attachment system. An example of this approach used a projective measure of broad aspects of adult attachment (the adult attachment projective) during brain scanning (Buchheim et al., 2006). In this pilot study of 11 women, line drawings intended to activate the attachment system (illness, solitude, separation, and abuse) were presented to subjects during brain imaging. The authors reported that subjects with organized (as compared to disorganized) attachment patterns showed increased activity in the right amygdala, left hippocampus, and right inferior frontal gyrus—areas hypothesized to be important in the attachment system. Allied research on the brain basis of thinking about other minds (mentalization) is also beginning to dissect the brain basis of complex social emotional thinking (Pelphrey, Morris, Michelich, Allison, & McCarthy, 2005; Saxe, 2006). Findings suggest that specific regions in the medial prefrontal cortex and temporal cortex mediate aspects of emotional empathy and collaborative behaviors. In the following section, we describe attempts to specifically understand the areas of the brain associated with parental attachment by presenting emotionally charged infant stimuli during brain imaging. These studies lay the groundwork in understanding a new parent's response to the cry of her child. Like the subtlety of language, the infant's cry may provoke a cascade of parenting behaviors—ranging from anxiety to empathy—correlated to the cry's duration and intensity, responses akin to the complex give and take of other social attachments. Indeed "parenting" brain circuits, which are activated by baby stimuli, overlap with circuits that regulate other social attachments, and might be even more active in parents during the early postpartum than at other times of life.

Parental Brains and Baby Cry Stimuli

The first studies of brain activity when mothers listen to infant cries were carried out by Lorberbaum and colleagues. Building on the thalamocingulate theory of maternal behavior in animals developed by MacLean (1990), they initially predicted that baby cries would selectively activate cingulate and thalamus in mothers (ranging from 3 weeks to 3.5 years postpartum) exposed to an audiotaped 30-second standard baby cry, not from their own infant (Lorberbaum et al., 1999). They later expanded their hypotheses to include the MPOA/BNST and its connections, including its indirect connections to motivational circuitry (Lorberbaum et al., 2002). In their first study (Lorberbaum et al., 1999), a group of four mothers were studied for their response to 30 seconds of a standard cry compared with 30 seconds of a control sound consisting of white noise that was shaped to the temporal pattern and amplitude of the cry. With cry versus control sound, the four mothers showed increased activity in the subgenual anterior cingulate and right mesial prefrontal/orbitofrontal using a fixed effects data analysis. In a methodologically more stringent follow-up study, brain activity was measured in 10 healthy, breastfeeding, first-time mothers with infants 1–2 months old. While they listened to standard infant-cry recordings compared to similarly cry-shaped control sounds, brain activity in many candidate parenting centers was revealed using a random effects imaging analysis, in which posterior regions were not imaged (Lorberbaum et al., 2002). Activated regions included the anterior and posterior cingulate, thalamus, midbrain, hypothalamus, septal regions, dorsal and ventral striatum, medial prefrontal cortex, right orbitofrontal/ insula/ temporal polar cortex region, and right lateral temporal cortex and fusiform gyrus. Additionally, when cry response was compared with the inter-stimulus rest periods, instead of the control sound (which some mothers judged to be aversive), the amygdala was active.

Hypothesizing that gender and experience would affect the neural responses to baby sounds including baby cry and laughter, Seifritz and colleagues (Seifritz et al., 2003) studied four groups: mothers and fathers of children under age 3, and non-parent males and females, with 10 subjects in each group. They used an event-related fMRI design, which measures brain response to brief 6–s events. Over the entire sample, intensity-matched baby sounds of crying, laughing, and "neutral" sounds (white noise pulsed at 5-Hz with an averaged frequency spectrum similar to the infant vocalizations) produced more brain activity in bilateral temporal regions. These regions might be important for hearing processes (Heshyl's gyrus and tem-

poral poles), processing human vocalizations, and empathic emotion processing (see below). They also reported that women as a group, including
parents and non-parents (but not males), had a decrease in activity in response to both baby cry and laughter in the subgenual anterior cingulate
cortex. This finding is, however, contrary to the Loderbaum and Swain
studies (Lorberbaum et al., 1999; Lorberbaum et al., 2002; Swain et al., 2003,
2004; Swain, Leckman, Mayes, Feldman, & Schultz, 2005). This highlights
the role of stimulus choice in these experiments; it also emphasizes the
importance of not viewing the anterior cingulate as one structure without
subdivisions. It is also possible that 6-second versus 30-second stimuli have
very different meanings to new parents as there may be nonlinear or biphasic
anterior cingulate responses. Finally, within-group analyses showed that
parental brains were activated more to infant crying than laughing in the
right amygdala, while the non-parents' response was greater for infant laughing than crying (Seifritz et al., 2003). These within-group results suggest a
potential change in amygdala function with being a parent, although there
was no direct comparison of parents to non-parents. Are parents more sensitive to their child's cry as the result of evolutionary processes that emphasize the primacy of survival and nurture over the invitation to reciprocity
via laughter? If so, at what developmental stage (in both parent and infant)
does the quality of the relationship to the child take precedence over simple
survival? These distinctions are unresolved and await the inclusion of more
nuanced parental measures that will make future studies more insightful.

In an attempt to further understand the neurocircuitry underlying
emotionally laden parenting behavior and parent–infant attachment, we and
our colleagues have been studying new parents across a range of experiences, temperaments, and parent–infant interaction styles. For example,
Swain and colleagues (Swain et al., 2003) reported on a comprehensive interview and self-report assessment and fMRI brain imaging (using own infant
cry stimuli) of postpartum mothers and fathers, across experience from novice
to multiple pregnancy families. In this design, inspired by Lorberbaum and
colleagues, parents listened to 30-second blocks of infant cries generated by
their own infant, as well as a "standard" cry and control noises matched for
pattern and intensity. Parents were seen at 2–4 weeks and 12–16 weeks
postpartum. These times were chosen to coincide with the transforming

experience of having a baby, and known to be associated with increased tendency for parents to be highly preoccupied in the early postpartum period (Leckman et al., 1999), as described in earlier sections.

In work similar to Loberbaum's, these investigators hypothesized that parental responses to their own baby's cries would include specific activations in thalamo-cortico-basal ganglia circuits believed to be involved in human ritualistic and obsessive-compulsive thoughts and behaviors discussed above (Baxter, 2003; Leckman et al., 2004). Swain and colleagues also reasoned that emotional alarm, arousal, and salience-detection centers, including amygdala, hippocampus, and insula (Britton et al., 2006; LeDoux, 2003) would be activated by baby cry stimuli. In a group of first-time mothers (n = 9) at 2–4 weeks postpartum, own-baby-cry stimuli compared with other-baby-cry activated regions of the midbrain, basal ganglia, cingulate, amygdala, and insula (Swain et al., 2003). Preliminary analysis of the parental interview data shows that mothers were significantly more preoccupied than fathers, which was reflected in the relative lack of activation for fathers in the amygdala and basal ganglia (Swain et al., 2004). In the group of primiparous mothers, given the same stimuli at 3–4 months postpartum, amygdala and insular activations were not evident, and instead medial prefrontal cortical and hypothalamic (hormonal control) regions were active (Swain et al., 2004). This may reflect a change in regional brain responses as the parent–infant relationship develops and mothers learn to associate their infant cries less with alarm and anxiety and more with social behaviors and habit systems.

Parental Brains and Baby Visual Stimuli

Several groups are using baby visual stimuli to activate parental brain circuits (Bartels & Zeki, 2004; Leibenluft, Gobbini, Harrison, & Haxby, 2004; Nitschke et al., 2004; Ranote et al., 2004; Strathearn, Li, & Montague, 2005; Swain et al., 2003) with a variety of designs, parent populations, and infant age.

Hypothesizing that reward and emotion circuits, which are important for aspects of romantic love (Bartels & Zeki, 2000), might also be involved in maternal love, Bartels and Zeki used photographs of own, familiar, and unfamiliar infants (9 months to 3.5 years of age) as stimuli for parental brain circuits (Bartels & Zeki, 2004). They measured brain activity in 20 healthy mothers while viewing still-face photographs of their own child compared to age-matched photographs of other same-aged children. There was increased activity in the midbrain (periaqueductal gray and substantial nigra regions); dorsal and ventral striatum; thalamus; left insula; orbitofrontal cortex; sub-, pre-, and supra-genual anterior cingulate; and superior medial prefrontal cortex. There were also increases in the cerebellum, left fusiform, and left occipital cortex, but decreases in the left amygdala. Bartels and Zeki also compared mother brain responses of own child versus familiar child to the best friend versus familiar friend in order to control for familiarity and positive affect, and argue that responses were unique to the own-child stimuli. They suggested that parent–infant attachment may be regulated by a push-pull mechanism that selectively activates motivation and reward systems, while at the same time suppressing circuits responsible for critical social assessment and negative emotions (Bartels & Zeki, 2004).

In a related study using photographs of much older children (5 to 12 years old), mothers viewed pictures of their own and other children's faces during fMRI and were asked to press a button to indicate identity (Leibenluft, Gobbini, Harrison, & Haxby, 2004). Some social cognition regions that were not activated in the Bartels and Zeki study (2004) were significantly activated in this study, including the anterior paracingulate, posterior cingulate, and the superior temporal sulcus. How can we understand the recruitment of social assessment pathways in a task that, prima facie, appears related to the motivation-reward system associated with attachment? This may be explained by the use of much older children, which might involve a different set of circuits relevant to those particular relationships. It may also be that the cognitive task interacts with affective responses to face images in some way (Gray, 2001). Differences in child photo affective facial expressions (happy vs. neutral vs. sad) may also constitute a confounding factor. Another possible reason for differences between studies is that sample populations and their relationships likely differ in important ways. Although all of the studies were of "normative" parent populations, most studies only screened for clinical psychiatric disease. It appears that different populations may process infant cues in different ways.

In another study focusing on parents' brains using visual stimuli, Nitschke and colleagues studied six healthy, primiparous mothers at 2–4 months postpartum as they viewed smiling pictures of their own and unfamiliar infants. They reported orbitofrontal cortical activations that correlated positively with pleasant mood ratings. In contrast, areas of visual cortex that also discriminated between own and unfamiliar infants were unrelated to mood ratings (Nitschke et al., 2004). Perhaps, as they suggest, activity in the orbitofrontal cortex, which may vary across individuals, is involved with high-order dimensions of maternal attachment.

With the innovative and perhaps more realistic and ethologically appropriate use of videotaped infant stimuli, Ranote and colleagues conducted a similar experiment (Ranote et al., 2004). In their study, 10 healthy mothers viewed alternating 40-second blocks of their own infant's video, a neutral video, and a video of an unknown infant. For these women, there was significant activation in the "own" minus "unknown" infant comparison in the left amygdala and temporal pole. These researchers interpreted this circuit as regulating emotion and theory of mind regions relating to the ability to predict and explain other people's behaviors. Certainly, this fits with fMRI experiments on biological motion, which activate similar regions (Morris, Pelphrey, & McCarthy, 2005). It is important to note that all of these visual paradigms used to examine differences between one's own infant and unfamiliar infants employ a complex set of brain systems necessary for sensory perception, identification, and emotional response. Yet it now appears from a number of studies that, despite the multisensory complexities of audiovisual stimuli, meaningful analysis of fMRI data is possible. For example, there seems to be a striking intersubject synchronization among emotion-regulating brain areas responding to audiovisual cues during observation of the same scenes of an emotionally powerful movie (Hasson, Nir, Levy, Fuhrmann, & Malach, 2004). Also, the intensity with which subjects perceive different features in a movie (color, faces, language, and human bodies) was correlated with activity in separate brain areas (Bartels & Zeki, 2004). Finally, regional activity between brain areas that are known to be anatomically connected has been shown to be simultaneously active during movie viewing (Bartels & Zeki, 2005). This work suggests that movies used as more naturalistic baby stimuli for parents may also be used to develop a functional architecture of parenting brain systems. Perhaps related decision-making can also be studied with interactive stimuli in future parent–infant brain imaging work.

Finally, Strathearn and colleagues have also been studying healthy mother–infant dyads using fMRI to examine maternal brain regions activated in response to visual infant facial cues of varying affect (smiling, neutral, and crying). They have completed a pilot study of eight healthy, right-handed mothers without a history of psychiatric impairment or child maltreatment. Their infants were between 3 and 8 months of age. Strathearn and his colleagues assessed serum oxytocin levels sequentially from the mothers during a standardized period of mother–infant interaction, during which they acquired videotapes of the infants' facial expressions. Maternal brain activity was then assayed with fMRI in response to the facial images of the mother's own infant compared with familiar and unknown infant facial images (Strathearn, Li, & Montague, 2005). Areas of significant activation unique to own-infant viewing included brain reward areas with dopaminergic projections (ventral striatum, thalamus, and nucleus accumbens), areas containing oxytocin projections (amygdala, bed nucleus of the stria terminalis, and hippocampus), the fusiform gyrus (involved in face processing), and bilateral hippocampi (involved in episodic memory processing). Further, a positive, but nonsignificant trend in this small sample was seen in serum oxytocin concentration before and after mother–infant interaction (prior to scanning), suggesting a possible correlation between brain activation and peripheral affiliative hormone production. A further study, which was limited to the presentation of crying infant faces, revealed activation of the anterior cingulate and insula bilaterally (Strathearn, Li, & Montague, 2005).

Across visual and auditory sensory stimuli thus far used in parent imaging studies, a number of crucial convergences in brain responses are evident. Although baby cries may be aversive compared with baby pictures, considerable overlap in activation of motivation, arousal, and reward circuits is not too surprising since, for example, parents are still generally compelled to approach a crying infant—perhaps in anticipation of reward. It also makes sense that common social cognition circuits would be involved. In particular, it is interesting to consider the common activation of the precuneus cortex in parents responding to own-child stimuli across visual and auditory stimuli (Leibenluft, Gobbini, Harrison, & Haxby, 2004; Swain, Leckman, Mayes, Feldman, & Schultz, 2005). This fits with the rapidly expanding literature on the importance of this region for episodic memory retrieval necessary for recognizing familiar auditory and visual social stimuli, as well as self-referential mental imagery (Cavanna & Trimble, 2006; Gobbini & Haxby, 2006; Lundstrom, Ingvar, & Petersson, 2005; Lundstrom et al., 2003; Nakamura et al., 2001; Todorov, Gobbini, Evans, & Haxby, 2006).

Careful use of a variety of baby stimuli to activate parent brains, along with correlations of parental brain activity with psychometric parameters, will help in the understanding of these circuits. It may also be helpful to include comprehensive measurements of parent physiology during infant response. In addition to understanding normal parental behavior, this field promises to elucidate abnormalities of parental circuitry that may be manifest in postpartum depression and anxiety. Such understanding may suggest optimal detection and treatment strategies for these conditions that have profound deleterious effects on the quality of parent–infant interactions, and the subsequent long-term health and resiliency of infants. These studies will also inform our understanding of social circuits important for empathy across a range of relationships. In particular, the basic approach-avoidance paradigm that favors proximity to favorable stimuli and distance from aversive ones may be replaced by a more nuanced position in which social judgment or mentalization regulates this paradigm within the context of a relationship and its consequent reward. In other words, it may be advantageous to approach a person despite the presence of aversive stimuli—a frown or a look of pain—when the result is greater social attachment. Taken further, this aspect of brain imaging may help illuminate the distinction between normative parental functioning that approaches a crying baby compared with parental functioning at risk for neglect and abuse in the same context.

NONGENOMIC INFLUENCES ON MATERNAL BEHAVIOR

Thus far, several experimental interventions in rats have been shown to have effects on aspects of maternal behavior, including licking and grooming, high-arched-back nursing, and aggression toward an intruder. More recently, other rodent maternal behaviors have also been systematically evaluated (Pryce, Bettschen, & Feldon, 2001). In general, these findings suggest that maternal behavior in the days following birth serves to program the subsequent maternal behavior of the adult offspring as well as establishing the pups' level of hypothalamic-pituitary-adrenal responsiveness to stress (Denenberg, Rosenberg, Paschke, & Zarrow, 1969; Francis, Diorio, Liu, & Meaney, 1999; Levine, 1975). This complex programming also appears to influence aspects of learning and memory. Further, many of the brain regions implicated in these experimental interventions are the same as those identified in the knockout gene and earlier lesioning studies. Although we review in detail a series of recent rodent studies, investigations in social primates also highlight the importance of early mothering in determining how the daughters will mother (Harlow, 1963; Suomi & Ripp, 1983). It is also clear that the effects of early maternal deprivation in primates may be difficult to reverse, such that many maternally deprived monkeys are able to function under normal conditions as adults but are unable to cope with psychosocial stressors (Suomi, Delizio, & Harlow, 1976).

Handling and brief separations (15 minutes per day) from pups

Repeated handling of pups in conjunction with brief maternal separations induces more licking and grooming by the rat dams (Liu et al., 1997). The handling procedure used in the Liu study involved removing the mother and then rat pups from their cage, placing the pups together in a small container, and returning the animals 15 minutes later to their cage and their mothers. The manipulation was performed daily for the first 21 days of life. This manipulation resulted in more than a doubling of the time the dam spent licking and grooming her pups. The licking and grooming behavior is also highly correlated with high-arched-back nursing postures.

As adults, the offspring of mothers that exhibited more licking and grooming of pups during the first 10 days of life showed reduced plasma adrenocorticotropic hormone (ACTH) and corticosterone responses to acute restraint stress, as well as increased hippocampal glucocorticoid receptor mRNA expression, and decreased levels of hypothalamic corticotropin-releasing factor (CRF) mRNA (Liu et al., 1997; Plotsky & Meaney, 1993). Subsequent studies by the same group of investigators have shown that the offspring of these high licking and grooming mothers also show reduced acoustic startle responses, and enhanced spatial learning and memory (Ladd et al., 2000; Liu, Diorio, Day, Francis, & Meaney, 2000).

Handling and prolonged separations (3 hours per day) from pups

In contrast, repeated handling of pups in conjunction with prolonged maternal separations induces deranged maternal behavior, including a reduction in licking and grooming by the rat dams and reduced maternal aggression. Similarly, the adult offspring show increased neuroendocrine responses to acute restraint stress and airpuff startle, including elevated levels of PVN CRF mRNA and elevated plasma levels of ACTH, corticosterone, and steroid mRNA. These animals also show an increased acoustic startle response, and enhanced anxiety or fearfulness to novel environments (Ladd et al., 2000; Ladd, Huot, Thrivikraman, Nemeroff, & Plotsky, 2004).

Handling and early adoption within first 3 to 6 hours

Early adoption has been found to be associated with increased maternal licking behavior (Barbazanges et al., 1996). In the same study, early adoption within the first 3 to 6 hours after birth was found to prevent the prolonged stress-induced secretion of corticosterone evident in early separated offspring that were returned to the nest with their biological mother. Similarly, as adults the early-adopted pups demonstrated lower novelty-induced locomotion and improved recognition performance in a Y-maze compared to the early-separated offspring. However, later adoption at either 5 or 10 days resulted in a prolonged stress-induced corticosterone secretion, increased the locomotor response to novelty, and disrupted cognitive performance in the adult offspring. This has been further supported by work on maternal separation of mice, which suggests a role for nerve growth factor to mediate the effects of external manipulations on the developing brain (Cirulli, Berry, & Alleva, 2003).

NONHUMAN PRIMATE MODELS

Comparable findings have been reported in rhesus and squirrel monkeys exposed to varying degrees of maternal deprivation (Levine, 2005; Suomi, 1997). Indeed, the behavioral profiles of mistreated monkeys (normative reactivity with normal care versus high-stress reactivity with disrupted maternal care) were remarkably similar to Bowlby's original description of anxious versus secure attachment in human infants (Suomi, 1995). In a non-human primate brain imaging study, Rilling and colleagues showed that separation of juvenile rhesus monkeys from their mothers was associated with activation of cortical brain circuits that are susceptible to stress hormones (Rilling et al., 2001). In addition to behavioral effects, separation from mothers may be associated with a range of adverse physical health outcomes. One suggestion of this comes from the work of Kinkead and colleagues, who have demonstrated a link between neonatal–maternal separation and dysregulation of the central and peripheral control of respiration (Kinkead et al., 2005).

A bridge between low licking and grooming parenting in rodents and circumstances of abuse and neglect in humans is provided by the work of Maestripieri and colleagues on nonhuman primate models of parenting. In one report on rhesus monkeys, the experience of abuse during the first month of life was associated with earlier female reproductive maturation and interest in infants (Maestripieri, 2005). This may be interpreted to provide an animal model of human teenage pregnancy, with all the associated possible negative consequences for the female's own health, the health of her offspring, and for ability to parent. Perhaps maternal behavior in this model is modulated by stress-response systems, as suggested by studies of macaques that showed a link between maternal behaviors, stress, serum cortisol, and infant development (Bardi & Huffman, 2006; Coplan et al., 2006). Early life stressors, as modeled with variable foraging (that is, when food is not readily available at all times), is also reflected in effects on neuronal integrity, metabolism, membrane structure, glial function, and cerebral glutamate content, as measured with magnetic spectroscopy in the brains of bonnet macaque monkeys, in the same brain regions implicated in trauma–related psychiatric disorders in humans, including the hippocampus (Mathew et al., 2003).

These animal models appear to fit with human population studies in which children exposed to abuse also manifest higher levels of cortisol and catecholamine stress hormones, as insecure infant attachment correlates with cortisol reactivity to environmental stress (Gunnar, Brodersen, Nachmias, Buss, & Rigatuso, 1996).

CROSS-FOSTERING STUDIES

It has been observed that rodent mothers display naturally occurring variations in maternal licking/grooming and arched-back nursing (Francis, Diorio, Liu, & Meaney, 1999). Since the licking/grooming behavior occurs most frequently before or during arched-back nursing, the frequencies of these two behaviors are closely correlated among mothers. In a subsequent cross-fostering study, investigators determined that the amount of licking and grooming that a female pup receives in infancy is associated with how much licking and grooming she provides to her offspring as a new mother (Francis, Diorio, Liu, & Meaney, 1999). They also reported that the low licking and grooming dams could be transformed into high licking and grooming dams by handling. Most impressively, they also found that this change was passed on to the next generation—that is, that the female offspring of the low licking and grooming dams became high licking and grooming mothers if they were either cross-fostered by high licking and grooming dams or if they were handled. The converse was also true, namely that the female offspring of the high licking and grooming dams became low licking and grooming mothers if they were cross-fostered by low licking and grooming dams.

These naturally occurring variations in licking, grooming, and arched-back nursing have also been associated with the development of individual differences in behavioral responses to novelty in adult offspring. Adult offspring of the low licking, grooming, and arched-back nursing mothers show increased startle responses, decreased open-field exploration, and longer latencies to eat food provided in a novel environment (Francis, Diorio, Liu, & Meaney, 1999).

Furthermore, Francis and coworkers demonstrated that the influence of maternal care on the development of stress reactivity was mediated by changes in gene expression in regions of the brain that regulate stress responses. For example, adult offspring of high licking, grooming, and arched-back nursing dams showed increased hippocampal glucocorticoid receptor mRNA expression, and increased expression of NMDA receptor subunit and brain-derived neurotrophic factor mRNA, as well as increased cholinergic innervation of the hippocampus (Francis, Diorio, Liu, & Meaney, 1999). In the amygdala there are increased central benzodiazepine receptor levels in the central and basolateral nuclei. In the PVN there is decreased CRF mRNA in the PVN. These adult pups also show a number of changes in receptor density in the locus ceruleus, including increased alpha2 adreno-receptors, reduced GABA A receptors, and decreased CRF receptors (Caldji, Francis, Sharma, Plotsky, & Meaney, 2000).

In related work by Francis and colleagues, oxytocin receptor binding levels were examined in brain sections from high and low licking, grooming, and arched-back nursing animals sacrificed either as nonlactating virgins or during lactation (Francis, Champagne, & Meaney, 2000). Examination of the MPOA and the intermediate and ventral regions of the lateral septum disclosed that oxytocin receptor levels were significantly higher in lactating females compared with nonlactating females. Lactation-induced increases in oxytocin receptor binding were greater in high compared with low licking, grooming, and arched-back nursing females in the BNST and ventral region of the septum. Francis and colleagues suggest, therefore, that variations in maternal behavior in the rat may be reflected in and influenced by differences in oxytocin receptor levels in the brain. Similar systems are described in nonhuman primates (Winslow, 2005).

In sum, despite genetic constraints, data from animal studies indicate that the interval surrounding the birth of the rat pup or the rhesus infant is a critical period in the life of the animal that likely has enduring neurobiological and behavioral consequences. In particular, the nature of early caregiving experiences can have enduring consequences on individual differences in subsequent maternal behavior, anxiety regulation, and patterns of stress response through specific neuropharmacological mechanisms reviewed in Weaver and colleagues (Weaver, Diorio, Seckl, Szyf, & Meaney, 2004). Thus, cycles of neglect may alter the HPA axis (Shea, Walsh, Macmillan, & Steiner, 2005) and persist across generations. Yet, there may be hope that stress response systems may be corrected in just one generation of improved parenting. Further, there may even be opportunities to correct a malfunctioning stress system in adulthood, as suggested by a recent report that early-life epigenetic programming of the glucocorticoid receptor gene in the hippocampus can be reversed in adulthood via infusion of a modulator of hippocampal gene expression (Weaver, Meaney, & Szyf, 2006).

In the final section of this review we consider whether there is any evidence in human studies for enduring effects of early life experience in humans.

EARLY LIFE EXPERIENCE, RISK, AND RESILIENCY

Increasing clinical and epidemiological data support the view that exposure to early adverse environments underlies vulnerability to altered physiological responses to stress and the later expression of mood and anxiety disorders (Ambelas, 1990; Brown, Bifulco, & Harris, 1987; Kendler, Gardner, & Prescott, 2002, 2006). Among the most important early environmental influences is the interaction between the primary caregiver and the infant. Building on the early work of Bowlby (1969) and colleagues, efforts to characterize this reciprocal interaction between caregiver and infant and to assess its impact have provided a powerful theoretical and empirical framework in the fields of social and emotional development (Cassidy & Shaver, 1999). Over the past 30 years, clear evidence has emerged that significant disturbances in the early parent–child relationship (reflected in such things as child abuse and neglect or insecure attachments) contribute to an increased risk for developing both internalizing and externalizing disorders over the entire life (Sroufe, 2005; Sroufe, Carlson, Levy, & Egeland, 1999). While early adversity and insecure attachment may not be a proximal cause of later psychopathology, it appears to confer risk. Conversely, longitudinal studies of high-risk infants suggest that the formation of a special relationship with a caring adult in the perinatal period confers a degree of resiliency and protection against the development of psychopathology later in life (Werner, 1997).

A growing body of evidence, similar to the findings observed in rodents by Liu, Francis, and colleagues (Francis, Diorio, Liu, & Meaney, 1999; Liu et al., 1997), indicates that human caregivers' levels of response to their children can be traced in part to the caregivers' own childrearing histories and attachment-related experiences (Miller, Kramer, Warner, Wickramaratne, & Weissman, 1997). Caregivers' attachment-related experiences are hypothesized to be encoded in internal working models of self and others that establish styles of emotional communication that either buffer the individual in times of stress or that contribute to maladaptive patterns of affect regulation and behavior (Bretherton & Munholland, 1999). In the next section, we review the results of early-intervention programs with high-risk families. The focus is primarily on interventions begun in the pre- or perinatal period and that included random assignment to either the experimental intervention group or to a comparison group.

Early Interventions to Reduce Insecure Attachments

Based on the empirical work suggesting the critical importance of early parent–infant relationships, at least seven home visitation studies with random assignment have been reported that have aimed to reduce rate of relationship disturbances between high-risk mothers and their infants (Anisfeld, Casper, Nozyce, & Cunningham, 1990; Bor, Brennan, Williams, Najman, & O'Callaghan, 2003; Heinicke et al., 1999; Jacobson & Frye, 1991; Juffer, Hoksbergen, Riksen-Walraven, & Kohnstamm, 1997; Lieberman, Weston, & Pawl, 1991; Sadler, Slade, & Mayes, 2006; Slade, Sadler, & Mayes, 2005; van den Boom, 1995). Six of the seven studies focused on populations of low socioeconomic status (SES), and one focused on mothers who adopted children of different nationalities. Six out of the seven interventions reported reductions in the rates of insecure attachment; Bretherton and Mulholland (1999) reported fewer negative attachment behaviors. Five of these home visitation programs employed health-care professionals as visitors, and one employed a combination of nurses, paraprofessionals, and nonprofessionals. Four studies began in the prenatal period (Anisfeld, Casper, Nozyce, & Cunningham, 1990; Heinicke et al., 1999; Jacobson & Frye, 1991; Sadler, Slade, & Mayes, 2006; Slade, Sadler, & Mayes, 2005). The duration of the programs varied, with two programs lasting only 3 to 4 months, another lasting on average 8.5 months, and the remainder lasting between 12 and 24 months. Unfortunately, only one of these studies has examined long-term effects on child emotional and behavioral adjustment. Bor and colleagues (Bor, Brennan, Williams, Najman, & O'Callaghan, 2003) found that maternal attitude at 6 months is an independent risk factor for behavioral problems at 5 years in both boys and girls. At present, it seems evident that the quality of infant–mother attachment is malleable. Nevertheless, while the emerging signs are compelling, we await clear evidence of the long-term impact of such adjustments on risk, resiliency, and later psychopathology.

Early Interventions to Improve Child Behavioral Adjustment

Thus far there have been at least three selective intervention studies with random assignment and prenatal initiation and at least one-year duration focused on child behavioral adjustment. The first set of studies was based on an intervention model that included home visits, parent meetings, and medical care (Brooks-Gunn, Klebanov, Liaw, & Spiker, 1993; McCarton et al., 1997). It showed early effects at 2 and 3 years of age that attenuated by 5 years of age. A second intervention that also included home visits by nurses, parent meetings, and medical care showed less of an effect early on at 4 years of age but that became significant at 5 and 6 years of age (Guteilus, Kirsch, MacDonald, Brooks, & McErlean, 1977; Guteilus et al., 1972). Finally, a third set of studies that included home visits by nurses that began prenatally and continued for 30 months has shown a remarkable number of positive outcomes as late as 15 years of age (Olds et al., 1997; Olds et al., 1998; Olds et al., 1999). For example, this nurse home-visitation program developed by Olds and coworkers reduced the number of subsequent pregnancies and the use of welfare, as well as instances of child abuse and neglect and criminal behavior on the part of low-income, unmarried mothers for up to 15 years after the birth of the first child. These studies by Olds and colleagues provide some of the strongest evidence to date that early intervention can make a difference in the lives of high-risk children. Although the mechanism by which these effects are achieved remains in doubt, Olds and colleagues have argued that one key element is the length of time between the first and second pregnancies by the mothers participating in the home visitation program (Eckenrode et al., 2000; Olds et al., 1999). On average, the time to the second pregnancy was more than 60 months in the experimental group that participated in the home visitation program and less than 40 months in the comparison group. This suggests that there was a greater maternal investment in the children who were in the Nurse Home Visitation Program compared to the children born to the comparison mothers. Over the three separate randomized control trials with different populations and contexts, there was less abuse, and improved infant emotional and language development (Olds, 2006).

In sum, data from selective early-intervention programs support the notion of a "critical period" in infancy that has far-reaching behavioral consequences. Thus far, the most compelling data suggest that these early intervention programs are likely to reduce a variety of maladaptive outcomes, such as early involvement in the juvenile justice system, as well as improve proximal infant outcomes such as safety and language/emotion development. Less clear is the impact of these early interventions on the later rates of depression and anxiety disorders as the children reach maturity. Nor is it clear what effect these early intervention programs have on an individuals' stress response, susceptibility to drug abuse, or on the capacity to become adequate parental caregivers themselves. It is also worth noting that none of these selective early-intervention programs has monitored maternal preoccupations or any physiological measures of adaptation to parenthood as possible proximal predictors of individual differences in outcome or benefit from intervention.

CONCLUSIONS

Becoming a parent requires an understanding of the needs of infants, who are dependent, developmentally immature, and needful of the care and protection of an adult who has their interests and wants as a core preoccupation. The transition to being parents and providing parental caregiving is reflected in a set of highly conserved behaviors and mental states that may reflect both an individual's genetic endowment and the experience of being cared for as a child. Indeed, while we have focused on the process of adults' becoming pregnant and anticipating the birth of their child, there are many other forms of parenting, including adoption, foster care, step-parenting, grandparenting, teaching, and mentoring. Each involves a specialized use of biobehavioral repertoires related to parenting, and each probably involves these highly conserved affiliative systems that permit us to become preoccupied and focused on caring love relations.

Behavioral, genetic, and neurobiological studies in model mammalian systems have the potential to inform clinical practice, particularly early intervention programs for high-risk expectant parents. To paraphrase Winnicott, "good enough" genes combined with "good enough" parental care are needed to ensure positive outcomes in childhood and beyond. Among these positive outcomes is a resiliency to subsequent adversities in life and the capacity to be a good enough parent for the next generation. Consequently, it is possible that effective early-intervention programs may have consequences for generations. Measures of "primary parental preoccupations" may be useful in future early-intervention programs as an index of change within a key domain of functioning.

Furthermore, the connection between primary parental preoccupation and the capacity to mentalize must be further clarified in future clinical studies. Just as the normative functioning of the former may produce positive outcomes in child development, a recent study indicates that the quality of parental mentalization helps promote secure attachment in children (Fonagy & Bateman, 2006; Fonagy, Steele, Steele, & Holder, 1997). It seems unlikely that in the highly conserved system of the parent–infant dyad that the quality of parental preoccupation, attachment, and mentalization would exist as unrelated systems, especially when one considers the overlap and redundancy in the neurobiological circuits underlying them.

Viewing parenting as an interaction among genes, past parenting, current experience, psychological state, neurobiological salience systems, and environmental constraints brings many disciplines to the study of parenting. No one discipline even within the social, or even basic, sciences can lay claim to studies of parenting as its primary domain of expertise. Parenting by its very nature is a multidisciplinary study. Close collaboration between clinicians and those who develop parent–infant intervention programs has been long-standing. But the "new science" of parenting brings together basic scientists—neurobiologists, geneticists, neuroimagers—with psychoanalysts, cognitive and social psychologists, social scientists studying attachment, anthropologists, obstetricians, and pediatricians. The special focus on how adults make room for their new infant is concerned not only with the development of healthy babies but also with helping adults make the transition to their new role, and to understanding the genetic, biologic, and psychological contributions to that transition. Future studies should permit the examination of how successful early-intervention programs influence brain development, problem-solving abilities, and stress response, as well as vulnerability to later psychopathology.

ACKNOWLEDGMENTS

Aspects of this work were supported by The Institute for Research on Unlimited Love and the National Alliance for Research on Schizophrenia and Depression supported JES. The Korczak and Harris Foundation and grants from the National Institutes of Health, MH49351, HD03008, RR06022, and MH30929, supported this research for JFL. The work is also supported by a grant from the Irving Harris Foundation and grants from the National Institute on Drug Abuse (RO1 DA-06025) and by a Research Scientist Development Award to LCM (KO2 DA-00222). Material in this paper has also appeared in chapters by our research group, including Leckman et al., 2004, Leckman & Herman, 2002; Mayes et al., 2005, and Swain et al., 2007.

REFERENCES

Ambelas, A. (1990). Life events and the onset of mania. *British Journal of Psychiatry, 157,* 450–451.

Anderson, B. J., Vietze, P., & Dodecki, P. R. (1997). Reciprocity in vocal interactions of mothers and infants. *Child Development, 48,* 1676–1681.

Anisfeld, E., Casper, V., Nozyce, M., & Cunningham, N. (1990). Does infant carrying promote attachment? An experimental study of the effects of increased physical contact on the development of attachment. *Child Development, 61*(5), 1617–1627.

Barbazanges, A., Vallee, M., Mayo, W., Day, J., Simon, H., Le Moal, M., et al. (1996). Early and later adoptions have different long-term effects on male rat offspring. *Journal of Neuroscience, 16*(23), 7783–7790.

Bardi, M., & Huffman, M. A. (2006). Maternal behavior and maternal stress are associated with infant behavioral development in macaques. *Developmental Psychobiology, 48*(1), 1–9.

Baron-Cohen, S., & Wheelwright, S. (2004). The empathy quotient: An investigation of adults with Asperger syndrome or high functioning autism, and normal sex differences. *Journal of Autism and Developmental Disorders, 34*(2), 163–175.

Bartels, A., & Zeki, S. (2000). The neural basis of romantic love. *Neuroreport, 11*(17), 3829–3834.

Bartels, A., & Zeki, S. (2004). The neural correlates of maternal and romantic love. *Neuroimage, 21*(3), 1155–1166.

Bartels, A., & Zeki, S. (2005). Brain dynamics during natural viewing conditions: A new guide for mapping connectivity in vivo. *Neuroimage, 24*(2), 339–349.

Baxter, L. R., Jr. (2003). Basal ganglia systems in ritualistic social displays: Reptiles and humans; function and illness. *Physiology and Behavior, 79*(3), 451–460.

Benoit, D., Parker, K. C., & Zeanah, C. H. (1997). Mothers' representations of their infants assessed prenatally: Stability and association with infants' attachment classifications. *Journal of Child Psychology and Psychiatry, 38*(3), 307–313.

Bidder, R. T., Crowe, E. A., & Gray, O. P. (1974). Mothers' attitudes to preterm infants. *Archives of Disease in Childhood, 49*(10), 766–770.

Bor, W., Brennan, P. A., Williams, G. M., Najman, J. M., & O'Callaghan, M. (2003). A mother's attitude towards her infant and child behaviour five years later. *Australian and New Zealand Journal of Psychiatry, 37*(6), 748–755.

Bornstein, M. H. (1995). Parenting infants. In M. Bornstein (Ed.), *Handbook of Parenting*, vol. 1. Mahwah, NJ: Erlbaum.

Bowlby, J. (1969). *Attachment and Loss, Vol. 1. Attachment.* London: Hogarth Press.

Bretherton, I., & Munholland, K. A. (1999). Internal working models in attachment relations: A construct revisited. In J. Cassidy & P. R. Shaver (Eds.), *Handbook of Attachment: Theory, Research, and Clinical Implications.* Vol. 150 (pp. 89–111). New York: Guilford.

Britton, J. C., Phan, K. L., Taylor, S. F., Welsh, R. C., Berridge, K. C., & Liberzon, I. (2006). Neural correlates of social and nonsocial emotions: An fMRI study. *Neuroimage, 31*(1) 397–409.

Brockington, I. (2004). Postpartum psychiatric disorders. *Lancet, 363*(9405), 303–310.

Brooks-Gunn, J., Klebanov, P. K., Liaw, F., & Spiker, D. (1993). Enhancing the development of low-birthweight, premature infants: Changes in cognition and behavior over the first three years. *Child Development, 64*(3), 736–753.

Brown, G. W., Bifulco, A., & Harris, T. O. (1987). Life events, vulnerability and onset of depression: Some refinements. *British Journal of Psychiatry, 150*, 30–42.

Buchheim, A., Erk, S., George, C., Kachele, H., Ruchsow, M., Spitzer, M., et al. (2006). Measuring attachment representation in an fMRI environment: A pilot study. *Psychopathology, 39*(3), 144–152.

Caldji, C., Francis, D., Sharma, S., Plotsky, P. M., & Meaney, M. J. (2000). The effects of early rearing environment on the development of GABA-a and central benzodiazepine receptor levels and novelty-induced fearfulness in the rat. *Neuropsychopharmacology, 22*(3), 219–229.

Cassidy, J., & Shaver, P. R. (1999). *Handbook of Attachment.* New York: Guilford.

Cavanna, A. E., & Trimble, M. R. (2006). The precuneus: A review of its functional anatomy and behavioural correlates. *Brain, 129*(Pt. 3), 564–583.

Champagne, F. A., Chretien, P., Stevenson, C. W., Zhang, T. Y., Gratton, A., & Meaney, M. J. (2004). Variations in nucleus accumbens dopamine associated with individual differences in maternal behavior in the rat. *Journal of Neuroscience, 24*(17), 4113–4123.

Cirulli, F., Berry, A., & Alleva, E. (2003). Early disruption of the mother–infant relationship: Effects on brain plasticity and implications for psychopathology. *Neuroscience and Biobehavioral Reviews, 27*(1–2), 73–82.

Clutton-Brock, T. H. (1991). *The Evolution of Parental Care.* Princeton, NJ: Princeton University Press.

Coplan, J. D., Smith, E. L., Altemus, M., Mathew, S. J., Perera, T., Kral, J. G., et al. (2006). Maternal–infant response to variable foraging demand in nonhuman primates: Effects of timing of stressor on cerebrospinal fluid corticotropin-releasing factor and circulating glucocorticoid concentrations. *Annals of the New York Academy of Sciences, 1071,* 525–533.

Corsini, C. A., & Viazzo, P. (1997). *The decline of infant mortality: The European experience, 1750–1990.* The Hague: Kluwer Law International.

Decety, J., & Grezes, J. (2006). The power of simulation: Imagining one's own and other's behavior. *Brain Research, 1079*(1), 4–14.

Denenberg, V. H., Rosenberg, K. M., Paschke, R., & Zarrow, M. X. (1969). Mice reared with rat aunts: Effects on plasma corticosterone and open field activity. *Nature, 221*(175), 73–74.

Dunn, J. B. (1977). Patterns of early interaction: Continuities and consequences. In H. R. Schaffer (Ed.), *Studies in mother–infant interaction* (pp. 321–347). London: Academic Press.

Eckenrode, J., Ganzel, B., Henderson, C. R., Jr., Smith, E., Olds, D. L., Powers, J., et al. (2000). Preventing child abuse and neglect with a program of nurse home visitation: The limiting effects of domestic violence. *Journal of the American Medical Association, 284*(11), 1385–1391.

Egeland, B., & Sroufe, L. A. (1981). Attachment and early maltreatment. *Child Development, 52*(1), 44–52.

Entwisle, D. R., & Doering, S. G. (1981). *The First Birth: A Family Turning Point.* Baltimore, MD: Johns Hopkins University Press.

Feldman, R., Weller, A., Leckman, J. F., Kuint, J., & Eidelman, A. I. (1999). The nature of the mother's tie to her infant: Maternal bonding under conditions of proximity, separation, and potential loss. *Journal of Child Psychology and Psychiatry, 40*(6), 929–939.

Feygin, D. L., Swain, J. E., & Leckman, J. F. (2006). The normalcy of neurosis: Evolutionary origins of obsessive-compulsive disorder and related behaviors. *Progress in Neuropsychopharmacology and Biological Psychiatry, 30*(5), 854–864.

Field, T., Healy, B., Goldstein, S., Perry, S., Bendell, D., Schanberg, S., et al. (1988). Infants of depressed mothers show "depressed" behavior even with nondepressed adults. *Child Development, 59*(6), 1569–1579.

Fleming, A., Vaccarino, F., Tambosso, L., & Chee, P. (1979). Vomeronasal and olfactory system modulation of maternal behavior in the rat. *Science, 203*(4378), 372–374.

Fleming, A. S., O'Day, D. H., & Kraemer, G. W. (1999). Neurobiology of mother–infant interactions: Experience and central nervous system plasticity across development and generations. *Neuroscience and Biobehavioral Reviews, 23*(5), 673–685.

Fleming, A. S., Steiner, M., & Corter, C. (1997). Cortisol, hedonics, and maternal responsiveness in human mothers. *Hormones and Behavior, 32*(2), 85–98.

Fleming, A. S., Vaccarino, F., & Luebke, C. (1980). Amygdaloid inhibition of maternal behavior in the nulliparous female rat. *Physiology and Behavior, 25*(5), 731–743.

Fonagy, P., & Bateman, A. (2006). Mechanisms of change in Mentalization-Based Treatment of borderline personality disorder. *Journal of Clinical Psychology, 62,* 411–430.

Fonagy, P., Steele, H., Steele, M., & Holder, J. (1997). Attachment and theory of mind: Overlapping constructs? *Association of Child Psychology and Psychiatry Occasional Papers, 14,* 31–40.

Francis, D. D., Champagne, F. C., & Meaney, M. J. (2000). Variations in maternal behaviour are associated with differences in oxytocin receptor levels in the rat. *Journal of Neuroendocrinology, 12*(12), 1145–1148.

Francis, D. D., Diorio, J., Liu, D., & Meaney, M. J. (1999). Nongenomic transmission across generations of maternal behavior and stress responses in the rat. *Science, 286*(5442), 1155–1158.

Gobbini, M. I., & Haxby, J. V. (2006). Neural systems for recognition of familiar faces. *Neuropsychologia, 45*(1), 32–41.

Goodman, S. H., & Gotlib, I. H. (1999). Risk for psychopathology in the children of depressed mothers: A developmental model for understanding mechanisms of transmission. *Psychological Review, 106*(3), 458–490.

Gray, J. R. (2001). Emotional modulation of cognitive control: Approach-withdrawal states double-dissociate spatial from verbal two-back task performance. *Journal of Experimental Psychology: General, 130*(3), 436–452.

Greenberg, M., & Morris, N. (1974). Engrossment: The newborn's impact upon the father. *American Journal of Orthopsychiatry, 44*(4), 520–531.

Gunnar, M. R., Brodersen, L., Nachmias, M., Buss, K., & Rigatuso, J. (1996). Stress reactivity and attachment security. *Developmental Psychobiology, 29*(3), 191–204.

Guteilus, M. F., Kirsch, A. D., MacDonald, S., Brooks, M. R., & McErlean, T. (1977). Controlled study of child health supervision: Behavioral results. *Pediatrics, 60*(3), 294–304.

Guteilus, M. F., Kirsch, A. D., MacDonald, S., Brooks, M. R., McErlean, T., & Newcomb, C. (1972). Promising results from a cognitive stimulation program in infancy. A preliminary report. *Clinical Pediatrics, 11*(10), 585–593.

Hansen, S., Harthon, C., Wallin, E., Lofberg, L., & Svensson, K. (1991). Mesotelencephalic dopamine system and reproductive behavior in the female rat: Effects of ventral tegmental 6-hydroxydopamine lesions on maternal and sexual responsiveness. *Behavioral Neuroscience, 105*(4), 588–598.

Harlow, H. F. (1963). The maternal affectional system of rhesus monkeys. In H. L. Rheingold (Ed.), *Maternal Behavior in Mammals* (pp. 254–281). New York: Wiley.

Hasson, U., Nir, Y., Levy, I., Fuhrmann, G., & Malach, R. (2004). Intersubject synchronization of cortical activity during natural vision. *Science, 303*(5664), 1634–1640.

Heinicke, C. M., Fineman, N. R., Ruth, G., Recchia, S. L., Guthrie, D., & Rodning, C. (1999). Relationship-based intervention with at-risk mothers: Outcome in the first year of life. *Infant Mental Health Journal, 20*(4), 349–374.

Hrdy, S. B. (2000). *Mother Nature: Maternal Instincts and How They Shape the Human Species.* New York: Ballantine Books.

Insel, T. R., & Harbaugh, C. R. (1989). Lesions of the hypothalamic paraventricular nucleus disrupt the initiation of maternal behavior. *Physiology and Behavior, 45*(5), 1033–1041.

Jacobson, S. W., & Frye, K. F. (1991). Effect of maternal social support on attachment: Experimental evidence. *Child Development, 62*(3), 572–582.

Juffer, F., Hoksbergen, R. A., Riksen-Walraven, J. M., & Kohnstamm, G. A. (1997). Early intervention in adoptive families: Supporting maternal sensitive responsiveness, infant–mother attachment, and infant competence. *Journal of Child Psychology and Psychiatry, 38*(8), 1039–1050.

Kendler, K. S., Gardner, C. O., & Prescott, C. A. (2002). Toward a comprehensive developmental model for major depression in women. *American Journal of Psychiatry, 159*(7), 1133–1145.

Kendler, K. S., Gardner, C. O., & Prescott, C. A. (2006). Toward a comprehensive developmental model for major depression in men. *American Journal of Psychiatry, 163*(1), 115–124.

Kinkead, R., Genest, S. E., Gulemetova, R., Lajeunesse, Y., Laforest, S., Drolet, G., et al. (2005). Neonatal maternal separation and early life programming of the hypoxic ventilatory response in rats. *Respiration Physiology & Neurobiology, 149*(1–3), 313–324.

Koob, G. F., & Le Moal, M. (1997). Drug abuse: Hedonic homeostatic dysregulation. *Science, 278*(5335), 52–58.

Ladd, C. O., Huot, R. L., Thrivikraman, K. V., Nemeroff, C. B., Meaney, M. J., & Plotsky, P. M. (2000). Long-term behavioral and neuroendocrine adaptations to adverse early experience. *Progress in Brain Research, 122*, 81–103.

Ladd, C. O., Huot, R. L., Thrivikraman, K. V., Nemeroff, C. B., & Plotsky, P. M. (2004). Long-term adaptations in glucocorticoid receptor and mineralocorticoid receptor mRNA and negative feedback on the hypothalamo-pituitary-adrenal axis following neonatal maternal separation. *Biological Psychiatry*, 55(4), 367–375.

Leckman, J. F., Feldman, R., Swain, J. E., Eicher, V., Thompson, N., & Mayes, L. C. (2004). Primary parental preoccupation: Circuits, genes, and the crucial role of the environment. *Journal of Neural Transmission*, 111(7), 753–771.

Leckman, J. F., & Herman, A. E. (2002). Maternal behavior and developmental psychopathology. *Biological Psychiatry*, 51(1), 27–43.

Leckman, J. F., Mayes, L. C., Feldman, R., Evans, D. W., King, R. A., & Cohen, D. J. (1999). Early parental preoccupations and behaviors and their possible relationship to the symptoms of obsessive-compulsive disorder. *ACTA Psychiatrica Scandinavica. Supplementum*, 396, 1–26.

LeDoux, J. (2003). The emotional brain, fear, and the amygdala. *Cellular and Molecular Neurobiology*, 23(4–5), 727–738.

Leibenluft, E., Gobbini, M. I., Harrison, T., & Haxby, J. V. (2004). Mothers' neural activation in response to pictures of their children and other children. *Biological Psychiatry*, 56(4), 225–232.

Levine, S. (2005). Developmental determinants of sensitivity and resistance to stress. *Psychoneuroendocrinology*, 30(10), 939–946.

Levine, S. (Ed.). (1975). *Psychosocial factors in growth and development*. London: Oxford University Press.

Lieberman, A. F., Weston, D. R., & Pawl, J. H. (1991). Preventive intervention and outcome with anxiously attached dyads. *Child Development*, 62(1), 199–209.

Liu, D., Diorio, J., Day, J. C., Francis, D. D., & Meaney, M. J. (2000). Maternal care, hippocampal synaptogenesis and cognitive development in rats. *Nature Neuroscience*, 3(8), 799–806.

Liu, D., Diorio, J., Tannenbaum, B., Caldji, C., Francis, D., Freedman, A., et al. (1997). Maternal care, hippocampal glucocorticoid receptors, and hypothalamic-pituitary-adrenal responses to stress. *Science*, 277(5332), 1659–1662.

Lorberbaum, J. P., Newman, J. D., Dubno, J. R., Horwitz, A. R., Nahas, Z., Teneback, C. C., et al. (1999). Feasibility of using fMRI to study mothers responding to infant cries. *Depression and Anxiety*, 10(3), 99–104.

Lorberbaum, J. P., Newman, J. D., Horwitz, A. R., Dubno, J. R., Lydiard, R. B., Hamner, M. B., et al. (2002). A potential role for thalamocingulate circuitry in human maternal behavior. *Biological Psychiatry*, 51(6), 431–445.

Lundstrom, B. N., Ingvar, M., & Petersson, K. M. (2005). The role of precuneus and left inferior frontal cortex during source memory episodic retrieval. *Neuroimage*, 27(4), 824–834.

Lundstrom, B. N., Petersson, K. M., Andersson, J., Johansson, M., Fransson, P., & Ingvar, M. (2003). Isolating the retrieval of imagined pictures during episodic memory:

Activation of the left precuneus and left prefrontal cortex. *Neuroimage, 20*(4), 1934–1943.

MacLean, P. D. (1990). *The Triune Brain in Evolution: Role in Paleocerebral Functions.* New York: Plenum.

Maestripieri, D. (2005). Early experience affects the intergenerational transmission of infant abuse in rhesus monkeys. *Proceedings of the National Academy of Sciences USA, 102*(27), 9726–9729.

Mathew, S. J., Shungu, D. C., Mao, X., Smith, E. L., Perera, G. M., Kegeles, L. S., et al. (2003). A magnetic resonance spectroscopic imaging study of adult nonhuman primates exposed to early-life stressors. *Biological Psychiatry, 54*(7), 727–735.

McCarton, C. M., Brooks-Gunn, J., Wallace, I. F., Bauer, C. R., Bennett, F. C., Bernbaum, J. C., et al. (1997). Results at age 8 years of early intervention for low-birth-weight premature infants. The Infant Health and Development Program. *Journal of the American Medical Association, 277*(2), 126–132.

Miller, L., Kramer, R., Warner, V., Wickramaratne, P., & Weissman, M. (1997). Intergenerational transmission of parental bonding among women. *Journal of the American Academy of Child and Adolescent Psychiatry, 36*(8), 1134–1139.

Minde, K., Shosenberg, N., Thompson, J., & Marton, P. (1983). Self-help groups in a nursery follow-up at one year. In J. Call, E. Galenson, & R. Tyson (Eds.), *Frontiers of Infant Psychiatry* (pp. 264–272). New York: Basic Books.

Morris, J. P., Pelphrey, K. A., & McCarthy, G. (2005). Regional brain activation evoked when approaching a virtual human on a virtual walk. *Journal of Cognitive Neuroscience, 17*(11), 1744–1752.

Nakamura, K., Kawashima, R., Sugiura, M., Kato, T., Nakamura, A., Hatano, K., et al. (2001). Neural substrates for recognition of familiar voices: A PET study. *Neuropsychologia, 39*(10), 1047–1054.

Nitschke, J. B., Nelson, E. E., Rusch, B. D., Fox, A. S., Oakes, T. R., & Davidson, R. J. (2004). Orbitofrontal cortex tracks positive mood in mothers viewing pictures of their newborn infants. *Neuroimage, 21*(2), 583–592.

Numan, M., & Insel, T. R. (2003). *The Neurobiology of Parental Behavior.* New York: Springer-Verlag.

Olds, D., Henderson, C. R., Jr., Cole, R., Eckenrode, J., Kitzman, H., Luckey, D., et al. (1998). Long-term effects of nurse home visitation on children's criminal and antisocial behavior: 15-year follow-up of a randomized controlled trial. *Journal of the American Medical Association, 280*(14), 1238–1244.

Olds, D. L. (2006). The nurse-family partnership: An evidence based preventative intervention. *Infant Mental Health Journal, 27*(1), 5–25.

Olds, D. L., Eckenrode, J., Henderson, C. R., Jr., Kitzman, H., Powers, J., Cole, R., et al. (1997). Long-term effects of home visitation on maternal life course and child abuse and neglect. Fifteen-year follow-up of a randomized trial. *Journal of the American Medical Association, 278*(8), 637–643.

Olds, D. L., Henderson, C. R., Jr., Kitzman, H. J., Eckenrode, J. J., Cole, R. E., & Tatelbaum, R. C. (1999). Prenatal and infancy home visitation by nurses: Recent findings. *Future Child, 9*(1), 44–65, 190–191.

Pedersen, C. A., Caldwell, J. D., Walker, C., Ayers, G., & Mason, G. A. (1994). Oxytocin activates the postpartum onset of rat maternal behavior in the ventral tegmental and medial preoptic areas. *Behavioral Neuroscience, 108*(6), 1163–1171.

Pedersen, C. A., & Prange, A. J., Jr. (1979). Induction of maternal behavior in virgin rats after intracerebroventricular administration of oxytocin. *Proceedings of the National Academy of Sciences USA, 76*(12), 6661–6665.

Pelphrey, K. A., Morris, J. P., Michelich, C. R., Allison, T., & McCarthy, G. (2005). Functional anatomy of biological motion perception in posterior temporal cortex: An FMRI study of eye, mouth and hand movements. *Cerebral Cortex, 15*(12), 1866–1876.

Plotsky, P. M., & Meaney, M. J. (1993). Early, postnatal experience alters hypothalamic corticotropin-releasing factor (CRF) mRNA, median eminence CRF content and stress-induced release in adult rats. *Brain Research. Molecular Brain Research, 18*(3), 195–200.

Pryce, C. R., Bettschen, D., & Feldon, J. (2001). Comparison of the effects of early handling and early deprivation on maternal care in the rat. *Developmental Psychobiology, 38*(4), 239–251.

Ranote, S., Elliott, R., Abel, K. M., Mitchell, R., Deakin, J. F., & Appleby, L. (2004). The neural basis of maternal responsiveness to infants: An fMRI study. *Neuroreport, 15*(11), 1825–1829.

Rilling, J. K., Winslow, J. T., O'Brien, D., Gutman, D. A., Hoffman, J. M., & Kilts, C. D. (2001). Neural correlates of maternal separation in rhesus monkeys. *Biological Psychiatry, 49*(2), 146–157.

Sadler, L. S., Slade, A., & Mayes, L.C. (2006). Minding the baby: A mentalization-based parenting program. In J. G. Allen & P. Fonagy (Eds.), *Handbook of Mentalization-based Treatment* (pp. 271–288). Chichester, UK: Wiley.

Saxe, R. (2006). Uniquely human social cognition. *Current Opinion in Neurobiology, 16*(2), 235–239.

Seifritz, E., Esposito, F., Neuhoff, J. G., Luthi, A., Mustovic, H., Dammann, G., et al. (2003). Differential sex-independent amygdala response to infant crying and laughing in parents versus nonparents. *Biological Psychiatry, 54*(12), 1367–1375.

Shea, A., Walsh, C., Macmillan, H., & Steiner, M. (2005). Child maltreatment and HPA axis dysregulation: Relationship to major depressive disorder and post traumatic stress disorder in females. *Psychoneuroendocrinology, 30*(2), 162–178.

Sheehan, T. P., Cirrito, J., Numan, M. J., & Numan, M. (2000). Using c-Fos immunocytochemistry to identify forebrain regions that may inhibit maternal behavior in rats. *Behavioral Neuroscience, 114*(2), 337–352.

Sichel, D. A., Cohen, L. S., Dimmock, J. A., & Rosenbaum, J. F. (1993). Postpartum obsessive compulsive disorder: A case series. *Journal of Clinical Psychiatry, 54*(4), 156–159.

Slade, A., Sadler, L., & Mayes, L. C. (2005). Minding the baby: Enhancing parental reflective functioning in a nursing/mental health home visiting program. In L. Berlin, Y. Ziv, L. Amaya-Jackson, & M. Greenberg (Eds.), *Enhancing Early Attachments: Theory, Research, Intervention, and Policy* (pp. 152–177). New York: Guilford.

Squire, S., & Stein, A. (2003). Functional MRI and parental responsiveness: A new avenue into parental psychopathology and early parent–child interactions? *British Journal of Psychiatry, 183*, 481–483.

Sroufe, L. A. (2005). Attachment and development: A prospective, longitudinal study from birth to adulthood. *Attachment and Human Development, 7*(4), 349–367.

Sroufe, L. A., Carlson, E. A., Levy, A. K., & Egeland, B. (1999). Implications of attachment theory for developmental psychopathology. *Developmental Psychopathology, 11*(1), 1–13.

Stern, D. N. (1974). Mother and infant at play: The dyadic interaction involving facial, vocal, and gaze behaviors. In M. Lewis & L. A. Roseblum (Eds.), *The Effect of the Infant on Its Caregiver* (pp. 187–213). New York: Wiley-Interscience.

Strathearn, L., Li, J., & Montague, P. R. (2005). An fMRI study of maternal mentalization: Having the baby's mind in mind. *Neuroimage, 26*(Suppl. 1), S25.

Suomi, S. J. (1995). Influence of Bowlby's attachment theory on research on non-human primate biobehavioral development. In S. Goldberg, R. Muir, & J. Kerr (Eds.), *Attachment Theory: Social, Developmental, and Clinical Perspectives* (pp. 185–201). Hillsdale, NJ: Analytic Press.

Suomi, S. J. (1997). Early determinants of behaviour: Evidence from primate studies. *British Medical Bulletin, 53*(1), 170–184.

Suomi, S. J., Delizio, R., & Harlow, H. F. (1976). Social rehabilitation of separation-induced depressive disorders in monkeys. *American Journal of Psychiatry, 133*(11), 1279–1285.

Suomi, S. J., & Ripp, C. A. (1983). A history of motherless mothering at the University of Wisconsin Primate Laboratory. In M. Reite & N. Caine (Eds.), *Child Abuse: The Non-human Data* (pp. 49–78). New York: Alan R. Liss.

Swain, J. E., Leckman, J. F., Mayes, L. C., Feldman, R., Constable, R. T., & Schultz, R. T. (2003). The neural circuitry of parent–infant attachment in the early postpartum. *American College of Neuropsychopharmacology, 114*, 192.

Swain, J. E., Leckman, J. F., Mayes, L. C., Feldman, R., Constable, R. T., & Schultz,

R. T. (2004). Neural substrates and psychology of human parent–infant attachment in the postpartum. *Biological Psychiatry, 55*(8), 153S.

Swain, J. E., Leckman, J. F., Mayes, L. C., Feldman, R., & Schultz, R. T. (2005). Early human parent–infant bond development: fMRI, thoughts and behaviors. *Biological Psychiatry, 57*(8), 112S.

Swain, J. E., Lorberbaum, J. P., Kose, S., & Strathearn, L. (2007). The brain basis of early parent–infant interactions: Psychology, physiology and *in vivo* functional neuroimaging studies. *Journal of Child Psychology and Psychiatry, 48*(3–4), 262–287.

Swanson, L. W. (2000). Cerebral hemisphere regulation of motivated behavior. *Brain Research, 886*(1–2), 113–164.

Todorov, A., Gobbini, M. I., Evans, K. K., & Haxby, J. V. (2006). Spontaneous retrieval of affective person knowledge in face perception. *Neuropsychologia, 45*(1):163–173.

Trevarthan, C. (1979). Communication and cooperation in early infancy: A description of primary intersubjectivity. In M. Bullowa (Ed.), *Before speech: The beginning of interpersonal communication* (pp. 321–347). Cambridge, UK: Cambridge University Press.

van den Boom, D. C. (1995). Do first-year intervention effects endure? Follow-up during toddlerhood of a sample of Dutch irritable infants. *Child Development, 66*(6), 1798–1816.

van Leengoed, E., Kerker, E., & Swanson, H. H. (1987). Inhibition of post-partum maternal behaviour in the rat by injecting an oxytocin antagonist into the cerebral ventricles. *Journal of Endocrinology, 112*(2), 275–282.

Weaver, I. C., Diorio, J., Seckl, J. R., Szyf, M., & Meaney, M. J. (2004). Early environmental regulation of hippocampal glucocorticoid receptor gene expression: Characterization of intracellular mediators and potential genomic target sites. *Annals of the New York Academy of Sciences, 1024*, 182–212.

Weaver, I. C., Meaney, M. J., & Szyf, M. (2006). Maternal care effects on the hippocampal transcriptome and anxiety-mediated behaviors in the offspring that are reversible in adulthood. *Proceedings of the National Academy of Science USA, 103*(9), 3480–3485.

Werner, E. E. (1996). Vulnerable but invincible: High risk children from birth to adulthood. *European Child and Adolescent Psychiatry, 5 Suppl. 1*, 47–51.

Werner, E. E. (1997). Vulnerable but invincible: High-risk children from birth to adulthood. *Acta Paediatrica Suppl., 422*, 103–105.

Werner, E. E. (2004). Journeys from childhood to midlife: Risk, resilience, and recovery. *Pediatrics, 114*(2), 492.

Winnicott, D. W. (1956). Primary maternal preoccupation. In *Collected Papers: Through Paediatrics to Psycho-Analysis* (pp. 300–305). New York: Basic Books, 1975.

Winnicott, D. W. (1960). The theory of the parent–infant relationship. *International Journal of Psycho-Analysis, 41,* 585–595.

Winslow, J. T. (2005). Neuropeptides and non-human primate social deficits associated with pathogenic rearing experience. *International Journal of Developmental Neuroscience, 23*(2–3), 245–251.

Zeanah, C. H., Benoit, D., Barton, M., Regan, C., Hirshberg, L. M., & Lipsitt, L. P. (1993). Representations of attachment in mothers and their one-year-old infants. *Journal of the American Academy of Child and Adolescent Psychiatry, 32*(2), 278–286.

Zeanah, C. H., Scheeringa, M., & Boris, N. (1994). Parenting styles and risks in the vulnerable infant. *Current Opinion in Pediatrics, 6*(4), 406–410.

Part III

MENTALIZATION IN PRACTICE

Chapter 10

Mentalization as a Frame for Working with Parents in Child Psychotherapy

Arietta Slade

As can be seen from the breadth of the contributions to this volume, the construct of mentalization has generated enormous interest among a diverse group of clinicians and researchers. As I will describe in this chapter, the constructs of mentalization and reflective functioning can also be applied to a particular aspect of child treatment, namely the ancillary work with parents that is an essential part of any psychoanalytically oriented child psychotherapy. In particular, I believe that effective work in this domain invariably involves engaging a parent's capacity to mentalize in relation to the child. While until recently most clinicians would have used different terms to describe what happens in successful parent work, I will suggest that this is actually a very useful and helpful way to think about this aspect of child treatment, because what we attempt to do, in a variety of direct and indirect ways, is to help the parents hold the child in mind. We do this by helping them develop a reflective stance in relation to the child, and in relation to their own experience as parents.

WORKING WITH PARENTS IN CHILD PSYCHOTHERAPY

Virtually all child therapists work, in some way or other, with the parents of the children they treat in psychotherapy. This work takes many forms, such as separate meetings with parents as an ongoing part of the treatment, direct work with the parents *instead of* work with the child, or inclusion of parents in the therapy sessions themselves. These are but a few of the many permutations that are typically part and parcel of this work, all of which arise in some organic way out of the process of an ongoing treatment.

Despite its ubiquity, there has to date been little articulated theory of the nature and purpose of this critical aspect of child treatment within the psychoanalytic literature,[1] and little comprehensive examination—within either the clinical or theoretical literature—of the complex issues involved in this work. Notable exceptions are the work of Saralea Chazen (2003), Kate Oram (2000), Pat Pantone (2000), Carol Wachs and Linda Jacobs (2006), and Kelly and Jack Novick (Novick, J. & Novick, K. K., 2001, 2002; Novick, K. K. & Novick, J., 2002a, 2002b, 2005), along with Diana Siskind (1987, 1997), who in her wonderful book *Working with Parents* (1997), puts it simply and pungently:

> When we review the literature on the therapist's work with the parents of child patients, it quickly becomes apparent that this is a neglected subject. It is surprising that this topic has failed to be represented as a complex and important treatment issue, one requiring a theoretical framework and careful discussion of its clinical application. (p. 4)

Siskind wonders about "this shrinking away" from difficult areas of our work, noting that "we write about everything that passes our consciousness" (p. 5), and yet not this. Indeed, it is very interesting to think about why this work has received so very little attention in the vast literature on child psychotherapy and psychoanalysis.

One of the great ironies of the relative absence of attention to parent work in the literature is the fact that experienced therapists, almost without exception, acknowledge that creating a working alliance with parents is crucial to successful work with a child. The more disturbed the child or the family, the more this is the case. In addition, not only is parent work very important, it is often very difficult; the work with children is *easy* relative to the work with parents. Child work can be fun, it can be tedious, it can be exhausting, or it can be exhilarating, but its parameters are well established. And it is organized, almost without exception, around play. Parent work, by contrast, is so challenging not only because of its inherent complexity, but also because of the fact that there are few if any adequate conceptualizations of its purpose.

Most parents bring children to therapy so that they can be "fixed." They may or may not have any interest in trying to figure out who the child is and what makes him tick, and they may or may not have an interest in thinking about their own emotional life as it pertains to the inner life of the child. When they do, of course, the work can be enormously productive and inherently rewarding. The effect on the child is palpable. But so often the parent and therapist have subtly competing agendas. While therapists may view parent sessions as intrinsic to helping provide a more sustaining holding environment for the child (which may in some cases mean working very directly to curtail a parent's toxic behaviors and interactions), the parents may view these sessions as open season to criticize and complain about the child. In addition, work with parents is often fraught with transference and countertransference issues, all played out within the framework of a relatively amorphous and poorly defined treatment situation. For instance, making a transference interpretation to a parent who is feeling rivalrous and inadequate in the face of the child's developing relationship with the therapist will be possible only in the most evolved parent–therapist relationships—and yet these dynamics often come to the fore early in a therapist's relationship with a family. Similarly, the therapist's feelings of identification with the child and competitiveness with the mother can derail a treatment in very short order.

Child therapists are faced with a number of crucial questions with respect to parent work: What is the aim of work with parents? How does the therapist see herself and her role within the framework of this process? What is the nature of the complex web of relationships among the child, the therapist, and the parents, all separate, but profoundly interconnected?

THE HISTORY OF APPROACHES TO WORKING WITH PARENTS

Much of the neglect and confusion within the psychoanalytic literature on parent work can be understood by examining the history of psychoanalytic theories of development and treatment. Child therapy and psychoanalysis were first described in the 1930s by Anna Freud (1966–1980) and Melanie Klein (1932). Consistent with their belief in the importance of addressing the intrapsychic conflicts of children as the means to promoting symptom relief, little attention was paid to the involvement of parents in the child's treatment. Mrs. Klein reportedly found any involvement with parents to be highly annoying and irrelevant (Karen, 1998). And according to what is likely an apocryphal story, Dorothy Burlingame was supposed to have suggested a set of guidelines for working with parents at the Anna Freud Centre (Alice Colonna, personal communication, January 2002). She purportedly suggested three routes to dealing with parents: (a) ignore them, (b) take the children away from them, and (c)—the most difficult and least advisable—work with them.

These ideas are obviously inconsistent with the child guidance model that was to emerge from the Anna Freud Centre in the 1950s; indeed, Anna Freud was well aware of the need to establish ongoing relationships with parents. The *child guidance model* refers to a loosely defined approach to parent work, one in which the therapist meets with parents in order to gather information on circumstances in the child's everyday life, help caregivers understand their child's development, develop strategies to manage behavioral problems, and contextualize their children's difficulties. But in this model, as it originally emerged, the work with parents was hardly an intrinsic part of the therapy. The therapeutic frame of the work with the child, the engagement with his interior life, was sacred. This thinking was embedded in an equally sacred notion, namely that the child could change while his environment did not, or that he could somehow change his environment as he progressed in treatment.

Not infrequently—since this model was so often simply not adequate—therapists would (and obviously still do) end up working in an analytic fashion with parents *alongside* the child's therapy; this transmutation of the child guidance model reflects therapist's need to bring the parents' conflicts to the fore as a means of helping the child. But here, too, there was relatively little theory to guide this kind of work, and it often became two almost parallel therapies. Oftentimes, when this failed, the parent was referred for individual psychotherapy of his or her own as an adjunct to the child's therapy. While this is often an entirely appropriate and crucial recommendation, a parent's individual treatment cannot—for reasons that will be described in the sections that follow—supplant parent work.[2]

In recent years, largely as a function of the fact that the focus within psychoanalytic developmental psychology has shifted from an internal to a relational perspective, with the infant viewed as powerfully shaped by his primary relationships, child therapists have begun to work more directly with parents. Because it is no longer possible to think of the child's internal world as *distinct and separate from his ongoing relational* experiences, and because psychoanalytic clinicians now see the child's sense of his own mind and his self-experience as dyadically and triadically created, parent work has slowly became a more essential aspect of child therapy. According to the scant literature in this area, the shape of this work can vary greatly. Some authors, notably Pantone (2000), and Wachs & Jacobs (2006), suggest that with certain kinds of child patients, the work should be focused primarily on the parents, with little or no emphasis on individual child work. Others, like Oram (2000), recommend involving the parents in the child's therapy, including them in dyadic work. It is my sense, however, that most child therapists continue to work in a way much more consistent with the traditional model of ancillary or concomitant work with the child's therapist. But views on the aim of this work vary. The Novicks maintain that it is possible and advisable for the child's therapist to engage the parent in analytically oriented ancillary work with the child. This work involves exploration of the parent's conflicts vis-à-vis the child, and is likely to be grounded in discussion of the parent's childhood relationships and the projections and projective identifications arising from internalized object representations. The majority of child therapists, however, see the aim of such work as focused on the *child*, as helping the parent to better understand the child, and view such deepening empathy and engagement as crucial to creating changes in the parent–child relationship and in the internal life of the child (see Siskind, 1997; and Slade, 1999). While this approach may touch upon the parent's own history, the latter is not the primary aim of this kind of contemporary parent therapy.

What I wish to argue here is that what many psychoanalytically oriented child therapists are attempting to do in their work with parents is to enhance parents' mentalizing capacities. That is, they are working to help the parent contemplate and make sense of the child's internal experience, and to grow to appreciate the multiple links between the child's behavior and his or her mental states. For most therapists, these aims have not been articulated precisely in this way, although it does not seem at all a stretch to place parent work in this context. Indeed, mentalization theory provides a most useful theoretical frame for parent work. And, given the advent of recent clinical applications of mentalization theory (Bateman & Fonagy, 2004), this framework provides specific ways to target and think about enhancing parental reflective functioning. Presumably, clearer conceptualizations will result both in less ambiguity about this kind of work, and more success in its implementation.

My appreciation of the relevance of mentalization theory to parent work began with my work with Michael, a boy who first came to see me when he was 3, now over 10 years ago. I have written about this work elsewhere (Slade, 1999), but I will briefly describe my work with Michael's mother. I began by seeing Michael and his mother together in parent–child psychotherapy, an approach dictated by Michael's age and the nature of his difficulties. As our work progressed, I also began to see Michael's mother individually. The focus of these sessions was almost exclusively her relationship with Michael. For five years, I saw Michael once or twice weekly; I also saw his mother every other week. Slowly, Julie began to understand Michael, and, more importantly, began to understand her own complex dynamics as they pertained to her interaction with him. What began as a discussion of Michael's biological disruptions gradually evolved into a textured discussion of the intersection of their inner lives. As her work deepened, and particularly as she began to be able to put into words the many meanings Michael had for her, he began to flourish in all ways, most notably in the development of the symbolic function.

When I began to think about what had happened in my work with Julie (which I think happens in child therapies all the time), I was helped by my background in attachment theory and research. I had from the beginning thought of my work with Julie as aimed at helping Michael feel more secure in relation to her, and as strengthening the flexibility and integrity of their attachment relationship. But what I began to realize was that I had in part done this by *engaging her capacity for reflective functioning* in relation to Michael. Over the course of our work, she had developed the capacity to *mentalize* his experience. This was what I came to think had been central in our work; without thinking about it consciously, I had been helping her think reflectively about her child. The more I thought about this, the more I began to think that much of what we do with parents generally is to try and engage the parent's reflective capacities. Ultimately, I found this subtle reframing of the aim and function of parent work both helpful and organizing.

I want to emphasize that I am trying to *describe what I believe many child therapists are already doing, but often intuitively and unconsciously.* The *unconscious* aspect of this is, I believe, what needs to be remedied; articulated guiding constructs are critical to our finding our way through the complex maze of working with parents. Thus, it is my hope that by trying to make these processes more conscious, and by articulating basic principles and conceptualizations, we can actually begin to develop ways of thinking about parent work that are more clear, coherent, and conceptually grounded than what we have today.

REFLECTIVE FUNCTIONING

The construct of reflective functioning (RF) was introduced over 10 years ago by a team of psychoanalytically oriented attachment researchers, Peter Fonagy, Miriam Steele, Howard Steele, and Mary Target (Fonagy & Target, 1996; Fonagy, Steele, Moran, Steele, & Higgitt, 1991; Fonagy et al., 1995). Reflective functioning can be understood narrowly as the capacity to understand one's own and others' behavior in terms of underlying mental states and intentions, and more broadly as a crucial human capacity that is intrinsic to affect regulation and productive social relationships. In just over 10 years, Fonagy and his colleagues have developed an extraordinarily rich and complex body of theoretical, clinical, and research work that elaborates the central importance of this "Interpersonal Interpretive Mechanism" (Fonagy, Gergely, Jurist, & Target, 2002) in promoting secure and healthy personal and relational adaptations across a range of contexts. The more that human beings are able to *mentalize*, or envision mental states in the self or other, the more likely they are to engage in productive, intimate, and sustaining relationships, to feel connected to others at a subjective level, but also to feel autonomous and of separate minds (Fonagy et al., 2002).

While all human beings are born with the capacity to develop the reflective function, *early relationships* create the opportunity for the child to learn about mental states, and determine the depth to which the social environment can ultimately be processed (Fonagy et al., 2002). A mother's capacity to hold in her own mind a *representation* of her child as having feelings, desires, and intentions *allows the child to discover his own internal experience via his mother's re-presentation of it.* A mother's capacity to make meaning of the child's experience will make him meaningful to himself, and allow her to go beyond what is apparent, beyond the concrete, and to instead make sense of the child's behavior in light of mental states, of underlying, likely unobservable, changing dynamic intentions and emotion. This helps the child begin to symbolize, contain, and regulate his internal experience, and to develop coherent and organized representations of self and other. This also helps the parent contain and regulate her own internal experience *as well as her behavior.*

In many instances (and we see this often in our consulting rooms) this process is derailed, often with dire consequences for the child.

> If the caregiver's capacity is lacking in this regard, the version of itself that the infant encounters is an individual conceived of as thinking in terms of physical reality rather than mental states. If the child finds no interpersonal alternative where he is conceived of as mentalizing, his potential in this regard will not be fulfilled. In cases of an abusive, hostile, or simply totally vacuous relationship with the caregiver, the infant may deliberately turn away from the mentalizing object because the contemplation of the object's mind is overwhelming, as it harbors frankly hostile or dangerously indifferent intentions toward the self. (Fonagy et al., 1995, p. 257)

Under such circumstances, the experience of holding the other in mind becomes fraught and terrifying for the child.

In Fonagy's view, mentalization is a crucial *human* capacity central to the development and maintenance of a range of social relationships. What most child therapists are working with, however, is the specific domain of *parental reflective functioning* (Slade, 2005). This term refers to the mother's (or other caregiver's) capacity to reflect on the current mental state of the child and upon her own mental states as these pertain to her relationship with her child, as opposed, for instance, to her capacity to reflect upon her childhood relationship with her own parents. These two different forms of reflective functioning are likely to be closely linked. A parent's capacity to mentalize in relation to her child is highly correlated with outcomes of significant relevance to the child's social and emotional development. Parents who are high in reflective functioning are more likely to have secure children (Slade, Bernbach, Grienenberger, Levy, & Locker, 2005). Furthermore, parental reflective capacities are correlated with positive caregiving practices in mothers (Grienenberger, Slade, & Kelly, 2005). Parental reflective functioning is also predictive of the child's capacity to play and symbolize (Fonagy & Target, 1996; Slade, 1999). These findings make quite evident how crucial it is that child therapists engage and enhance parental reflective capacities as an adjunct to individual work with the child.

EVALUATING PARENTAL REFLECTIVE FUNCTIONING

As I will elaborate in the next sections of this paper, one of the primary aims of parent work is to help parents develop a reflective stance. As described by Fearon and his colleagues (Fearon et al., 2006),

> the heart of good mentalizing is not so much the capacity to always accurately read one's own or another's inner states, but rather a way of approaching relationships that reflects an expectation that one's own thinking and feeling may be enlightened, enriched, and changed by learning about the mental states of other people. In this respect, mentalizing is more like an attitude than a skill, an attitude that is inquiring and respectful of other people's mental states, aware of the limits of one's knowledge of others, and reflects a view that understanding the feelings of others is

important for maintaining healthy and mutually rewarding relationships. (p. 215)

It is this attitude that child therapists wish to elicit in parents.

Some parents, however, have little or no capacity to mentalize when
they bring their child for treatment. This is frequently marked by the
parents' attention to the child's behavior, with little appreciation of the
mental states that might underlie or provoke such behavior. Such parents
speak of the child or of themselves in ways that are devoid of mental state
language, and that emphasize behavior, physical traits, or personality but
fail altogether to consider internal experience. These are parents who
present the child therapist with a litany of the child's misbehaviors, or who
define the child in terms of characteristics that appear to them largely im-
mutable (i.e., "She's just a bad seed"). These nonmentalizing narratives
are accompanied by descriptions of coercive and controlling interactions
(Fearon et al., 2006).

In some instances, parental representations of the child and his experience are manifestly self-serving and even bizarre. For instance, here is a
description offered by the parents of 5-year-old Luke during their first evaluation session with me:

> There's something rather inhuman about him—there's an ab-
> sence of warmth, human feeling, fellow feeling. He has deformed
> the family life and marriage. On a bad day, he's violent, ungov-
> ernable, and underemployed.

> He is without that current that passes between parents and chil-
> dren. . . . Never a moment where there's a bond . . . he's at-
> tached in a way that doesn't strike us as normal . . .

> He's an animal, a psychopath.

Aside from the obviously troubling quality of these descriptions, there is no
suggestion in any of these comments of an interest in the child's mind. And
it is easy to imagine how disrupted the interactions between Luke and his
parents might be given their minimal understanding of his experience.

Some parents use mental state terms to describe themselves or their child, although these often seem hackneyed and superficial. While the description of mental states is in and of itself not an indication of reflective functioning, it is a crucial building block in the development of a reflective stance, and for some parents accurately recognizing even the most basic mental states in themselves or in the child can be an enormous accomplishment.

The development of the reflective or intentional stance is marked by the capacity to see behavior *as a function* of underlying mental states or intentions. We can think of a parent as reflective *once they manifest the capacity to link the child's (or parent's own) internal state to behavior or to other internal states.* "He threw a tantrum in the store (behavior) because he was tired and hungry (physical state), and I'd been dragging him around all day and he was sick of it (mental state)." "She didn't sleep all night because she'd been so frightened by how angry I'd gotten at her." When work with parents in child psychotherapy is going well, we begin to see such shifts from a behavioral to a reflective stance. For instance: "Oh, so maybe he's been running away from me when I pick him up at school because he can't bear for me to know how much he's missed me!" rather than "How can I get him to stop running away when I'm trying to get him in the car after school?"

The reflective stance refers to the capacity to understand the nature of mental states, as well as to appreciate their dynamic nature and interpersonal functions. Thus, for instance, a reflective individual understands that mental states, by their very nature, can be disguised, or opaque to the outsider. They understand that mental states change over time. They understand the *dynamic* nature of mental states: my feelings can affect the way my child feels, and vice versa. In addition, with reflectiveness comes increased accuracy in the capacity to make sense of mental states. So many times parents misread intentions and motivations; often our work results in their becoming more accurate and sensitive readers of their children's feelings and desires. Finally, the capacity to maintain a reflective stance (or at least have that as a goal!) can be inherently regulating for the parent, and helps them to contain and modulate their own intense feelings and fantasies.

In their work on the development of mentalization-based treatments, Fonagy and his colleagues (see Allen & Fonagy, 2006, Bateman & Fonagy, 2004) have noted that mentalizing is most compromised in moments of high-intensity negative affective arousal. Failures in mentalization often set in motion cycles of nonmentalizing interactions, which are typified by mutual efforts at control and coercion, rather than cooperation and mutual recognition.

As an example of the difference between mentalizing and nonmentalizing interactions, imagine the following: It is early evening, and a mother has just finished work. She stops to pick up her 2-year-old child from daycare, where he has spent the whole day. She has nothing to prepare for dinner, and so stops at the supermarket to pick up a few things. Even as she pulls her car into the supermarket parking lot, her child starts to fuss and whine.

Let us imagine Mother #1, who quickly recognizes (probably long before they even get to the supermarket) that her child is hungry, tired, and just wants to get home, and *that his fussy behavior is indicative of these underlying affects and desires.* He has missed her, and is not happy about having to run an errand, one that will only further distract his already harassed and distracted mother. Because she is mentalizing, because she recognizes the *meaning and intention of her child's "mis"behavior,* she will probably start trying to regulate his distress long before it escalates. She will verbally acknowledge that he doesn't want to go to the store, that he just wants to go home and eat dinner, and that he has had a long day and misses her. She will give him something to eat as soon as he starts asking for food (rather than worrying about his spoiling his dinner. He is hungry *now.*) She will recognize right away that this will have to be a very short shopping trip. If he starts to tantrum despite all these efforts to anticipate his dysregulation, she will stop and try to settle him down by comforting him physically, giving voice to his feelings, and trying, in whatever ways she can, to balance his needs with the reality of her mission. This does not mean that she will abandon her own goals, but that she will attend to the regulation of his needs along with her own.

Contrast this with Mother #2, who feels angry as soon as she picks up on her child's displeasure about the shopping trip, and so does little to anticipate or regulate his building distress. Thus, by the time he starts to fuss, she is already agitated, and denies all of his (increasingly annoying) requests for food, demands to get out of the cart, and so on. She is determined to get all the things she needs, and as she moves methodically through the aisles, his distress escalates. Within moments, the child is in a full tantrum, arching his whole body back, poised for a complete meltdown. In complete frustration, she mutters (or yells) "You're doing this on purpose! You're trying to drive me crazy! You never let me do what I need to do!" Her grip is too tight and her jaw clenched when she lifts him out of the cart when they are ready to leave. By the time they get to the car, both mother and child are completely exhausted, dysregulated, and distinctly out of sync. This exemplifies a nonmentalizing interaction, with both partners attempting to coerce and control the other. While the child's attempts at coercion are largely reactive at this point, they will in due course be internalized, and he will be as coercive, controlling, and nonmentalizing as his mother.

From the start, Mother #1 was able to reflect on her child's current mental state and adjust her behavior and expectations in accord with that mental state. Mother #2 found the dysjunction between their distinct desires and intentions intolerable, and had great difficulty holding her child's (equally legitimate and understandable) intentions in mind. As she overrode her child's mental state, his distress escalated, as did hers. Finally, in her anger, she handles him roughly and misattributes malevolent intent to him. Thus she not only behaves insensitively (because she is not using his mental states to guide her behavior), but she also obliterates his self experience by projecting her own feelings and desires onto his. Much of what we do in our work with parents, I believe, is try to help parents behave *and think* more like Mother #1 and less like Mother #2, by helping them mentalize or reflect upon the meaning and intention of their child's behavior.

Some parents are capable of making sophisticated, complex, and sometimes surprising links between their own and their child's internal experience. For instance, here is a highly reflective mother describing an interaction with her toddler:

> Sometimes she gets *frustrated and angry* (child mental state) in ways that I'm *not sure I understand* (understands the opacity of her child's mental state). She points to one thing and I hand it to her, but it turns out *that's not really what she wanted* (child mental state). It *feels very confusing to me* (mother mental state) when *I'm not sure how she's feeling* (mother's mental state affected by child's), especially when she's upset (child behavior). Sometimes *she'll want to do something* (child mental state) and I won't let her because

it's dangerous, and *so she'll get angry* (transaction between mental states). I may try to pick her up and she obviously *didn't want to be picked up because she's in the middle of being angry* (appreciation of the process of child's mental state) and I interrupted her. In those moments it's *me who has the need to pick her up and make her feel better*, so I'll put her back down (distinguishes own needs from those of child).

I think it would be fair to say that it is unusual to hear talk like this from parents in our consulting rooms, at least in the early phases of treatment; when we do, it is likely that we are dealing with a relatively flexible and healthy family system, one that permits more complex and dynamic work. I recently had the experience of meeting a mother who—within minutes of our first session at the start of an evaluation of her 5-year-old son—described the child's current behavior *in light* of traumatic events he had experienced in his early childhood. It was instantly clear to me that this mother saw her child *as a psychological being*, despite the fact that her child's behavior was enormously troubling and infuriating to her, and that she felt guilty for her own part in her child's unhappiness. As I have gotten to know this mother, I have been impressed again and again with how eager she is to understand her child, and how readily she is able to adapt her behavior and expectations in line with these insights. In clinical practice, it is more often the case that mothers and fathers find it very difficult to enter their child's experience as a means of understanding them, and instead resort to blocking out or distorting their child's internal life, resulting in distress and dysjunction all around (see Coates, 2004).

WORKING WITH PARENTS

In the section that follows, I will describe some of the ways that I try in my work with parents to create a context in which they can slowly shift from a physical to a reflective stance, from nonmentalizing to mentalizing narratives, and from cycles of nonmentalizing interactions to cycles of mentalizing interactions. In part, this occurs via a process of identification with me as the reflective parent. In parent work, *I hold the child in mind for the parent as a mentalizing being*, as a person whose feelings and behaviors are inextricably interrelated, and whose feelings and behaviors are inextricably intertwined with theirs as a parent. Most importantly, I see the child's behavior as *meaningful*. Hopefully the parent will come to internalize this view of the child, which will in turn allow them to hold this in mind for the child. He can then begin to experience himself as a meaningful, connected, and feeling person, who then can begin to symbolize, rather than act.

As mentioned briefly above, Fonagy, Fearon, and their colleagues (Fearon et al., 2006) have described this kind of work as "reframing nonmentalizing narratives," or interrupting cycles of nonmentalizing interactions in which one party in the interaction (here the parent) has—in her failure to mentalize—responded in a controlling and coercive fashion with the child. Only when these nonmentalizing narratives are reframed in the language of mental states can the parent begin to *respond* to the child's internal experience rather than to her own projections.

In the sections below, I describe what I think are some of the component parts of this work.

The Creation of a "Playspace"

All work with parents begins with the creation of an environment of reflectiveness; that is, we create a context for symbolization and meaning making on the part of the parent. As we know from Winnicott (1971), helping the parent feel safe enough to mentalize, to envision, name, and play with mental states depends upon the creation of a playspace (see too Fonagy & Target, 1996; Slade, 1994). This is an odd term to use in thinking about parent work, which sometimes feels like a war zone, but it is actually a helpful metaphor to keep in mind.

Creating this playspace begins with our inviting the parent to participate in the treatment. This means that, from the beginning, we frame the therapeutic process to parents in such a way that they see their sessions with us as equally *intrinsic* to the treatment as are individual sessions with the child. This often means that we have to confront our own desires to keep the child all to ourselves, and challenges our implicit rescue fantasies, both of which inherently disparage the parent. These sessions need to be regularly scheduled, and frequent enough to move beyond reporting and catching up. Involving parents in this way raises a number of complex issues regarding confidentiality and boundaries. While it is of course crucial to preserve the safety of the child's relationship with the therapist, such exigencies cannot be used as a justification for avoiding work with parents.

Understandably, many parents come to treatment with the fantasy that the therapist, as the expert, is going to either tell them what to do, or point out their abject failures in parenting. (In this sense, we ourselves risk engaging in a cycle of nonmentalizing interactions with them.) Upending this expectation of obtaining both advice and judgment (or reframing the nonmentalizing narrative) is crucial, because under the best of circumstances the parent and therapist are collaborators in discovering who the child is and what he thinks and feels. In some very real way parents know the child better than we ever will; it is our job to bring that knowledge and understanding into their relationship with the child. Most parents want help in improving their relationship with the child, no matter how far such wishes may be from consciousness. They have come to us often because they feel lost, helpless, worried, and guilty, or because they are overwhelmed by feelings for the child that they cannot manage or articulate. If we can keep this in mind in inviting them to participate in the treatment, they can see us as helpful and facilitating, not judgmental.

In my experience, it is often difficult for less-experienced therapists to incorporate parent work into child treatment in an ongoing way. This is often because they are a little intimidated by parents, unsure of what to do, or just overwhelmed by keeping track of all the pieces of the work. It may also have to do with the fact that they are often not yet parents themselves, and so are more identified with the children, and less certain about how to establish a connection with the parents. Many therapists (and not just beginning ones) struggle with countertransferential feelings in these situations, such that they inadvertently side with the child as victim of parental distortions and cruelty. While aspects of this identification with the child are crucial to his finding safety in the therapeutic relationship, the therapist's relationship with and empathy for the child should not preclude attempting to establish a working relationship with the parent.

Holding the Parent in Mind

Creating an environment in which the parent can begin to hold the child in mind depends upon our capacity to first—and throughout the treatment—hold the parent in mind. Parents who are unable to reflect upon their children's internal experience have often had disrupted and traumatizing early relationships themselves, and our capacity to bear these parental distortions within the countertransference depends upon our remembering this. We must first be able to hear and tolerate the *parents'* experience of the child. Creating an empathic bond that evolves from an understanding of the parents' intersubjective experience of parenting is critical to the formation of each parent's capacity to recognize the child as separate and having a mind of his own.

Parents' feelings about the child make sense to *them* in a profound way. Parents often come to treatment feeling very badly about their children (and themselves as parents) and we need to sit with these awful feelings and understand them. We don't try to talk them out of these feelings (he's not bad, he's just curious), we listen to and try to make sense of them. We hold the parent's experience *for* them, however intolerable or distorted it may seem to us. For some parents, the experience of being held in mind by *anyone* is extremely rare. Thus, our willingness to hold and represent the parent's experience of parenting *this particular child* creates an empathic bond that is critical to the development of the parent's capacity to mentalize.

In this sense, the parent's willingness to hold the child in mind is often the *end* rather than the beginning of the process. As my colleague Steve Tuber put it (personal communication, November 2002), it can be an act of generosity for a parent to contemplate the child's mind, and they must be supported and heard in order to take this leap. This means that we must listen to what it is like for parents in "hot" or difficult moments with the child. It will also involve our learning—at some point, or at multiple points—their *own* story, so that the *meaning* of their failures in holding and empathy become a crucial, reflected-upon part of the dialogue, and of our own understanding.

Model the Reflective Stance

Both creating a playspace and keeping the parent in mind are first steps in establishing a solid working alliance with parents. Most essential to the work, however, are the ways in which we use our meetings with parents to *model the reflective stance.* We struggle to penetrate the opacity and complexity of the child's experience, and we try to symbolize it. We play with it, we wonder about it, we search for the right metaphors to make the child "sensible" to the parent. And we iterate—again and again—the essential aspects of reflective awareness. We talk about feelings, we link them to behavior, continuously underscoring the links between behavior and mental states ("Maybe he's up in the middle of the night because he was afraid when you were away.") We talk about the transient nature of feelings: they will change (and become more tolerable) over time. We note the relations between a parent's mental state and those of her child. ("So maybe your daughter is so angry and hurtful to you because she has been frightened by your sad feelings.") We try to be accurate in our descriptions of mental states, and to convey the complexity of emotional experience. ("So 'enraged' doesn't really capture what you were feeling; perhaps you were frightened and helpless and frustrated.") We understand what we don't know about another's internal experience. And we model curiosity and openness to discovering it—there are no easy answers, there is only a process of discovery. We are continuously attempting to reframe nonmentalizing narratives.

One of the things we hope to accomplish by *re*-presenting the child to the parent in a reflective way is to mobilize their appreciation and recognition of the child's mental experience. Providing metaphors for the child's experience is one way that we bring the child alive for the parent, galvanizing both the attachment system as well as more sensitive caregiving. Let me provide a brief example. I was working with the parents of 5-year-old Luke. As briefly mentioned above, these were parents who found it very difficult to envision Luke's internal experience. About a year into treatment, their marriage began disintegrating in brutal and—for Luke—terrifying ways. I was trying to communicate to the parents how their increasing acrimony was shattering his basic sense of integrity, leaving him open to intense and frightening internal experiences and fantasies. In the effort to avoid each other, both parents were taking off for days at a time without notice; such random and unexplained comings and goings were quite disorienting for Luke. I hoped to articulate Luke's experience in a way that would override their hatred for each other and mobilize their concern.

I searched for a metaphor that would aptly communicate how important it was for them to create a predictable and organized world for him, and how intolerable their overt hostility was for him. In order to do this, I used a vivid and emotionally charged metaphor that I hoped would crystallize for them just how much pain he felt at the great uncertainty, rage, and chaos in his life. As he himself said, when I mentioned that his parents' comings and goings were so hard to understand, "It's MORE than I can understand."

In my meeting with the parents, I told them about an interview I'd seen on TV in which a firefighter had described his experience of trying to orient himself in the immediate aftermath of September 11. He was among those desperately struggling to free a small group of firefighters buried in the rubble that had once been the base of a central stairwell. He radioed to the trapped men for help in locating them; he wanted landmarks, orienting points. His trapped comrade radioed out: "We're right at the corner of West Street and Franklin. That corner, right there." The firefighter wept in recounting the story: "I knew that neighborhood like the back of my hand. I *know* where West and Franklin is. It wasn't there. It was gone." The basic landmarks that would lead him in this desperate situation had completely disintegrated. "It's like that for Luke," I said. "Everything that he knows is gone. And you have to give him the anchors, to create the order out of a universe that for him has exploded completely." It was my hope that—by using such a vivid metaphor to describe the depth of Luke's disorientation— I might be able to evoke their desire to nurture and protect him.

It is very common and natural for parents to ask for advice during the course of their work with us. Within the framework of a reflective model, advice always derives from understanding. That is, what you do with your child, or what I suggest you do with your child, depends entirely upon how we understand the emotional context of a particular situation. What I am helping you do is develop a way of thinking about and understanding your child; *what to do* will flow easily from that. Sally Provence, a wise and gifted child analyst, put it this way: "Don't just do something. Stand there and pay attention. Your child is trying to tell you something."

The child therapist is always trying to help parents wonder what that *something* is. For most parents, curiosity about their child's experience, and a recognition that such experiences are separate from their own, emerges slowly, and often comes in moments of suddenly wondering: "Gee, I wonder why he did that? Oh, so maybe *that's* how she was feeling." Because it leads to understanding, the simple act of imagining the child's experience—even briefly—can be momentous and transforming of a parent's representation of the child. And it is only after the parent is engaged in wondering that developmental guidance and knowledge takes on real meaning and vitality.

Marie came to me in complete and abject despair. She felt as if she had really begun to hate her 3-year-old daughter, Leslie, whom she described as intensely aggressive, provocative, and hyperactive, traits that were especially pronounced in *their* relationship. I met several times with Marie to try to get a sense of what was going on, wondering to myself what might have gone so quickly wrong in this dyad. When I finally met Leslie, I was indeed impressed with her energy, intensity, and willfulness. But both Marie and I were surprised when Leslie refused to let her mother leave the room. She clung to Marie and whimpered; her mother, of course, did not leave, and Leslie proceeded to play out a range of fears, notably abandonment. This child—who wished to be so big and scary, and who was in fact often so very frightening to her mother—turned out to be very frightened herself. The mother looked quite astonished, and did not for a second miss the implications of her daughter's play.

I scheduled an appointment with the mother for the following week. As I returned to my desk, however, I happened to glance out my office window. I saw the following scene unfold in the parking lot: Marie had buckled Leslie in her car seat, but—having forgotten something in the waiting room—pulled up to the office door, thinking Leslie was safe in her car seat. While Marie got out of the car and walked to the office door, Leslie quickly darted out of her car seat and jumped out of the car. By the time Marie got back in her seat, Leslie was standing directly *in front* of the car, a large SUV. Just as Marie engaged the engine, she saw her (small!) daughter, directly in the car's path. She immediately jammed on the brakes and flew out of the car. In a terrified fury, she screamed and roughly yanked her daughter to the side and practically threw her into her car seat. The terrified mother was also terrifying.

When the mother returned the following week, we had two different things to talk about: how frightened her daughter was, and how frightening she could be in her anger. Marie, who had largely seen herself as a victim of Leslie's torments, could begin to appreciate her role in frightening her daughter and in provoking her acting out. What was most striking, however, was the change in this mother's affect as we talked. She softened, she relaxed, and she began to see her child *more sympathetically and more psychologically. She began to wonder what went on in her mind.* Leslie was no longer a demon to her, but a frightened child. She began to imagine her child in quite a different way. Unfortunately, Marie did not return to see me after this session, and failed to pay her bill. Perhaps my seeing *her* as aggressive and her daughter as frightened was simply unbearable.

Working at a Level the Parent Can Manage

It is crucial to work at a level the parent can manage. In the beginning, many parents use few mental state words to describe their children, or their descriptions of their children's emotional life are full of distortions and misattributions. They indicate to the therapist in many ways that emotional experiences are too live and intense to be contemplated. In these instances, the parents' capacity to reflect upon the child's mental experience often begins with the simple understanding of their child's particular way of physically regulating himself; that is, while they cannot talk about mental states, they may be able to talk about physical states. This aspect of the child's internal experience can be approached with some neutrality, and can often be very helpful to parents, who may find it difficult to recognize even physical states, or levels and trajectories of arousal in their children. Thus, for instance, a parent experiences her child as being wild and out of control, without any sense of the triggers and patterns of his dysregulation. Developing a basic understanding of regulatory processes can be a starting point in developing a reflective stance in the parent (see Slade, 1999).

With parents who have a very hard time imagining their child's internal experience, it can often be helpful to focus very specifically on "hot" or what Pine (1985) would call "affectively supercharged moments" in the interaction. As Fonagy and others have noted (Allen, 2006; Fearon et al., 2006), mentalization is most difficult during moments of negative affective arousal. As happened in my discussions with Marie, described above, there is enormous value in getting into the nitty-gritty of what actually happened between parent and child; slowly trying to understand the "hot spots" often leads to the affect, the dysregulation, and ultimately paves the way to greater understanding of the transaction between and interdigitation of child and parent mental states.

Flexibility

There is no single format for conducting parent sessions. Rather, *reasoned* flexibility is key. This is not a monolithic or simple approach, but rather a way of *thinking about and framing* the work. Sometimes the therapist may decide to bring a parent into the child's session (with the child's permission, of course). Sometimes she will decide to alternate dyadic and individual sessions. Sometimes she will meet alternately with parent and child, or have regular, concomitant sessions with the parent. I have had experiences in which I realized that bringing the parent into a session with the child was toxic to the child, and that—no matter what my intentions—I could not protect the child. Sometimes the moments of transition in the waiting room become critical moments of translation and reformulation. Many of the decisions about which of these approaches is suitable in a given clinical situation will rest upon the developmental stage of the child, the issues he or she is dealing with, and an assessment of the parents' capacities. But because child therapists are, among other things, trying to create shifts within the relationship, these variations remain dynamic ways to bring about change. In his book, *The Motherhood Constellation*, Stern (1995) notes that once you introduce parents into the psychotherapeutic situation, the work can seem messy, "impure," and chaotic. But when theoretically guided, carefully thought out, and respectful both of the child's boundaries and needs, as well as the parent's need for support and understanding, this work is not messy, but developmentally appropriate.

There are of course times when it is nearly impossible to do any productive work with parents at all. I have worked, as all child therapists have, with parents whose narcissism and fundamental detachment from the child (whether manifest in entanglement or disengagement) meant that I couldn't engage them in even the most basic wondering. The story is set, the die is cast; my attempting to shake or challenge this story (i.e., to reframe the nonmentalizing narrative) would disrupt my relationship with the child and threaten the treatment. In these cases, I do what I can with the child and hope that she can grow up and away very soon. I hope that the parents will "catch" my reflective stance, and I look for little windows to get through to them. Sometimes this seems like so little, but I try to keep in mind the understanding and pleasure that can come out of a single moment of true reflectiveness.

What Reflective Parent Work Is Not

It is important to briefly consider what this type of parent work is *not*. It is not individual therapy for the parent. One of the most common occurrences in working with very disrupted families and disrupted relationships is that the therapist refers the parent for her or his own separate individual therapy. While this may sometimes be very necessary, and can actually help a parent separate her experience from that of her child, it cannot replace ancillary or concomitant work with parents. To do so obscures critical opportunities to work *on the relationship* and specifically to address the parent's capacity to come to know the child *through the therapist's eyes, and his or her particular vision of the child.* Individual therapy is usually about the parent, and not the relationship. While individual treatment may be helpful, what the parent *also* needs is to find a way to understand the child, and the child's individual therapist is in a unique position to facilitate this discovery. The child therapist is not conducting psychotherapy with the parent, but is trying to directly intervene in facilitating the parent–child relationship, using her understanding of the child as the lynchpin.

In line with this perspective, parent work is also not *primarily* about understanding the parent's conflicts in relation to the child (Novick, J. & Novick, K. K., 2001, 2002; Novick, K. K. & Novick, J., 2002a, 2002b). While such understanding may well, and perhaps always should, emerge from the parent's struggle to understand her child, such insights are *secondary* to the processes described here. Similarly, while a couple's dynamics may become an issue when working with a mother and father together, one is generally trying to use one parent's understanding of the child to inform the other's, rather than focus upon discrepancies in their views, and the conflicts that result from these discrepancies. While a couple's conflicts will of course be an issue in certain circumstances, they can hopefully be addressed in such a way that the child's mind—as it exists in dynamic relation to the minds of his parents—can remain the focus of the work.

Parent work is not the same as family therapy. Family therapy is inherently about understanding and thus changing family systems. While family systems are certainly affected by reflective parent work, it is the *particular relationship that a child therapist has with a child and with his mind* that is central to change in this model. The parent develops a different understanding not only of the child's affects and intentions, but also of his development, as it underlies and indeed motivates certain desires and beliefs. Such are the unique contributions of this sort of approach. From a technical and theoretical point of view, its closest "cousin" is infant–parent psychotherapy (Fraiberg, 1980; Lieberman, Silverman, & Pawl, 1999). In fact, the reflective model I have described here can be applied to many aspects of clinical work with children and their parents. As an example, interdisciplinary teams at the Yale Child Study Center have been applying these same principles in developing mother–infant reflective parenting programs for both high- and low-risk families (Slade, 2007; Sadler, Slade, & Mayes, 2006; Slade, Sadler, deDios-Kenn, Webb, Ezepchick, & Mayes, 2005; Slade, Sadler, & Mayes, 2005; see too Grienenberger et al., (2004). Likewise, Fonagy and his colleagues (Fearon et al., 2006) have developed the SMART model (Short-term Mentalization and Relational Therapy), which aims to enhance reflective functioning in children and their families.

CLOSING COMMENTS

In a recent paper, Sheldon Bach (2001) described the child's experience of being held in mind by a parent in a most poetic way:

> A person's specific memories and experiences are like individual beads that can achieve continuity and gestalt form only when they are strung together to become a necklace. The string on which they are assembled is the child's *continuous existence in the mind of the parents*, which provides the continuity on which the

beads of experiences are strung together and become the *neck-lace of a connected life.* (p. 748)

When we work with parents, we are helping them gather the pearls that they have dropped, or perhaps not even seen, and to once again or even for the first time string them together in a single, coherent, strand. This gift to the child is *the necklace of a connected life.*

AUTHOR'S NOTE

This paper evolved from a presentation originally made to the Canadian Association for Psychoanalytic Child Therapists in association with the Toronto Child Psychoanalytic Program, on September 28, 2002. Revised versions were presented to psychoanalytic institutes in and around the New York metropolitan area, including the Institute for Psychoanalytic Training and Research, the Postgraduate Center for Mental Health, the Westchester Center for the Study of Psychoanalysis and Psychotherapy, and the William Alanson White Institute. I would like to thank the many colleagues who helped shape my thinking along the way, particularly Mary Target, Peter Fonagy, Steve Tuber, Arnold Zinman, and Phyllis Beren. An earlier version of this paper appears in F. N. Busch (Ed.), *Mentalization: Theoretical Considerations, Research Findings, and Clinical Implications* (New York: Analytic Press, 2008).

NOTES

1. The same could be said for virtually all child therapy approaches. See Target, Fonagy, Slade, Cottrell, & Fuggle (2005).

2. Likewise, family therapy is sometimes recommended in these circumstances (Asen, 2007; Kerr & Bowen, 1988; White & Epston, 1990). While this work is in principle different from parent work, it may—by virtue of its potential to disentangle the child from family projections and distortions—have similar positive effects on the child, and on the parent's capacity to see the child as having a mind of his own.

REFERENCES

Allen, J. G. (2006). Mentalization in practice. In J. G. Allen & P. Fonagy (Eds.), *Handbook of mentalization-based treatment* (pp. 3–30). Chichester, UK: Wiley.

Allen, J. G., & Fonagy, P. (Eds.). (2006). *Handbook of Mentalization-based Treatments.* New York: Wiley.

Asen, E. (2007). Multi-contextual multiple family therapy. In L. Mayes, P. Fonagy, & M. Target (Eds.), *Developmental science and psychoanalysis: Integration and innovation* (pp. 293–307). London: Karnac.

Bach, S. (2001). On being forgotten and on forgetting one's self. *Psychoanalytic Quarterly, LXX,* 739–756.

Bateman, A. W., & Fonagy, P. (2004). *Psychotherapy for borderline personality disorder: Mentalization based treatment.* Oxford, UK: Oxford University Press.

Chazen, S. (2003). *Simultaneous treatment of parent and child.* London: Jessica Kingsley Publishers.

Coates, S. W. (2004). After September 11, 2001: The parent's reflective capacity as mediator and moderator. Paper presented at the annual meeting of Division 39, The American Psychological Association, Miami, FL, March 19, 2004.

Fearon, P., Target, M., Sargent, J., Williams, L. W., McGregor, J., Bleiberg, E., & Fonagy, P. (2006). Short-term mentalization and relational therapy (SMART): An integrative family therapy for children and adolescents. In J. G. Allen & P. Fonagy (Eds.), *Handbook of mentalization-based treatment.* Chichester, UK: Wiley.

Fonagy, P., & Target, M. (1996). Playing with reality: I. Theory of mind and the normal development of psychic reality. *International Journal of Psycho-Analysis, 77,* 217–233.

Fonagy, P., Gergely, G., Jurist, E., & Target, M. (2002). *Affect Regulation, Mentalization, and the Development of the Self.* New York: Other Press.

Fonagy, P., Steele, M., Steele, H., Leigh, T., Kennedy, R., Mattoon, G., & Target, M. (1995). Attachment, the reflective self, and borderline states: The predictive specificity of the Adult Attachment Interview and pathological emotional development. In S. Goldberg, R. Muir, & J. Kerr (Eds.), *Attachment Theory: Social, Developmental, and Clinical Perspectives* (pp. 223–279). Hillsdale, NJ: Analytic Press.

Fraiberg, S. (1980). *Clinical Studies in Infant Mental Health: The First Year of Life.* New York: Basic Books.

Grienenberger, J., Popek, P., Stein, S., Solow, J., Morrow, M., Levine, N., et al. (2004). The Wright Institute Reflective Parenting Program workshop training manual. Unpublished manual, The Wright Institute, Los Angeles, CA.

Grienenberger, J., Slade, A., & Kelly, K. (2005). Maternal reflective functioning and the caregiving relationship: The link between mental states and mother–infant affective communication. *Attachment and Human Development, 7*, 299–311.

Karen, R. (1998). *Becoming Attached: First Relationships and How They Impact Our Capacity to Love.* New York: Oxford University Press.

Kerr, M., & Bowen, M. (1988). *Family Evaluation.* New York: Norton.

Lieberman, A. F., Silverman, R., & Pawl, J. (1999). Infant–parent psychotherapy: Core concepts and current approaches. In C. H. Zeanah (Ed.), *Handbook of Infant Mental Health* (pp. 472–485). New York: Guilford.

Novick, J., & Novick, K. K. (2001). Parent work in analysis: Children, adolescents, and adults. Part I: The evaluation phase. *Journal of Infant, Child, and Adolescent Psychotherapy, 1*, 55–77.

Novick, J., & Novick, K. K. (2002). Parent work in analysis: Children, adolescents, and adults. Part III: The middle and pretermination phases of treatment. *Journal of Infant, Child, and Adolescent Psychotherapy, 2*, 17–41.

Novick, K. K., & Novick, J. (2002a). Parent work in analysis: Children, adolescents, and adults. Part II: Recommendation, beginning, and middle phases of treatment. *Journal of Infant, Child, and Adolescent Psychotherapy, 2*, 1–27.

Novick, K. K., & Novick, J. (2002b). Parent work in analysis: Children, adolescents, and adults. Part IV: Termination and post-termination phases. *Journal of Infant, Child, and Adolescent Psychotherapy, 2*, 43–55.

Novick, K. K., & Novick, J. (2005). *Working with Parents Makes Therapy Work.* New York: Jason Aronson.

Oram, K. (2000). A transitional space: Involving parents in the play therapy of their children. *Journal of Infant, Child, and Adolescent Psychotherapy, 1*, 79–98.

Pantone, P. (2000). Treating the parental relationship as the identified patient in child psychotherapy. *Journal of Infant, Child, and Adolescent Psychotherapy, 1*, 19–38.

Sadler, L. S., Slade, A., & Mayes, L. C. (2006). Minding the baby: A mentalization-based parenting program. In J. G. Allen & P. Fonagy (Eds.), *Handbook of mentalization-based treatment* (pp. 271–288). Chichester, UK: Wiley.

Siskind, D. (1987). *The Child Patient and the Therapeutic Process: A Psychoanalytic, Developmental, and Object Relations Approach.* Northvale, NJ: Jason Aronson.

Siskind, D. (1997). *Working with Parents: Establishing the Essential Alliance in Child Psychotherapy and Consultation.* Northvale, NJ: Jason Aronson.

Slade, A. (1999). Representation, symbolization, and affect regulation in the concomitant treatment of a mother and child: Attachment theory and child psychotherapy. *Psychoanalytic Inquiry, 19*, 797–830.

Slade, A. (2005). Parental reflective functioning: An introduction. *Attachment and Human Development, 7*, 269–281.

Slade, A. (2006). Reflective parenting programs: Theory and development. *Psychoanalytic Inquiry, 26,* 640–657.

Slade, A., Bernbach, E., Grienenberger, J., Levy, D., & Locker, A. (2002). Addendum to Reflective Functioning Scoring Manual: For use with the Parent Development Interview. Unpublished manuscript. The City College and Graduate Center, City University of New York.

Slade, A., Grienenberger, J., Bernbach, E., Levy, D. W., & Locker, A. (2005). Maternal reflective functioning and attachment: Considering the transmission gap. *Attachment and Human Development, 7,* 283–292.

Slade, A., Sadler, L., & Mayes, L. C. (2005). Minding the baby: Enhancing parental reflective functioning in a nursing/mental health home visiting program. In L. Berlin, Y. Ziv, L. Amaya-Jackson, & M. T. Greenberg (Eds.), *Enhancing Early Attachments: Theory, Research, Intervention, and Policy* (pp. 152–177). New York: Guilford.

Slade, A., Sadler, L., de Dios-Kenn, C., Webb, D., Ezepchick, J., & Mayes, L. (2005). Minding the baby: A reflective parenting program. *Psychoanalytic Study of the Child, 60,* 74–100.

Stern, D. N. (1995). *The Motherhood Constellation.* New York: Basic Books.

Target, M., Fonagy, P., Slade, A., Cottrell, D., & Fuggle, P. (2005). Psychosocial therapies of children. In G. Gabbard, J. Beck, & J. Holmes (Eds.), *Concise Oxford textbook of psychotherapy* (pp. 341–352). Oxford, UK: Oxford University Press.

Wachs, C., & Jacobs, L. (2006). *Parent-Focused Child Therapy: Attachment, Identification, and Reflective Functioning.* New York: Rowman & Littlefield.

White, M., & Epston, D. (1990). *Narrative Means to Therapeutic Ends.* New York: Norton.

Winnicott, D. W. (1971). *Playing and reality.* London: Tavistock Publications.

Chapter 11

Critical Moments as Relational Moments

Kimberlyn Leary

This chapter tells a story from a very different domain of clinical practice—that of negotiation and mediation. Using an interdisciplinary approach, I inquire into the relational milieu favorable to dialogue that occurred as part of an effort to negotiate a cease-fire in a civil war in Aceh, Indonesia. My research occurred in the context of a study designed to investigate the role of what I call *critical moments* in dispute resolution. Mentalization was applied as a post-hoc frame to understand the relational activity in which mediators engaged in order to sponsor a discussion between guerilla fighters from the Free Aceh Movement (GAM) and the Republic of Indonesia under the auspices of the Henri Dunant Centre (HDC), an international, nongovernmental organization dedicated to conflict management. Thus this chapter aims to extend the idea of mentalization into a new arena and to suggest that the recognition and use of critical moments depends upon mentalizing interactions.

This chapter represents a form of applied psychoanalysis: psychoanalytic concepts undergird this narration of a story about change under uncertain conditions. While a negotiation scenario is a far cry from a clinical session, the work depicted here shows how the effort to understand one's self in interaction with others is germane to practice disciplines such as that of conflict transformation. Intentions, attitudes, subtle relational cues, and dispositions—all elements that make up what developmental psychoanalysts call "mentalization"—play an underappreciated role in negotiation. Recognition of this opens possibilities for fruitful cross-talk among analytic clinicians, negotiators, and mediators.

Mentalization is a concept that is particularly relevant to negotiation in several respects. First, mentalization depends upon being open and open-minded, a willingness to recognize others, and a capacity to avoid assuming with too much certainty that we know what others think and believe. Second, mentalization is consistent with an appreciation of how seemingly rational arguments and discourse are often influenced by emotional factors. Third, mentalization promotes an attitude of accepting that we have something to gain from others, and that others can help us to reflect upon and reevaluate our own point of view. Finally, as will be discussed below, mentalization can be synergistic when people engage in it mutually, resulting in the emergence and discovery of new and unexpected directions. All of these aspects of mentalization can be seen in the specific negotiations that will be discussed in this chapter. Let me begin with some background to this inquiry and to the actual negotiations that will function as my "case example."

SETTING THE STAGE

On August 15, 2005, the Republic of Indonesia and the Free Aceh Movement signed a peace agreement that is widely believed to be the most credible opportunity to date for ending a civil war that has been waged for 30 years and has claimed more than 9,000 lives. Although peace-making efforts began in 2000, the tsunami that decimated the region in 2004 put Aceh on the international stage, making it politically desirable for both sides to advance toward a more decisive settlement.

An opportunity to explore the role of critical moments in negotiation presented itself when I was invited to study the first intervention process that was initiated in Aceh to de-escalate this armed conflict. This occurred in the context of my appointment as a Visiting Scholar at the Program on Negotiation at Harvard Law School.

My training as a psychoanalyst was preceded by postdoctoral work at the University of Michigan Psychological Clinic studying the therapeutic alliance in psychoanalytic psychotherapy. With colleagues there, I studied audiotapes and transcripts of many psychotherapy sessions in order to ascertain those specific factors that enhanced the development of the therapeutic alliance. This work culminated in a series of projects that ultimately focused on the process of negotiation we observed in the exchanges that occurred in psychotherapy. Wanting to better understand the nature of influence and the theories that account for its vicissitudes, I joined the Program on Negotiation as a Visiting Scholar where, in time, my work came to involve the study of *critical moments*—those decisive moments in which influence is exerted. As part of this project, I was invited to interview the participants at the political talks held in January 2001, discussions that were a prelude to the conversations that resulted in decisive movement toward a cease-fire process in Aceh. Identified as a psychologist-psychoanalyst, I met with representatives from the rebel leadership (GAM) currently in exile in Stockholm, with members of the Indonesian government, and with the Henri Dunant Centre, the international nongovernmental organization that facilitated the discussions. Before I proceed with a description of the material that came from the interviews on critical moments, I will describe the terms of the conflict that has resulted in this long-standing civil war.

BACKGROUND

The terms of this conflict, as with all conflicts, were complex. The rebels' stated objective was independent statehood, based on a claim of distinct ethnic and cultural identity. The Indonesian government had vowed to uphold its territorial integrity, rejected Acehenese independence, and offered only autonomy. A further basis of the dispute was also undeniably economic, as Aceh is the site of tremendous wealth in natural resources. Both sides have been accused of gross human rights violations.

THE FIRST MOVEMENTS TOWARD DIALOGUE

The precipitant for dialogue occurred when the HDC essentially inserted itself into the conflict, ultimately brokering a cease-fire in 2002. This particular effort had been assessed as a negotiation failure, as it had yielded only an interim agreement. However, key features originating from this dialogue—plans for GAM to be transformed from a fighting force to a political movement—were incorporated into the cornerstone of the 2005 peace agreement, making the success and failure of this negotiation effort rather more ambiguous to determine.

Most efforts to understand decisive shifts in negotiations reflect top-down applications of frameworks to existing case material. Negotiation specialists have suggested that developing effective theory about these exchanges could be enhanced if the distinctive perspectives of practitioners and disputants could be included. Developing this kind of knowledge base requires that one examine a negotiation process in some detail. In my research, participants were invited to provide a first-person account of historical events in the manner of an oral history or a clinical consultation. The result is a thick description of particular experiences; in this case, of moments deemed critical, and as so defined by the participants themselves. I should also like to emphasize that my commentaries about these moments are intended as discovery-oriented and speculative, opening up questions for future inquiry rather than stabilizing or fixing answers.

THE BEGINNING OF DIALOGUE

As in a clinical consultation, it is important to understand the history of the presenting problem and the patient's efforts to cope before the effort to secure help. Here the key players were the HDC, who initiated the first attempt to convene the combatants, and the experts the Centre invited during the structured conversations that took place later on. My aim here is to tell a story of how the intervention took shape while using the respondents' own words to convey the importance of their efforts to be mindful of themselves in the context of differently constituted others. It was my sense that what occurred can be captured more precisely as a form of online mentalization, unfolding in real time.

Historically, a turning point in the Aceh hostilities occurred in 1999 when the HDC, then a newly organized, independently funded nongovernmental organization, identified Aceh as a site for intervention. Martin Griffiths, HDC's director and former United Nations Assistant Secretary General for Human Rights, and Louisa Chan-Boegli, a physician who had previously worked for the United Nations High Commission on Refugees, were at the center of HDC's project in Aceh.

Martin Griffiths described the ethos of the Centre during its early days: "As a new organization, we thought a humanitarian organization ought to be concerned about reducing conflict, instead of just providing assistance and protection during it." The organizational culture of the HDC seems to have had an important impact on the way the HDC formulated its role. The agency is small and relatively free of bureaucracy, factors that allow decisions to be made quickly. The Centre's founding values include innovation and flexibility, giving rise to a style of facilitation that is perhaps best described as intuitive, improvisational, and deeply relational. These values are fully consistent with the kind of open-mindedness that promotes mentalization.

From the start, the HDC was able to engage with the Indonesian central government at its highest levels. This was due to chance circumstances. Director Martin Griffiths describes what took place:

> One of our consultants had written a book on Asian values a couple of years before, and one of the people he'd interviewed was [Indonesian President Abdurrahman] Wahid and his family. What he did was to sit in the outer corridors of the presidential palace waiting for a meeting, obviously not getting one. Eventually, he simply left a copy of the book, went back to his hotel, and was almost immediately phoned by the daughter of President, to say, "Oh yes, that book, great, are you here? Please come back." . . . As a result of that, we got a meeting with the president. It was just one of those things, and huge credit goes to [him] for his incredible persistence.

> That was the first piece of chance, and the second thing was that . . . Gus Dur [aka President Wahid] had just come into power. He was a maverick . . . he was much more open to new approaches, much more tolerant in his general approach to people. Because of him, of course, we were then able to be in touch with senior ministers.

Dr. Louisa Chan-Boegli believed that the HDC had an opportunity to create an external forum for dialogue between the two belligerents, with the aim of trying to reduce the conflict directly. Griffiths initially resisted:

> I thought that the government of Indonesia, which I didn't know particularly well at the time, would be very unwilling to have a dialogue with the GAM abroad. It seemed like an odd thing for a government so sensitive on sovereignty issues to do, even with somebody like Gus Dur in charge of the government. We had only been alive, by that time, for about two and a half months. And we'd never done this sort of stuff before. We were particularly untutored at that time in these sorts of processes. [But] Louisa, she was very convincing, and very compelling.

The HDC moved forward, vigorously pursuing efforts to engage the Indonesian government and GAM representatives. Though technically a neutral, the HDC clearly stood for something. Chan-Boegli explained:

> Although we wanted to see ourselves as without any viewpoint, I think that we did very much have a point-of-view. . . . What we were for was a dialogue process. That is already taking a certain stance, because there are people on both sides who are not willing to come to a dialogue process. The second thing is that we wanted to stop the violence. Having said that, we did try our best not to pass any judgment on either side. That was the true meaning of our being neutral or impartial. . . . If we're not going to have violence, what was needed was a certain set of things to happen, and since there was nobody recognizing independence, it was futile to fight an independence war.

Once again, one can hear in this honest self-reflection and recognition of different points a view a spirit that would encourage mentalization to flourish.

Setting up meetings between the GAM and the Indonesian government took place over the course of many months. Winning the government's agreement to participate in the meeting was viewed as "facilitation" and not as a negotiation. Louisa Chan-Boegli reports that she persuaded HDC's director, Martin Griffiths, to send her to Stockholm for a final effort to engage the GAM:

> It meant something to the GAM that I took time at Christmas to go out there. There were a couple of things which to them were important. One was the withdrawal of troops, of course. I used everything possible. Finally at three a.m. [I discovered] one of the things that was important and one that seemed a very small thing. One of the GAM ministers had a full-time job as a doctor in a hospital and he had just taken a new clinic post, and for him to set aside working days during the week to come to a meeting in Geneva was a big deal. He had to negotiate with his bosses to get time off. It bothered him that the government was dictating the dates: "We can come to Geneva on this date, but not that date." And I said, Okay, we'll take into consideration that logistic problem for you. And that was a sign that we acknowledged the importance of his work. It was a key thing. I said "You know, I understand. I've been a doctor myself and I understand. We'll try to accommodate as much as possible." And he said, "Okay, I'll try on my side too." And he did. He did keep his word. So you see, we have to do a lot of other things besides getting to the point.

As these vignettes indicate, dialogue efforts of this sort are frequently chance events that require improvisational flexibility and application of influence that is often exerted subtly and in relational terms. Respondents conveyed their sensitivity to the person approaching them and proved willing to give and accommodate to the extent that key others were able to accord them respect by virtue of attempting to sustain a matrix of respect and hope that change was possible.

ARRANGING A PLACE AT THE TABLE: GENEVA, 2001

When GAM and government negotiators did meet in January 2001, they did so at the HDC's headquarters in Geneva. The participants around the table included GAM's Stockholm leadership (Hasan di Tiro, a descendant of Aceh's precolonial sultans, and Mahmood Malik, whom GAM considers to be its prime minister), and Indonesian government ministers, many of whom were career diplomats (including Desra Percaya and Hassan Wirajuda). HDC Director Martin Griffith and HDC staffer Louisa Chan-Boegli were joined by three internationally known experts whom they invited to participate as advisors to the HDC.

The HDC advisors were strategically chosen to equalize the proceedings. The HDC invited British Lord Eric Avebury (whose forebears had opposed Dutch colonialism in Aceh) and Hurst Hannum, Professor of International Law at the Fletcher School at Tufts University and author of a definitive book on sovereignty claims. The third expert was William Ury, a negotiation specialist from Harvard Law School who is currently the director of the Global Negotiation Project at Harvard, and coauthor of the influential negotiation text *Getting to Yes*.

Each of these experts brought distinctive talents to the meeting. Lord Avebury's presence was perceived as providing reassurance to the GAM. Hurst Hannum understood himself to have a specific role as well, as the international lawyer who was sympathetic to the minority concern, but also positioned to deliver the news that existing statutes did not permit the Acehenese a legal right to independence: "I was to tell them that the rest of the world was not on their side."

William Ury was expected to convene internal talks with each side aimed at helping the parties to fully explore the options open to them and to take a full accounting of the costs imposed by each solution.

The meeting itself was configured not as a negotiation per se but as a "workshop on substantive issues." This distinction was useful in several ways, particularly in justifying the inclusion of outside experts who were then free to give voice to assessments (e.g., that GAM had no international standing for its claims) that would have been corrosive if they came from the other side. Calling the meeting a workshop also related to other aspects of face-saving: a failed workshop would be considered to have different implications on the ground and in the international press than would the dissolution of talks considered to be negotiations for peace.

All of the proceedings took place at the HDC's headquarters, a beautiful old mansion just a few meters from Lake Geneva. The building was large enough for groups of delegates to meet together and was able to offer accommodations when a small caucus was desired. Participants also took their meals together, which had the added benefit of allowing for informal exchanges.

The most innovative proposal to come from the meetings, that GAM transform from a fighting force to a political movement, grew directly out of the workshops. Early in the workshop process, Ury and the facilitation team encouraged the parties to consider the deep structure of their wishes for independence or autonomy. For instance, the facilitators asked GAM to reflect on the fundamentals on which their identity was based (i.e., "Are you a political movement forced to use military means, or a military movement?"). Engaging in a series of "thought experiments," Ury invited the GAM to think through the obstacles that President Wahid would face if he were to grant Aceh the independence they desired. The reply came quickly, "He'd be in trouble but that's his problem." "No," Ury said, "that's *your* problem if you want him to make that speech." In this way, the workshop fostered mentalizing experiences where the relation between self and other was redefined and the parties were able to appreciate the genuine constraints under which representatives from the other side worked.

The facilitators advanced an interim solution: The parties would agree to disagree about the long-term status of Aceh. In the immediate term, they would cease hostilities and, as an intermediate step, GAM would move to transform itself into a political movement in the context of an integrated Indonesia. For GAM, becoming a political movement was a path to "decolonization." For the Indonesian government, this new direction was entirely consistent with the "autonomy" they had advanced for Aceh all along.

Martin Griffiths described what he observed as a critical moment:

> We were all gathered round a flip chart. . . . Bill [Ury] was still the center of this. Slowly GAM started gathering around us. We started to produce the formula which still survives. "You can get involved in a democratic process, it doesn't mean to say that you have to give up on independence, on the contrary, it's a way to it." We mapped out those principles, and it really jelled. Avebury was incredibly important as well, of course, as a wise man for the GAM. I think the key point was that the GAM was

engaging as a result of Bill's teaching. They were engaging with a new world of analysis and words and discourse.

The second thing about . . . gathering around that flip chart, was that there was a sense of excitement about it. They weren't just sitting back . . . they were engaged. There was a sense of energy there. I think we all felt, "My God, there is something here, something's happening. There's a sense of something being created, a new idea here which could be very, very valuable."

The emergence of this idea—that GAM would become a political movement advocating for its beliefs within the context of an integrated Indonesia—constituted a distinctive turning point. Autonomy and independence were now joined by a third possibility, interposed between the existing formulations. Though the mechanism for such a transformation was not explicitly addressed, the very idea of such a transformation can be thought of in psychoanalytic terms as offering a new potential space in which the impasse might soften. This critical moment can also be understood as an example of the synergistic effect of the mutual process of mentalizing.

TURNING POINTS IN THE ACEH-INDONESIA DIALOGUES

Druckman (2001) notes that progress in security negotiations often depends on the influence of factors outside or more distant from the negotiation process. This appears to have been the case with respect to the January 2001 dialogues. The central government's strong support for the dialogue process in general, and the HDC's efforts in particular, were clearly key features of the government's decision to participate in talks with the GAM at all.

The respondents I interviewed easily identified elements of the negotiation process, structure, and outcomes that they considered to represent critical moments. These include: the *political milieu* in Jakarta (and in Aceh) at the time the January 2001 talks were convened; the *Geneva venue*; the presence of the *international experts*; the use of a *workshop format*; the suggestion that *GAM could transform* itself from a fighting force to a political movement; and the *quality of the relational process* that occurred with respect to all of these domains. Although all of the critical moments identified were interdependent to an important degree (e.g., the design of the meeting as a workshop enabled a certain kind of relating that likely would not have occurred in a formal negotiation), the participants could also distinguish specific features of each type of critical occurrence.

The physical setting of the January 2001 meeting emerged as being crucial to the participants' sense of safety and security. Situating the meeting in Geneva, a neutral country, had political meaning. The physical attributes of the Centre's quarters were also important. With its accommodations for larger plenary sessions as well as smaller rooms for private discussions, the building provided an environment where leadership on both sides could explore ideas with the HDC team, away from their delegations. Concretely and symbolically, the Geneva venue conveyed a sense that there was space enough to contain the groups' mutual hostilities, and room to explore other alternatives.

The international experts appear to have been important in several ways. For the GAM, the presence of American and British experts signaled the possibility that their struggle might receive wider recognition (e.g., "This was the first time . . . that we knew the international community cared [about] what was going on in Aceh"). At the same time, the international experts did not threaten Indonesian sovereignty since they represented no international body and had no authority beyond that extended to them by the participants themselves.

HDC director Martin Griffiths described what happened:

[Hassan] Wirajuda took me aside and said, "You know, we've only agreed that these people would be here for the pre-meeting, not for the meeting." But I also said to Hassan that it was really important for Bill and me to be sitting together. . . . I said to Hassan, "I need this man's help; this is going to be a crucial meeting. You know, I haven't done much of this stuff, and this guy is really good, and so I want to have him next to me."

In the end, they compromised. During the formal talks, Bill Ury joined Martin Griffiths and Louisa Chan-Boegli at the facilitator's end of the table.

The other HDC advisors sat in the back, as observers. Some respondents believed that resolving this issue became a cornerstone to new trust. The use of the international experts was both the occasion of conflict *and* a direct instance of how a conflict might be managed.

Calling the meeting as a workshop also shaped the nature of the conversation that emerged. The suggestion that GAM could transform itself into a political party emerged directly from the workshop format. It is perhaps the most specific instance of a critical moment occurring during the January 2001 dialogues. The workshop created "potential space," and vetted for consideration possibilities that existed only in the subjunctive (e.g., "what if?" "how might?") (Pizer 1999). In so doing, the workshop format reassigned priority away from existing formulas to those that were emergent.

CRITICAL MOMENTS AS RELATIONAL MOMENTS

Each of these factors acquired substance in a relational context. For example, President Wahid's openness to dialogue was predicated upon his responsiveness to the HDC consultant who waited patiently throughout a long afternoon hoping to engage him personally. The Geneva venue and workshop format appeared to be pivotal because they permitted the participants to relate to one another in a range of contexts and in ways that underscored emergent proposals. The suggestion of a "third story" (Stone, Heen, & Patton, 1999)—that GAM become a political party—took shape in a spontaneous discussion around the flipchart.

All of the respondents, for example, commented on the "rapport," "chemistry," "good faith," and "sincerity" that existed during the meetings. Issues of face-saving were particularly critical during the dialogue given its import within the system of Asian values shared by both of the parties. The Acehenese had long been infuriated with the implication that Jakarta could grant freedom to Aceh. For Louisa Chan-Boegli the management of respect and recognition proved pivotal: "I said to the government [that] it would be important not to appear like you have something to give them, because they're very proud. They're very dignified. . . . So the government negotiators said, 'I'm here to listen to you.'" At least some of the GAM's concerns could be linked to issues of recognition, which is a basic element of mentalization.

The relational engagement among the participants was perhaps the most ambivalently regarded of all of the critical occurrences that were identified. Some respondents could explicitly identify the relevance of these psychological and relational factors as key. Others appeared distinctly uneasy with the notion that relational factors were more than a background influence. All of the community of practitioners referred frequently to the *expression of strong emotion and the intense interpersonal engagement* that occurred. Whether or not the participants saw things psychologically, the success of the negotiations needs to be understood in terms of an environment in which mentalization emerged and was welcomed.

As Hurst Hannum recalls,

One of the things I remember them saying in the fairly early stage, [as] they (GAM) were talking about the dire consequences of not reaching an agreement [was], "The war will start up again. A lot of people will be killed, there'll be one million refugees and the UN will intervene." I said, "Don't kid yourselves, nobody cares about Aceh." I said it in exactly those terms. And I don't know if the fact surprised them, or just the fact that I would say that would surprise them. But I think it made an impression. I certainly wasn't doing it just for effect. It was something I believed very strongly.

Louisa Chan-Boegli:

Every time they would come to Geneva, I would make a point of going to the airport myself, driving the car myself to get them. In the evenings I would sit down with them and have dinner with them—not only with the GAM side, but also with the government side, and then alternate.

Mahmood Malik:

Martin and Louisa are sincere, resourceful people. They work very hard, indeed. And at the time, I feel—how do I say it—I feel so sorry when I see they are so frustrated, you know. Sometimes my

347

decisions are very strong and they feel frustrated. I know that [laughter]. They are very frustrated—and I with them, also.

Desra Percaya

I miss her [Louisa]. She made everyone feel welcome. She was always there to greet the delegation when they arrived from the airport. This made a difference. Now when we go, there is nothing, no one.

TOWARD AN ACCOUNT OF "CRITICAL INFLUENCE"

Desra Percaya's reflections about "nothing" and "no one" speak powerfully to the role of "moments, words, and attitudes." The HDC configured its role to be that of "accompanying parties in conflict," and deployed a set of approaches to dialogue that were ad hoc, responsive, and able to accommodate to changing conditions. This, in turn, rested on the capacity of individual facilitators to develop close, collaborative relationships with the belligerents based on an extensive and deep knowing of the participants.

The experience of negotiation is often considered highly stressful, even by experienced practitioners. The prospect of negotiation not uncommonly invokes visceral reactions that many other forms of professional practice do not. A central component to these reactions is the perception of vulnerability. And it is especially the case when negotiators understand that human lives hang in the balance.

The facilitators here did considerably more than take into account the partisan perceptions of the parties. Their efforts extended well beyond the traditional tools of empathy and active listening. Indeed, the application of technique does not seem to describe the quality of their efforts adequately. On the contrary, their capacity to be influential rested on the ability to engage mentalizing capacities, as manifested in the attitudes they seemed to hold about themselves and, in turn, displayed toward the combatants and the conflict itself.

One of the most essential parts of such mentalizing attitudes is an acceptance that the work is deeply intimate, and that it implicates the mediator's identity and personal psychology. Negotiators and facilitators accurately sense that the work ahead will make complex and personal demands on them, even in the most dispassionate of interactions. This may be one reason why the effort directed at resolving disputes is regularly perceived as stressful by practitioners. To the extent that the facilitator expects to be deeply and personally engaged, she or he may be better prepared to live within the strong emotions stirred by the dialogue.

The mediators' self-report of their interventions indicated that each was acting quite naturally and in accord with the ways in which they were accustomed to comport themselves. Each was comfortable with using significant interpersonal pressure, albeit in different ways, to bring the parties together. Many of these efforts did not appear to be strategic or planned in the usual sense. Rather, each was willing to take advantage of whatever leverage presented itself in order to press their case for dialogue. Being open-minded and being flexible were crucial factors here.

"MORE THAN GETTING TO THE POINT"

The facilitators' capacity to be effective issued from a relational and mentalizing stance that they held throughout the dialogue process. They created a context of mindfulness about who the parties were at every moment, as members of identity groups, such as soldiers, diplomats, rebels, loyalists, and so on, and accorded them recognition as psychological persons. This occurred, for example, when Ury insisted to the GAM that President Wahid's problem was also the GAM's problem (if they wished him to make a speech favorable to their cause), and again when Louisa Chan-Boegli acknowledged the importance of the medical work of the GAM negotiator in scheduling the January 2001 dialogue.

In Martin Griffiths's skillful handling of the conflict, which involved the participation of international experts, he drew attention to *his* needs ("I haven't done much of this stuff and this guy is really good, and so I want to have him next to me"), demonstrating in real time how existing differences could be accommodated as well as how a given conflict might be managed. In addition, his statements reveal a mentalizing stance, specifically in identifying how one feels (and being able to differentiate it from how someone else might feel), and in being able to communicate honestly and forthrightly to others.

Thus, the relational architecture enabling the substantive discussions was laid down through a performance. These performances stood for and in lieu of collaborative relationships that existed only as emergent potentials.

The provisional agreements reached in Geneva were, of course, just that. The final documents codified little more than a set of intentions and were some distance from the facilitators' hopes of what might get accomplished. Here is Martin Griffiths again:

> We misjudged what we could get out of the talks. . . . GAM or the government said "Oh, sorry. We aren't coming here for a specific agreement on this stuff. We have to think about it." I'm not sure it was a bad thing in hindsight. We discovered that we weren't going to get more than understanding. That was an important moment for me when I realized that.

This is a wonderful mentalizing statement, a reflection on the difference between what Griffiths hoped and what actually was possible. An effective practitioner is able to hold contradictory attitudes regarding herself, acknowledging that she is both humble and arrogant. Certainly, one would be hard-pressed to consider the HDC's self-nomination to intervene in Aceh as anything less than ambitious. At the same time, the Centre's willingness to insert themselves into a conflict widely viewed as intractable quickly attracted attention, arguably enabling them to have more influence than had they assumed would be standard prerogatives accorded a new organization. Importantly, the facilitators (notably Ury, Chan-Boegli, and Griffiths) were not just hopeful that some agreement might be crafted. Rather, they treated agreement as something they were certain the parties could reach. Their unfaltering optimism that something beyond war was possible drove the dialogue process in decisive ways.

HDC Director Griffiths was humble as he reflected that the facilitators were never likely to get more than an agreement of understanding. Experiencing this as a failure-for-real, paradoxically, enabled him to appreciate anew that this understanding, in and of itself, also counted as an instance of the only success that was in fact possible. In this way, Griffiths's comments indicate that a relevant attitude is one that encompases the tension of humility and ambition.

It is within the tension of this dialectic that facilitators are able to re-constitute themselves and their mission. It is also within this tension that potentials exist for psychoanalytic practitioners to participate in an array of conversations that carry us beyond the consulting room. It is evident that mentalizing skills have a broad and pervasive import.

CODA

At an event held to honor his selection as the "Great Negotiator" for 2002 at the Program on Negotiation at Harvard Law School, Lakhdar Brahimi, the UN Special Envoy to Afghanistan, and later to Iraq, described nego-tiation in this way. "Moments, words, and attitudes," he said, "can make a difference. Situations evolve because of many, many factors . . . but from time to time you have one little touch that may make a difference." I have excerpted some of Brahimi's remarks from that afternoon in order to con-sider further what the study of mentalization and critical moments in ne-gotiation might encompass.

> You've got to accompany people who are in conflict even if you know that the likelihood of success is limited.

> I didn't go [there] to meet nice people. I have come to meet the thugs. The nice people are sitting in Paris. To stop the fighting, you've got to talk to the people who are doing the fighting no matter how horrible they are. This is the price of ending a con-flict like this.

> Understanding is the most important thing when you are dealing with people. You have got to make that effort to understand. . . . You need to be at the same time arrogant, because you want to solve problems that look insolvable, but you need also to be very, very humble. These are contradictory things, but I think if you look closely, you will see that it's not that much of a contradiction.

> Expertise is something that you need. When you are working on something . . . [there] you need more than expertise.

Brahimi brings a very different take to thinking about negotiation, an enterprise that is ordinarily viewed as a technical and rational process. Rather than emphasizing formal preparation, the effective practitioner knows the participants deeply, well beyond simple familiarity with their biographies. The interests he seeks to address are those that are sacred, rather than just important. The trade-offs that concern him are gut-wrenching, and include moral choices that must be acknowledged. Thus, Brahimi orients himself to something well beyond the tactics and strategies of dispute resolution. In so doing, he underscores the crucial import of the mentalizing attitudes the mediator brings to his or her work. These attitudes serve the function of helping practitioners to bear the inevitable tensions, discomfort, and even pain that occurs in the attempt to sponsor real change. This is the foundation of the "more than expertise" to which he refers.

In calling the work of negotiation "accompanying people who are in conflict," Brahimi also signals that negotiation is a relational activity. The inquiry here has suggested that some critical moments may be best appreciated as relational moments. What is critical at these junctures is the practitioner's capacity to respond flexibly to the emergent and intentional aspects of other people's behavior. This is the essence of mentalization, of course, and demonstrates its utility and unique value in framing the activities of practitioners from a range of intervention disciplines.

REFERENCES

Druckman, D. (2001). Turning points in international negotiation: A comparative analysis. *Journal of Conflict Resolution, 45*(4), 519–544.

Pizer, S. (1999). *Building Bridges: The Negotiation of Paradox in Psychoanalysis*. New York: Analytic Press.

Stone, D., Heen, S., & Patton, B. (1999). *Difficult Conversations*. New York: Viking Press.

Chapter 12

Metaphor, Activity, Acknowledgment, Grief

Mentalization and Related Transformations
in the Psychoanalytic Process

Stephen Seligman

This paper illustrates the emerging theories about mentalization and reflective functioning by presenting an analytic treatment of a patient with a chronic
traumatic history and masochistic-narcissistic character trends. She started out
in a nonmentalized state characterized by projective identification, psychic
equivalence, teleology, and a rather limited behavioral repertoire. As the case
progressed, she developed a more fluid psychological organization in which
she was able to see others' motives and imagine their states of mind, taking
them into account so as to be more flexible and with a wider and more
context-specific range of affects. Concurrently, she became more flexible,
empathic, and less compelled by her past and the correlated psychological
rigidities; her emotional range broadened and her practical experience became
somewhat more varied and pleasurable. Similarly, the transference became
less rigid and more open to interpretation, and the patient was more able to
take advantage of the directly supportive aspects of the analytic situation. In
tandem with this, the analyst became freer and more emotionally available.

This all emerged from a mix of change processes including traditional
interpretation of the transference, the past, and the patient's extra-analytic

relationships; working out transference-countertransference interaction, affect regulation, a particular metaphor that facilitated a transition to more direct and mentalized functioning, grief and mourning triggered by the death of a close relative of the patient, and progress through intercurrent extra-analytic life events. As these evolved, they converged in supporting the development both of mentalization and evolving senses of subjectivity/ intersubjectivity. The patient became more self-reflective, more aware of the difference between her own psychic reality and external reality, and concurrently became able to conceive of the distinction between her own mental life and the others' experiences. The issues taken up in this volume serve as touchpoints to observe the evolving treatment outcome.

When we first met, Harriet J. was in her fifties, an administrator in an agency for emotionally disturbed children. She was pleasant in her demeanor and appearance, and I felt she was "a good person." A bit nondescript, she seemed lively and articulate enough, interested but apprehensive. She was consulting a couple of analysts, and I was pleased that she chose me. We agreed to meet twice weekly.

Ms. J. had become disenchanted with an analyst that she had seen for several months. She felt that he was cool and unresponsive. I was sympathetic, but Harriet's presentation of herself as mistreated seemed exaggerated. She *could* refer to her own internal experiences of frustration and strong and romantic wishes to be close to him, and even appreciated his plausible technical reasons for being restrained, but this was awareness without reflection. Whatever she knew about herself was disconnected and overridden by having an ax to grind.

This intimated a dilemma that is common with certain patients: Something felt right about Harriet's account of the analyst at the same time that her responses were driven by her own internal rigidities. I managed to restrain myself from enacting either of the twin temptations of joining her in blaming the analyst or taking up the underlying sense of grievance, and things went along well for a while. Ms. J. had been in a submissive marriage with a man who turned out to be a drug abuser, and who had ultimately died of drug-related illness. Hardly anyone had appreciated how devastating this had been for Harriet, even though the marriage had ended a decade ago. She told me that she found my under-standing this to be quite moving and helpful.

GETTING SNAGGED: A TRANSFERENCE-COUNTERTRANSFERENCE BIND

But when Harriet returned from a vacation, she was shocked to see my charge for her week away, although I had already explained that this ar-rangement was standard in my practice. She felt hurt and angry: indeed, she insisted that I was betraying our avowed purpose of helping her enjoy life, since I must be reminding her that she had to put me first even after she had been able to "give herself" this special trip. She accused me of overlooking her conscientiousness and concern for our work together. I agreed that my billing her might seem one-sided. But as I acknowledged that it was a way of conducting business that worked better for me than any of the alternatives, I maintained that it was nonetheless not a matter of deni-grating her commitment to treatment. This, however, only served to in-tensify her anger, and she became more harsh and one-sided in her criticism of me.

I tried different responses, including trying to explain myself further and trying to confront, gently I thought, Ms. J.'s difficulty seeing that I might have my own requirements without this reflecting my attitude about her. At times, although I sympathized with Harriet's sense of being mistreated, I attempted to add that the force of her reaction might have sources in her own history and psychology. I had been hearing about her ongoing sense of grievance with several friends, and I suggested that there might be a pattern here from which we might learn.

But this too only served to amplify Ms. J.'s anxiety and hostility, along with a rather rigid and quite belligerent side of her. In retrospect, I see that these attacks left me feeling quite pressured, annoyed, and guilty, and I became rather flatfooted. In addition, my efforts to help her see that her reactions might reflect her own past experience overlooked how difficult it was for her to see realities other than those driven by her strong emotions. Despite my having written on the dangers of premature interpretation (Seligman, 2002), I was overly persistent in taking this tack. Not surpris-ingly, this hardened and intensified her conviction that I was pursuing my own agenda, since she felt that I was keeping her talking about her bad experience with me when she wanted to "move on." I was calling attention to myself and insisting on running the show rather than helping her feel better.

In this atmosphere, my interpretations served as a form of reflexive self-protection *for me* in the face of some persistent bewilderment and irritation. I became grumpier and more negative than I usually am with patients. It felt like Harriet was boxing me in, keeping me from being the kind of analyst I want to be. I felt misdescribed and misrecognized, not so much because I felt criticized but because I couldn't find myself in the rather nasty account that she was offering—try as I might. I was thus left with the common dilemma of either complying with projections that felt wrong, or contesting them in a way that left me an outsider, and here leaving someone whom I had hoped to help stranded with her own helplessness and desperate anger.

TECHNICAL IMPLICATIONS OF CONCEPTUALIZATIONS ABOUT TRAUMA, PROJECTION, AND FAILURES OF MENTALIZATION

There are many perspectives that we can bring to bear on this situation: This is kind of projective identification and mutual enactment that is so common, especially with patients whom we end up calling sadomasochistic, borderline, and narcissistic. The analyst is caught between identifying with one or another side of the controlled-controlling, abuser-abused dyad that is so constitutive of the patient's object relations. It seems clear to me, again in retrospect, that Harriet was evoking in me her own sense of being pushed around, minimized, railed at, and dismissed, feelings that resembled her own traumatic experiences, present and past.

Before going on to describe some of the subsequent evolution of the case, I want to restate and elaborate four particular points that the work with Harriet illustrates, which are illuminated by taking up the emerging thinking on mentalization along with more established strands in the analytic lore and literature. These are the compulsion to project; the emergence of transference as a state of mind without reflective functioning; the dangers of premature interpretation; and the pressure for, and perhaps requirement that the analyst engage in repetitive enactments in the transference-countertransference, a development that most often re-evokes some of the patient's traumatic experiences (if not the analyst's).

Overall, Harriet could not allow for the fact that I had needs and requirements of my own, instead insisting on the peremptory reality of her idea that I was punitive and considered her unworthy. As far as the part of her mind that mattered, I *simply was someone who was judging and punishing her.* There was no other possible reality. Although Ms. J. could be quite an intelligent and thoughtful person, her stance here was quite closed and impervious to new information. She could not "play with reality," but was instead stranded in a state of concrete psychic equivalence, both embattled and alone (Fonagy & Target, 1996).

Thus in the grip of unmentalized, powerful affects—fear, longing, and danger—Harriet couldn't make use of everyday mental procedures for correcting "misperceptions." Under such conditions, patients take their subjective experience as if it were entirely "real," the whole story, without reflective thinking: No matter what information the patient may have about the analyst's reliability, honesty, concern, and so on, the compelling reality of the subjective experience overrides anything else that the patient might "know." So, no matter what Harriet knew about my good intentions, even when she felt, as she did, that I was a caring person, she couldn't think of me as having anything but cruel motives when it came to the fee, and this dominated her experience. The theory of other minds no longer applied. This transference was thus characterized by an *impairment of reflective functioning, of mentalization, of the reality sense.* By thinking of the absence of objectivity as an aspect of a psychic state, rather than as a capacity for accuracy, we can better differentiate transference as a metacognitive variant from its other conditions—transference as distortion, as desire, as developmental possibility, and so on.

For Harriet, only one affectively charged internal representation system—only one "emotional reality"—could exist at any given moment, and the other had to be projected with great force and certainty. Although apparently a thoughtful and responsible person, she lacked a true theory of mind in those areas where strong, self-related affects were involved. It was either her or "them." With Harriet, this was a ubiquitous pattern; she could regale me with stories about friends who were mistreating her, denouncing them while professing to be helpless to make any changes. She couldn't bear to be aware of her dependence on these friends, both as people whose companionship she badly needed, and as necessary objects for the projection of her own persecutory objects, without whom she would have to face her own needs and fears of being humiliated and out of control. This pattern was repeated in the transference.

PREMATURE INTERPRETATION, "NARCISSISTIC RESISTANCES," AND THE BREAKDOWN OF METACOGNITION

This all well illustrates certain pained and angry reactions to apparently accurate interventions, responses that we often think of as "resistance." People lacking reflective functioning cannot conceptualize any alternative explanation of their subjective (if actually reified) realities. Further, any suggestion that there might be alternatives may well be experienced as abandonment, since it disrupts the implicit assumption that everyone sees the world in the same way. Even analytically correct and tactful interpretations in such situations can lead to heightened, self-protectively aggressive reactions, despite their apparent accuracy. The resistance is to the otherness of the analyst as much as to the content of the interpretation.

In addition, the confrontation that is often unavoidable in many analytic interpretations may also be taken as an accusation that the patient is "crazy," or at least has defective judgment about what is real. In this way, as in others, the emerging sense of threat both amplifies and is amplified by internal, persecutory objects, and a vicious cycle can ensue. Projective identifications and other maneuvers often externalize the persecutory phantasies, which may in turn be further amplified by the responsive, if potentially destructive, actions of the analyst. In addition, further anxieties about the exposure of underlying states of disintegration or loss of reality are also mobilized.

Overall, under such psychic conditions, trusting oneself or anyone else is difficult because there isn't a sense of things persisting beyond the moment, and there is no reliable sense that psychic reality is only that, which makes bad feelings especially problematic. Under the "meta-assumption" that fantasies and feelings are as real as other people, painful experiences cannot be conceived as something just in the mind; they are *hyperreal*, and cannot be contained as subjective experience. (Indeed, this category does not exist.) Thus, as so many analysts have noted, they have to be relocated outward, and splitting and projection are necessary to preserve psychic equilibrium in the face of overwhelming affects and phantasies. Such projections may well further reinforce paranoid states, as the external world appears to be highly dangerous. At the same time, as she is left with her dependent feelings, the patient may experience herself as especially vulnerable to the power of the analyst, since she badly needs his help. The patient also needs the relationship with the analyst to provide an object for the projected psychic dangers, such as abandonment, betrayal, and attack, all of which present themselves in Harriet's case. Thus, a vicious cycle may well ensue in which the attachment intensifies the sense of fear and danger, which in turn intensifies the dependent feelings, and so on. With patients who have been traumatized, especially those with disorganized attachments, there is already a predisposition to link attachment and insoluble fear (Hesse & Main, 2000). Overall, the emerging constellation is likely to constitute a threat of the repetition of the trauma. This was the case for Harriet.

PITFALLS AND PROGRESS WITH MS. J.

With all this in mind, I can now say that I was initially overly attentive to the content of Harriet's projections, rather than attending to the danger of considering alternative views of reality. She was under such psychic duress that these interpretive comments would intensify the fear that her sense of reality was being undermined by a punitive but needed caretaker, from whom she could not extricate herself. This dynamic often stalls therapeutic progress with patients with serious characterological problems who have not developed the capacity of reflecting on their own internal reality as anything other than the whole world.

In such situations, the self-protective, self-punitive, and fearful sources of the disruptive, rageful, and withdrawing responses should not be neglected: Life without metacognition is psychically risky. Often, understanding how the patient's reactions *do make sense from her perspective* can be helpful, along with acknowledgments that each of us has a different point of view, each of which may have merits. This can have the effect of introducing the possibility that there *are* two minds in the room, if only at a rather concrete and halting level. Also, shifts into and out of affect regulation, mentalization, and reflective functioning should be carefully tracked by the therapist, and noted for the patient when helpful.

Along these lines, it helped Harriet when I communicated my growing understanding that my interpretations about the "content" of the transference were challenging her fragile sense of the authority of her own thinking. I might say, for example, that I could understand how she might feel that I was telling her that my view of things was better than hers and that would leave her with the impossible choice of having to accept something that felt wrong to her or having to give up on a therapy that meant a lot to her. Interpretation-like comments will be helpful, if at all, when the patient begins to shift from concretization to mentalization. Therapists will be well-advised to track the moment-to-moment ebbs and flows of such shifts.

In situations like these, Pine's (1985) maxim about striking when the iron is cold is a useful one. When the iron is hot, that is, when the transference is more fully engaged and the affects are intense and saturated, the analyst's interpretive formulations remain useful, but primarily for his or her undisclosed thinking. Since the countertransference in these situations is often very pressured and challenging, these thoughts may provide a regulatory antidote to our own feelings of helplessness, frustration, rage, loneliness, and guilt, if they are not abused in a self-serving way.

Still, despite the slight gains that arose from my shift in timing interpretations, I realized they were not going to untie the knot here. I came to feel, reluctantly, that I would have to make what felt to me to be a concession to protect the prospect of an ongoing therapeutic alliance. I proposed that at this point, Ms. J. could take four cancellations each year without charge, and that we might revisit this matter in the future if it seemed timely. The sense of concession was neither about my authority nor about my pocketbook, but because I felt that I was acting in response to pressure to comply with the projection that I had done something greedy that had to be redressed, rather than having come to feel that this was the right thing to do. I have come to realize, sometimes regrettably, that these matters may well have to be worked out in actions, rather than reflection, at these stages of such cases; this may in fact be inevitable and also may be useful at times.

As all of this proceeded, things did soften somewhat. Although still aggrieved, Harriet began to recall how ignored she had felt as a child. Harriet's mother married her father after his first wife died, leaving him to care for their 3-year-old son. Although the courtship was romantic, things changed dramatically after the marriage. By the time Harriet was born, her mother was bereft of her earlier pleasures and the romance gave way to depression in the drab workaday. The brother was always getting into trouble, and then persecuting Harriet, but her pleas for help were ignored. Her own wishes and talents were not acknowledged and she was rarely allowed to feel that her own perceptions and feelings mattered. When she came home with a good report card, for example, her brother would tease her in front of friends and family, sneering that "she liked school." No one protected her. Whatever emerging pride remained was squashed; and she became a meek, self-effacing "good girl," without a voice of her own, retreating into numb compliance.

A very vivid, even gory, memory emerged poignantly. When Harriet was about 6, she came home to see her beloved cat dying on the street, after having been hit by a car. The horrific image of his still breathing body remains fixed in her mind. Still, even as she stood watching, she was discouraged from saying anything. Subsequently, she was never given an opportunity to grieve or even talk about what had happened, including her inchoate suspicion that her brother had coaxed the cat into the street. We gradually appreciated how Ms. J. had felt completely, even brutally, discounted in the past, as in the transference. This led to halting insight about how she felt that she had to dramatize her suffering as the only way to justify her wishes and perceptions, since she otherwise believed that neither her own thinking nor her anger could be justified. We also, slowly, thought about how her harsh self-criticism, her criticism of others, and her feelings of deprivation worked together. High-volume complaint and hard-edged grievance were the only form in which she could imagine being heard.

Here, Harriet was beginning to become more aware of her own motives, including those implicated in her compensatory and defensive character style. This synergized with the historical reconstruction. Coming to see one's experiences as having a history, with patterns and continuities over time, is a step in the development of a personal sense of subjectivity. Reflecting on one's own mind as something other than "objective" reality is a central feature of feeling like a separate person with a mind of one's own (see, for example, Britton, 1992; Caper, 1997; Coates, 1998; Fonagy, 2000; Fonagy, Gergely, Jurist, & Target, 2002; Seligman, 2000, 2002; Slade, 2000; Stern, 1985, among many others).

The beginning of mentalization in Ms. J. is illustrated in what might otherwise seem like a minor detail: Ms. J. had called to accept an invitation to a party for an old friend who had recently become ill. She asked the friend to call back. When the call was not returned promptly, Ms. J. felt miffed, imagining that her friend was being vindictive since he felt snubbed by her prior to the illness, even though she knew that he was preoccupied by his condition. She then said, "*I believe this, and I don't believe this.*" Harriet's declaration of self-reflective doubt about a projection (supported by powerful emotion) that she had been treating as a fact, illustrates the emergence of capacity for mentalization, or, in the contemporary Kleinian terms of Ronald Britton (1999), an ability to distinguish between beliefs and facts.

METAPHOR, COMMUNICATION, AND METACOGNITION

Let me now return to the further flow of the case, so as to illustrate another aspect of this emergence of Ms. J.'s sense of subjectivity and intersubjectivity, this time in a transitional process supported by the fortuitous emergence of a metaphor that helped us look at her uses of suffering.

Harriet came into one session holding a biography of Joan of Arc. When I noticed it, she told me how she had immediately grabbed it in the bookstore, since she had chosen Joan as her confirmation saint as a teenager, aware that it was unconventional, although without an explicit sense of the resonance of her own suffering to her heroine's. She was quite affected by this now. At the time, however, no one in her family had displayed the slightest interest in her originality or self-expression. She now tearfully recounted how crushingly disappointed she felt.

I was intrigued by all this, seeing how the story of Saint Joan captured the important themes of redemptive and heroic suffering that were so important for Harriet, along with the fate of a pure and misunderstood woman who was betrayed by a powerful man, here the King of France, who first supported her and then abandoned her (just as, she felt, I had). As we began to talk about how suffering was a key part of her identity, I also let her know that I believed that her choice of Joan must have expressed her own sense of decency and creativity. I felt this quite spontaneously, and it was touching to both of us for me to say it.

This helped us talk *about her experience* in a way that, for better or for worse, circumvented some of the onus that Harriet associated with the usual analytic attention, but very much had the feeling that she was speaking from inside herself, in her own voice. In addition, Harriet's projection of her self-representation into the Saint Joan story gave me a way to communicate my respect for Ms. J.'s struggle and my appreciation of her suffering, in a sublimated way that touched her longings but neither overwhelmed her nor exacerbated her predisposition to feel patronized. This was all at some distance from the cycle of idealization and disillusionment that had prevailed in the transference. In addition, my attention to the positive affects was useful here. Analysts are sometimes unnecessarily constrained and neglect the progressive possibilities in appreciating positive affects associated with key internal representations of self and other. Contrary to what some have taken for granted, this does not have to preclude attention to the threatening and overwhelming negative ones.

There is another quite important and more personal element that I must now add. I had a special interest in Saint Joan, spurred by two extraordinary films, one by Robert Bresson (1962) and one by Carl Theodor Dreyer (1928). I didn't mention this in the first session when Harriet brought the book, but she may well have seen the gleam in my eye, or heard the enthusiasm in my voice. After a session or two and some mulling it over, I told her about the silent Dreyer film, which is quite extraordinary.

Some time later, Harriet watched it. It includes an utterly stunning performance by Antonin Artaud as a rock-hard, imperious judge, and a protracted scene of Joan burning at the stake, in which her ecstatic agony is remarkably conveyed by the facial expression of the great French actress Maria Falconetti.* Harriet and I talked about this scene, sharing our awe of it, especially of the suffering that was embodied. The aestheticization of

---

* I am grateful to Ruth Bittner for correcting an earlier error about which actor played this role.

this extraordinary pain, excruciating, masochistic, and noble, served to help Ms. J. approach and regulate her own such affects and fantasies. Thinking about these images together offered the possibility of a containment of something primitive, and may well have been the most suitable way to approach it at this point. The narratives and metaphors functioned something like language might in another case. (See Ferro, 2002, for a contemporary Bionian elaboration of this kind of analytic activity, and, of course, Winnicott's [1951, 1971] conceptions of the transformational potentials of play and the transitional space.) We did in fact talk about such themes as, for example, how Joan was compelled to choose to suffer, that were quite immediate and personal for Harriet, in a way that would not have been possible without the background of the Saint's story.

Thus, the Joan of Arc metaphor served both to evoke and organize Ms. J.'s inner life, providing a position from which she could take a self-observing perspective that was otherwise precluded in the more psychically threatening arena of direct interpretation. The metaphor played a transitional function, a kind of "me-not me" language, that allowed for a dialogue of subjectivity without Ms. J. having to be fully explicit that she was talking about herself, to me. As she was able to do this, she could take further steps toward reflective collaboration in the analytic process.

Overall, two dynamic change processes were proceeding simultaneously: the explicit process of reflecting together on the patient's psychology, and the implicit process of building a sense of her subjectivity amidst the intersubjective world in which one person has an interest in the other's mind. At the same time that direct themes were mediated by the Saint Joan story, an ongoing process of emergent intersubjectivity was proceeding in our shared interest. The use of the metaphor provided the opportunity for us to talk about a Harriet-like character as a third person, in a transitional space that supported symbolization and self-reflection (Benjamin, 2004; Ogden, 1994; Winnicott, 1951). It was a bit like playing with a child, or sharing enthusiasm about some object on the street with a younger baby. (Everyday examples abound, as when a toddler and his father stop on the street, the child tentatively pets a dog, and the father says, "Nice doggie!" while looking at the boy, who fully understands that his dad is talking about the animal.)

Such shared enthusiasm about a third object is part of the normal process of an infant's coming to experience her own subjectivity. Trevarthen (1980) has called this process, "secondary intersubjectivity," in which the developing sense of having one's own mind in a field of others is supported when two people share attention to a third object. The infant has come to know that the father is seeing the same dog, but from a different vantage point. Harriet and I were quite involved in such a dialogue, in which her mind was a focus of our attention, but in which my own subjectivity was marked by my particular interest, in a generally affirmative atmosphere globally defined by my overall attentiveness in the analytic effort. In the presence of my own distinct but linking interest, my own recognition of Ms. J.'s experience underlined the novel experience of being understood from someone else's perspective, while staying involved with that other person.

It may be that it was an exceptionally fortuitous convergence that led Ms. J.'s interest in Saint Joan to converge with my own, but I do believe that many analyses progress through similar creative processes that may not be so obvious yet are nonetheless variations on such formats, acting as transitions to an emergent intersubjectivity, often proceeding implicitly and in the background. I would add that I could not have offered this account while I was talking with Harriet about Joan of Arc, and I sometimes wondered if I was just passing the time.

THINKING ABOUT REALITY: LOOKING AT OTHERS WITH A SHARED PERSPECTIVE

As this evolved, Ms. J. was continuing to talk about her interpersonal entanglements. She continued to offer stories of how particular "so-called friends" were mistreating and exploiting her. I was often able to elaborate and appreciate her viewpoint, but she was nonetheless disappointed when I wasn't enthusiastic about her sense of grievance. In listening to her, I found myself in the familiar bind, sympathetic to her distress, but rendered unable to offer my perspective on how she was exacerbating, if not causing, her difficult position. I often encountered an inflexible, demanding, and angrily anticipating rejection of even the smallest hope that her own wishes must be accommodated, in place of her making those wishes known.

Eventually, we could find some common ground in talking together about her friends' psychologies. I would notice how her friend Sarah, for example, only called when she needed something, and Ms. J. felt acknowledged and a bit relieved. Over time, I might add that Sarah seemed to be a very nervous person who couldn't think of other people because she was so preoccupied with her own needs. In addition to the direct value of these ideas, this lending of my mind helped Harriet because she could become more dependent on me in actuality, while helping to build a constructive, idealized sense of our evolving relationship. It also engaged us further in the emergent intersubjective format of thinking together about a third person, a situation with which Harriet had very little experience. There was a softer and more collaborative quality to this talk, as it hovered on the edge of aggressive criticism and empathic understanding, with projection now more contained and less compelled.

In this atmosphere and mode of relating, there were new opportunities to think about how Harriet's behavior was evoking others' reactions. As we were joined in critiquing her friends and colleagues (fairly, I hope), we could talk with greater freedom about Ms. J.'s own role—a process that expanded her sense of agency as it developed some insight. She also got to practice a kind of observation of others' minds, which provided some alternative to her more solipsistic, paranoid reversal of her own persecutory self-criticism, dominated as it was by projection. Overall, this further expanded the sense of an authentically dyadic process, rather than a closed and persecutory and depriving interpersonal world. Things were getting a little less binary, a little more intersubjective, a little less projective and alien. The space of the Joan of Arc metaphor was migrating toward current reality, so that we could really talk about *Harriet*.

This was now elaborated as Ms. J. became involved as a successful and well-respected leader in a reorganization at her workplace. Sometimes with my help, sometimes on her own, she strategized about adversaries whom she anticipated might denounce her, rather than engaging in purely projective, masochistic protestations. While I usually fell short of providing strategic advice, I did help her sort out the tactical questions, along with paying careful attention to how her own tendency to feel aggrieved in a self-referential way—"to take things personally"—might get in her way. Overall, she was less beset by the pressure to project and then respond antagonistically to her own harsh self-criticism, of which she was becoming somewhat more aware.

GRIEF, DIFFERENTIATION, INTEGRATION

As Ms. J. became freer to think about her friends' and colleagues' foibles along with her own, she also became more able to assert herself efficiently—both in pursuing some long-deferred pleasures, and in taking more direct and explicit positions with others. She eventually got a more appealing job that allowed more personal freedom in a place where her own skills gave her more leverage to negotiate a better deal for herself. She took longer and more imaginative vacations, and started some new friendships in which her wishes were respected. She celebrated her newfound agency quite enthusiastically; at times, she would now self-reflectively take the risk of alienating others with whom she had been friendly. This meant, in practice, that she went too far sometimes, and when she asked me, I let her know that I did indeed think this. She now could tolerate criticism without feeling compelled to attack the critic. In this climate, it became more possible to link this exaggerated assertiveness to her anxieties, and to her sense that she could not find a response to her own wishes anyway, since she never had. This insight built a synergy with her increasing success at negotiating interpersonal and professional situations.

Although there were many such situations, this change was seen most poignantly and powerfully in her evolving relationship with her brother. Excluding some other developments, I will now describe this in some detail, wanting to make some observations about the linkage of grief, internalization, personal integration, and the development of mentalization. Although Harriet had long felt hurt and angry with her brother, she had kept in touch, visiting whenever she returned to their home city, where he still lived. When he became ill with a potentially life-threatening illness, she offered advice based on expertise that she had acquired when a friend had a similar condition. Although her brother and his family signaled that they had a different approach, she persisted, and he eventually stopped returning her phone calls and emails, as did his children, to whom she had been close. She was informed that his illness was not immediately fatal, but was otherwise cut off from the rest of those who represented her last blood ties to her original family.

She was quite offended, so much so that she never considered that she might have taken some liberties or that she might have done better to take her brother's obstreperous character, of which she was well aware, into account in approaching this matter. But as time went on, she did wonder that her own pride had gotten in her way. Some time later, she learned that her brother's condition had worsened, and she called him to say that she would be in their area and that she hoped that she could visit.

Surprisingly, he called back quite promptly, and tenderly thanked her for calling. Stunning Harriet, he told her how much he had missed her, despite how much pain there had been between them. He added that he always thought that she would call and apologize, and that he didn't realize how strong she was. They were both really stubborn, he said, he guessed "it ran in the family." Harriet was equally forthcoming, and did travel to see him. Mr. J. continued to soften as he contemplated death, and in later talks he told Harriet that he was remembering some of the cruel things that he had done to her, and that he regretted it. This extraordinary turn of events was quite moving, providing acknowledgment, reparation, and an even further amplified sense that interpersonal relationships might work out with some justice and reconciliation.

As Mr. J. became more ill, things became even more poignant. Memory and gratitude mingled with grief, anger, and regret, both about the current loss and the ways that the past limited the person Harriet could become, and whom she had been. She made a number of unexpected links between the present and the past, including wondering, in an emotionally convincing way, whether she had sought in her roguish and cruel husband an echo of her brother, from whom she always fruitlessly sought protection. Over time, the tone of her talk about her brother and his family was marked with an appropriately subdued satisfaction, as the mutual recognition and reconciliation proceeded, but this was mingled with a resignation and melancholy about what was not to be—a complexity of emotion hardly ever seen in Harriet. (See Mitchell, 2000, and Dent, 2006, for an exploration of the way analysts have neglected sibling relationships.)

There were parallel developments in the transference. Ms. J., for example, without my prompting, told me that she had come to see that my way of handling the fee policy didn't mean that I didn't care about her. She still felt that I hurt her, and that I had showed her my worse side, but also that I had since changed. Mostly she was angry and sad that it couldn't have been different, that there was so much time wasted. She added that her own way of seeing herself as exploited made it impossible for her to see that maybe that it was my own way of handling things, rather than something that had to do with her; speculating about my mental life, she thought that maybe this was a sensitive area for me. Although I suppose I could say that this account doesn't fully capture her own projections and the like, I'm not sure whether this isn't as accurate a description as any other, and it does, in any case, show the development of a two-person sense of how things were unfolding, marked by disappointment and even grief, rather than the ever-present and closed system of persecution.

Some months later, Harriet's brother died. After the funeral, Harriet told me about how things had gone, noting how she was approaching things in a new way. She started the session saying that she had "borrowed a page from" my book; she finally understood about how to use silence. At a family dinner after the funeral, her niece brought her one of her brother's shirts, which she had asked for as a memento. But the young woman brought it into the restaurant right before the dinner, which put Harriet in the position of having to carry it around, rather than waiting until afterward. She found this thoughtless and was offended. She responded, however, by just not saying anything, noting that she would have, in the past, complained and gotten nasty, which, she said, would have just "made me hate myself for the rest of the week." After a moment, her niece offered an apologetic response, and took the shirt back to her car, where Harriet picked it up after the dinner.

This moment, minor as it was, reflected an important change in Harriet's psychology, including fairly sophisticated self-reflection and new capacities to regulate and think about feelings (Jurist, 2005; Schore, 1994). The "borrowing a page" from the analyst's book marks a shift from *projective* identification to the more constructive *introjective* identification, in which the attributes of the other can be used to enhance the self, rather than be overridden in the compulsion to protect the self from its own destructive demons.

Later in the session, Harriet described her sister-in-law's growing depression. The widow was complaining that no one was respecting her own Judaism on this awful occasion. However, although her father had been

369

Jewish, she had no religious training and had adopted Harriet's brother's Christian practice. After the funeral, the family just went home and put on the ballgame and sat around watching, without even talking about her dead brother; "If they're such big Jews," Harriet said, "Why not sit shiva?"

After a while, I wondered aloud whether Harriet might consider her own admonitions, that she was putting other people down but not thinking about her own loss; maybe she was still in shock, or maybe it was hard to be on her own with all of this. She mostly got mad at me, and told me more about how I didn't understand how problematic her sister-in-law was.

But, after the session, she left a phone message with a very different tone, from which I now quote at some length.

> I know that I was busy fighting with you today. What I said did matter to me, but the thing is I wanted to thank you at the end for bringing me to a much better place, which was talking about what I didn't get, which was uhhhm . . . like you said, to sit shiva with, wouldn't it have been nice if that had happened, and I could have done that for my brother with my family. It brings me to a better place inside of myself. And perhaps now that you've articulated that for me, it's something that I can do for myself at least, a little better than I've been doing it. . . . So thank you, that's a very big gift . . . [At this point, Harriet paused with a friendly, sardonic, and somewhat anxious chuckle.] I won't fight with you *in my mind* for at least a few hours. [Emphasis mine]

Ms. J. seemed sadder but wiser, but also happier and more flexible. She was capable of optimism, gratitude, and even humor, amidst grief. She still struggled to keep herself from succumbing to the influence of others, or feeling abandoned and aggrieved, and then, ultimately, quite bad about herself. But this was less peremptory, and her emotional and behavioral repertoire had expanded and become more flexible and efficient.

Grief marks a space between oneself and one's objects. As Freud (1917) declared, mourning is the antidote to a state of absorption in another with whom one has an unsatisfactory relationship, where the other haunts the inside of the self, hated but needed, persecutory but invisible, blocking access to the actual world. Mentalization—having one's own mind—is both a source and an outcome of the often painful, but potentially exhilarating, process of becoming available to other people, to one's own history and interior life, to one's voice and one's actual body, and consequently, to life's opportunities and pitfalls.

REFERENCES

Benjamin, J. (2004). Beyond doer and done to: An intersubjective view of thirdness. *Psychoanalytic Quarterly, 73*, 5–46.

Bion, W. R. (1962). A theory of thinking. *International Journal of Psycho-Analysis, 43*, 306–310.

Bresson, R. (1962). *The Trial of Joan of Arc.* (Film)

Britton, R. (1992). Keeping things in mind. In R. Anderson (Ed.), *Clinical Lectures on Klein and Bion.* New York: Routledge, 1992.

Britton, R. (1999). *Belief and Imagination: Explorations in Psychoanalysis.* New York: Brunner-Routledge.

Caper, R. (1997). A mind of one's own. *International Journal of Psycho-Analysis, 78*, 265–278.

Coates, S. (1998). Having a mind of one's own and holding the other in mind: Commentary on paper by Peter Fonagy and Mary Target. *Psychoanalytic Dialogues: A Journal of Relational Perspectives, 8*(1), 115–148.

Dent, V. (2006). The bright forms shining in the dark: Sibling dynamics in A. S. Byatt's "The Chinese Lobster." Paper submitted for publication.

Dreyer, C. T. (1928). *La Passion de Jeanne d'Arc* (The Passion of Joan of Arc). (film)

Ferro, A. (2002). *In the Analyst's Consulting Room.* New York: Brunner-Routledge.

Fonagy, P. (2000). Attachment and borderline personality disorder. *Journal of the American Psychoanalytic Association, 48*(4), 1129–1146. Hillsdale, NJ: Analytic Press.

Fonagy, P., & Target, M. (1996). Playing with reality: I. Theory of mind and the normal development of psychic reality. *International Journal of Psycho-Analysis, 77*, 217–234.

Fonagy, P., Gergely, G., Jurist, E. J., & Target, M. (2002). *Affect Regulation, Mentalization, and the Development of the Self.* New York: Other Press.

Freud, S. (1917). Mourning and melancholia. *Standard Edition, 14*, pp. 239–258.

Hesse, E., & Main, M. (2000). Disorganized infant, child and adult attachment: Collapse in behavioral and attentional strategies. *Journal of the American Psychoanalytic Association, 48*(4), 1097–1128.

Jurist, E. L. (2005). Mentalized affectivity. *Psychoanalytic Psychology, 22*(3), 426–444.

Mitchell, J. (2000). *Mad men and medusas: Reclaiming hysteria and the effects of sibling relations on the human condition.* London: Allen Lane and Penguin Books.

Ogden, T. H. (1994). The analytic third: Working with intersubjective clinical facts. *International Journal of Psycho-Analysis, 75*, 3–20.

Pine, F. (1985). *Developmental Theory and Clinical Process.* New Haven, CT: Yale University Press.

Schore, A. (1994). *Affect Regulation and Origin of the Self.* Hillsdale, NJ: Erlbaum.

Seligman, S. (2002). Attachment, intersubjectivity, and self-reflectiveness: Implications of the convergence of emerging attachment theory with psychoanalysis. Presentation at the annual James Grotstein lecture, Los Angeles, June 15.

Seligman, S. (2000). Clinical implications of attachment theory. *Journal of the American Psychoanalytic Association, 48*(4), 1189–1196.

Slade, A. (2000). The development and organization of attachment: Implications for psychoanalysis. *Journal of the American Psychoanalytic Association, 48*(4), 1147–1174.

Stern, D. N. (1985). *The Interpersonal World of the Infant.* New York: Basic Books.

Trevarthen, C. (1980). The foundations of intersubjectivity: Development of interpersonal and cooperative understanding in infants. In: D. R. Olson (Ed.), *The Social Foundation of Language and Thought: Essays in Honor of Jerome Bruner.* New York: Norton.

Winnicott, D. W. (1951). Transitional objects and transitional phenomena. In *Through Paediatrics to Psychoanalysis: Collected Papers* (pp. 229–242). New York: Brunner-Mazel.

Winnicott, D. W. (1971). *Playing and Reality.* New York: Basic Books.

Chapter 13

Birth Mother, Adoptive Mother, Dying Mother, Dead Mother

Karen Gilmore

The ideas of Peter Fonagy, Mary Target, and their collaborators (Fonagy, Gergely, Jurist, & Target, 2002) have been widely disseminated and absorbed into psychoanalytic thinking, enriching it both theoretically and clinically. Their myriad contributions have informed my ideas about development and have directly influenced my work in the consulting room. Some have become so fundamental and—in my work with certain patients—so complementary to the psychoanalytic endeavor that I am hard-pressed to imagine how I could have done without them. Nevertheless, I do not see their ideas as constituting a new psychoanalytic agenda, as they (Fonagy et al., 2002) and others (Sugarman, 2003) have suggested. Rather, I see them as highlighting the crucial role of the interpersonal surround in the development of the mind, and the requirement of interpersonal or intersubjective nutriment for the establishment of certain intrapsychic processes, as well as of boundaries between psychic reality and the external world. I am struck in much of their writing by the emphasis on the development of cognitive capacities and its reverberations on the regulation of inner life. As a modern ego psychologist, I find this a sympathetic point of view, one that further enriches, rather than replaces, the "hypercomplex" system of the human psyche (Green, as cited in Sandler, 2000), a system that incorporates drive and the unconscious, is deeply rooted in the body, and functions in a dynamic interaction with the multiple other systems contributing to human development. The work around *reflective function* and *mentalization* distinguishes itself as a cohesive and evolving opus, illuminating a hitherto neglected arena with an impact on psychoanalytic research, clinical theory, and technique (Slade, 1999; Sugarman, 2003).

For a child analyst with an interest in early development, Fonagy and his colleagues' contributions elaborating the emergence of the child's mind and experience of self in the context of the interpersonal world provides a fascinating perspective on an aspect of development that—while fully described in the developmental psychology literature (see Fonagy et al., 2003)—has been relatively ignored within psychoanalysis. Their detailed examination of the child's mind in the stage between 2 and 5 years of age, and their explication of the crucial role of a more mature other in facilitating the child's move from psychical equivalence to the pretend mode (Fonagy & Target, 1996), contribute in significant ways to understanding the powerful transformation of the mind during the oedipal phase. Moreover, their exegesis suggests that the transformations of thinking that facilitate the passage through this crucial nodal point in development set the direction of future, emergent capacities that will in turn promote resilience in later development.

I likewise appreciate their emphasis (Fonagy et al., 2002) on the ways that the challenges of the adolescent expansion of thinking expose faults in the prior foundation for reflective capacity, separation–individuation, and sense of self. The vulnerable adolescent is easily overwhelmed both by the complexity of the world opened up to him by his own expanding mind and by the demands upon him to disengage from his childhood objects whose presence essentially stabilized his projections. Traditional psychoanalytic contributions have focused primarily on the importance of the body, instinctual life, and the new challenge of an unprecedented upsurge in sexual and aggressive feelings during these two nodal points in development (i.e., the Oedipus and adolescence). Fonagy and his colleagues' emphasis on the crucial evolution of cognitive capacities, as well as on the essential presence of more mature objects to facilitate the progression toward symbolic capacity, self-reflection, and development of the self addresses a critical and somewhat neglected feature of both developmental epochs. They also beautifully describe the specific redress that psychoanalytic treatment provides in creating a transitional space where psychical reality can be consigned to the inner world and productively contemplated.

THE CASE OF MR. N.

I would like now to introduce the case of Mr. N. in order to illustrate the clinical utility of these ideas. I chose this case because the facts of Mr. N.'s history are weighted against the kind of developmental experience that would create self-reflective capacity. Indeed, as I came to know him, his lack of access to meaning in his emotional life and inner world and his grave difficulty "mentalizing" raw and unthinkable thoughts (as opposed to enacting them) were powerful interferences in his using his analysis for anything but the latest manifestation of what he termed his "rotten core."

Mr. N. came for treatment at age 28 with no prior contact with any mental health professional except for the referring analyst, a family friend. A big, imposing man with the body habitus of a college athlete gone to seed, Mr. N.'s presentation was distinguished by a pervasive estrangement from his own mind, associated with disruption of the function of thinking, such that he regularly became mired in paralyzing ruminations and doubting. In every aspect of his life, he felt stymied and frustrated, unable to pursue his own desires or even to know what it was he wanted. A graduate of a top-tier college, he had been unemployed for almost a year after a failed attempt to embark on a career in business, a direction pursued at the behest of his father and ultimately experienced as entirely unsuitable for him. He had submitted to the pressure of the woman he had dated since high school to finally wed, but continued to feel deeply ambivalent about her despite her impressive pedigree, beauty, brains, and apparent unswerving commitment to him.

In our early meetings Mr. N. readily revealed his history, some of which he almost never spoke of to anyone; clearly, he was responsive to an atmosphere of interest in his mind although he himself seemed almost entirely unable to think about his own thoughts. I came to see that his ready provision of the history that follows, which of course has been subjected to my revision, was an astute resistance to his unconscious experience of our relationship as a potential disruption of his adaptation (Green, in Sandler, 2000), as well as a subtle denial of its presence as a force to be reckoned with. In the course of a few months, I learned the broad outlines of the following.

Mr. N. was adopted at birth by a brilliant academician and self-made millionaire and his wife, whose aristocratic family violently disapproved of the marriage. His mother died when he was 15 years old after a 10-month decline due to a brain tumor. Mr. N.'s adoption was rarely discussed in the family and had been mentioned to his own wife only once. Similarly, his mother's life and her death were infrequently mentioned.

While the importance of his adoption and his mother's prolonged illness and death was acknowledged by Mr. N., he immediately conveyed to me that his complicated relationship with his much revered, awe-inspiring, immensely successful father was the center of his seemingly well-remembered life. He recalled, as a very little boy, his daily vigil, mitt in hand, for his father's return from work, so that they could play catch together, as they did whenever possible. He also admitted that he suffered miserably when he was separated from his parents, as he was routinely when they traveled. He recalled himself stricken with worry about his fathers' safe return, and confessed with uneasiness that, despite the absence of any religious exposure, he typically engaged in prayers for his father's life, offering up his mother as sacrifice. Indeed, his focus was consistently on his father, whom he idealized and dreaded.

Over time, he was nonetheless able to recognize his father's cruel torment of both himself and his mother throughout his childhood over his academic performance. His father arranged for professional reading tutors when Mr. N. was barely 4 and insisted that Mr. N.'s homework be closely supervised by his mother and then checked by himself when he returned from work. This resulted in daily battles punctuated by his father's withering sarcasm, demands for perfection, and belittling of wife and son. Scathing denunciations of Mr. N.'s stupidity, his carelessness, and his colossal time wasting were regular fare. Even outside the academic arena, Mr. N.'s father demonstrated a remarkable lack of understanding of his son's mind, in both its particular and general features. For example, he erupted in rage when Mr. N., at age 8, did not know how to direct him by car to a sports activity. Incidents such as these were commonplace.

From early in his development, Mr. N. showed considerable athletic talent, which he knew that his father admired. He pursued a number of sports, but for reasons unconvincing even to himself gave them up one by one. An avid hockey and baseball player, he was scouted as a young adolescent for professional baseball, but, feeling somehow cognitively overwhelmed by the sport, he quit playing, much to his father's disappointment. Similarly, while recruited by college coaches for varsity teams in two sports, he insisted on giving up the one both he and his father valued and ended up in a sport whose culture felt entirely alien to him, on and off the field.

Mr. N.'s early adolescence saw the confluence of several crucial developments. For one, he matured early and was fully developed by age 13 and one-half. The physical transformation into a 6 foot, burly and bearded young man seemed to happen over a single summer and was accompanied by a huge internal upheaval, with an upsurge of sexual feelings as well as an uneasy awareness of his physical power relative to his peers. Of course, this was accompanied by a quantum shift in the expectations of the surrounding environment. Second, his relationship to his mother, already eroded by his identification with his father, became more strained as his squeamishness about physical contact with her peaked with puberty.

Tragically, this estrangement coincided with the subtle changes in his mother's mental status which, in retrospect, were harbingers of her fatal illness. Initially, these changes evoked exasperation in Mr. N., since they were amplifications of her usual histrionic reactions—for example to minor physical injuries—that had traditionally elicited disdain from his father. However, when he returned home after a month away in sports camp, he found her clearly altered and was informed that she had a brain tumor. As she rapidly declined, his father made him a proposition: they could decide together to go ahead with temporizing surgery because "anything was possible," and a cure might be discovered in the time they gained. This surgery, which Mr. N. had no choice but to endorse, briefly returned the mother's mental status to normal, but left her partially paralyzed and, from my patient's perspective, gruesomely altered physically and "weirdly" disinhibited. Over the next eight months, she slowly recapitulated at home what had happened rapidly before, becoming fully demented and finally comatose until her death in early summer. During that year the patient applied to boarding school, which his mother had opposed, and left for school in the fall.

Even within the analysis, Mr. N. could hardly tolerate thinking about his experience of his mother's long decline. Her room was next door to his and she was attended by a nurse and his devoted father, who, throughout her illness, immediately went to her room after work and ate his meals there. To Mr. N., she was bizarre and alien looking and, because she was now indifferent to her former standards of propriety, he was routinely exposed to her partial nudity. He actually stopped entering the room at all during her last months, but despite his avoidance he was reminded of her presence by sounds and odors and, of course, by his father's steadfast visits.

Much of Mr. N.'s time during that year was spent in the family's newly remodeled "teen lounge" basement, a space where he had occupied himself for hours as a younger boy, practicing goals with his hockey stick. Mr. N. had his first experience of intercourse in that room during his mother's illness. At his mother's memorial service, Mr. N. recalled that he was inexplicably terrified that his adopted status would be mentioned and tremendously relieved when it was not. Immediately following, his father consoled him by suggesting with enthusiasm that they go to the mall where he could "buy anything he wanted." Somewhat later in treatment, Mr. N. described how, soon after his mother died, his father accompanied him to an athletic tournament out of state and allowed him to rent a pornographic video, which they watched together in the hotel room. He was deeply mystified and embarrassed in describing this event about which not a single word was exchanged with his father.

Mr. N.'s father continued to torment him at boarding school, arriving like a vengeful deus ex machina to remove him to a nearby hotel in order to direct the rewriting of his papers. However, Mr. N.'s overall experience of boarding school was of liberation and fun: for the first time he was surrounded by countless "siblings" and a peer-driven culture to which he responded with great enthusiasm. Whatever difficulty had troubled him when apart from his parents was no longer in evidence and he described no apparent mourning process. He shed tears only once, when his father announced early in the following spring that he was going to marry an old family friend.

Mr. N. observed that he lacked any interest in the academic aspect of school, and discovered, as if it were a revelation, that if he didn't do the work and simply admitted it, there was little price to pay. His considerable talent as an athlete was a great asset as it defined his peer group and provided him status. His academic record was spotty, but due to his father's academic prestige and his own considerable athletic credentials, Mr. N. was admitted to a top college where his father held a prestigious post. There his sense of engaging in a charade escalated as he concocted one scheme after another to fool his teachers into accepting late assignments, inadequate preparation, and so on. He reported with a mixture of satisfaction and dismay that he played his part in the deception to the hilt. In fact, he viewed the construction of elaborate ruses as the most impressive accomplishment of his college experience. (It led him to seriously consider and very briefly pursue acting as a career, despite his father's disdain for such a choice.) Overall, his college life was marked by substance abuse, wild and reckless behavior, and consistent lack of self-regard. An emblematic example is the story of his excellent, highly touted first chapter for his senior thesis, which he completely undermined by doing no further work until the night before it was due. His one demonstration of judgment was his decision to take a year off from school following a drunken spree during which he put his head through a window. This year off, spent literally on the other side of the world, was notable for its success, complete sobriety, and demonstration of leadership, group spirit, and responsibility.

Mr. N.'s history contains elements that readily serve to illustrate the role of attachment, reflective function, and mentalizing capacity on personality. Moreover, as I grew to know him, the traumatic impact of his adoption in all its repercussions, his father's verbal abuse, his mother's illness and her death were increasingly elucidated, as was his pattern of drug and alcohol use and vulnerability to dissociation, evidence of which emerged still later in the analysis. Here I would like to address these features and show how the use of Fonagy and his colleagues' concepts proved helpful in thinking about Mr. N.'s developmental history and in preparing me for the rocky course of the relationship. I believe these circumstances—the adoption constellation (which includes the responses of all parties to the event), abusive parenting, prolonged parental deterioration, and parental death—are particularly suited to illuminate the impact of certain kinds of disturbances of key relationships in childhood on mental structure and ego capacities. These ideas provided most help in considering the general features of his mind and his thinking and served to contextualize the exploration of his complex enactments and the manifestations of his sadomasochistic fantasy, rageful self-destructiveness, and unconscious identification with his dying mother. Their ideas brilliantly illuminate the way that developmental trauma alters the emergence of ego capacities, which in turn affects the expression of conflict and defense.

ADOPTION AND ATTACHMENT

Adoption has certainly been a topic of interest to psychoanalysts and attachment researchers, and is almost inevitably a part of any child clinician's practice. While its actual frequency in the population is estimated at roughly 2%, it has been reported to comprise between 4 and 30% of children presenting to clinic and between 10 and 15% of children in residential treatment (Brodzinsky & Schechter, 1990; Wieder, 1977). Moreover, adoption fantasies are universal and are represented in the myths and literature of every society, and of course are the premise of Oedipus's story. Here I wish to examine the intrapsychic elaboration of actual adoption at birth, the topic of a number of psychoanalytic papers and studies (Brinich, 1980, 1995; Gilmore, 1995; Nickman, 1985; Wieder, 1977, 1978) and psychodynamic research (Brodzinsky, Smith, & Brodzinsky, 1998).

At least for the clinical subgroup that we see in our offices and clinics, adoption at birth poses a powerful mental challenge for both the adoptee and the adoptive parents, and directly impacts the nature of their bond, despite the absence, for the adoptee, of a remembered event of abandonment, rejection, and loss. Furthermore, the fact of adoption has an ongoing influence on personality development in the adoptee, especially in regard to self-development, predisposition to anxiety, self-esteem regulation, superego structure, object relations, and resolution of adolescent challenges in regard to identity consolidation and sense of personal agency (Brinich, 1980; Brodzinsky & Schechter, 1990; Hoopes, 1990). As I hope to elaborate in what follows, it has been my experience that the fact of adoption can interfere with the development of self-reflective capacity because, very much like the impact of abuse and neglect, adoption poses the impossible challenge of thinking about unthinkable decisions by the people who are assumed to unconditionally love and cherish the child.

The idea that adoption constitutes a particular type of loss is a central thesis of this literature. Brodzinsky, Smith, & Brodzinsky (1998) have written persuasively about the common features of adoption and loss, suggesting that loss and bereavement offer a useful model for considering the internal struggle of the adoptee and the adoptive parents. The mourning process in the adoption situation is greatly complicated by the unique features of adoption loss. These include its evolving, shifting meaning in the mind of the developing child, its voluntary nature, the environmental collusion to minimize its importance, and the usual absence of concrete information and experience of the biological parent. These factors combine with the awareness that the lost parents are likely alive, haunting the adoptive family's mental lives like ghosts. From a psychoanalytic point of view, such circumstances lend themselves to split parental, especially maternal, representations (Brinich, 1980; Siegal & Siegal, 2001; Weider, 1977), and to persistent infantile fantasies about rejection and abandonment that are layered over but never fully reworked throughout development (Frankel, 1991; Nickman, 1985). Since information is typically imparted beginning in the toddler period, these fantasies often retain an anal coloration (Weider, 1977). In addition, because of the toddler's immature mental capacities, an excess of aggression is often deflected onto the adoptive mother (Sherick, 1983) with ongoing impediments to the resolution of ambivalence (Brinich, 1995).

The specific impact of adoption on the analytic relationship and the transference has also been addressed in some of the literature (Blum, 1983; Nickman, 1985; Weider, 1977a, 1977b, 1978). In work with this patient, where the phrase "what relationship?" formed the nidus around which we gradually came to understand the many facets of the transference, the absent biological mother emerged as a kind of "hole" transference; this "hole-object" is present yet absent, incomprehensible, and inexpressible (Gerzi, 2005; Quinodoz, 1996). The implication here is that reflection and relationship are not possible because the abandonment exceeds comprehension and containment; the object creates a black hole in the mind of the individual that is reenacted in the transference relationship. The corresponding experience of the adoptive parents has long been recognized in the literature (e.g., Blum, 1983; Brinich, 1995; Sherick, 1983; Siegal & Siegal,

2001), perhaps more so as prolonged struggles with infertility in pursuit of biological conception have become the common prologue (Apfel & Keylor, 2002). The particular prior circumstances of long, arduous, and potentially damaging infertility work-up and treatments heighten the comparable experience of loss and damaged self-esteem in the minds of the adoptive parents—loss of the idealized biological child, loss of a sense of adequacy as man or woman and as competent spouse, loss of a nonutilitarian, pleasure-oriented sexual relationship, and so on. These losses become woven into the usual anxieties of adoptive parents about their child as the adoptee's capacities, deficits, and personality emerge over time (of course in a complex interaction with these very anxieties). Especially problematic for the adopted child is the adoptive parents' idealized fantasy of the lost biological child, to whom the adoptee is forever unequal (Sherick, 1983; Siegal & Siegal, 2001). This idealized imago contributes, as a kind of ghostly point of comparison, to a barrage of anxieties that I have encountered directly in some adoptive parents and indirectly in the analysis of their children. Moreover, these anxieties proliferate as if objectively based, and include the worry that the child is alien, manifests traits derived from facts and fantasies about the birth parents, is bound to repeat the devalued and depraved behavior of the birth parents, is never going to fully accept them as the real parents, and so on. The fantasy of the absent idealized biological child can thus cast a shadow on the adoptee and have an impact comparable to a scarring sibling rivalry, but is instead more like shadow-boxing with only an "absence" for a sparring partner.

My focus on this aspect of the adoptive experience—that is, the adoptive parents' ongoing and evolving view of their actual child as compared to the absent biological child—developed during the course of my work with Mr. N. both as his own unconscious fantasy and as a countertransference reaction. Mr. N. knew he was adopted from uneducated, working-class parents when his adoptive parents were in their late thirties and had been married for over a decade. At a later point in treatment, when Mr. N. and his wife were themselves trying to conceive, his father confirmed that he and Mr. N.'s mother had had an extended struggle with infertility. Nonetheless, Mr. N.'s own conscious reverie about what he called the "prologue" of a baby's life was confined to thoughts about his biological parents. Gradually, after exploring with him how awful that was, I was able to suggest to him that it was perhaps more unbearable still to think about his adoptive parents, to recognize from his own current experience how much they wanted a biological child! He was nobody's first choice!

What Mr. N. described as his father's "hard-ass" approach to child-rearing could now be presented to him as his representation of his father's urgent and desperate attempt to force his adoptive son's mind to function like his own, like his "own son's" mind. The requirement seemed to be to succeed as his father had done, or not at all. Here it seemed that Mr. N.'s "reflective capacity" had been defensively deployed to rationalize his father's behavior as an outgrowth of his own difficult childhood, warding off his anxiety that his father's behavior was a measure of his specific disappointment in him. It was nonetheless possible to show Mr. N. that his own persistent anxiety that he was not his father's son, that he was stupid and could not understand, reflected an internal pressure-cooker where autonomous thinking was impossible. He struggled constantly with an ongoing internal diatribe against wastefulness and laziness; urgent and continuous work was maintained as the wished-for ideal to which he provocatively submitted and then quickly and decisively defied and caricatured. Yet the thought that his father was specifically comparing him to an idealized fantasy of his own biological child was too awful to contemplate; while interpreted, it remained unintegrated into Mr. N.'s experience.

Mr. N. gradually came to see that both he and his mother had been brutalized by a man whom he simultaneously hated and worshipped. Any attempt on his mother's part to offer him something that might interest him was scoffed at and demeaned by both father and son in a sadomasochistic alliance. Mr. N.'s educational experience was colored by his rage and sense of inadequacy; when he escaped his father's continuous tyrannical control in high school, he became a master disappointer, full of potential in the eyes of every new teacher, actively engaged in an artful prolongation of expectation through prevarication and excuses, and inevitably disappointing in his consistently meager delivery. His mostly unconscious but astonishingly powerful oppositional stance was his secret weapon; to it was sacrificed any personal stake he might have and it acted to waste everything his father invested in: athletics, educational and career opportunities, money, time— and, inevitably, treatment.

PARENTAL ILLNESS AND DEATH, AND ATTACHMENT

Of course, parental death in childhood has an obvious impact on the child's attachment security and, depending upon the age of the child, the family circumstances, and the availability of the surviving parent. The reverberations of this disruption on attachment patterns can be profound. I think it is fair to say that the old controversy over the young child's capacity to mourn has been put to rest with the recognition that the child's stage of development when the parent dies shapes the process of mourning (Frankiel, 1994), a process that inevitably differs in some details from the adult's. Furthermore, this process depends upon the availability of the human environment to support the immature capacities of the child. Like many other processes humans are subject to (including psychoanalysis), the child's trajectory qualitatively deviates from the adult's on the basis of the child's current mental organization, total or partial actual dependency, and ongoing age-appropriate and specific needs for objects to sustain and nurture intrapsychic development. The bereaved child loses such an irreplaceable object with the death of one parent and, of course, may suffer a double loss, as the surviving parent's functioning becomes compromised by his or her own mourning process. The common observation of unresolved grief in adults who lost a parent in childhood (Bowlby, 1963) attests to the tremendous challenge that such an unnatural event poses for the child and the surviving parent.

In cases where the death is preceded by a long period of incapacitating illness with an unclear outcome, the experience of parental loss is further complicated. It is a type of "ambiguous loss" (Boss, 1999), defined as one where either the finality is uncertain or the loss involves the deterioration or sudden interruption of the person's mental life without cessation of physical life. With a brain-damaged person, this has been aptly described as "personality death" (Feigelson, 1993) that leaves the onlooker to grapple with the "death in life" (Tennyson, quoted in Feigelson) of a familiar and beloved other. The survivors of this particular type of loss are confronted with a "double," who presents "illusory sameness. . . . The sense of reality is adumbrated, cast in shadow, and [in cases where physical life persists indefinitely] a 'mourning process without end' is set in motion" (p. 334). The profound experience of uncanny anxiety with its creepy sense of estrangement from the familiar is an ego state imposed on the mind, as it were, by the devastating transformation of the object. When this exposure occurs in childhood or adolescence, the burden on the child is quite staggering. It may be usefully compared to the terrifying experience of parental alteration in the context of abuse, which Fonagy and his colleagues (Fonagy, Moran, & Target, 1993) so persuasively argued can dramatically interfere with thinking and reflective capacity. Like the child abused by a trusted adult in a family setting, the child in the situation I am describing may not only have to contend with a frightening and threatening transformation of a familiar object, but also with an environment that conspires to foster denial and splitting, that cannot facilitate appropriate expression of pain and loss, and that insists on maintaining a caricature of optimistic family life.

Unique to the circumstances described here is that the mind made incomprehensible is, in fact, no longer present; it is supremely indifferent. It is a special variant of Green's "dead mother," that is, the depressed or bereaved mother who is present but who has completely disengaged from her child. It is more closely captured by Sekoff's (1999) "deadening object":

> It is the zombie, the walking dead who seek out the living to add them to their deadened numbers. These "undead" with their stiffened gait, decomposing flesh, and relentless gaze seem to need the living—as if envying the existence of those who still inhabit the light and walk freely. (p. 121)

Not surprisingly, Mr. N. was himself unable to think back on the terrible reverberations of this exposure for a 14-year-old boy, as it must have been experienced at that age, with its impact on developmental challenges, particularly in regard to object removal, sexuality, and superego modifications. In the present, he could only condemn himself, and, as I came to see, live out his own "death in life" as expiation. Mr. N.'s capacity to think about his own mind was here most dramatically compromised.

As I hope to show further in what follows, Fonagy and his colleagues' elaboration of the vicissitudes of mentalization in development has usefully informed work with this patient. Mr. N.'s history was replete with impediments to reflective function and indeed his analysis was a continuous struggle to promote his capacity to reflect on and impart meaning to his experience, to facilitate his tolerance of his need for others, and to promote the transformation of the psychic equivalence mode (which largely dominated his experience) to a better differentiation of internal and external reality. The idea that the therapeutic action hinges on the provision of a space where enactments can be mentalized is a valuable addition to our understanding of cure (Fonagy et al., 2002). It is a crucial complement to the complexity of psychoanalytic clinical thinking that has also proved invaluable in the clarification of this man's defenses (including his defensive deployment of non-reflectiveness and pseudostupidity), his instinctual life, identifications, mood disturbances, altered ego states, and narcissistic collapse.

THE ANALYSIS

Mr. N. scheduled himself into a five times per week analysis with what I came to understand was his usual initial impulse to immerse himself or, as he put, "drink from a fire hose"; he was an active and respectful participant and he seemed genuinely committed to speaking what was on his mind. Over time it became clear that he himself believed that he was describing how he thought and thinking about how he felt for the first time in his memory. However seductive such a formulation may be, I came to appreciate the many defensive functions of his apparent openness and naiveté. For one, he masked his spiteful rejection of his father's demands with a kind of helpless befuddlement so that he often appeared guileless and confused before authority. He also defied the aspect of his maternal representation that threatened to make him a "sucker" by attending to his "feelings" and suggesting that his inner experience was both meaningful and important. The strength of his need to ridicule and disavow his own inner life formed a wily and omnipresent threat to our work, one that brought the loyalty conflict between mother and father directly into the transference. One peculiar manifestation of this conflict was that, despite his considerably greater reflective capacity over the course of treatment, content directly bearing on his mother remained opaque to him, although quite clear to me. He reacted to my pointing out such connections as if struck dumb by their obviousness and his blindness to them. Of course, this awestruck posture (the paternal transference) perpetuated his covert resistance to seeing connections himself. Similarly, when I first suggested to him that some of his thoughts referred to *our* relationship, he said, with no trace of irony, "What relationship?" I was a doctor whose agenda he embraced cooperatively and to whom he was grateful and eager to talk, but that was not really a "relationship." This query, "what relationship?" was eventually recognized as intrinsic to the nature of his object representations and was encapsulated in his most troubling symptom, discussed below, which had yet to appear in the analysis.

I hasten to add that Mr. N. had many relationships with friends and family. But I increasingly recognized that while he would describe features of a few key people, he was apparently unable to speak of relationships as dynamic, coherent entities in which he participated as a co-creator and which served to meet his conscious and unconscious needs. It was as if his actions played no part in shaping the nature of his relationships, reflected nothing about his feelings for others, and, most typically, were only in response to *their* agenda. It took many years of work for him to recognize that even when his cooperative facade had cracked, he was still engaging in his analysis as if it were not for him. As these observations about his current relationships and the transference accrued and as I came to learn more about his family life, a fundamental aspect of his childhood experience came into focus: his father was unable to tolerate the unfolding of his own interests and capacities without urgent and preemptive interventions to control and shape him. However painful, it was helpful for him to understand that, in relation to the most central figure in his life, he had known little interest in his own thoughts, little active concern for his feelings, and little opportunity to elaborate his anxieties into meaningful mental content. Over time, I suggested to him that he operated as if his designated job was to fill a vacancy left by the unborn biological child, one whose imagined features had nothing to do with himself, and to whose life course he repeatedly submitted and then stubbornly and ragefully refused, even as his abject gratitude and devotion indentured him. Here, I could invoke as evidence his own recognition that the idea of the imposter was a pervasive mental construct that colored his self-experience and informed his interest in acting.

I also suspected that, behind the all-consuming relation to his father, he was enacting the void and the deceit of his maternal objects, who also "promised but didn't deliver." While his elaboration of his relationships remained sketchy at best, he periodically became obsessed by individuals who were altered. For example, he spent months ruminating about one friend who was in the midst of a psychotic episode and another whose sudden intolerance and irritability suggested (to me) that he was suffering from depression. Unable to disengage his own sense of reality from his friends' distortions and attacks, unable to believe that they were not "deliberately playing with [his] mind," he conveyed his bafflement and confusion, which only found resolution in quasi-paranoid constructions or despair about his own worth. I understood this, at least in part, as a re-creation of his response to his mother's awful transformation, and wondered if it resonated with her earlier failure to maintain her intersubjective engagement with him under his fathers' regime. Attempts to show these connections to Mr. N. were greeted with that familiar mixture of awe and indifference that served to make him impenetrable to all "adult" pronouncements.

Interestingly, Mr. N. had an abiding fantasy, amounting to a fantasy of cure, about military service, again in emulation of his father whose own military experience had always been presented in glowing terms. Mr. N. spoke wistfully about the total abdication of self and inner life to an ultimate authority, wedded to the opportunity to kill others with abandon. Here the sacrifice of an independent mental life was essential for survival and the aggression attendant on such submission found a ready and honorable outlet. Juxtaposing that idea with another fantasied formulation, that of his father as the Wizard of Oz, the beloved imposter of children's literature, suggests that, on some level, Mr. N. also imagined he had the upper hand with his father all along but was unwilling to draw back the curtain for fear of losing him.

Nonetheless, the degree to which his mother was unable to modulate his father's harsh campaign and protect her son was incorporated in Mr. N.'s sense of her as submissive, weak, and devalued. Moreover, the absence of dialogue about his adoption left him unassisted in the evolution of narrative fantasy about his origins and unable to think about his own experience. I will describe shortly how all these elements emerged in the transference relationship and consigned me to impotence.

Early on, I observed that Mr. N.'s range of emotion was constricted in a curious way. He easily "got amped," as he put it, frustrated nearly to the point of apoplexy by random service people or his wife when she was clumsy or naive. Indeed, getting "amped" in interactions with his father was the current bread-and-butter of their exchanges, with these rants routinely ending in shared hilarity. His withering mockery of his father's domineering obsessions was both funny and rageful. However, in other contexts, this state seemed more consistently negative, despite the trivial nature of the stimulus. His outrage and indignant incomprehension were time-consuming and time wasting, absorbing and distracting, and seemed to simultaneously recreate the dynamic with his father as it served to perpetuate his defiant paralysis. But what of other feelings? Guilt and punitive self-destructiveness abounded, but Mr. N.'s repertoire was otherwise meager and his expression of tender emotion, loving attachment, enthusiasms, desire, or sorrow was consciously dampened because the accompanying "sucker feeling" immediately alienated him from his emotion and introduced a false note. These were the feelings associated with his mother, connected to rare, idealized memories of vacationing with her and sharing a mutual pleasure in the natural world. As I searched for "our relationship" and for his feelings for me, I was aware of my own anxious feelings of maternal solicitude, and the disturbing sense that, in his view, yielding to me "suckered" him into a profoundly compromising, foolish, and ultimately devastating aloneness, a "one-way street" where he alone was wanting and needing and I was aloof and distant.

At this juncture, Mr. N.'s bland disavowal of the transference stood in some contrast to his enthusiasm for treatment and his ostensibly eager participation. We were both then surprised that he responded to my first two-week absence, occurring about 10 months into the treatment, by saying upon my return, "Don't ever do that again!" He said he had heard of this kind of thing—namely, the patient unraveling in August—happening in psychoanalysis, but he was shocked that it happened to him. Unfortunately, our opportunity to examine this striking reaction was followed in short order by the September 11 attacks. I believe these two events, although vastly different in actual significance, were psychically experienced as comparably devastating because they demonstrated, in a kind of one-two punch, my failure to protect him from sadistic attack from within and without. It was as if the sequence actualized his mother's abandonment of him to the sadomasochistic, apocalyptic excitement of her prolonged coma and his father's unmodulated domination . . . and there was no laughter to be had at the end.

The two events ushered in a complex and persistent enactment that jeopardized the treatment and seemed intractable. And while the process of analysis involved the consideration of many facets of this behavior, the enactment became by its tenacity a real threat to our work, exerting the same destructive power as elsewhere in his life. Furthermore, my ability to understand and to share my understanding with Mr. N. were greatly attenuated by its most salient manifestation: his absence.

Mr. N. began to miss appointments. His absences, which were unannounced and lasted as long as three weeks, began directly after 9/11, as if in retaliation for my prior absence that temporally ushered in that catastrophe. Nonetheless, over time this correspondence became less clear and I was unable to see a pattern in his comings and goings. Many seemed random and incomprehensible. The more prolonged absences that occurred, early in this second phase of the analysis, seemed timed to his wife's business trips and had a recognizable form that he himself was able to elucidate. He anticipated a scheduled trip with a growing feeling of excitement and an uncharacteristically open and frank fondness for her. After much exploration, it became clear that the "benders" that then ensued to fill the time of her absence had been going on for years. He would contact his dealer, obtain copious quantities of alcohol and cocaine, and isolate himself in his shuttered and dark apartment, only maintaining enough contact with his wife to guarantee her ignorance. While prostitutes and pornography were sometimes included in these episodes, he admitted some time later that what he more regularly sought out were video recordings of real deaths—beheadings, throat slashings, and even the death of a father killed while his child watched. He was mesmerized and tormented by these images, which festered in his mind. Nonetheless, Mr. N.'s conscious experience was that he looked forward to his wife's absences as alluring opportunities to indulge in his obsessions and to be himself in all his "darkness." He assiduously protected these episodes from his wife's and father's detection by the unfailing reversal of his state when circumstances demanded it. That he succeeded so well in this, despite the total obliteration of day and night and disruption of patterned behaviors, was at least in part a reflection of his wife's willingness "not to notice." Not noticing and not recognizing how utterly lost he felt were the crimes of his mothers.

As if to inform me of that experience, Mr. N. seemed likewise oblivious to the impact of his disappearances on me. He had no thoughts about what I might be thinking or feeling in his absences, which at times were most remarkable for their unpredictability. He did begin to anticipate with dread that I would be interested in finding a way to understand them, and that I viewed them as infused with meaning about himself. He was able to consider, but without full conviction, that the anticipatory excitement around his wife's business trips was a transformation and a denial of his unbearable anxiety and incipient depression, and that he medicated himself with drugs and alcohol both to deaden himself and to transform the rageful but terrifying fantasies of his wife's violent death into something exciting and mesmerizing. He could recognize his identification with his mother in his recurrent retreat to coma and, after several years, he could see that guilty feelings about his terrible failure to "go into that room" were part of his current stasis and renunciation of life. The siren call of the zombie mother that he had resisted as a boy was now too powerful; his joining her in living death was proof of the seductive deceit of the "sucker(ing) mother." When his use of drugs and alcohol, those deadly transformations of mother's succor, diminished and finally ceased over the next two years, his "benders" were transformed into "lock-ins" in which the fabric of daily life similarly unraveled as he played video games and mostly slept. He was able to tell me that during these episodes he anticipated his appointments with me with unarticulated dread and was relieved as the time to depart for my office came and went and he could continue undisturbed in his twilight state and my absence.

Understanding this enactment in terms of its meaning for our relationship was slow in coming. Even when he recognized the lock-in as a precipitous plummet into depression where time was obliterated and his ties to living others were reduced to the barest thread, he was compelled to exclude me and to deny me the power to succor him and to make him come back to life. As for me, any satisfaction in his sobriety and hope that the treatment was taking hold were repeatedly undone, and by the fourth year of treatment, they gradually gave way to a feeling of disorientation. I was increasingly aware of my countertransference responses of incomprehension, anxiety, and helplessness as his disappearances relentlessly recurred and extended, creating in me a comparable feeling of nameless dread. "What relationship?" It was as if we had no connection, as if I were nothing to him, like the birth mother he didn't think about and whose abandonment of him he insisted was pure "luck." Or like the adoptive mother who could not have really wanted him and who could as easily take him as leave him. Or like the dying mother whose transformation into a weird zombie threatened his connection to the world as she slowly failed to recognize him and know him. Or like the really dead mother whose abandonment reverberated in his expanded adolescent mind with all his prior abandonments. But I was also the container for his own helpless and abandoned feelings as he negated my importance and meaning with each missed hour and left me feeling as untethered to the world as he felt. The aggression toward me was disavowed and trumped by his pervasive self-destructiveness as he continued to thwart any activity that might lead to productive work, including most of all the analytic work. I was left to contemplate my hunches and hypotheses alone.

Despite its absence from any acknowledgment in his verbal communication, I became more keenly aware of how much anger and despair was being expressed in this behavior. I recognized that each time he came and went I tacitly colluded with an analysis that was, in his words, "half-assed" and therefore not true and not his own. I suggested to him that his disappearances rendered me a ghostly and ineffectual presence: I became his mother. I was the mother of his early childhood who perpetuated his feelings of estrangement and despair at finding no protection from his father. I was the mother of his adolescence who did not protect him from exposure to her terrible death. In response to these interpretations, he was able to recall his greater need to distance himself from his mother as puberty brought sexuality to the fore with its complicated relationship to his adoption and the newly challenged incest taboo. He recognized that his father's silence and failure to address his adolescent son's retreat from any contact with his dying mother once again left him alone with unbearable feelings, complicated by the developmental amplification of his instinctual life and his fundamental exclusion from his parents' relationship. I underscored that the frightening link between sexuality and death reinforced the split in his mental life, making sexuality exclusively the domain of darkness, deceit, and destruction. These and many other issues were opened up through this period but then lost in the meaning-defying interruptions.

What seemed to finally make an inroad into this entrenched behavior was my painful decision to end the treatment. This decision was based on my growing experience of the analysis as chaotic and even senseless, and myself as impotent and irrelevant, unable to meaningfully engage this repetitive enactment and translate it into thought. Here the idea that the therapeutic action of psychoanalysis rides on such a transformation is apt. Unfortunately, in this case repeated attempts to understand his behavior did not deplete the force of his destructive drive to repeat it. This resonated profoundly with his painful description of a glorious day of deep sea fishing where he battled a magnificent fighting fish for hours, finally defeated it, and then in the moment where he could graciously and respectfully return it to the sea, instead casually and indifferently killed it. So, after a full year where, despite his new sobriety, this persistent symptom got better and worse but did not progress in a meaningful way toward resolution, I told Mr. N. the treatment must end. I said that I recognized that it had benefited him consequentially; his drug abuse had ceased, he had proceeded with a two-pronged career plan that incorporated both his own and his father's preferences, he had tolerated the discomforts of an infertility work-up and his wife had become pregnant, and he was now able to contemplate the future. We both knew that more treatment was indicated, but I was concerned that the analysis had become the arena of waste—of time, money, talent, and good intentions—and at this point it was the repository of his self-destructiveness. Moreover, I had been shut out of his contemplation of many important issues, such as the entire realm of his sexuality and his thoughts and feelings about a pregnancy or lack thereof, with the possibility or loss of the possibility of a genetically related person known to him for the first time in his life. What felt like an even more densely meaningful exclusion from the analysis was his decision to inquire about his biological parents at the adoption agency that managed his adoption, rationalized by an interest in his medical history. Such pervasive exclusion was, needless to say, multiply determined but unanalyzable without the patient "coming into the room" and being with me. This was made all the more poignant because, immediately preceding his last extended absence, he had described a hypnogogic image of me "drawing him in" that seemed inexplicably overwhelming in its power as if he could not escape his dependency; this was followed by weeks of nonattendance. Here of course the impulse behind his absence was obvious, but unworkable without his participation.

Was Mr. N. transformed by what had to be experienced as a threat of imminent abandonment? The picture was immediately complicated by a number of events that occurred in rapid succession following my announcement that the treatment come to an end, including the violent suicide of one of the friends mentioned earlier, Mr. N.'s own diagnosis with an operable but quite deadly malignancy, and his access to information about his birth family. The last mentioned brought with it the unexpected and extraordinary information that he had a twin brother and that this brother was chosen to remain with his biologic parents. While the import and reverberations of these events have yet to be understood, their immediate effect was to shake my resolve to end the treatment.

However, what eventually led me to modify my position with some conviction was the emergence of intense, believable affect in the sessions. Perhaps it was because life and death were abruptly and dramatically restored to external reality by my statement, embedded as it was in a rush of powerful, real life and death events; like this hectic, "fire hose" onslaught of reality, my statement was not only a thought but actually a seriously intended action. Certainly the immediate transformational impact can be considered from a number of vantage points, including the idea that some patients in the borderline spectrum improve when their actualizations are concretely interrupted by the analyst (Abend, Porder, & Willick, 1983, 1988). It did seem as if what Mr. N. called my "line in the sand" made me the "external waker or disturber" of his comatose dream-state (Lewin, 1955) in which I had heretofore been incorporated as a day residue, especially as the absent object. My unwillingness to continue in sham psychoanalysis seemed to jolt my patient back into his own life, where the thought of losing me, our relationship, and our work together really mattered.

Nonetheless, despite his initial renewed compliance, we agreed and soon observed that the multiple demands imposed by school and family precluded a full analytic schedule. His life now required that he balance many obligations, a challenge he was formerly unable to manage and one that offered an infinite series of excuses and rationalizations for missing appointments. I acknowledged that a modified treatment ran counter to his "fire hose" experience and made explicit my concern that either treatment arrangement (psychoanalysis or psychotherapy) seemed to invite his need to undermine the process. I nonetheless proposed that sustaining our relationship in a more modest arrangement might make it possible for him to actually attend his sessions and tolerate his feelings.

A shift to a sitting-up, twice-weekly psychotherapy might seem to be an acknowledgment that this man had been, all along, too ill for psychoanalysis, that the induced regression was too disorganizing, and that his destructiveness, unleashed in the transference, was too deadly. However, Mr. N. was able to make significant gains in the five years on the couch, and in the ensuing ongoing psychotherapy he has made it clear that he has a far deeper understanding of himself. Certainly, my internalized voice vies with his father's and, he reports, can often hold sway against meaninglessness and despair. At times, he says, with pleasure, that it feels as if it is his own voice and his own capacity to reflect on his experience. He agrees that it is primarily in the examination of his attachment to me that the intensity of his ambivalence is too unmanageable, and ruptures his capacity to think and to remain in contact. The layering of his transference feelings, incorporating the absent biological mother, now further complicated by her "Sophie's choice" of his twin, the adoptive mother in all her incarnations, and his abusive and yet devoted adoptive father, make future analytic work—with its unique access to these depths—both optimal but challenging indeed. In the interim, the psychotherapy may consolidate the current gains and strengthen his capacity to tolerate his feelings without being overwhelmed by them.

REFERENCES

Abend, S., Porder, M., & Willick, M. (1988). A response. *Psychoanalytic Inquiry, 8,* 438–455.

Abend, S., Porder, M., & Willick, M. S. (1983). *Borderline Patients: Psychoanalytic Perspectives.* New York: International Universities Press.

Apfel, R., & Keylor, R. (2002). Psychoanalysis and infertility: Myths and realities. *International Journal of Psycho-Analysis, 83,* 85–104.

Blum, H. P. (1983). Adoptive parents: Generative conflict and generational continuity. *Psychoanalytic Study of the Child, 38,* 141–163.

Boss, P. (1999). *Ambiguous Loss: Learning to Live with Unresolved Grief.* Cambridge, MA: Harvard University Press.

Bowlby, J. (1963). Pathological mourning and childhood mourning. *Journal of the American Psychoanalytic Association, 11,* 500–541.

Brinich, P. M. (1980). Some potential effects of adoption on self and object representations. *Psychoanalytic Study of the Child, 35,* 107–133.

Brinich, P. M. (1995). Psychoanalytic perspectives on adoption and ambivalence. *Psychoanalytic Psychology, 12,* 181–199.

Brodzinsky, D., Smith, D., & Brodzinsky, A. (1998). Children's adjustment to adoption: Developmental and clinical issues. *Developmental Clinical Psychology and Psychiatry,* Vol. 38. Thousand Oaks, CA: Sage Publications.

Brodzinsky, D., & Schechter, M. D. (Eds.). (1990). *The Psychology of Adoption.* New York: Oxford University Press.

Feigelson, C. (1993). Personality death, object loss, and the uncanny. *International Journal of Psycho-Analysis, 74,* 331–345.

Fonagy, P., Moran, G. S., & Target, M. (1993). Aggression and the psychological self. *International Journal of Psycho-Analysis, 74,* 471–485.

Fonagy, P., Gergely, G., Jurist, E., & Target, M. (2002). *Affect Regulation, Mentalization, and the Development of the Self.* New York: Other Press.

Fonagy, P., & Target, M. (1996). Playing with reality: II. The development of psychic reality from a theoretical perspective. *International Journal of Psycho-Analysis, 77,* 459–479.

Fonagy, P., Target, M., Gergely, G., Allen, J. G., & Bateman, A. W. (2003). The developmental roots of borderline personality disorder in early attachment relationships: A theory and some evidence. *Psychoanalytic Inquiry, 23,* 412–459.

Frankel, S. A. (1991). Pathogenic factors in the experience of early and late adopted children. *Psychoanalytic Study of the Child, 46,* 91–108.

Frankiel, R. (1994). Do children mourn? A controversy. In R. Frankiel (Ed.), *Essential Papers on Object Loss.* New York: New York University Press.

Gerzi, S. (2005). Trauma, narcissism, and the two attractors in trauma. *International Journal of Psycho-Analysis, 86,* 1033–1050.

Gilmore, K. (1995). Gender identity disorder in a girl: Insights from adoption. *Journal of the American Psychoanalytic Association, 43,* 39–59.

Green, A. (1986). The dead mother. In *On Private Madness* (pp. 142–173). London: Hogarth Press.

Hoopes, J. (1990). Adoption and identity formation. In D. Brodzinsky & M. Schecter (Eds.), *The Psychology of Adoption* (pp. 144–166). New York: Oxford University Press.

Lewin, B. (1955). Dream psychology and the analytic situation. In D. Lewin & B. Schwartz (Eds.), *Selected Writings of Bertram D. Lewin* (pp. 264–290). New York: The Psychoanalytic Quarterly, Inc., 1973.

Nickman, S. L. (1985). Losses in adoption: The need for dialogue. *Psychoanalytic Study of the Child, 40,* 365–398.

Quinodoz, D. (1996). An adopted analysand's transference of a 'hole-object.' *International Journal of Psycho-Analysis, 77,* 323–336.

Sandler, J., ed. (2000). *Clinical and observational psychoanalytic research: Roots of a controversy: André Green and Daniel Stern.* London: Karnac Books.

Sekoff, J. (1999). The undead: Necromancy and the inner world. In F. Kohon (Ed.), *The dead mother: The work of André Green* (pp. 109–127). London: Brunner-Routledge, The New Library of Psychoanalysis, 36.

Sherick, I. (1983). Adoption and disturbed narcissism: A case illustration of a latency boy. *Journal of the American Psychoanalytic Association, 31,* 487–513

Siegel, A. M., & Siegel, R. N. (2001). Chapter 11: Adoption and the enduring fantasy of an idealized other. *Progress in Self Psychology, 17,* 129–147.

Slade, A. (1999). Representation, symbolization, and affect regulation in the concomitant treatment of a mother and child. *Psychoanalytic Inquiry, 19,* 797–830.

Sugarman, A. (2003). A new model for conceptualizing insightfulness in the psychoanalysis of young children. *Psychoanalytic Quarterly, 72,* 325–356.

Wieder, H. (1977a). On being told of adoption. *Psychoanalytic Quarterly, 46,* 1–21.

Wieder, H. (1977b). The family romance fantasies of adopted children. *Psychoanalytic Quarterly, 46,* 185–200.

Wieder, H. (1978). On when and whether to disclose about adoption. *Journal of the American Psychoanalytic Association, 26,* 793–811.

Chapter 14
<hr>

On Having to Find What You Don't Know How to Look For

Two Perspectives on Reflection

Donnel B. Stern

MENTALIZATION THEORY AND RELATIONAL DISSOCIATION THEORY: COMMONALITIES

In their important 2002 book, Fonagy, Gergely, Jurist, & Target (2002) tell us that it is their intention to link psychic development and philosophy of mind, "to capture and specify the process by which infants fathom the minds of others and eventually their own minds." That is, "we fathom ourselves through others" (p. 2). Mind is created, not inborn, and it is created by the interaction of the baby with the parenting ones. Mind is an interpersonal construction, a product of a certain very particular kind of reflected appraisal.

This is music to my ears, with my roots in the interpersonal developmental thinking of Harry Stack Sullivan. As a matter of fact, the account by Fonagy, Gergely, Jurist, and Target is remarkably similar to Sullivan's; and where it differs, it could serve as a creative specification and elaboration of Sullivan's thinking.

There are many other areas where the work of Fonagy, Target, and their collaborators overlaps with my own views. They argue for the continuing centrality of verbal meanings in psychoanalysis and psychotherapy, for instance, while simultaneously making it abundantly clear that a large proportion of the most important events in the clinical situation take place outside the reach of verbal language, and may never be brought within it. This is also a position I favor. We all also agree that mind or self is inevitably fragmented. Philip Bromberg (2006, in press; Chefetz & Bromberg, 2004), and I (Stern, 1997, 2003, 2004, 2006) each express that point with an updated version of Sullivan's (1953) personifications, "me" and "not-me." Fonagy, Target, and their colleagues prefer "self," a term that for them refers to the part of one's sense of who one is that, because it connects to inborn potentials, is authentic and real; and "alien self," a sense of oneself as "other" that comes about because it is not connected to the inborn potentials of the constitutional self.

But despite all of these explicit areas of overlap, there are aspects of nonmentalizing or emergent mentalization that are crucial to the analytic process and that have not been fully addressed in the mentalization literature. The issues arise around the issue of mutual enactments. I went into the conference at which this paper was presented feeling, on the basis of the writings of Fonagy, Gergely, Jurist, and Target (2002), that they and I place our emphasis differently in considering the value of these unconscious entanglements with our patients, especially the value of the analyst's experience at such times.

But at the conference, both Fonagy and Target told me in conversation that, on the basis of listening to my paper, they agreed with everything I said. This was heartening to me, but also puzzling, since I had read the mentalization literature to say something else. And so I went back to that literature after the conference. It turned out that I still read it the same way, although my sense of the magnitude of the difference had been tempered by my personal exchanges with the writers.

I think the explanation for this state of affairs must be something like this: In any one work, no writer can say everything that he or she believes. Many meanings that are not possible to explore in any one work nevertheless fall within a writer's perspective. Fonagy and Target and their collaborators have not explicitly presented the aspect of their views that might make our apparent differences vanish. Nevertheless, they believe we all hold the same views about the significance of enactments and of the nature of the analyst's experience at those times. Perhaps these writers simply have not had a reason to express those views in explicit terms.

Even if the authors of mentalization theory practice in a way that already recognizes the points I make in this chapter, though, the points have not yet been made explicit in the mentalization literature. I explain in this chapter how the position taken about mutual enactments by Fonagy and his colleagues in their 2002 book appears to differ from mine. By the end of the chapter, I hope that readers will be in a better position to evaluate the issue for themselves.

MENTALIZATION AND MUTUAL ENACTMENT

Everyone agrees that the analyst's mentalization is compromised during mutual enactments. When analysts are blindly involved in unconsciously motivated relatedness with their patients, they can mentalize neither their own experience nor their patients'. The term *enactment*, as a matter of fact, might just as well be defined as the mutual inability of patient and therapist to mentalize.

From the perspective of mentalization theory, during an enactment, because the analyst reacts directly to the patient's projective identification, the patient's expectation that the inside world and the outside world must be the same—that is, of psychic equivalence—is reinforced. If, on the other hand, the analyst is able to accept the patient's projective identification without reacting directly to it, and especially if the analyst can convert it into a mentalization that can then be given back to the patient, an enactment does not take place. The patient is encouraged to move just a bit further from psychic equivalence toward the beginning of reflective function.

Now, what I am about to present is the point that the mentalization literature suggests to me, and that, in person, the authors of that theory told me they do not intend: From the perspective of mentalization theory, no matter how understandable mutual enactments may be, and no matter how sympathetic we are to the analyst's role in them (and Fonagy, Target, and their collaborators are very sympathetic), mutual enactments are regrettable to the extent that they interrupt the analyst's capacity to mentalize.

Let me offer illustrations of what I took to be these views, in two brief quotations from the 2002 book.

[I]t is necessary to accept that in order for the patient to stay in mental proximity, the therapist *must occasionally allow herself* to become the vehicle for the alien part within his self. If she is to be of any use to him, she has to become what he needs her to be. Yet if she becomes that person fully, she can be of no help to him. She *aims for a state of equipoise* between these two positions—*allowing herself to do as required yet trying to retain in her mind as clear and coherent an image of the state of his mind as she is able to achieve.* (p. 370; emphasis added)

The therapist is portrayed as being in control of the enactment: she "must occasionally allow herself to become the vehicle for the alien part within his self." This is not something that is portrayed to be happening *to* the analyst; she "allows" it. It seems to be assumed in this passage that the therapist has the ability to select the clinical stance toward the patient that she thinks is best. In this "state of equipoise," she allows "herself to do as required yet [tries] to retain in her mind" a clear and coherent image of the patient's mind.

And now consider this passage:

Some enactments on the part of both therapist and patient are an inevitable part of this work, since the patient cannot remain psychologically close to the therapist without externalizing the alien parts of the self. It is at these moments, when the therapist is enacting the split-off parts of the patient's experience, that the patient's true self may be most accurately observed. *Sadly, almost invariably the therapist will have extreme difficulty in communicating insight and understanding at such times. It is far more likely, in the middle of such turmoil, that the therapist's rage or terror or both will obscure her vision of the patient.* (p. 14; emphasis added)

In this description, the analyst's participation in an enactment of the patient's alien self is presented as if it is regrettable. Participating in an enactment, however inevitable or unavoidable it may sometimes be, deprives the analyst of the tools she needs to be useful to the patient.

As far as I am concerned, the problem with enactments is not that, "Sadly, almost invariably the therapist will have extreme difficulty in communicating insight and understanding at such times." What is destructive is not the compromise of certain parts of the therapist's professional conduct; what is destructive is the therapist's indefinite unreflectiveness. Enactments are the only form in which dissociated material can be represented, and as such they are often the single most important source of information about the patient, especially in the case of traumatized patients. The important aim for a therapist in the grip of an enactment is not to find some way to regain his usual capacity to offer insight and understanding. The important aim, even the crucial one, is for the therapist to understand the unconscious impact of the patient on him, and then to use his knowledge of this impact, and of his own disequilibrium, to grasp parts of the patient's experience that the patient has no way to put into words. Most of the experience that the analyst must grapple with at these times is unformulated (Stern, 1983, 1997, in press a), as all dissociated experience is, and all of it is highly charged with affect. Sometimes, in fact, that experience is virtually nothing *but* affect, affect that can feel completely inchoate to the patient.

I hasten to say that Fonagy, Target, and their colleagues are quite tolerant of those times when the analyst's capacity to mentalize her own countertransference fails. These analysts know that, at times, they will be blindly involved in enactments—especially, of course, with more disturbed patients. Their writings are replete with examples of enactments that are presented in a way deeply sympathetic with therapists who find themselves participating in interactions shaped by various disavowed aspects of their patients' minds. Along with many others, Fonagy, Target, and their colleagues understand these enactments to be the effects of the patient's projective identifications, a familiar defense employed periodically by almost everyone, but the habitual defense of those with borderline personality organization.

But I nevertheless read the mentalization literature to say that, no matter how accepting the attitude about being drawn into enactments may be, enactments must be understood as failures—entirely understandable failures, yes, but failures nonetheless. They must be seen as failures because the analyst has not been able to use the part of his mind that, in a better or less challenging world, *could* have been used to maintain his capacity to offer understanding.

In making these points, I certainly do not mean to deny that there is plenty of room in mentalization work for the productive use of enactments. If a patient stays in treatment following a mutual emotional storm, the mentalization of the experience behind the enactment, especially the affect, would be the most important and immediate clinical goal for any analytic therapist, certainly including the theorists of mentalization. The point I want to emphasize is that the therapist's unconscious affective involvement with the patient, very often reflected in less than fully controlled clinical conduct, is not itself understood to be productive and desirable. I read the mentalization literature to say that the content of the analyst's part of the enactment is less crucial than I believe it is.

THERAPEUTIC ACTION IN RELATIONAL THEORY

From most relational perspectives, the analyst is continuously involved in an unconscious way with the patient. There is no part of the mind that exists apart from the influence of the other. Every one of the analyst's thoughts and feelings, and all of her conduct, are constructed by her, and are therefore personal, and open to the patient's unconscious influence. Even those parts of the analyst's conduct that she selects or constructs on the basis of a theory of technique are personal, because of course every choice could have been made otherwise, and no theory of technique prescribes what we actually do from one moment to the next in anything more than a very loose way. Whatever content is being discussed is also being played out in some way in the therapeutic relatedness; and this means that, if analysts assume that their interpretations are nothing more than what they appear to be at face value, they are liable to be participating in ways that do not illuminate the transference but instead reinforce it. And so, without realizing it, it happens that the analyst of a masochistic patient makes sadistic interpretations of masochism; the analyst of a seductive patient who is nevertheless fearful of sexuality makes seductive interpretations of the patient's fear; the analyst of a narcissistically vulnerable patient interprets the narcissism in a way that wounds the patient's self-regard.

But this is only half the point. Just as inevitably as the patient unconsciously affects the analyst, the analyst unconsciously influences the patient. From this point of view, the relationship is understood to take place between two unconsciously intertwined subjectivities. There is no refuge in the analyst's mind from the patient's influence, no socially isolated perch from which to observe.

One point that becomes immediately apparent for analysts working from this perspective is that the motivation for mentalizing with patients is liable to be just as complicated as the motivation for any other intervention, and just as likely to be part of a mutual enactment, visible or not. Telling a patient he seems angry, sad, or pleased about something, for instance, can serve any number of purposes, many of them the analyst's own purposes, developed at least partially, and unconsciously, in reaction to the patient. And it's not only the *content* of the analyst's reflection that may be an unconscious participation in an ongoing enactment, of course; it's even more likely to be the *manner* in which the content is delivered, which may occur entirely outside the analyst's awareness. Or, for whatever reason, the analyst's perception of his manner may be quite different than the patient's. And when it comes to mentalizing one's *own* reactions and sharing the process with the patient, even if one's reactions seem innocuous at face value, the situation is fraught with complication. We all know that the same words take on different emotional resonances, depending on the context within which they are spoken and the expressive qualities with which they are given voice. The exercise of the analyst's reflective function can never be assumed to be a simple or straightforward matter.

I should add, too, that, while it is certainly the case that these ongoing mutual enactments are liable to be most dramatic and disturbing in the treatment of borderline patients, I don't mean my remarks to be specific to work with those patients. What I am saying is meant to apply to all treatments. It is likely that the clinical difficulty for the therapist, and her level of discomfort, decline with milder psychopathology, but the principles are the same. The therapist can certainly *hope*, in other words, that her interventions have a particular impact on the patient; but she can never rely on her conscious intentions alone. She must always be asking herself *what else* than she knows might she might be doing or saying. *How else* might she be involved with the patient than she has considered? What role might her seemingly neutral clinical conduct be playing in that involvement? From a relational perspective, it is as crucial for the therapist to be continuously curious about the unconscious meanings in her own experience as it is for her to be curious about those in the patient's.

THE INTERPERSONAL FIELD

The mutual influence I have described tends to lock the two participants into certain reciprocal patterns of experience and conduct. It does not matter to me what term we use for the field of influence comprised by the inter-relation of these two subjectivities. Sullivan's (e.g., 1953) term was "the interpersonal field," although he meant something slightly different than we mean today; Mitchell (1988) called it "the relational matrix"; Wolstein (1959) referred to "the transference-countertransference interlock." There are others. Whichever term we choose, the point is that the clinical situation is mutually constructed and conducted, though asymmetrical (Aron, 1996). That is, while maintaining roles that differ in expertise, clinical experience, power, and so on, patients and therapists also relate in a mutual way, as two human beings. Even if they wanted to, they could not do otherwise. For this reason, the patient's transference tends to draw the analyst into a certain kind of countertransference; and the analyst's transference has the same effect on the patient. Over time, these patterns become what Wolstein (1959) called "interlocks," which in more modern language we know as mutual enactments. Both parties play roles in maintaining these rigid patterns.

It follows from this point of view that the therapist's expertise cannot be rooted in an invulnerability to the patient's influence, or in an ability to grasp the nature of the patient's influence and resist being transformed by it. Sometimes therapists indeed are invulnerable, but that is not necessarily a state to be desired. We need our vulnerabilities. And sometimes therapists do sense the patient's influence before responding to it. That, too, though, is not always such a good thing, because it can sometimes deprive patients of their habitual ways of making relationships, what one writer (Feiner, 1982) has called their "ticket of admission."

The analytic expertise that allows us to practice over many decades without burning out grows from a special kind of acceptance of our vulnerability, and a consequent ability to observe how we *have already been* influenced. To reach something new, we must usually find a way to transcend or deconstruct the old; and to do that often, or even usually, requires that, without our awareness, we create the old in the therapeutic relatedness and then make it visible, available for reflection by both patient and analyst. To articulate the old *is* to create the new. Like water rushing in to fill a newly empty space, the new comes about by itself, in a way we may not even be able to imagine, when room is made for it by our reflection on the old.

Now, this point suggests that mutual enactments are not necessarily undesirable. In fact, I think that is right. As I said before, what is undesirable is not the enactment itself, but the therapist's indefinite unreflectiveness about it. But let me be very clear: To say that enactments are not necessarily undesirable does not imply that therapists are free of their customary responsibilities: *of course* it would be unacceptable for us to take an "anything goes" attitude toward our patients; *of course* we must be as aware as we can of when the patient is feeling too unsafe.

If, without conscious intention, we must create the old in the therapeutic relatedness and then make it visible, then the most important question is, What happens to make it possible to reflect on the old, on what has been invisible? What makes it possible, that is, for the new to leap into being? Whatever this is, it is not reflection. Reflection is an outcome. By the time you can reflect on the old, it has already lost its bite. New reflection opens up other areas for consideration and change, and in that way the process of change proceeds outward, in ripples. It is often, but not always, the case that taking advantage of the therapeutic potential of new perceptions requires their mentalization. But the process begins in something that comes before reflection. The process begins in something that makes reflection possible.

My candidate for this "something" is the development of a new perception of the other. I might add, incidentally, that I am not alone in taking this position (see Bromberg, 1998, 2006).

The new perception in question may be the analyst's new perception of the patient, or it may be the patient's new perception of the analyst. That happens, too. Most often, as in the example I will offer below, it is difficult to say who had the new perception first. But whatever the origin of a new perception of the other, once you have it, especially when the affective tone of that perception is different from the tone of the previous relatedness, you can't *help* relating to the other in a new way. You couldn't relate in the old way if you tried—at least, not authentically. Among other freedoms that become available at such a moment is the freedom to mentalize what is newly visible, and therefore first accessible to mentalization. The new perception itself remains to be mentalized, of course; but, more often than not, it is also now possible to reflect on the unseen bonds that had constricted the therapeutic relatedness into the patterns of the preceding enactment.

ILLUSTRATION

I had met with a very bright middle-aged professional man three times a week for a year and a half. Ron was enthusiastic about beginning an analysis, which he was doing with the hopes of reigniting his career, which had been spectacular but was now sputtering. Although I had expected to enjoy working with him, shortly after we started I found myself dreading Ron's sessions. He was seldom openly angry or dissatisfied, but he frequently told me that my skill was inadequate and that I was not warm enough in manner. He made these observations very politely, but I felt the bite of them; and he treated me in a way that conveyed his criticisms even when he wasn't stating them. He told me repeatedly that his primary interest in life was to be as generous and kind as possible to his wife and children. He also participated, apart from the family, in numerous personal and political activities. I often admired the commitment behind many of these activities, familial and extra-familial alike; but what struck me most regularly and forcefully about them was his presentation of each one as another evidence of his virtue. There was a continuous and subtle suggestion that his virtue was notable, especially when compared to others—and I felt that "others" in this case certainly included me.

Any attempt on my part to point out things in his experience that might complicate this picture (for example, less lovely affects) was met with a rueful smile and a demurral. Ron really wished he could identify what I saw in his experience, he would say, but he just could not. In the meantime, his wife, who seemed quite unreasonable to me when Ron began treatment, flew into daily, seemingly unprovoked rages at him. It was not long, though, before I thought I understood how she felt. Ron's virtue, and especially his advertisement of it, most particularly his smiling "patience" in the face of others' frustration with him, was itself a provocation.

Ron's critical observations of me were perfectly accurate, of course, because my reaction to the way he treated me was to feel irritated with him. I felt that way much of the time I was with him. I was often cool and distant, and I was certainly unsuccessful in the pursuit of what he called his "feelings," which, as far as I could see, were limited to two registers: warm, loving, and appreciative; or mournful and sad, a reaction to the regrettable absence of warmth, love, and appreciation in others. I didn't know which I disliked more, him with me or me with him. And yet, of course, I also felt that I should be finding a way of working with this state of affairs. I felt interested in whatever I could learn about what was happening between us; but I also felt guilty and self-critical.

I knew that my patient's reactions and my own were interlocked. But as is usually the case, knowing this in the abstract was not enough to help me out of the field's grip. I talked with Ron many times about his dissatisfaction with me, and about the kind of relatedness that had come to exist between us. I told him that we needed to find a new way to see what was transpiring between us. Naturally, he asked how we should do that. I did my best to answer the question, but nothing I said seemed to set us on a new path. Ron did begin to tell me, though, that this kind of relatedness had taken place elsewhere in his life, including in his relationship with his wife. He usually dealt with it by ending the relationship, he said, although, for various reasons, he had not done that in his marriage. He spoke often about leaving treatment, but he agreed that it would be better not to do that if instead we could find a way to come out the other side of what was going on between us.

At least now we were sometimes agreeing that we had a mutual problem. Sometimes, the patient could accept that it was possible that his wife and I were not merely unreasonable and persecutory. He was willing to go this far, I think, because he saw that I took his distress seriously, even though he also still felt that I was culpable. But we didn't have a convincing way to characterize this problem, which therefore remained mutual in only a hypothetical way. It was clear to me that, without getting some traction in real experience, even the glimmerings of collaboration between us about the issue were not going to keep the treatment going for long.

The beginning of a break in the deadlock came about one day when the patient was once again talking about his doubts about continuing in treatment. This time, though, he did not say it with anger, but with regret.

He looked different to me, helpless, despairing. He said he didn't want the same thing to happen yet again: another relationship abandoned because of his dissatisfaction with it. In response, I said something to him that I had said more than once before: I told him I felt sure that our relationship was somehow mirroring a significant relationship from his past, though I did not know which one. But this time, responding (I think) to Ron's changed demeanor, I made the point more softly, and with my own feelings of regret. I added that I, too, must be involved in maintaining what was transpiring between us, that I couldn't imagine how it could be otherwise.

I did not invite discussion of the nature of my involvement. If Ron had asked me about it, I would have told him that, for the time being, I thought it made most sense to talk about his experience, and for me to investigate the impact of my history on my own. I might also have added that, while such a discussion did not seem to me to be the best course at the moment, at some time in the future, perhaps that would change.

But none of this was necessary. In fact, before I had spoken I had gauged that Ron would understand and accept what I said as an expression of my regret, not as a statement of my willingness to talk about my past. It turned out I was right. But when I say that I "gauged" Ron's response, I don't mean that I actually formulated this meaning in my mind. Nor did I formulate until a few minutes later the part of this moment that surprised me most: my confidence that I could trust Ron not to use what I said as one more reason to criticize me. This was a new perception of Ron, and I would not have had it unless he had somehow treated me differently, in some small way I could not specify. And so it seems likely that he had also perceived me differently. Something between us had shifted.

At this point, Ron began telling me more about his relationship with his father than I had yet heard. His father had been much more continuously and severely critical, unnecessarily brutal really, than Ron had let me know to that point. Ron told me that his hatred and fear of his father had therefore been more intense, and more troubling to him, than he had related before. Within a few minutes it was clear to me that my patient had suffered much more than I had understood.

Later, I asked Ron what he knew about why he hadn't told me more about this aspect of his relationship with his father. He said he hadn't been aware of hiding it, but that when it began to come out of him, he realized that he had always been ashamed of having been treated this way, and that it was his shame that had kept him silent about it. I was glad Ron mentalized this shame, because it was better coming from him. But if he hadn't described it, I would have, because the feeling had been palpable in the room.

It wasn't long before his shame and rage at having been humiliated by his father could be linked to the way he felt I treated him and the way he treated me. Having been so ashamed, he had wanted to shame me—and he had—by making it clear that he was more decent and loving than me. He would not descend to his father's overt sadism; yet it was not long before he appreciated the irony that his "goodness" was its own form of sadism. For Ron, I, of course, had been his father; and for me, he had been a member of my own family. As is always the case in emotionally intense enactments, our dissociations had been reciprocal.

This session and those that came after it indicated to me that the treatment would probably not founder, and it has not. We have moved on to Ron's longings for his father (and for me) that his rage and humiliation had always obscured.

I do not have the space to take up the crucial question of *why* the new perceptions became available to Ron and me when they did. I have addressed that matter elsewhere (Stern, 2003, 2004, in press b). It is a very knotty problem. I believe that, while there are indeed some significant things that can be said about the reasons for new perceptions, there is a mystery at the heart of the matter. Seldom if ever do we really know exactly why new perceptions and the interactive freedom they herald arrive when they do.

It is not clear to me whose new perception of the other came first. This is the best account I can offer: Ron would not have spoken to me with the regret he showed if he were seeing me, at that moment, as the sadistic father. I responded immediately to this new feeling on his part, and a new perception of *him* also awakened in *my* mind. It would be true to say that, prior to my new ways of seeing Ron, I wanted badly to be able to treat him differently. But that desire was born less of an empathic grasp of Ron's need for a different response than it was of the narcissistic injury I was suffering of being a bad analyst.

Once I perceived Ron differently, whether I *wanted* to treat him differently or not was immaterial. You might say I was *drawn* to treat him differently; or you might even say I *had* to. I certainly no longer would have been able to treat him as I had just a few minutes earlier; nor could I have rid myself of my sudden empathic appreciation of Ron's situation, even if I had wished to do so—which, of course, I didn't. This is the kind of moment that inspired my title: I found what I hadn't known how to look for. I didn't make it happen; I was taken by it. In my experience, that is how all mutual enactments end. We must put ourselves in the best position we can, which we do by not giving up our attempt to do analytic work; but after that, we can only wait for freedom to arrive.

Of course, only a small proportion of our opportunities for reflection with our patients grow from the breach of a mutual enactment. It is nevertheless worth noting that there are very often moments when it becomes possible for us to say something new to our patients, something we could not have said a few minutes before. Many of the best interpretations arise in this way. I think the principle governing the appearance of novelty in the experience of either the patient or the analyst is always the same, whether we are talking about the new perceptions that break up intense enactments or the everyday appearance in the analyst's mind of reflections she has not had before: To *say* something new requires that you *be* something new. Sometimes you must change considerably, as I had to with Ron; and sometimes the changes are so subtle that we do not even notice them. We are always in the position of having to find what we don't know how to look for, even when we don't know it.

Was there a better way to learn about Ron's humiliation and longing than to have been personally and deeply involved with him the way I was? I believe, actually, that this part of Ron's experience might very well not have come to light if it had not been enacted. I hope I do not seem the least bit flippant about the seriousness of the issue of the analyst's unconscious involvement. I feel quite serious about it. We must protect our patients. The atmosphere of safety—not absolute safety, but enough—is crucial. But I also believe that the analyst's unconscious involvement is consistent with some of the most significant kinds of analytic discipline. Keep in mind that I was able to build and maintain enough of a collaboration with Ron that he stayed in treatment with me until we were able to do the work I have described.

I do what I can, within the limits of my job, to avoid arousing unnecessary pain, and to relieve it when it has become unavoidable. But emotional pain comes with the territory. We all know this, but I think the point is especially clear if you believe, as I do, that dissociated experience is unformulated experience. Dissociated experience cannot be represented, consciously or unconsciously; it has yet to attain a shape articulated clearly enough to allow representation. Such experience is therefore unavailable in any symbolic form. Mutual enactments are our only route of access to these parts of our patients' minds; as they end, the experience can finally be given symbolic representation. The fact that enacted experience is unformulated means not only that we must find what we don't know how to look for, but also that, in a very important sense, *what we are looking for does not exist until we find it.* We must come to know a part of our subjectivity that was not even a presence in our minds until it was created in unconscious reciprocity with the patient.

We must respect the danger posed by mutual enactments. I know that with Ron things could have gone differently; he could have left treatment in despair. In situations such as this one, we work on the razor's edge. This is one time that the old saw is true: if enactments don't kill you, they make you stronger.

CODA

If there is a genuine difference between my views and mentalization theory, it has to do with the degree of centrality we assign to the nature of the analyst's experience in enactments and the kind of clinical use we make of that experience. After carefully considering the question, I do still think it is likely that there is, in fact, a difference in emphasis in our work and the way we think— but I am also impressed with how much we share. I am glad to have had the opportunity to think about these questions, and certain matters are clearer to me as a result of my exchanges with colleagues at the conference and afterward. I can't imagine a better reason to hold a meeting such as this one.

REFERENCES

Aron, L. (1996). *A Meeting of Minds: Mutuality in Psychoanalysis.* Hillsdale, NJ: Analytic Press.

Bromberg, P. M. (1998). *Standing in the Spaces: Essays on Clinical Process, Trauma, and Dissociation.* Hillsdale, NJ: Analytic Press.

Bromberg, P. M. (2006). *Awakening the Dreamer: Clinical Journeys.* Hillsdale, NJ: Analytic Press.

Chefetz, R. A., & Bromberg, P. M. (2004). Talking with "me" and "not-me": A dialogue. *Contemporary Psychoanalysis, 40*, 409–464.

Feiner, A. H. (1982). Comments on the difficult patient. *Contemporary Psychoanalysis, 18*, 397–411.

Fonagy, P., Gergely, G., Jurist, E. L., & Target, M. (2002). *Affect Regulation, Mentalization, and the Development of the Self.* New York: Other Press.

Mitchell, S. A. (1988). *Relational Concepts in Psychoanalysis.* Cambridge, MA: Harvard University Press.

Stern, D. B. (1983). Unformulated experience. *Contemporary Psychoanalysis, 19*, 71–99.

Stern, D. B. (1997). *Unformulated Experience: From Dissociation to Imagination in Psychoanalysis.* Hillsdale, NJ: Analytic Press.

Stern, D. B. (2003). The fusion of horizons: Dissociation, enactment, and understanding. *Psychoanalytic Dialogues, 13*, 843–873.

Stern, D. B. (2004). The eye sees itself: Dissociation, enactment, and the achievement of conflict. *Contemporary Psychoanalysis, 40*, 197–237.

Stern, D. B. (2006). Opening what has been closed, relaxing what has been clenched: Dissociation and enactment over time in committed relationships. *Psychoanalytic Dialogues, 16*(6), 747–761.

Stern, D. B. (in press a). Dissociation and unformulated experience. In P. F. Dell, J. O'Neil, & E. Somer (Eds.), *Dissociation and the Dissociative Disorders: DSM-V and beyond.* American Psychiatric Association Press. Also in R. Meares & P. Nolan (Eds.), *The Self in Conversation*, Vol. IV. Sydney, Australia: ANZAP Books, in press.

Stern, D. B. (in press b). Shall the twain meet? Metaphor and dissociation. *Psychoanalytic Inquiry.*

Sullivan, H. S. (1953). *The Interpersonal Theory of Psychiatry.* New York: Norton.

Wolstein, B. (1959). *Countertransference.* New York: Grune & Stratton.

Chapter 15

"MENTALIZE THIS!"

Dissociation, Enactment, and Clinical Process

Philip M. Bromberg

Despite differences in emphasis, there is a shared sensibility among analysts interested in self-states and dissociation (e.g., Bromberg, 1998a, 2006; Chefetz, 1997, 2000; Chefetz & Bromberg, 2004; Howell, 2005; Stern, 1997, 2003, 2004), and those whose contributions have focused on mentalization and reflective functioning (for a full bibliography see Fonagy, Gergely, Jurist, & Target, 2002). I am speaking of a sensibility that recognizes human related-ness as the essence of selfhood and as the key element in both normal de-velopment and therapeutic growth.

SELF-STATES AND DISSOCIATION

The Capacity to Feel Like One Self While Being Many

A human being's ability to live a life that allows both authenticity and self-reflection requires an ongoing dialectic between the separateness and unity of one's self-states; crucially, this dialectic must allow each self to function optimally without foreclosing communication and negotiation between them. When all goes well, a person is only dimly or momentarily aware of the individual self-states and their respective realities because each functions as part of a healthy illusion of cohesive personal identity—an overarching cognitive and experiential state that is felt as "me." Each self-state is part of a functional whole, informed by a process of internal negotiation with the realities, values, affects, and perspectives of the others. Each aspect of self has its own degree of access to the various domains of psychic functioning (e.g., capacity to feel and tolerate the pressure of one's needs and wishes, capacity to judge what is adaptive social behavior, capacity to love, capacity to act from a sense of one's values as well as from a sense of purpose, capacity to maintain object constancy in relationships, and capacity to mentally bear the experience of intrapsychic conflict). Despite collisions and even enmity between aspects of self, it is unusual for any one self-state to function totally outside of the experience of "me-ness," exiled from human relatedness—that is, without the participation of the other parts of self.

In a relatively coherent personality, dissociation is a healthy, adaptive function of the human mind—a basic process that allows individual self-states to function optimally (not simply defensively) when full immersion in a single reality, a single strong affect, and a suspension of one's self-reflective capacity is exactly what is called for or wished for. I am referring to times requiring concentration, single-mindedness, task orientation, or full surrender to a pleasurable experience. "Under normal conditions, dissociation enhances the integrating functions of the ego by screening out excessive or irrelevant stimuli" (Young, 1988, pp. 35–36). In other words, the process of dissociation is basic to human mental functioning and is central to the stability and growth of personality. It is intrinsically an adaptational talent that represents that which is most human in what we refer to as "consciousness."

Trauma and Defensive Dissociation

As part of its evolutionary function dissociation serves also as a defense, but a defense unlike any other. As made clear by Harry Stack Sullivan (1940, 1953) it is not just a different name for the process that Freud called repression. Repression as a defense is responsive to *anxiety*—a negative but regulatable affect that signals the potential emergence into consciousness of mental contents that may create unpleasant, but bearable, intrapsychic conflict. Dissociation as a defense, is responsive to *trauma*—chaotic, assaultive flooding by unregulatable affect that takes over the mind, threatening the stability of selfhood and sometimes sanity. Intrapsychic conflict becomes experientially unbearable, not just unpleasant. Why unbearable? Because the disjunction that takes place is not between inharmonious mental contents, but between alien *aspects of self*—between self-states that are so discrepant that they cannot coexist in a single state of consciousness without potential destabilization of self-continuity.

Trauma and anxiety differ not only in the "quantity" (the intensity) of the affect involved, but are qualitatively different with respect to the tasks required of the mind. In other words, traumatic affect is not anxiety with its volume turned up. It is an affective flooding intense enough to disrupt thought because it is *inherently chaotic*. The primary source of the chaos is a mental apparatus that is attempting to function beyond its capacity because the different self-experiences the mind is being asked to contain and resolve as internal conflict are non-negotiable for that person at that moment. When holding more than one self-experience at a time is too threatening, dissociation is enlisted by the mind as the most adaptive means of relieving affective chaos. To paraphrase Sullivan (1953), "anxiety permits gradual realization of the situation in which it occurs . . ." but the effect of trauma "reminds one in some ways of a blow on the head, in that it simply wipes out what is immediately proximal to its occurrence" (p. 152). Indeed, it is fairly clear that what is most responsible for wiping out here-and-now experience that is "immediately proximal" to the occurrence of trauma is the automatic triggering of dissociation as a defense.

When functioning as a defense, dissociation *controls* traumatic experience that cannot be regulated, and does so by impairing cognitive ability to process input from a dehumanizing relationship or event that threatens selfhood. Each domain of self comes to define a discontinuous constellation of unsymbolized reality, now guarded against input by the others through the autohypnotic process that supports dissociation. Defensive dissociation shows its signature through disconnecting the mind from its capacity to perceive that which feels too much for selfhood to bear. It reduces what is in front of someone's eyes to a narrow band of perceptual reality that lacks emotionally personal relevance to the self that is experiencing it ("whatever is going on is not happening to *me*"). What is drained of personal relevance are the here-and-now interactions that feel too de-stabilizing to safely allow cognitive processing. Because self-coherence has become a liability to self-stability it has become no longer adaptive to "feel like one self while being many." The mind's spontaneous ability to re-flectively hold another person's subjectivity in the context of your own—a here-and-now phenomenon—is compromised, which in turn impairs the broader capacity for intersubjectivity, thus highlighting a central link between dissociations and the concept of mentalization. The individual is largely unable to see himself reflectively through the eyes of an "other" because self-state *differences* that formerly were able to coexist adaptively are now separated hypnoidally so that each can play its own protective role—each state's individual "truth" unimpeded by input from other self-states (or from other people).

The gaps between dissociated aspects of self must be linked by human relatedness in order for the experience of intrapsychic conflict to be pos-sible. Conversely, it should be understood that because the ability to expe-rience intrapsychic conflict is not always present, the clinician's immediate goal must be to use the therapeutic relationship to help his patients trans-form self-experience into something more than islands of "truth"—to help them become able to "stand in the spaces" between self-states so that reli-ance on the protection of dissociation is replaced by a capacity to feel inter-nal conflict as bearable.

The overarching principle of clinical work is to enable a person to move from experiencing his patterns of behavior as who he *is*, to experi-encing them as something that he *does*. In classical language, what is called ego-syntonic must become ego-alien, leading to increasing development of what has been called an "observing ego"—the agreed-upon criterion for the therapeutic action of psychoanalytic treatment. From a postclassical perspective, I see what has been called the development of an observing ego as the patient's increasing ability to hold and process internal commu-nication between disjunctive self-states without such communication being automatically foreclosed by defensive dissociation. Regardless of a patient's personality style or diagnosis, *every* treatment process, through the dyadic dissociative phenomenon we call *enactment*, engages what is unsymbolized as well as symbolized in both the analyst's mind and the patient's as part of increasing a patient's capacity to process intrapsychic conflict. In this regard every analyst might well consider the potential applicability to all of his patients of what Janet (1907) said about the manifestation of dissociation in *hysteria*—that if it is "a mental malady, it is not a mental malady like any other . . . [but] a malady of the personal synthesis" (p. 332).

DISSOCIATION AND MENTALIZATION

Standing in the Spaces

What Janet (1907) called "personal synthesis" is best described as fluid self-state communication. As I have stated elsewhere (Bromberg, 1993), "health is the ability to stand in the spaces between realities without losing any of them" (p. 186). "Standing in the spaces" is my shorthand way of describing a person's relative capacity to make room at any given moment for subjective reality that is not readily containable by the self that he experiences as "me" at that moment. This capacity is what distinguishes creative imagination from fantasy and allows the possibility of compromise, interpersonal negotiation, and intrapsychic conflict.

People who are able to reflect on someone else's subjective experience of them in the context of their own self-experience—people who can "stand in the spaces"—are relating intersubjectively, an extraordinary process that Peter Fonagy, Mary Target, and their colleagues believe is mediated by a developmental achievement they have aptly termed the capacity for "mentalization." This capacity allows a person to reflect on disjunctions between his own self-experience and the way he seems to exist in the mind of an "other," without having to automatically sequester these disjunctions in disconnected self-state islands of reality in order to prevent them from communicating freely. Or to put it another way, the capacity to mentalize makes it less likely that the mind will automatically enlist dissociation to protect its stability when confronted with "otherness."

Self-reflective recognition of an other's subjectivity has become a topic of great interest to contemporary clinicians, researchers, and theorists representing different analytic schools of thought. A central focus has been on how best to facilitate the cognitive symbolization of unprocessed affective experience—experience that Wilma Bucci (1997) calls "subsymbolic," that

Donnel Stern (1997) conceptualizes as "unformulated," that I call "dissociated," and that, if you add the context of memory, includes terms like nondeclarative and procedural.

"Mentalize This!"

Now let me tell you why the title of this chapter ends with an exclamation point: "Mentalize This!" is intended to signify the inevitability of collision between subjectivities that is intrinsic to a therapist's effort to do his job. Negotiation between collision and safety is at the heart of psychotherapeutic change and is the central issue underlying what we call the therapeutic action of psychoanalysis. It is the analyst's commitment to the joint processing of *collisions* between subjectivities that brings the process of mentalization most into focus. This commitment requires the analyst to be as attuned as possible to a patient's shifting equilibrium between affective safety and affective overload (especially in the area of developmental trauma), and most of this chapter is going to address the issue of that shifting balance.

When I chose the title I hoped that most readers would have either seen or at least have heard about the film *Analyze This* (1999). I thought it was likely because it was really a very popular movie among therapists; most everyone I know who saw it enjoyed it, including me. And since I never can leave well-enough alone, I tried to think about why therapists tended to like it, which is what led me to the idea for the title. The tagline of the film is "New York's most powerful gangster is about to get in touch with his feelings. YOU try telling him his 50 minutes are up." The title of the movie is of course spoofing the tradition that the analyst holds the high cards because his role is always deferred to by the patient. The fact that Robert De Niro, as patient, is also a Mafia Don, gives new meaning to the term "resistance." It gives him the power, at any given moment, to "level the playing field"—at gunpoint. To De Niro, his reluctant therapist, played by Billy Crystal, is "other," and vice versa—about as "other" as anyone could imagine. Neither has any familiarity with what goes on in the mind of someone like the other, but for very different reasons they each need the relationship to "work," thus fearing the other's potential power. Intersubjectivity does not exist, it has to be earned. Each starts off behaving dissociatively, as if the other is an object to be managed because there is no common ground for intersubjective negotiation. Because the interpersonal threat that each attributes to the other is perceptually dissociated before it can become traumatic, their mental processes do not allow reflective relatedness. Thus, an interpersonal/relational "impasse" is initially created in which neither person can reach the other intersubjectively. The price paid for this temporary safety is emotional deadness and relational stagnation as spontaneity is preempted by predictability.

By unlinking the mind from the sensorium and thus from reflective perception of dyadic affective experience that is potentially destabilizing to self-continuity, a person exists in a dissociated state of consciousness, isolated from the danger of directly experiencing an other's otherness. As soon as dissociation creates self-states that are proactively serving this protective function, selfhood becomes a sequestered cocoon regardless of what self-state it embodies at a given moment. The crucial point is that when self-state coherence is replaced by a dissociative cocoon, the person exists in a state of consciousness in which he has insufficient simultaneous access to his range of self-states to allow authentic interchange with the subjectivity of others. Without self-state coherence *he is only partially alive*; other people are simply actors in whichever mental representation of reality defines the self-state that exists at the moment. Whatever the patient's state of dissociated reality may be, the person to whom the patient is relating will be interpersonally "tailored" to fit the image of the internal object that is necessary to insure affective stability.

Translated into language I've used in previous writing (Bromberg, 1995), Crystal and De Niro start as two solitary people in a large empty ballroom, each trying to move as if dancing with the other, apparently oblivious to the absence of shared "music." At those moments one hears mainly the presence of the absent music—the palpable absence of the sound that Khan (1971) writes is "heard with the eyes," the recognizably *alive* melody of authentic self-experience that stems from the relational wholeness that Winnicott (1949) called psyche-soma. When this melody is missing, both the "lyrics" and the interpersonal context in which they are spoken feel "off," because each partner in his own way has become more of a visitor than an inhabitant of his own psychosomatic existence. If and when the melody is restored, it becomes the music of intersubjectivity—"dance music"—and infuses the lyrics of a deadened relationship with life.

A positive therapeutic outcome seems unlikely in *Analyze This* because both characters see one another as a source of potential harm or trauma. Crystal fears being murdered if he pushes the wrong button in De Niro; De Niro fears being forced to get in touch with dissociated feelings about his relationship with his father and being flooded with shame if Crystal recognizes his vulnerability to being exposed as a person who is still his father's "little boy." However, something unexpected takes place *between* De Niro and Crystal that makes otherness and selfhood become negotiable. Each finds that the other's mind is interesting in a way he had not anticipated and begins to get curious about it. Also, the fact that they both have a sense of humor modulated the degree to which they experienced one another *only* as a source of potential harm or trauma.

One thing that made the film so delicious to me was that it had the felt rightness of a real therapy relationship, and a good one at that. Its rightness is independent of whether the boundaries of the characters' relationship are untraditional. Their personal encounters are stormy and potentially dangerous, but they are both able to hang-in even though each wants to throw in the towel many times. At first it is De Niro who makes the "hanging-in" possible because when he doesn't like what is going on he doesn't hold back verbally, which then forces Crystal into the open because hiding would make things worse for him. Unexpectedly, De Niro's openness becomes infectious, and as this happens each of them begins to experience the other as a real person to whom he can relate personally rather than as an entity who is just "saying things." For each one, the "other" became a person who is open to hearing and thinking about what *he* is experiencing, even though the other might not like it. In the language of my title, each begins to confront the other's subjectivity with his own, as if to say, "Mentalize THIS!"

Enactment, Collision, and Negotiation

The key moment in the film takes place when Crystal, as a therapist, confronts De Niro about hiding his feelings, and challenges him to face them. De Niro finally breaks down sobbing, after which he turns to Crystal and, with a look on his face that starts as murderous rage and then, almost imperceptibly, becomes *simultaneously* shadowed with admiration, De Niro delivers what is deservedly the most quoted line in the film:

"YOU . . . YOU . . . . YOU'RE GOOD! YOU'RE *REALLY* GOOD*.*" Crystal, not knowing if he is about to be shot for being so "good," stands there, mumbling disclaimers about his expertise, and looking as though he doesn't know what De Niro means. But De Niro persists, and in that moment, they join one another in co-creating a new and potentially therapeutic reality within which negotiation between isolated subjectivities begins to replace the dissociative cocoon. What makes a transition from the cocoon to eventual intersubjective communication most possible is De Niro's state of mind shifting from fear camouflaged as trust to a genuine coexistence of formerly unbridgeable aspects of self—one organized by anger and the other by admiration, each expressed authentically. Despite the fact that these self-states do not yet cohere in the form of conflict and ambivalence, they are simultaneously contained as a mind–body phenomenon that is indeed expressible in the here-and-now. De Niro's masterful delivery of the two opposite meanings contained in "You . . . You . . . You're good! You're *really* good," although initially confusing to Crystal, is what initiates the co-construction of shared mental space in which their respective subjectivities begin to communicate.

What permits intersubjectivity to develop out of enactment, even at a moment such as this, is the "fear system" (LeDoux, 1996) being activated under safe (but not *too* safe) conditions. When those conditions are present, the analytic relationship repeats the failures of a patient's past but does something more than just repeat them. The "something more" facilitates self-state coherence and is what allows an enactment to become the context for therapeutic growth in which something *new* emerges out of what patient and analyst do in an unanticipated way. I've called these unanticipated relational events "safe surprises" (Bromberg, 2006) because it is only through surprise that a new reality—a space between spontaneity and safety—is co-constructed and infused with an energy of its own. Edmund Burke (1757), who considered this phenomenon as a kind of "safe shock," wrote:

> If the pain and terror are so modified as not to be actually noxious; if the pain is not carried to violence, and the terror is not conversant about the present destruction of the person . . . they are capable of producing delight; not pleasure, but a sort of delightful horror, a sort of tranquility tinged with terror. . . . Its

highest degree I call *astonishment*; the subordinate degrees are awe, reverence, and respect . . . distinguished from positive pleasure." (p. 165)

It is that thin but negotiable line between unanticipated, *containable* shock, and the unanticipated, *uncontainable* shock of trauma that separates what is perceived as potentially overwhelming from what is perceived as a safe surprise. The therapeutic process requires patient and analyst to "stand, together, in the spaces between realities and move safely, but not *completely* safely, back and forth across the line" (Bromberg, 1999, p. 64). Something transformational takes place between Crystal and De Niro, which, because it is a safe surprise rather than a traumatic shock, allows them to begin to communicate intersubjectively. What is it?

De Niro's reaction contains different emotions and the shadows of different self-states in one facial expression and one tone of voice, but these are not synthesized into a unitary self-experience that can be experienced as intrapsychic conflict or named. So too for Crystal. But because the disjunctive mental states can coexist, neither state has to be denied as real, which allows the formation of a joint mental space in which dissociation is sufficiently surrendered to permit each person to reflect on the other's mind experiencing his own, and for that joint experience to become amenable to negotiation. For each person, the other becomes more than an "object" to be managed. The dyadic impact of a safe surprise is what allows an enactment to be more than a repetition of the past, as well as a central ingredient in the therapeutic facilitation of mentalization.

The analyst's ability to provide a safe environment is not in itself the source of therapeutic action. While the analyst must indeed be trying not to go beyond the patient's capacity to feel safe in the room, it is an inevitable impossibility for him to succeed, and it is because of this impossibility that therapeutic change can take place. Collisions between the analyst's and the patient's subjectivities reflect externalized self-state differences in what is experienced as reality within the internal world of the patient, and there is no way to avoid these clashes of subjectivity without stifling the emergence, in both patient and analyst, of dissociated self-states that need to find a voice.

Mentalization depends on whether an individual is able to experience the other as holding him in mind, whether lovingly, agreeably, disagreeably, hatefully, or bewilderingly, to name just a few possibilities. Ronald Laing (1962) points out that "confirmation" of one's identity does not depend on the other's approval of you, but on their "recognition" of you—their accurate perception of you as you experience yourself. In a paper titled "Help! I'm Going Out of Your Mind" (Bromberg, 1998b), I explored the question of what it is that makes being held in mind so important, and part of my answer addresses the reason that attachment theory *itself* is so important.

A person's core self—the self that is shaped by early attachment patterns—is defined by who the parental objects both perceive him to be and deny him to be. That is, through relating to their child as though he is "such and such" and ignoring other aspects of him as if they don't exist, the parents disconfirm the relational existence of those aspects of the child's self that they dissociate. This makes the disconfirmed aspects of the child's self relationally non-negotiable because the subjective experiences that organize those self-states can't be shared and compared, communicatively, with how they appear to another mind. The main point is that disconfirmation, because it is relationally non-negotiable, is traumatic by definition, and I believe accounts for much of what we call developmental trauma—or, as it is sometimes named, "relational trauma."

Distinct from developmental trauma is massive trauma—the kind of gross invasion of mind and body associated with mental, physical, and sexual abuse, or with the kind of sudden, unanticipated, and unspeakable horror to which New Yorkers were subjected on September 11, 2001. I've worked with people who have been through each kind of trauma and have found that individuals who came to me because of having suffered massive trauma in adulthood, but who also had a developmental history of pronounced disconfirmation, were typically more debilitated by the later event than were victims of adult-onset trauma who did not have such a developmental history. I've also observed that an individual who has a background of developmental trauma is more likely, eventually, to become a "difficult patient" even if he doesn't start out that way. No matter how successful that person may be in certain areas of his life, and no matter how well put together he may seem when first meeting him, you can be sure there is more there than meets the eye.

Just a few words about how I account for this. For every human being, the preservation of self-continuity has the highest evolutionary priority. In order for self-continuity to remain stable while one is growing up, any person, at least to some extent, will continue to enact the procedurally learned early attachment patterns upon which his core self rests. Why? Because the way any person is seen in the mind of an other must reflect the core self that was "his parent's child." For most people the need to be "your parents' child" evolves during the process of living, and is reshaped so that the relational patterns defining the core self are built upon, modified, and integrated into a configuration of individuality that is largely nondissociative.

However, if parts of the self were systematically disconfirmed early in life, the task of continuing to exist in the mind of another person (and thereby in his own eyes) as the same self that was "his parent's child," is a much more complicated and difficult task because it includes having to dissociate those self-states that are disjunctive with it. Those parts tend to remain cognitively unsymbolized. They are organized as islands of affective reality that cannot be modified by conflict resolution because they are sequestered. But they have a life of their own—a life that shapes a person's destiny at least as much as, and often more than, the "me" that can be thought and put into words. The "not-me" parts of self must become amenable to self-reflection by being cognitively and linguistically symbolized in a relational context before they can become part of what the person feels as "me."

Until that happens, the "not-me" parts continue to hang around and enact dissociatively what cannot be thought or said, making trouble both for the patient and for people in his life. Because they are affect-driven voices from parts of the self that were disconfirmed relationally, their presence is communicated without a shared cognitive context that could allow the affect to develop consensually negotiated meaning.

Enactment is a process that takes place in a "cocoon built for two." This cocoon certainly is not unique to the analytic relationship. A patient has had plenty of experience with it before ever meeting his analyst, but it is in the analytic relationship that there is finally a chance to make use of it in a new way. Because it is dissociated, it pulls both patient and analyst into it like a pair of moths drawn to a flame. Each person is insulated from intersubjectivity, at least for a while. This leads almost inevitably to repetitive collisions between the patient's subjectivity and that of the analyst. Yet *because* they are repetitive they hold a powerful therapeutic potential— the potential to generate a process of relational negotiation that becomes increasingly intersubjective.

A therapeutic posture that systematically tries to avoid collisions of subjectivities is eventually experienced by a patient as disconfirming. The patient feels that the analyst is not really holding him in mind. He comes to feel this because the analyst is not feeling personally the impact of the dissociated parts of the patient's self that are trying to find relational existence. Because the analyst is not reacting "personally" to him, the patient's dissociated self-states are robbed of a human context in which to be recognized and come alive. And it is by their coming alive that mentalization best occurs.

The De Niro/Crystal example brings this into high relief. At the most productive point in their relationship, each is communicating affectively, not just in words, that he is holding the other in mind; that is, each demonstrates by his personal reaction to the other that the other's state of mind is recognized. Although this creates anxiety in both of them, it permits them to process together what is taking place in the here-and-now. Yes, it is edgy. It could result in their breaking apart at any point, which for Crystal means literal "termination." But it doesn't. What does happen leads to a stronger intersubjective connection that allows the danger of breaking apart to become itself amenable to dialogue. It's equivalent to what we see as a patient's growing ability to "work in the transference."

The point of the De Niro/Crystal vignette is not that mentalization is all about confrontation, but rather that increased capacity for mentalization requires increased confrontation with the subjectivity of an other's mental states. The balance between affective safety and seeing ourselves as others see us is a constantly shifting one, and it is the analyst's attunement to these shifts, not the proper application of technique, that allows increased mentalization to take place. The best work is always done when collisions happen unexpectedly, because the process of negotiation that increases mentalization is much more experience-near. Let me show you what I mean through some of my own case material.

ROSEANNE

My patient, whom I've named Roseanne, is a woman whose sense of self had been badly damaged in childhood by a disturbed, sadistic father who took pleasure in acting as if there were something wrong with her mind to think that someone as loving as he would ever want to hurt her. Those who remember the Charles Boyer/Ingrid Bergman film will know what I mean when I say she had been systematically "gaslighted." Attachment theorists would describe Roseanne as a prime example of the disorganized/disoriented type of insecure attachment—extremely dissociative, with a vulnerability to annihilation anxiety that was apparent from day one. The vignette is about something that happened between us about four years into our work, at a point when I had become angry with her but did not recognize the extent of it, which is a central issue in the vignette. I knew consciously only about my growing "impatience" with Roseanne's state of hopelessness, particularly because it seemed to become most vocal at the very moments I felt real progress was being shown. At such times, her hopelessness felt almost spiteful—an insistence that she was exactly the same as she had always been, that what happened was nothing new, and that analysis had changed nothing. In the face of what I saw as ample evidence of her growth, I was feeling more and more helpless and uncomfortable. I could sense another part of her trying to find a voice, but my efforts to enable it to speak were always greeted with both hopelessness and bewilderment about my crazy misunderstanding. I did not at that time see the shadow of "Daddy" hovering over me because I was experiencing her "hopeless self" *only* as getting in my way, and telling myself that the part of Roseanne that was being masked at those moments would emerge if it refused to be bullied into silence. My fantasy of "unmasking" Roseanne was to apply equally to me, as we entered an intense new phase of our enactment.

The incident took place about fifteen minutes into a session, after she had reported an encounter that, to me, showed a clear ability to trust people more than she acknowledged. Just as I was thinking about whether to say something about that, she began speaking in her predictably hopeless voice about the futility of ever trusting anyone to take care of her because eventually they would use her for their own deceitful purposes. At that moment I said something I'm sure I wouldn't have if I had been able to predict what was to follow.

I was feeling, once again, that I had been tantalized and then deprived. But knowing her history with her sadistic father, I was always concerned about triggering affective flooding if I addressed anything *in our relationship* that she could hear as an accusation. This time, as if by magic, a story popped into my mind—a story I had heard many years before but had never forgotten. Somehow it felt like the perfect metaphor to capture this moment with Roseanne, and I even told myself that because it was a metaphor she and I could play with it without risking what might happen if I spoke about the two of us directly. I didn't recognize how closely this metaphor overlapped her dissociated *internal* reality; nor did I come close to being suspicious about its sudden appearance in my mind. So, with great equanimity, I delivered it.

The story was so penetratingly close to the reality of some dreaded "not-me" parts of her that she had no time to protect herself dissociatively when it emerged so suddenly. At one level the story is about sadism, and my telling it at all, much less so unexpectedly, certainly contained sadism on my part. However, it also pulled me more deeply into an already long-standing enactment between us, but this time I was not able to avoid getting dirty as a player in Roseanne's internal drama. Unlike her real father, I was to know firsthand what being abusive felt like—I *became* that object. I didn't just "understand" her futility about ever trusting anyone to take care of her because eventually they would use her for their own deceitful purposes; I recognized from her point of view the function it served because I could feel personally the value to Roseanne of always being vigilant. I had been experiencing her "hopeless self" only as a spoiler because it had become noxious to me, but now I also knew its "user value." Now to the story.

I said to Roseanne that there was something about her image of hopelessness of ever being "taken care of" by another person that made me think of a story I once heard about a little girl who was told by her father that she was going to receive something very special on her next birthday, 10 months from then, but she was not to know what it was and mustn't ask. Being a very good girl, she kept herself from looking in the closet and most certainly did not ask Daddy any questions. But 10 months was such a long time. Nevertheless, the day did arrive and the little girl was filled with great excitement. She could hardly sit still. Sure enough, Daddy entered the room holding a very large box that was wrapped in gold paper and tied with a bright red ribbon and bow. It was so beautiful! "Daddy! Daddy! Can I open it now?"

"No," replied Daddy. "But why? I've been so good!" "I told you that you are not to know what it is and that you mustn't ask. That hasn't changed.

Some day, when the time is right, you will be allowed to open the box. Meanwhile, we will put it in the closet just as it is, and you can look at the box anytime you want to." The good little girl was disappointed beyond words, but she knew better than to protest.

Four years went by. (Yes, I was unaware it was the exact length of time that Roseanne and I had been working together.) Several times a week she went to the closet and gazed hopefully at the box—as if somehow it might open itself if she wished hard enough. Then one day, she did something she never thought possible; she went to the closet and took the box down from the shelf. Closing her eyes and holding her breath because the excitement was so great, she tore off the red bow, ripped off the beautiful gold paper, and opened the box. It was empty!

Roseanne's face contorted into a mask of horror. Her body seemed to shrink until it was almost lost in the chair in which she sat, and her clothes looked like a masquerade—a costume of adult sophistication covering a bewildered and terrified child. I experienced her as recoiling from my story as if it were an instrument of torture. Her voice became a plaintive whimper. Her entire being had changed; to say that she became frightened is to deny the full impact of the experience. It was more than simply a shift in affect. She *was* the child of her sadistic father; and I, at that moment, *was* the father of that child.

I heard myself as if I was a character in a play mouthing a line—a line that went, "I'm sorry I scared you, and I can see my story wasn't a good idea, and blah, blah, blah"—but I knew I had lost all feeling of relatedness and was just trying to do "the right thing" by finding the right words. But just at the point when the "right words" were starting to fail me, the terrified child was gone as suddenly as she had appeared, leaving me in a state of consternation.

What came over me at that moment I don't have language for, but something reconnected me with my human feelings. Perhaps it was similar to what Ronald Laing (1962) described when a woman he was treating perceived his emotional withdrawal and said "in a very small voice, 'Oh, please don't go so far away from me.'" Laing wrote that each of the "right" therapeutic responses he could think of felt distant and inhuman, and that the only thing he could say to his patient was "I am sorry" (pp. 95–96).

Well, that's what *I* said at that moment, but this time I said it because I meant it. I wanted the part of her that was technically no longer there but

429

whom I felt had still to be listening—the terrified child—to hear me as well. I told her I saw a very little girl come out, with horror on her face, and that even though she went back inside, I did see her come out. I said that if she was listening I wanted her to know that I was sorry I scared her. I said that I could understand her being scared because it was so different from anything I usually say to her, and that I had said it so suddenly that it of course shocked her, which was not a good thing for me to do. She had been holding her breath while I was talking, and when I paused, she exhaled, nodded to me that she had heard what I said, and the session ended on that note.

Roseanne appeared for her next session with a distinctly malicious gleam in her eye. "Admit it," she needled. "You didn't know what happened last time, and you didn't know what to do, and you were trying to hide it. But you couldn't and it's killing you. I want it to kill you! I want to rip you open so you can't hide anything. I want to live inside you. I want to feel your heart beat so I can feel mine beat. I know you're thinking right now! Stop thinking! I *hate* your mind."

"I'm not feeling too good about it myself, right now," I replied. I told her that I could see, now, how I was taking care of her as a patient in the same way her father took care of her as a child. "Yeah," she replied (much to my relief), "That's how my father always took care of me. Nothing felt real, and I thought that was normal. I'm always forgiving him, but your story was too close to the truth that everything he gave me I had to suffer for, and in the end it was only an empty box. When you told me the story, part of me got the point right away and appreciated what you were trying to do; but if I showed you that, it would be like admitting you were right; that I could see how I was treated, and worse, I could see that maybe it's how I treat you. And then I wouldn't be able to stay in a safe place anymore. I don't know if I'm really less stuck now, but I know you want it to be true so you *act* like it's true. You act like it's me who feels it, when it's really you. It makes me crazy . . . well, maybe not crazy anymore, just confused."

I mumbled something like, "Just because someone who matters thinks he knows what's right for you doesn't make it true; but that's a new thought and you don't trust it, so it's even *more* scary to have it."

Over the next months we continued processing this event together, and the increase in my own range of consciousness allowed me to access and to speak with her about an aspect of my experience that I was becoming more and more aware of.

I told her I had been thinking about what might have been going on with me that allowed me to tell her that story without thinking at all about what it would be like for her to hear it. I told her that I'd begun to realize I was releasing myself from something I hadn't even been aware I felt trapped by: That in recent months it had become more and more difficult for me to squash my own excitement about what I could see taking place in our work. I felt her growth, and felt more and more entitled to have it openly acknowledged so that I didn't have to always keep my good feelings about it pushed down inside me. I said that I also realized, now, that in the last months before that session I had begun to question whether my total commitment to taking care of her safety was keeping me from . . . here I paused—I was going to say "keeping me from being myself" but what came out was, "keeping me from having a birthday party, and getting a present that I'm allowed to open. *You* know what present I mean."

"Sure I do. The present was for me to tell you that I was getting better. Do you blame *me* that you didn't get the present?" I said that I *had* blamed her, but I didn't realize it because I didn't want to see myself as so "needy." I told her I was remembering that for months before that session I had been making a lot of "innocent" comments about her growth and her new potential, that probably were hints about the present I felt I should get. She said she knew that, but had "forgotten" it because she hated me when I did that and wanted to hurt me. I replied that maybe the way she tried to hurt me was to make me feel helpless like her parents did to her, and that I did often feel foolish about my excitement when she told me I was being "crazy."

In the following months we began to look together not only at *my* contribution, but also at hers, and the more we spoke the more our minds constructed meaning—cognitive meaning that was made real by being linked to affective meaning. She could at last begin to think her personal history into the here-and-now, rather than just feel it in her body. She began to reflect on her past and comprehend what she had needed to do to her mind and her ability to feel alive, in order to cope with it.

She spoke about her fear that if she acknowledged any change I would try to take it over. I offered the possibility that as I felt more and more constrained, I became, without realizing it, little Roseanne—needing to break free of *my* "good girl" self—and she became more and more her controlling father. I was finally able to say to her that my bursting out at that moment was not only coming from needing to "be myself" but from actually hating a part of her—the part that behaved as if I were her father wearing his "nice guy" mask. "Well, the truth is," I said, "I did want to feel like a nice person. It was a shock to realize that what led me to scare you was hatefulness that had been eating away at me little by little, and I hadn't even known it was there."

"Good!" she retorted. "Remember when I told you I hated your mind? That I needed you to feel and stop thinking? That I wanted to rip you open and live inside you? Remember? So why wouldn't you feel eaten away little by little?" And then she added with a wicked giggle, "If I ate you all at once there wouldn't be anyone left to love."

I've found the concept of mentalization so salient to my own perspective on this event that I want to end by quoting from the first of the two "Playing with Reality" papers that Fonagy and Target published in 1996:

> Only when the mode of pretence comes gradually to be integrated with the experience of psychic reality corresponding to external reality, where the thought suddenly becomes for real, do terrifying conflicts arise. This is partly because feelings are felt to be enormously powerful because so real, and partly through an increasingly clear awareness of the mental state of the other. (p. 227)

Their last point touches directly on Roseanne's boundary issue, and her felt wish to cannibalize my mind and know it from the inside. The separate existence of my mind became too terrifying for her at that moment because she could not, to use Fonagy and Target's words, "play with reality." It also helps clarify why my "empty box" story led to triggering her terror, which, for the moment, increased her dissociated reliance on the hypervigilant, mistrustful self to protect the various child parts. For the young child, Fonagy and Target (1996) write, "the difference between the equivalent and pretend mode has to be clearly marked. . . . If this is not ensured, it quickly becomes clear just how threatening the isomorphism of internal and external realities can become for the child" (p. 220). The authors then go on to remind us of how easy it is

> to overlook the fact that the child may only be able to reflect on thoughts and feelings about real-life events during play if an adult is there to provide a necessary frame, and insulate him or her from the compelling character of external reality. The very young child's understanding of minds may be developmentally advanced in play, because of the segregation of this from external reality, and the avoidance of the sense of encroachment that they otherwise experience between thought and reality. (pp. 220–221)

To illustrate how threatening the overlap of internal and external realities can become for a child, these authors provide a lovely vignette from normal development, with which I will end the chapter:

> A 4-year-old boy was read a ghost story by his mother. Although the story was not expected to be particularly frightening, he was visibly shaken by it. The mother quickly offered a reassurance: "Don't worry, Simon, it didn't really happen." The child, clearly feeling misunderstood, protested in reply: *"But when you read it, it did really happen to me!"* (Fonagy & Target, 1996, p. 220)

REFERENCES

Bromberg, P. M. (1993). Shadow and substance: A relational perspective on clinical process. In *Standing in the Spaces: Essays on Clinical Process, Trauma, and Dissociation* (pp. 165–187). Hillsdale, NJ: Analytic Press, 1998.

Bromberg, P. M. (1995). Psychoanalysis, dissociation, and personality organization. In *Standing in the Spaces: Essays on Clinical Process, Trauma, and Dissociation* (pp. 189–204). Hillsdale, NJ: Analytic Press, 1998.

Bromberg, P. M. (1998a). *Standing in the Spaces: Essays on Clinical Process, Trauma, and Dissociation.* Hillsdale, NJ: Analytic Press.

Bromberg, P. M. (1998b). "Help! I'm going out of your mind." In *Standing in the Spaces: Essays on Clinical Process, Trauma, and Dissociation* (pp. 309–328). Hillsdale, NJ: Analytic Press, 1998.

Bromberg, P. M. (1999). Playing with boundaries. In *Awakening the Dreamer: Clinical Journeys* (pp. 51–64). Mahwah, NJ: Analytic Press, 2006.

Bromberg, P. M. (2006). *Awakening the Dreamer: Clinical Journeys*. Mahwah, NJ: Analytic Press.

Bucci, W. (1997). *Psychoanalysis and Cognitive Science: A Multiple Code Theory*. New York: Guilford.

Burke, E. (1757). *A philosophical enquiry into the origin of our ideas of the sublime and the beautiful*. London: Penguin Group, 1998.

Chefetz, R. A. (1997). Special case transferences and countertransferences in the treatment of dissociative disorders. *Dissociation, 10,* 255–265.

Chefetz, R. A. (2000). Disorder in the therapist's view of the self: Working with the person with dissociative identity disorder. *Psychoanalytic Inquiry, 20,* 305–329.

Chefetz, R. A., & Bromberg, P. M. (2004). Talking with "me and not-me": A dialogue. *Contemporary Psychoanalysis, 40,* 409–464.

Fonagy, P., & Target, M. (1996). Playing with reality: I. Theory of mind and the normal development of psychic reality. *International Journal of Psycho-Analysis, 77,* 217–233.

Fonagy, P., Gergely, G., Jurist, E. L., & Target, M. (2002). *Affect Regulation, Mentalization, and the Development of the Self*. New York: Other Press.

Howell, E. F. (2005). *The Dissociative Mind*. Hillsdale, NJ: Analytic Press.

Janet, P. (1907). *The Major Symptoms of Hysteria*. (1st ed.). New York: Macmillan.

Khan, M. (1971). "To hear with the eyes": Clinical notes on body as subject and object. In *The Privacy of the Self* (pp. 234–250). New York: International Universities Press, 1974.

Laing, R. D. (1962). Confirmation and disconfirmation. In *The Self and Others* (pp. 88–97). Chicago: Quadrangle Books.

LeDoux, J. E. (1996). *The Emotional Brain*. New York: Touchstone.

Stern, D. B. (1997). *Unformulated Experience: From Dissociation to Imagination in Psychoanalysis*. Hillsdale, NJ: Analytic Press.

Stern, D. B. (2003). The fusion of horizons: Dissociation, enactment, and understanding. *Psychoanalytic Dialogues, 13,* 843–873.

Stern, D. B. (2004). The eye sees itself: Dissociation, enactment, and the achievement of conflict. *Contemporary Psychoanalysis, 40,* 197–237.

Sullivan, H. S. (1940). *Conceptions of Modern Psychiatry*. New York: Norton.

Sullivan, H. S. (1953). *The Interpersonal Theory of Psychiatry*. New York: Norton.

Winnicott, D. W. (1949). Mind and its relation to the psyche-soma. In *Collected papers: Through paediatrics to psycho-analysis* (pp. 243–254). London: Tavistock, 1958.

Young, W. (1988). Psychodynamics and dissociation. *Dissociation, 1,* 33–38.

ACKNOWLEDGMENTS

The conference that led to the development of this volume was held at the City College of New York on September 15 and 16, 2005. Jointly sponsored by the Doctoral Sub-program in Clinical Psychology at the City University of New York, the Anna Freud Centre, University College London, and the Yale Child Study Center, the conference was made possible by a grant from the FAR Fund; further support was graciously provided by the Center for Mental Health Promotion. We are enormously grateful to the FAR Fund, which has contributed so generously to our doctoral training program over the past five years; the Fund's broad support has had a galvanizing effect on faculty and students alike. We are also grateful to Jenny and Gary Cox-Steiner of The Center for Mental Health Promotion, who have come through time and again to support individual doctoral students in their efforts to make sense of the breadth and complexity of human attachments. A huge debt of gratitude is also due Ms. Emily Bly, the then second-year doctoral student who coordinated the conference. She was responsible for organizing the extraordinary effort that was required to advertise the conference nationally and internationally, shepherd and organize the presenters, and finally for seeing to the directing, entertaining, and feeding of the nearly 600 attendees. For her good humor, endless resourcefulness, incredible efficiency, and extraordinary competence we are both grateful and humbled. Thanks also to the many other students in the doctoral program who were so enormously helpful in the days leading up to the conference, and on the day of the conference itself, especially Marjorie Frosch, Teresa Lopez-Castro, Olga Poznansky, and Yianna Ioannou. Finally, thanks to the members of our doctoral faculty who moderated the panels and added their voices to those of our invited speakers: Diana Diamond, Steven Tuber, Paul Wachtel, and Lissa Weinstein. As members of the doctoral training program faculty, we are blessed to work side by side with an exceptional group of colleagues, and we deeply appreciate the entire faculty's support of the conference. And of course a huge thank you goes to our families, for tolerating and even at times appreciating what it is that we set out to do.

Each of the editors had responsibility for one section of this volume. All of us, however, read and reviewed every chapter in the book. In addition, Sharone Bergner took the lead in pulling together all of our thoughts in the introduction, and Arietta Slade assembled the manuscript and prepared it for publication. It was a long journey from the conference to the book, and we are happy to say that it has been a wonderful and rewarding experience for us to work with the authors and with each other.

LIST OF CONTRIBUTORS

Kay Asquith, MA, *Anna Freud Centre*

John S. Auerbach, PhD, *James H. Quillen Veterans Affairs Medical Center, James H. Quillen College of Medicine, East Tennessee State University*

Anthony Bateman, MA, FRCPsych, *Barnet, Enfield, and Haringey Mental Health NHS Trust, University College London*

Rebecca Smith Behrends, PhD, *Yale University School of Medicine*

Sharone Bergner, PhD, *City University of New York, Institute for Psychoanalytic Training and Research*

Sidney J. Blatt, PhD, *Yale University School of Medicine*

Philip M. Bromberg, PhD, *William Alanson White Institute, New York University Postdoctoral Program in Psychotherapy and Psychoanalysis*

John F. Clarkin, PhD, *Weill Medical College of Cornell University*

Diana Diamond, PhD, *City University of New York, Weill Medical College of Cornell University*

Peter Fonagy, PhD, FBA, *University College London, Anna Freud Centre*

Glen Gabbard, MD, *Baylor College of Medicine*

György Gergely, PhD, DSc, *The Central European University, Budapest, Hungary*

Karen Gilmore, MD, *Columbia University Center for Psychoanalytic Training and Research, Columbia University College of Physicians and Surgeons*

Saul Hillman, MA, *Anna Freud Centre*

Jill Hodges, PhD, *Great Ormond Street Hospital for Sick Children*

Elliot L. Jurist, PhD, *City University of New York*

Jeanne Kaniuk, MSW, *Coram Family*

Otto Kernberg, MD, *Weill Medical College of Cornell University*

Kimberlyn Leary, PhD, ABPP, *Harvard Medical School, Cambridge Health Alliance*

James F. Leckman, MD, *Yale Child Study Center*

Kenneth N. Levy, PhD, *Pennsylvania State University, Weill Medical College of Cornell University*

Lisa Miller, MD, *Baylor College of Medicine*

Melissa Martinez, MD, *Baylor College of Medicine*

Linda C. Mayes, MD, *Yale Child Study Center, Anna Freud Centre*

Stephen Seligman, DMH, *University of California, San Francisco*

Arietta Slade, PhD, *City University of New York, Yale Child Study Center*

Howard Steele, PhD, *New School for Social Research*

Miriam Steele, PhD, *New School for Social Research*

Donnel B. Stern, PhD, *William Alanson White Institute, NYU Postdoctoral Program in Psychotherapy and Psychoanalysis*

James E. Swain, MD, PhD, *Yale Child Study Center*

Mary Target, PhD, *Anna Freud Centre, University College London*

Prakash Thomas, MD, *Yale Child Study Center*

Zsolt Unoka, *Faculty of General Medicine, Semmelweis University*

Frank E. Yeomans, MD, *Weill Medical College of Cornell University*

INDEX

abandonment, 326, 358, 362–363
  adoption felt to be, 380, 392
  in case study of Mr. N., 389, 392–394
  as issue in BPD, 147, 211
Aber, L., 123–124
abuse. *See also* trauma
  avoidance of thinking about mental
    states after, 171, 208, 314
  in case study of Mr. N., 376, 379, 383
  in case study of Ron, 409–410
  in case study of Roseanne, 426–428
  in case study of Sara, 184
  effects of, 19, 34, 204, 285
  effects of parental, 15–17, 27
  mentalization failure after, 18–19
  by trauma victims, 16
abuser–abused dyads, 186, 204, 356–358,
  365–366
acting out, 63, 74–76, 93
adaptive projective identification, 253–254
addictions, 31
  attachment's similarity to, 41n6, 217
adolescence, cognitive abilities in, 374–375
adoption, 284
  in case study of Mr. N., 376, 378–379,
    387–388
  effects of, 11, 380–383
  reflective functioning and parent–child
    relationships after, 6, 117–119,
    123–133
Adult Attachment Interview (AAI), 116,
  141

description of, 119–122
evaluation of RF from, 225–226
in measuring effectiveness of treatment,
  183–184, 188–189
in study of adoptive parent–child
  relationships, 117–119, 123–133
affect. *See* emotions
affect expression. *See also* facial expressions
  in *Analyze This* movie, 421–422
  failure to use and understand, 19
  infants' development of, 53–54, 54
  in mother–infant interactions, 53–54,
    65–67, 77n4
affect mirroring, 65–67, 72–73, 77n4
affect regulation, 90
  in BPD, 142, 207
  development of, 24–25, 73–76, 172
  failures of, 24–25, 359–360, 416
  family modeling of, 56
  in Harriet J. case study, 359–360, 364,
    369
  increasing through therapy, 104, 181,
    369
  lack of, 19, 395
  outside sources of, 62, 90
  prefrontal cortex in, 210–212
affect representations, in BPD, 142
affective safety, 12
affective states, 62–63, 73. *See also* mental
  states
agency, sense of, 93–94, 207, 366–367, 380
aggression, 171, 186, 381, 392

439